This collection of original essays offers a selection of contemporary scholarship intended to help define an agenda for future research in the field of international trade and finance. Written to honor Peter B. Kenen and following his work, the volume is divided into three parts: international trade theory, international monetary theory, and applied policy analysis. Trade issues addressed include the role of capital in standard trade models, welfare implications of economic integration, and the relationship between economic openness and the size of government. The monetary chapters include two related essays on the effects of exchange rates on economic activity and two essays on aspects of optimum currency area theory. Applied policy papers include two essays on industrial countries, two others on developing countries, and another on problems of transition in the successor states of the former Soviet Union. Also included is an essay by Paul Krugman assessing Kenen's lifetime of scholarly achievements.

T0312136

International trade and finance

International trade and finance
New frontiers for research

Essays in honor of Peter B. Kenen

edited by

BENJAMIN J. COHEN

University of California,
Santa Barbara

CAMBRIDGE
UNIVERSITY PRESS

CAMBRIDGE UNIVERSITY PRESS
Cambridge, New York, Melbourne, Madrid, Cape Town, Singapore, São Paulo

Cambridge University Press
The Edinburgh Building, Cambridge CB2 2RU, UK

Published in the United States of America by Cambridge University Press, New York

www.cambridge.org
Information on this title: www.cambridge.org/9780521580861

First published 1997
This digitally printed first paperback version 2005

A catalogue record for this publication is available from the British Library

Library of Congress Cataloguing in Publication data
International trade and finance : new frontiers for research :
essays in honor of Peter B. Kenen / [edited by] Benjamin J. Cohen.
   p. cm.
ISBN 0–521–58086–2
1. International trade. 2. International finance. I. Kenen,
Peter B., 1932– . II. Cohen, Benjamin J.
HF1379. I5813 1997
382 – dc21   96-49927
                                    CIP

ISBN-13 978-0-521-58086-1 hardback
ISBN-10 0-521-58086-2 hardback

ISBN-13 978-0-521-02204-0 paperback
ISBN-10 0-521-02204-5 paperback

Contents

Contributors

POLLY REYNOLDS ALLEN is Professor of Economics at the University of Connecticut. An expert on questions of monetary union and the ECU markets in Europe, she is coauthor of *Fundamental Determinants of Real Exchange Rates* (1995). In 1980 she and Peter Kenen collaborated on a major theoretical study entitled *Asset Markets, Exchange Rates, and Economic Integration.*

TAMIM BAYOUMI is an Economist in the Research Department of the International Monetary Fund. He was educated at Cambridge and Stanford Universities and has also worked at the Bank of England. His research interests cover a wide range of issues in international economic theory and policy, and he was coauthor with Peter Kenen of a 1993 article on monetary targeting in Europe.

BENJAMIN J. COHEN is Louis G. Lancaster Professor of International Political Economy at the University of California, Santa Barbara. His books include *In Whose Interest? International Banking and American Foreign Policy* (1986) and *Crossing Frontiers: Explorations in International Political Economy* (1991). He received his Ph.D. from Columbia University in 1963.

PATRICK J. CONWAY is Professor of Economics at the University of North Carolina in Chapel Hill. A 1984 Princeton Ph.D., he is a specialist in the economics of developing countries, focusing on the interaction of developing economies with broader systemic arrangements for international trade and finance. Among his numerous publications are *Economic Shocks and Structural Adjustments: Turkey after 1973* (1987).

KATHRYN M. E. DOMINGUEZ is Associate Professor of Public Policy at the University of Michigan and a faculty research fellow at the National Bureau of Economic Research. She is the author of *Exchange Rate*

Efficiency and the Behavior of International Asset Markets (1991) and coauthor of *Does Foreign Exchange Intervention Work?* (1993). In 1992 she collaborated with Peter Kenen on an article on intervention and exchange-rate behavior in the European Monetary System.

BARRY EICHENGREEN is John L. Simpson Professor of Economics and Professor of Political Science at the University of California, Berkeley. He is a research associate of the National Bureau of Economic Research and a research fellow of the Centre for Economic Policy Research in London. He has written many books and articles on international monetary issues, including most recently *Globalizing Capital: A History of the International Monetary System* (1996), and is coauthor with Peter Kenen of a 1994 essay on managing the world economy under the Bretton Woods system.

REUVEN GLICK is Vice President at the Federal Reserve Bank of San Francisco, where he serves as Chief of the International Studies Section of the Economics Research Department and also as Director of the Bank's Center for Pacific Basin Monetary and Economic Studies. A 1979 Princeton Ph.D., he has written extensively in the areas of international macroeconomic policy, Pacific Basin economic developments, and European integration. He is coeditor of *Exchange Rate Policy and Interdependence: Perspectives from the Pacific Basin* (1994).

LINDA S. GOLDBERG is Research Officer and Senior Economist at the Federal Reserve Bank of New York. A specialist on exchange-rate systems, she received her Ph.D. from Princeton University in 1988 and has taught at New York University. Her publications have focused mainly on foreign-exchange crises arising under controlled exchange-rate regimes, foreign-exchange systems in the former Soviet Union, and implications of exchange rates for producer investment and pricing decisions in industrialized and developing countries.

PAUL R. KRUGMAN is Ford International Professor of Economics at MIT, a research associate of the National Bureau of Economic Research, and, with Peter Kenen, a member of the Group of Thirty. Winner of the AEA's John Bates Clark Medal in 1992, he has published articles and books on a wide range of topics in international trade and finance, including *Geography and Trade* (1991) and *Currencies and Crises* (1992). His latest book, *Pop Internationalism*, appeared in 1996.

NANCY P. MARION is Professor and Chair of Economics at Dartmouth College. Her publications focus on international macroeconomics and finance, with an emphasis on the behavior of exchange-rate regimes. She received her Ph.D. from Princeton University in 1977.

CONSTANTINE MICHALOPOULOS is Senior Advisor for Europe and Central Asia in the World Bank and Adjunct Professor of Economics at American University. A 1966 Ph.D. from Columbia University, he has published extensively on trade and financial policy issues relating to development and countries in transition. He is coeditor of *Trade in the New Independent States* (1994).

ARVIND PANAGARIYA is Professor of Economics at the University of Maryland and codirector of the University's Center for International Economics. His many publications have addressed a variety of topics in international trade theory, trade policy, and economic integration. A 1978 Ph.D. from Princeton University, he is coeditor of *New Dimensions in Regional Integration* (1994).

DANI RODRIK is Rafiq Hariri Professor of International Political Economy at the John F. Kennedy School of Government, Harvard University. He is also a research associate of the National Bureau of Economic Research and a research fellow of the Centre for Economic Policy Research. His publications cover a wide range of topics relating to trade policy and economic reform in developing and transitional economies. A 1985 Ph.D. from Princeton University, he is coauthor of *Eastern Europe and the Soviet Union in the World Economy* (1991) and coeditor of *The Economics of Middle East Peace* (1993).

MARINA V.N. WHITMAN is Professor of Business Administration and Public Policy at the University of Michigan. Formerly Vice President and Chief Economist of the General Motors Corporation, she served as a member of the President's Council of Economic Advisors in 1972–73. She received her Ph.D. from Columbia University in 1962 and is the author of several books on international economic theory and policy, including *Reflections of Interdependence* (1979).

CLAS G. WIHLBORG is Felix Neubergh Professor in Banking and Financial Economics at the School of Economics and Commercial Law at Gothenberg, Sweden. He has also taught at New York University, the University of Southern California, the Claremont Graduate School, and the Wharton School. A specialist in the areas of international finance and macroeconomics, he received his Ph.D. from Princeton University in 1977.

Introduction

Benjamin J. Cohen

Peter Kenen received his doctorate from Harvard University in 1958. Four decades later, on the occasion of his sixty-fifth birthday, a group of his former students and collaborators present this collection of essays in his honor. Our intention is to offer a selection of contemporary work in international trade and finance that will not only salute a great teacher and scholar but also help in defining an agenda for research in the late 1990s and beyond. The title of our collection deliberately echoes a seminal volume of cutting-edge scholarship edited by Kenen – and also published by Cambridge University Press – in 1975 (Kenen 1975). As Kenen's first Ph.D. student, the privilege fell to me to edit and introduce this tribute to his many contributions to the field.

We begin with a brief essay by Paul Krugman highlighting some of Peter Kenen's more important achievements over a lifetime of outstanding research and writing. Although still as active and innovative as ever, Kenen has already distinguished himself as one of this century's most notable, not to say prolific, international economists. His influence has been felt in the development of both the trade and monetary sides of the field; and he has contributed work in applied policy analysis and political economy as well as pure theory. As Krugman's survey amply demonstrates, Kenen's many accomplishments demonstrate a span of vision that is as creative as it is unusual.

Like the main body of Peter Kenen's work, the remainder of the volume is divided into three parts: international trade theory, international monetary theory, and applied policy analysis. Although diverse, the individual chapters – all written expressly for this *festschrift* – accurately reflect both the breadth and the underlying coherence of Kenen's varied intellectual interests.

Leading off Part I, on trade theory, is an essay by Patrick Conway offering a retrospective look at Kenen's early – and, to some extent,

1

unjustly neglected – article on "Nature, Capital, and Trade" (Kenen 1965). In that paper, Kenen suggested that international trade theory might best be understood if the factor capital were viewed not as a direct input into production but rather as an activity that "improves" land and labor services – in effect, an ingenious extension of the standard 2×2 Heckscher–Ohlin (HO) model to incorporate a third factor, anticipating much subsequent development in the field. An effort to update that formulation within a general 3×3 (or $N \times M$) theoretical structure, Conway shows, only reinforces Kenen's conclusions that neither factor–price equalization nor identical technology is a necessary result of international trade. Kenen's formulation also provides a convincing explanation for the shortcomings of the traditional HO model in most recent empirical tests of trade patterns.

Next, Arvind Panagariya turns to the work of James Meade, who, as any of Kenen's former students can testify, was a major influence on Peter's own thinking about international trade and finance. Even before "Nature, Capital, and Trade," Panagariya notes, Meade had constructed a complete 3×3 model of trade in his 1955 monograph on *The Customs Union Issue* – in fact, the first welfare theoretic analysis of economic integration in a general-equilibrium setting. Much commented upon but poorly understood, the model is restated by Panagariya in more formal terms in order to underscore a number of critical implications, including the importance of both the level of tariffs in nonmember countries and the presence of flexibility in the terms of trade in evaluating the desirability of preferential trading arrangements. Meade's model also casts some doubt on the validity of the "natural trading partners" hypothesis that has been much touted in the literature lately.

In Chapter 4, Dani Rodrik explores the relationship between the openness of an economy and the size of its government sector. Available evidence for a large sample of countries, he finds, overwhelmingly demonstrates a positive correlation between foreign trade and the level of public spending (both expressed as a percentage of GDP). The explanation for this striking empirical regularity, he suggests, lies in the heightened exposure to external risk characteristic of more open economies. Government can play a "sheltering" or stabilizing role to help insulate society against the vagaries of the global marketplace, including in particular a high degree of variability in the terms of trade.

Part II, comprising four chapters on international monetary theory, starts with a pair of related essays on the effects of exchange-rate behavior on real economic activity, both inspired by Peter Kenen's pioneering work in the early 1980s (Kenen and Rodrik 1986). In Chapter 5, Reuven Glick and Clas Wihlborg focus on trade flows and challenge the conventional presumption of a negative relationship between currency flexibility and import–export volumes. The problem, they argue, is the ambiguous relationship between exchange-rate variability and risk exposure under different types of currency regimes. In fact, the total macroeconomic risk that traders face need not increase, and may even decrease, with the degree of flexibility of exchange rates. Employing an original measure of nominal currency flexibility that depends on foreign reserve changes as well as exchange-rate variability, the authors conclude that the evidence lends no support to the view that firms face more risk, and therefore may trade less, when currencies float.

Linda Goldberg, by contrast, focuses on investment activity, which in many economies does appear to be highly sensitive to movements of the real exchange rate. The real question, she suggests, is what determines the *strength* of the exchange-rate effect, which clearly varies from country to country. The answer, she argues, is related to structural differences in export and imported-input exposures and in the industrial organization of exporting sectors. Applying an innovative theoretical model to a sample of six Latin American economies, she shows that countries with more concentrated export activity also tend to have the greatest exposure to exchange-rate movements through their reliance on imported inputs. While revenues are greatly influenced by currency fluctuations, therefore, input cost exposures tend to mitigate some of the corresponding effects on firm profitability and investment activity.

Chapters 7 and 8 are also closely related to one another, this time by a common interest in the theory of optimum currency areas (OCAs), another branch of the literature that has benefited from Peter Kenen's pioneering insights (Kenen 1969). Tamim Bayoumi and Barry Eichengreen address the choices of exchange-rate regime by individual countries. Analysis of data from industrial economies demonstrates that such choices have been heavily influenced by the kinds of structural variables traditionally highlighted by OCA theory, such as bilateral trade patterns, country size, and asymmetric shocks. The impact of such variables has been especially evident since the end of the Bretton Woods era. But other country characteristics not obviously associated with OCA theory have at times also played a critical role, particularly during the 1960s, and even more important have been systemic considerations reflecting the structure of global and regional currency arrangements. The choice of exchange-rate regime, they argue, cannot be fully understood except in the context of a broader model explicitly recognizing the interdependence of such national policy decisions.

Benjamin Cohen considers the implications of rapidly growing cross-border currency use and competition for traditional OCA theory which, reflecting conventional political geography, tends to define monetary arrangements in strictly territorial terms: physically distinct and mutually exclusive enclaves that are the explicit product of collective state action. Cross-border currency competition, by contrast, which is driven largely by market forces, creates new currency spaces ("regions") that are functional rather than geographic in nature – bounded not by territorial frontiers but rather by the range of each money's effective use and authority. After outlining the welfare implications of currency regions, Cohen addresses the issues that their existence poses for the creation of a formal monetary union as traditionally defined in OCA theory. The degree of symmetry between a proposed currency area and preexisting currency regions significantly influences the net gains of monetary union for participating countries.

Part III, devoted to applied policy analysis, includes two chapters on industrial countries, two on developing economies, and one on problems of transition in the successor states of the former Soviet Union.

In Chapter 9, Marina Whitman compares and contrasts labor-market institutions and processes in Europe, North America, and Japan, stressing the extent to which all industrial countries now appear to rely increasingly on "external" rather than "internal" adjustments in response to cyclical fluctuations and changing economic signals. Even Japan, which has traditionally placed most emphasis on diversification and reallocation of labor *within* firms rather than through external labor markets, is becoming more tolerant of American-style layoffs and increased rates of labor turnover as commercial and financial conditions vary. Such a shift, Whitman suggests, is in fact a rational management response to recent structural transformations in the global economy, including the deregulation of capital markets, technological catch-up, and intensifying competition across national borders. But in an argument reinforcing Dani Rodrik's conjectures in Chapter 4, she also suggests that by shifting more of the costs of adjustment from firms to workers, this trend in labor markets is likely as well to heighten demands for protection or other actions by government to reduce or cushion the transitional costs of adjustment for workers – precisely the sort of "sheltering" role that Rodrik evokes to explain the larger size of the public sector in more open economies.

Kathryn Dominguez focuses on monetary-policy coordination among the main industrial economies, a topic frequently addressed by Peter Kenen in recent years (Kenen 1988, 1989, 1990). For over twenty years the United States, Germany, and Japan – the Group of 3 (G–3) – have repeatedly pledged to coordinate their policy responses to shared macroeconomic problems, often in formal public agreements. But have they meant what they said? In a detailed evaluation of available data dating back to 1975, Dominguez finds little evidence of systematic or sustained coordination by the G–3 governments. Ironically, the United States, often thought to be most guilty of unilateralism in its foreign economic behavior, is found to honor its international commitments more often than either Germany or Japan. The latter, on the other hand, are found to respond more to U.S. policy changes, whereas Washington is generally unaffected by policy changes in Germany or Japan.

In Chapter 11, Polly Allen returns to a subject that she and Peter Kenen first addressed nearly two decades ago: the determinants of equilibrium exchange rates (Allen and Kenen 1980). Using the recently developed NATREX (Natural Real Exchange Rate) model, which stresses the "fundamentals" of investment, saving, and long-run flows of capital in exchange-rate determination, Allen reexamines Mexico's currency crisis of 1994–5. A peso crisis, she notes, was inevitable at some point, given the unstable trajectories of falling saving and an appreciating real exchange rate that were allowed to develop after 1987. The NATREX model identifies problems in the underlying fundamentals that have been largely ignored in discussions of the Mexican crisis.

Nancy Marion, too, is concerned with exchange-rate management in developing countries, seeking in particular to account for the recurrent devaluation cycles – periods of growing currency misalignment punctuated by periodic downward revisions – that seem endemic in countries like Mexico. Data from a sample of 17 Latin American countries, she argues, suggest that the size and timing of devaluations are in fact heavily influenced by the costs of rate adjustment relative to the costs of sustained misalignment. And what determines the magnitude of these costs? In a manner parallel to that of Bayoumi and Eichengreen in Chapter 6, Marion explores the role of key structural variables highlighted by traditional OCA theory, on the assumption that the same factors thought to influence the choice of exchange-rate regime might play a role in determining the size and timing of devaluations as well. Analysis confirms the importance of country size as well as both commodity and geographic concentration in foreign trade. Openness, on the other hand, appears to have surprisingly little effect on decisions to devalue – perhaps, Marion speculates, because greater openness increases the cost of rate adjustment as well as the cost of a given misalignment.

Finally, in Chapter 13, Constantine Michalopoulos addresses some of the difficult payments problems that have confronted many formerly communist countries since the end of the Cold War – yet another of the many subjects to which Peter Kenen has turned his attention (Kenen 1991). Focusing specifically on the members of the Commonwealth of Independent States (the CIS, comprising all the republics of the former Soviet Union except the Baltic nations of Estonia, Latvia, and Lithuania), Michalopoulos reviews recent trends in trade and payments within the CIS and evaluates alternative policy solutions that were attempted or might have been considered to alleviate the financing difficulties that most CIS countries have experienced. The remedy for their payments problems, he argues, must be sought along two tracks: first, more effective stabilization measures, to enhance the prospect of convertibility in the region; and second, a strengthening of institutional arrangements to permit efficient settlements through correspondent bank accounts. A multilateral clearing arrangement, though once a potentially appealing option, would no longer be appropriate in these countries' changed economic circumstances. Increased external financing, on the other hand, remains essential, but only if conditioned on continued progress in stabilization and structural reform.

In keeping with the spirit of inquiry that we all imbibed from Peter Kenen as his students or collaborators, each of the essays in this volume concludes with suggestions for further research. In this way we hope that the impact of Kenen's outstanding intellect and imagination, which we have all felt so profoundly in our own work, will continue to manifest itself in international economic scholarship for years to come.

REFERENCES

Allen, Polly R., and Peter B. Kenen (1980). *Asset Markets, Exchange Rates, and Economic Integration: A Synthesis*. Cambridge University Press.

Kenen, Peter B. (1965). "Nature, Capital, and Trade," *Journal of Political Economy* 73:5 (October), 437–60.

Kenen, Peter B. (1969). "The Theory of Optimum Currency Areas: An Eclectic View." In R. A. Mundell and A. K. Swoboda, eds., *Monetary Problems of the International Economy*, pp. 41–60. Chicago: University of Chicago Press.

Kenen, Peter B., ed. (1975). *International Trade and Finance: Frontiers for Research*. Cambridge University Press.

Kenen, Peter B., and Dani Rodrik (1986). "Measuring and Analyzing the Effects of Short-Term Volatility in Real Exchange Rates," *Review of Economics and Statistics* 68 (May), 311–15.

Kenen, Peter B. (1988). *Managing Exchange Rates*. London: Royal Institute of International Affairs.

Kenen, Peter B. (1989). *Exchange Rates and Policy Coordination*. Ann Arbor: University of Michigan Press.

Kenen, Peter B. (1990). "The Coordination of Macroeconomic Policies." In W. Branson, J. Frenkel, and M. Goldstein, eds., *International Policy Coordination and Exchange Rate Fluctuations*. Chicago: University of Chicago Press.

Kenen, Peter B. (1991). "Transitional Arrangements for Trade and Payments Among the CMEA Countries," *International Monetary Fund Staff Papers* 38 (June), 235–57.

CHAPTER 1

The practical theorist: Peter Kenen's contribution to international economics

Paul R. Krugman

Academic economists can achieve distinction in many ways. Some become innovative theorists, who re-imagine the world and give us a new language to discuss how it works. Some become sage advisers to the powerful, shaping policies and institutions by the force of their intellect. Some become servants to the profession – great teachers, or those invaluable academic statesmen who edit journals and guide centers of research. And a few masochistic economists even become academic administrators – a job somebody once described as being like trying to herd cats.

The extraordinary thing about Peter Kenen's career is that he has filled all these roles, and filled them all so very well. The theorist who wrote "Nature, Capital, and Trade" and "The Theory of Optimum Currency Areas" was also a key member of the famed Bellagio Group, which brought together policy-minded academics and intellectually inclined policymakers to discuss international monetary institutions with a depth and cogency that have never been matched. It goes without saying that Kenen's combination of analytical force and real-world acumen has made him one of the most influential teachers of his generation. But not content with these accomplishments, he has also directed the International Finance Section, which under his leadership has maintained to this day a unique role as a center for and publisher of policy-relevant research in international economics. And surely he deserves some academic version of the Purple Heart for not merely serving as provost of a university, but doing so at Columbia in 1969–70 – and emerging from that cauldron with his good humor intact.

A career so varied defies easy summary, especially given that in the midst of all his other activities Peter Kenen has somehow managed to write dozens of books and monographs and publish more than a hundred papers. Still, at the risk of being presumptuous I would suggest that there

7

is a distinctive Kenen modus operandi that informs many of his writings
– whether they were written for an academic or a policy audience.

To understand the quintessential Kenen contribution, one needs to
realize that economists and policymakers, each in their separate ways,
are inveterate oversimplifiers. Economists, of course, are always trying
to reduce the complexity of the world to something they can model. This
is an entirely appropriate goal. Sometimes, however, the pursuit of
simplicity, which is necessary, leads modelers to confuse beauty with
truth – to imagine that the simplest, most elegant model that seems to
yield insight about a phenomenon must also be an adequate framework
for discussing how that phenomenon actually works in practice. Often,
alas, factors that the modeler regards as inessential details turn out to
be crucial in reality. To take only one important example: the elegance
of the two-good, two-factor trade model, its ability to illustrate in so
compact a form so many principles of economic analysis, has seduced
many theorists into believing that so beautiful a model must also be
essentially true; yet the evidence is overwhelming that this model is too
simple to provide even a first cut at understanding the realities of world
trade.

Policymakers, in their own way, also seek more simplicity than the
world really offers. They want strong, clear ideas, and are averse to
hearing about awkward tradeoffs. (I am told that the European
Commission's EMU study, *One Market, One Money*, was originally intended as a survey of the costs and benefits of monetary union. After
looking at some early draft chapters, the higher-ups redefined it as a
survey of the benefits.) Yet many policy issues – above all, the kinds of
international monetary issues on which Peter Kenen has often worked –
have no ideal resolution; they must be viewed as a matter of making the
best compromise among competing objectives.

If there is a distinctive Kenen attribute, it is his ability to identify the
crucial piece that is missing in an oversimplified discussion, whether
among academics or among policymakers, and to supply that missing
piece. It is always, of course, an easy shot to tell people that they have
overlooked important complications. What takes real talent and insight
is not merely to say that a discussion is oversimplified but to propose a
useful way to correct it – to point out, for example, that the size of an
optimum currency area depends crucially on the fiscal institutions that
span regions (or fail to); that no matter how carefully worded, an international monetary agreement cannot produce a "rhinopotamous" that
reconciles fundamentally opposed objectives. One suspects that Peter
Kenen's uniquely broad experience has been crucial to his ability both to
point out the missing pieces and to supply them – for example, that he is

sensitive to institutional issues that other economists might miss because of his unusual experience in talking with people who really make policy, but that he is more conscious of the limits of institutional competence than many other international advisers because he is such a good analytical economist. Whatever the source of Kenen's ability to combine sharp-edged analysis with institutional realism, it is a very special talent indeed.

With these remarks as background, let me follow the outline of this book and highlight some (but by no means all!) of Peter Kenen's important contributions to the theory of international trade, international monetary theory, and the realities of international economic policy.

International trade theory

Peter Kenen began his career during the golden age of Heckscher–Ohlin trade theory – the era marked not only by the thorough analysis of the two-sector model but more generally by the development of techniques for thinking about general equilibrium in small-scale models. Two of Kenen's earliest papers, "On the Geometry of Welfare Economics" (1957) and "Distribution Demand, and Equilibrium in International Trade" (1959), were significant methodological contributions to that enterprise, offering analytical techniques for integrating the analysis of production with that of distribution.

More than a decade later, in his paper "Migration, the Terms of Trade, and Economic Welfare in the Source Country" (1971), Kenen returned to the two-factor model, making the point that assessing the effects of a shock depends crucially on taking into account the full general equilibrium consequences of that shock. The then-standard analysis of factor mobility found that emigration would lower the income of those who remained in the source country. Kenen pointed out that this analysis assumed a downward-sloping marginal product curve for labor, which was necessarily true only in the case of a closed economy. In an open economy facing given world prices, emigration would leave factor prices and hence the income of remaining residents unchanged. In an open economy facing a nonlinear offer curve, emigration might either improve or worsen the terms of trade (depending on the factor intensity of exports), producing first-order gains or losses rather than the second-order welfare effects asserted by the standard model. Finally, Kenen pointed out that it might be crucial to take into account the impact of the migrants on production and demand in the destination as well as in the source country, a point often forgotten to this day in analyses of factor mobility. All in all, the paper is an elegant application of classic trade theory, showing that Kenen was and is as good as anyone at ringing the changes on the two-factor model.

Kenen's most distinctive contribution to the theory of international trade, however, was his pioneering effort to go beyond the two-factor model, above all in "Nature, Capital, and Trade" (1965) and its sequel, "Toward a More General Theory of Capital and Trade" (1968).

To understand the motivation for these papers, it may be helpful to recall the peculiar state of international trade theory in the early 1960s. By that time the two-factor model had been polished into the beautiful structure it remains to this day – a structure that combines a pleasing minimalism in its basic approach with unexpected subtleties in its implications, providing in one package a sort of workout in basic economic principles, a set of useful metaphors for thinking about world trade, and a practical tool for analyzing certain kinds of policy problems. The combined simplicity and power of the 2×2 model had made it the dominant paradigm of international trade theory. Yet it was also clear that the model failed in important ways to account for the data. Most obviously, factor prices, then as now, were manifestly *not* equalized. Less obviously, it was hard to reconcile the evident importance of capital flows with the proposition that trade and capital mobility were perfect substitutes. Finally, Leontief's work on the factor content of trade had yielded the famous paradox that U.S. exports were labor-intensive.

The conflict between theory and evidence had put trade theorists in an awkward bind. They were reluctant to abandon the simplicity and elegance of their standard model, yet that model was clearly inadequate. What were they to do?

Peter Kenen's answer was to offer a new model that was more complex than 2×2, but still tractable, with two crucial features that moved it substantially closer to realism.

The first crucial feature of the model introduced in "Nature, Capital, and Trade" was that it included not two but three factors. The objection to models with more than two factors up to that point had been simply that they were too complicated; and indeed it is hard to say anything about the general properties of a 3-factor, 2-good model. Kenen, however, imposed an ingenious two-level structure that allowed him to avoid getting bogged down in algebraic complexity. At the lower level, capital was applied to the primary factors, land and labor, to produce "improved" land and labor; only at the higher level were these "improved" factors combined to produce final goods. It turned out that by imposing this structure Kenen had created a three-factor model which was as amenable to analytical treatment as the standard two-factor model.

It may be worth pointing out two other important features of this production structure. First, the lower level of Kenen's production model was, in effect, a version of the "specific factors" model that along with 2×2 and the basic Ricardian setup has become one of the workhorses of international economics – except that Kenen's work preceded by quite a few years the papers by Jones[1] and Samuelson[2] that are generally credited with introducing the specific factors model! Second, Kenen's approach, in a way, allowed him to have his cake and eat it too when it came to factor price equalization. In his model, the prices of "improved" factors *are* equalized by trade, because the upper level of the production structure is in effect Heckscher–Ohlin; but the prices of unimproved factors are not, because they also depend on the rate of return on capital.

The other crucial feature of Kenen's analysis was his insistence on viewing capital not as a physical factor of production comparable to land or labor, but rather as an Austrian-style stock of "waiting" – which he modeled as a sort of wage fund needed to transform stocks of labor and land into flows of factor services. The most important result of this point of view was that Kenen quickly concluded that human capital created by education was at least as important as the physical capital stock, a point that economists seem to need to rediscover every twenty years or so; and Kenen showed, once again well in advance of some of the papers that are often credited with discovering the point, that the Leontief paradox might well be resolved by using an inclusive measure that included human as well as physical capital.

"Nature, Capital, and Trade" did not become the canonical model of international trade – which is no surprise, because one can say that today there really is no canonical model, only a half-dozen special models that are frequently applied to different issues. (A modern international economist must be prepared to accept two or three contradictory sets of assumptions before breakfast). However, the paper played a crucial role in opening up trade theory to a wider set of concerns, and it remains widely read and taught (indeed, I have always taught Kenen's model in my graduate trade course as a classic demonstration of how strategic assumptions can reduce a seemingly hopeless problem to elegant tractability).

International monetary theory

International monetary theory has always been a subject driven more by current policy concerns than by the real side of international economics, and Peter Kenen's work is no exception. Kenen, however, has been closer to the actual concerns of policymakers than most of his colleagues; as a result, every major shift in the nature of those concerns (and this is a corner of economics in which the rules of the game seem to be rewritten every few years) has elicited from him a new theoretical analysis. One might, of course, imagine that models built to illuminate contemporary policy issues would lose their relevance as time passes. Those of us who play the game of "model the current controversy" have often found, however, that, although the issues move on, the model often has more staying power than you might have expected; and that has been especially true of Kenen's work.

One of the pleasures of writing this essay was reading through many (though not enough) of Peter Kenen's papers, and discovering jewels that I had never before encountered. One of those jewels is his early paper "International Liquidity and the Balance of Payments of a Reserve-Currency Country" (1960), a concise analysis of the "Triffin problem." Kenen set up a cleverly minimalist framework with hardly any moving parts: the United States holds gold but freely exchanges it for dollars held by central banks, and the rest of the world can use either dollars or gold as reserves, but its willingness to hold dollars depends on the amount of gold the United States is known to have backing those dollars. Using this simple framework Kenen not only showed that a gold-dollar standard is unsustainable in a world where dollar reserves grow faster than the gold stock; he also showed (long before catastrophe theory became briefly trendy) that the unraveling of the system would come suddenly: when the ratio of gold to dollars falls below a critical level, there will be a cumulative process in which central banks shift from dollars to gold, which reduces the gold reserves of the United States, leading to a further flight from the dollar, and so on.

A crucial aspect of the "Triffin" era concern over world reserves was, of course, the question of how large reserves needed to be. It seemed natural to suppose that the demand for reserves would increase with the size of world trade, but could more be said? Peter Kenen has not, it must be said, specialized in sustained econometric projects, but several times he has produced the crucial first-cut paper that launches an extensive empirical literature. He did just that with the essay he co-wrote with Eleanor Yudin, "The Demand for International Reserves" (1965), which went beyond simple money-multiplier stories about reserve demand. In the Kenen–Yudin framework the demand for reserves was assumed, instead, to arise from a precautionary motive – the desire to hedge against unfavorable shocks to the balance of payments. The framework was, as Kenen himself is the first to admit, oversimplified, but it opened the door to a long and productive research program.

Over the course of the 1960s the debate over international monetary institutions widened from its initial focus on the size and composition of reserves to a broader concern over the appropriate exchange regime. This debate has remained utterly relevant, and modern discussions of what came to be known as the "optimum currency area" continue to rely heavily on the three seminal contributions to the subject: Robert Mundell's 1961 article,[3] Ronald McKinnon's 1963 paper,[4] and Peter Kenen's "The Theory of Optimum Currency Areas: An Eclectic View" (1969).

Perhaps the best way to describe Kenen's contribution to this debate is to say that Mundell's and McKinnon's contributions, important as they were, offered what at least seemed to be quite one-dimensional analyses of the problem. Mundell argued that a currency area should be determined by the extent of labor mobility – end of story. McKinnon's analysis linked the size of optimum currency areas to the openness of regions to international trade – end of story (at least the way many people read it). What Kenen did was not only to point out that both factors matter, but to add two other crucial criteria, which vastly alter the practical analysis of proposals for fixed rates or currency union.

First, Kenen pointed out that a region may not suffer much from being part of a currency area, even if labor mobility is absent, if it has a highly diversified economy. The reason is that a diversified region is unlikely to suffer the large idiosyncratic shocks that would make exchange rate adjustments vital. This is not an abstract or old-fashioned argument – on the contrary, it is crucial in making the case for EMU. Realistic advocates of EMU acknowledge that Europe does not currently bear much resemblance to a Mundellian optimum currency area: there is not much labor mobility, and it will be a long time before there is anything like the geographic mobility that characterizes American workers. Nor can one really count on labor market "flexibility" to make it easy to achieve large adjustments in relative wage rates and price levels. But sophisticated EMU supporters point out with considerable justice that European countries are highly diversified economies with quite similar product mixes, and argue that, as a result, large "asymmetric" shocks requiring major changes in relative wages will be few and far between. Whenever they make this argument, they are (whether they know it or not) drawing on Peter Kenen's insights.

Second, Kenen pointed out that in practice it is essential to consider an institutional fact that international economists might like to ignore but cannot: the large role of taxation and spending, especially transfer payments, in modern economies. Because of this role, he argued, there are strong reasons why a currency area should coincide with the fiscal unit. On one side, to have a single fiscal unit sprawl across several currencies whose values fluctuate would create great technical difficulties for the central government: "ulcer rates in government are already far too high, and ought not to be increased unnecessarily"[5] (A decade later, the problems of administering Europe's Common Agricultural Policy, under which payments ended up being based on "green" exchange rates that differed from actual market rates, were a major motivation for the creation of the EMS.) On the other hand, Kenen reemphasized a point he had made in his earlier paper, "Toward a Supranational Monetary System" (1967): a region that is part of a unified fiscal system is likely to be able to cope with idiosyncratic shocks much more easily than one that it is not, receiving both automatic and discretionary transfers from the central government to carry it through its difficulties. Here is a point often emphasized by critics of EMU: if fiscal integration is crucial to monetary union, then Europe, with hardly any central budget other than the CAP, fails the test. And like the supporters of EMU, these critics are, whether they know it or not, drawing on Peter Kenen's insights.

It is also worth noting that a key element in all discussions of optimum currency areas has been the proposition that there is a cost to exchange rate variability – a cost that is due, at least in part, to the increased uncertainty imposed on international trade and investment. The measurement of such costs has always been elusive, and remains so to this day. Nonetheless, Peter Kenen and Dani Rodrik made a pioneering contribution to the empirical literature on this subject in 1986, in their effort to estimate the effects of volatility on trade flows, "Measuring and Analyzing the Effects of Short-Term Volatility in Real Exchange Rates."

While economists debated the relative merits of fixed and flexible rates, during the 1970s fixed rates in fact gave way to generalized floating. (Although the transition was driven by the force of events rather than deliberate policy, one may argue that the defense of the old regime was less determined than it might have been if economists had not been generally in favor of floating.) One response of economists was to try to develop new frameworks that might restore some order to the international monetary system; I will describe some of Peter Kenen's contributions to that debate in the next section of this essay. However, there was also a need to understand how the new system worked, for even though many economists had long advocated a move to flexible exchange rates, when the change actually happened it turned out that the profession was woefully unprepared for the realities of such rates in a world of high capital mobility.

Two questions in particular became particularly urgent. First, how did the tools of traditional macroeconomic policy operate under the new regime? Second, what role, if any, might exchange market intervention play as a policy tool?

It is important to realize that although the Mundell–Fleming model, which remains the workhorse of international macroeconomics, was already available in the 1970s, there was at the time considerable confusion over how to model both the mobility of capital and exchange rate determination. The Mundell–Fleming model was commonly stated as a *flow* model – that is, with capital flows depending on the interest differential. The job of equilibrating the foreign exchange market was commonly thought of as depending, even in the short run, on real adjustment: an incipient payments deficit would lead to a decline in the currency, which would stimulate net exports, directly acting to reduce the imbalance and indirectly stimulating the economy and hence raising interest rates. Intervention likewise was treated as a flow; its effectiveness depended inversely on the responsiveness of capital flows to interest differentials.

It was clear to most international economists that this was a crude and awkward framework. As a graduate student at the time, I can remember the sense of relief I felt when a group of papers – by Pentti Kouri, William Branson, Rudi Dornbusch, Lance Girton and Dale Henderson, and Polly Allen and Peter Kenen – offered a far cleaner approach based on Tobin-type financial modeling. In these new models financial markets were characterized by an instantaneous stock equilibrium, with no need to rely on real adjustment to occur moment by moment. The new models also brought a huge increase in the clarity of discussion over such once-tortured issues as the distinction between sterilized and unsterilized intervention (both were, like open-market operations, reshufflings of the central bank's portfolio; unsterilized intervention was a swap of domestic money for foreign bonds, sterilized a swap of domestic *bonds* for foreign bonds) and the potential role of forward-market intervention (which now could clearly be seen as very similar to sterilized intervention – I remember acing an interview at the IMF by explaining the equivalence). Finally, portfolio balance models offered at least one way to integrate the short run with the long run, to show how the market might enforce long-run current account balance. Although the portfolio balance approach to exchange rates had many creators, its most definitive statement was the 1980 book by Allen and Kenen, who also did the most thorough job of exploring its implications for macro policy – implications that were similar to, but more nuanced than, those of the Mundell–Fleming model.

The portfolio balance approach to the exchange rate does not loom as large on the scene now as it did fifteen years ago. (Tobin-type financial models have fallen out of favor in domestic macro as well.) Partly this is the result of a shift in concerns: international monetary economists now worry mainly about expectations of future exchange rates and far less about the wealth and portfolio rebalancing that was so emphasized in Allen and Kenen. Partly it is because of the evidence that has convinced many international economists that bonds in different currencies are close enough substitutes as to make sterilized intervention ineffective (although Kenen has remained unconvinced: his own sense of the lessons of history is that intervention matters more than most of his colleagues think). Partly it is also the result of the general debacle of empirical exchange rate models. Nonetheless, although the work of Kenen and others on this issue may not be read as much now as it was some years ago, it played a crucial role in clarifying the analysis of the macro-economics of floating exchange rates at a time when there was much confusion.

There have been many other Kenen contributions to international monetary theory, but I will mention only one more: his work on the microeconomics of international money, and in particular the role of the dollar. During the 1960s, when international monetary economics was preoccupied with the problems of reserve assets, the willingness of nations to hold dollar-denominated reserves was a crucial issue. With the transition to floating rates and the general increase in capital mobility (which makes stocks of reserves less important than the access of countries to world financial markets), that issue has been far less crucial – and has been largely ignored by most theorists. Nonetheless, the dollar continues to play a special and strategic role in the world economy, both in official and in private transactions. How should we think about this role? How durable is it? Peter Kenen, at least, has never lost sight of the importance of these questions; his 1983 Group of Thirty monograph, "The Role of the Dollar as an International Currency," remains one of the most insightful discussions of the subject.

Policy

Peter Kenen was a precocious entrant to the world of policy discussion. He was not yet 30 when he published a monograph on trade policy under the imprimatur of the Joint Economic Committee, and he was the youngest member of the original Bellagio Group, that remarkable academic-policymaker study group that met from 1964 to 1977.

By all accounts, during the 1960s the Bellagio Group was the Camelot of international monetary affairs, a unique time and place in which deep thought connected with the reality of actual policy. Peter Kenen played a key role in forging the special clarity of that group's contributions to the language and (sometimes) practice of policy, above all its justly celebrated formulation of the three-horned dilemma of reconciling adjustment, confidence, and liquidity. That dilemma remains as real as ever – ask the former Finance Ministers of the United Kingdom, Sweden, Mexico, . . .

In the end, of course, the fixed-rate system did collapse. The decade after the fall of Bretton Woods was marked by many conferences attempting to put together some more ordered system. Peter Kenen was a frequent participant in such conferences, but should not be blamed for their failure to accomplish much; as he himself noted in 1974, a reconstruction of something like Bretton Woods was simply not going to happen because "no major government saw reason to sacrifice national advantage in the interests of agreement. No government identified national destiny with the rehabilitation of the international system. None was able to say or believe that its own strength and security would be enhanced significantly by accepting limits on its freedom of action" ("Reforming the Monetary System: You Can't Get There from Here," 1974).[6]

In the less heroic age of international monetary policy that has prevailed since 1971, Peter Kenen has almost always been on the scene of important decisions (if largely invisible behind a cloud of cigarette smoke!), always giving good advice, occasionally having it taken. It is beyond my competence to document his role in any detail. I would like, however, to draw attention to two distinctive Kenen interventions in policy affairs that demonstrate how his special ability to combine rigorous analysis with a well-honed sense for institutions and policy can sometimes lead him to places other economists miss.

The first of these episodes involves the Third World debt crisis of the 1980s. When that crisis emerged there were many proposals for some kind of coordinated international solution; many of these proposals were grandiosely impractical, others simply silly. Early in the game, however, Kenen proposed a fairly simple and inexpensive plan for modest debt forgiveness, financed essentially by bootstrapping the market discount on the debt itself. At the time, the general reaction to the Kenen proposal was that it would not work, because the debt forgiveness involved was – most of us thought (I was working on the issue for the Council of Economic Advisers at the time) – simply not enough to make much difference. Meanwhile, any debt forgiveness that *was* large enough to matter was ruled out by the unwillingness of either creditor-country governments or their banks to accept the implied cost. The result was a seven-year period of muddling through, before the principle of debt forgiveness was finally accepted after all in 1989.

Here is the interesting point: when some debt forgiveness did take place under the so-called Brady Plan (misnamed, since the original plan was not really Brady's, and anyway made no sense; the template for the eventually successful deals was devised by Mexican officials), it turned out to be quite modest in practice. Nonetheless, each country that arranged a Brady deal quickly found its situation transformed, its access to international capital markets restored. It turned out, in other words, that the size of the debt reduction was not all that important: what really mattered was the psychological impact of a debt deal, the sense of putting the problem behind us. Nobody can know whether such a modest deal could have worked in 1983, but one may well argue that Peter Kenen, with his sense for the realities of international finance, may have had a better notion of what would work than those of us whose assessment of the problem was based exclusively on quantitative models.

The second episode, which is still in progress, involves the drive toward European monetary union. EMU has generated a vast research literature, much of it extremely high-quality. With few exceptions, however, first-rate researchers have paid little attention to the actual content of the Maastricht treaty; it has simply been assumed that if EMU does go through, European monetary affairs will subsequently be managed pretty much the same way they are in the United States (or perhaps in Germany). But as anyone who read Kenen's writings on optimum currency areas should have realized, the central banking institutions of such an area spanning a number of sovereign states with very little fiscal integration cannot simply behave like those of a centralized political unit. Who is worrying about how EMU will actually work, and whether the institutions created in the Maastricht treaty are up to the job? Well, Peter Kenen is – and he is almost the only world-class economist who is doing so. His "EMU after Maastricht" (1992) remains far and away the best guide for economists who want to know how this strange bird, which has repeatedly defied prediction of its demise, will actually behave.

In concluding this essay, let me strike a slightly regretful note. It seems to me that it will be a very long time before the world sees another Peter Kenen – that is, an economist who is able to integrate the theory and practice of international economics so seamlessly. This may seem a strange remark to make at a time when there are probably more smart economists in high-level positions than ever before – when Larry Summers is Deputy Treasury Secretary and Joe Stiglitz is Chairman of the Council of Economic Advisers. Still, in today's world the economist who wants to influence policy must be *political* – both in the limited sense of being expert at maneuvering through the intrigues of office politics and in the larger sense of being a partisan – in a way that Kenen has never been. Kenen rose to eminence in a very different environment, one in which (at least as far as international monetary affairs were concerned) the grand issues were regarded not as struggles for advantage but as problems to be solved in the common interest, in which what was good for the world monetary system was presumed to be good for America. In 1977 Kenen wrote ("Monetary Reform: An Overall View") about that era:

> When we look back upon what academics and officials, but especially academics, have written about international monetary problems in the last twenty-five years, one fact stands out. Without always knowing it, most of us have judged events, decisions, and proposals by an idealistic, cosmopolitan criterion. We have asked how far each step has taken us toward the creation of a world money to which national monies would be subordinated and by which they might someday be supplanted.

What international economist would now make such a statement? Not only would that sort of idealism immediately brand him as irrelevant, he might even worry slightly about receiving an unwanted package from some self-proclaimed patriot! For a time a more limited, purely European, sort of cosmopolitan idealism seemed to prevail in the discussion of EMU; but there, too, technocracy has given way to partisan politics and nationalism. The kind of world that produced a Kenen – that allowed an economist to enter the inner circle of policy discussion merely because he was brilliant, wise, and well-spoken, without asking whose side he was on – is no more.

But that is all the more reason why we should honor and value Peter Kenen, whose work did so much both to help us understand the world and to do a better job of managing it.

NOTES

1. Ronald W. Jones, "A three-factor model in theory, trade, and history," in Jagdish Bhagwati et al., eds., *Trade, Balance of Payments, and Growth* (Amsterdam: North-Holland, 1971), 3–21.
2. Paul Samuelson, "Ohlin was right," *Swedish Journal of Economics* 73 (1971), 365–84.
3. Robert A. Mundell, "The theory of optimum currency areas," *American Economic Review* 51 (1961), 657–65.

4. Ronald I. McKinnon, "Optimum currency areas," *American Economic Review* 53 (1963), 717–25.
5. Kenen, 1969.
6. This essay is included in *Exchange Rates and the Monetary System: Selected Essays of Peter B. Kenen* (1994).

Peter B. Kenen: A chronology of principal publications as of June 1996

Books and monographs

British Monetary Policy and the Balance of Payments, 1951–1957. Cambridge: Harvard University Press, 1960.

Giant Among Nations: Problems in United States Foreign Economic Policy. New York: Harcourt Brace, 1960 (reprinted with "Postscript," Chicago: Rand McNally, 1963).

Money, Debt, and Economic Activity. Englewood Cliffs, NJ: Prentice-Hall. Third edition, 1961 (with A. G. Hart); fourth edition, 1969 (with A. Entine and A. G. Hart).

United States Commercial Policy: A Program for the 1960s. Washington, DC: Joint Economic Committee, U.S. Congress, 1961.

The Reserve-Asset Preferences of Central Banks and Stability of the Gold-Exchange Standard. Princeton Studies in International Finance 10, International Finance Section, Princeton University, 1963.

International Economics. Englewood Cliffs, NJ: Prentice-Hall. First edition, 1964; second edition, 1967; third edition (with R. Lubitz), 1971.

Capital Mobility and Financial Integration: A Survey. Princeton Studies in International Finance 39, International Finance Section, Princeton University, 1976.

A Model of the U.S. Balance of Payments. Lexington, KY: Lexington Books, 1978 (in association with D. P. Dungan and D. L. Warner).

Exchange Rates, Domestic Prices, and the Adjustment Process. Occasional Paper 1, New York: Group of Thirty, 1980 (with C. Pack).

Asset Markets, Exchange Rates, and Economic Integration. Cambridge University Press, 1980 (with P. R. Allen).

Essays in International Economics. Princeton: Princeton University Press, 1980.

The Role of the Dollar as an International Currency. Occasional Paper 13. New York: Group of Thirty, 1983.

21

The International Economy. Englewood Cliffs, NJ: Prentice-Hall: First edition, 1985; second edition, 1989. Cambridge University Press: Third edition, 1994.

Financing, Adjustment, and the International Monetary Fund. Washington, DC: Brookings Studies in International Economics, 1986.

Managing Exchange Rates. The Chatham House Papers, Royal Institute of International Affairs, London, 1988; New York: Council on Foreign Relations Press, 1989.

Exchange Rates and Policy Coordination. Manchester, U.K.: University of Manchester Press, and Ann Arbor: University of Michigan Press, 1989.

EMU after Maastricht. Washington, DC: Group of Thirty, 1992.

Exchange Rates and the Monetary System: Selected Essays of Peter B. Kenen. Aldershot, U.K.: Edward Elgar, 1994.

Economic and Monetary Union in Europe: Moving Beyond Maastricht. Cambridge University Press, 1995.

Books edited

Trade, Growth, and the Balance of Payments: Essays in Honor of Gottfried Haberler. Chicago: Rand McNally, 1965 (with R. E. Caves and H. G. Johnson).

The Open Economy. New York: Columbia University Press, 1968 (with R. C. Lawrence).

International Trade and Finance: Frontiers for Research. Cambridge University Press, 1975.

The International Monetary System under Flexible Exchange Rates: Essays in Honor of Robert Triffin. Cambridge: Ballinger, 1981 (with R. Cooper, J. de Macedo, and J. van Ypersele).

Handbook of International Economics, Vols. I, II. Amsterdam: North-Holland, 1984, 1985 (with R. W. Jones).

Managing the World Economy: Fifty Years after Bretton Woods. Washington, DC: Institute for International Economics, 1994.

The International Monetary System: Essays in Memory of Rinaldo Ossola. Cambridge University Press, 1994 (with F. Papadia and F. Saccomanni).

Understanding Interdependence: The Macroeconomics of the Open Economy. Princeton: Princeton University Press, 1995.

Papers and professional publications

"On the Geometry of Welfare Economics," *Quarterly Journal of Economics* 71, 1957.

"Distribution, Demand, and Equilibrium in International Trade," *Kyklos* 12, 1959.

"International Liquidity and the Balance of Payments of a Reserve-Currency Country," *Quarterly Journal of Economics* 74, 1960.

"Economic Aspects of Private Direct Investment." In *Taxation and Operations Abroad* (C. L. Harriss, ed.). Princeton: Tax Institute, 1960.

"International Liquidity: The Next Steps," *American Economic Review* 53, 1963.

"Toward an Atlantic Capital Market," *Lloyds Bank Review*, July 1963.

"Development, Mobility, and Tariffs: A Dissenting Note," *Kyklos* 16, 1963.

"Measuring the U.S. Balance of Payments," *Review of Economics and Statistics* 46, 1964.

"Déséquilibres des Paiements et Etalon Monetaire International," Banque Nationale de Belgique, *Bulletin* 40, 1965.

"Trade, Speculation, and the Forward Exchange Rate." In *Trade, Growth, and the Balance of Payments: Essays in Honor of Gottfried Haberler* (R. Baldwin et al., eds.). Chicago: Rand McNally, 1965.

"Nature, Capital, and Trade," *Journal of Political Economy* 73, 1965.

"The Demand for International Reserves," *Review of Economics and Statistics* 47, 1965; and "Reply," 49, 1967 (with E. Yudin).

"A Suggestion for Solving the International Liquidity Problem," Banca Nazionale del Lavoro, *Quarterly Review* 76, 1966 (with F. Modigliani).

"Financing and Adjustment: The Carrot and the Stick." In *Maintaining and Restoring Balance in International Payments* (F. Machlup et al., eds.). Princeton: Princeton University Press, 1966.

"Toward a Supranational Monetary System." In *Issues in Banking and Monetary Analysis* (G. Pontecorvo, ed.). New York: Holt, Rinehart, and Winston, 1967.

"Toward a More General Theory of Capital and Trade." In *The Open Economy* (P. B. Kenen and R. C. Lawrence, eds.). New York: Columbia University Press, 1968.

"Private International Capital Movements." In *International Encyclopedia of the Social Sciences*. New York: Crowell-Collier, 1968.

"The Theory of Optimum Currency Areas: An Eclectic View." In *Monetary Problems of the International Economy* (R. A. Mundell and A. Swoboda, eds.). Chicago: University of Chicago Press, 1969.

"The International Position of the Dollar in a Changing World," *International Organization* 23, 1969.

"Flexible Exchange Rates," *American Economic Review* 57, 1969.

"Skills, Human Capital, and Comparative Advantage." In *Education, Income and Human Capital* (W. L. Hansen, ed.). New York: Columbia University Press, 1970.

"Migration, the Terms of Trade, and Economic Welfare in the Source Country." In *Trade, Balance of Payments and Growth* (J. N. Bhagwati et al., eds.). Amsterdam: North-Holland, 1971.

"Export Instability and Economic Growth," *Kyklos* 24, 1972 (with C. Voivodas).

"Convertibility and Consolidation: Options for Future Reform of the System," *American Economic Review* 62, 1972.

"Economic Policy in a Small Economy." In *Trade, Development and Planning* (W. Sellekaerts, ed.). London: Macmillan, 1974.

"The Balance of Payments and Policy Mix: Simulations Based on a U.S. Model," *Journal of Finance* 29, 1974.

"A Note on Tariff Changes and World Welfare," *Quarterly Journal of Economics* 88, 1974.

"Floats, Glides, and Indicators: A Comparison of Methods for Changing Exchange Rates," *Journal of International Economics* 5, 1975.

"Factor Use, Factor Ratios, and the Leontief Paradox," *Asian Economics* 16, 1976.

"A Comparison of Exchange-Rate Regimes: Stability, Profitability, and Speculation." In *Recent Issues in International Monetary Economics* (E. Claassin and P. Salin, eds.). Amsterdam: North-Holland, 1976.

"Flexible Exchange Rates and Monetary Autonomy," *Revista Internazionale del Scienze Economiche e Commerciali* 23, 1976.

"Portfolio Adjustment in Open Economies: A Comparison of Alternative Specifications," *Weltwirtschaftliches archiv* 112, 1976 (with P. R. Allen).

"Capital Mobility and the Integration of Capital Markets." In *Economic Integration* (F. Machlup, ed.). London: Macmillan, 1976.

"Debt Relief as Development Assistance." In *The New International Economic Order* (J. N. Bhagwati, ed.). Cambridge: MIT Press, 1977.

"Monetary Reform: An Overall View." In *International Monetary Relations after Jamaica* (F. Basagni, ed.). Paris: Atlantic Institute, 1977.

"Techniques to Control International Reserves." In *The New International Monetary System* (R. A. Mundell and J. J. Polak, eds.). New York: Columbia University Press, 1977.

"New Views of Exchange Rates and Old Views of Policies," *American Economic Review* 66, 1978.

"Who Thinks Who's in Charge Here: Faculty Perceptions of Influence and Power in the University," *Sociology of Education* 51, 1978 (with R. Kenen).

"Monetary Policy in Developing Countries." In *Conference on the Role of Monetary Policy in Developing Countries*. Banjul: Central Bank of the Gambia, 1978.

"The Transmission of Disturbances from Market to Planned Economies." In *Inflation in Planned Economies* (E. Neuberger and L. Tyson, eds.). New York: Pergamon Press, 1980 (with L. Tyson).

"The Analytics of a Substitution Account, Banca Nazionale del Lavoro," *Quarterly Review* 139, 1981.

"Intervention and Sterilization in the Short Run and the Long Run." *The International Monetary System under Flexible Exchange Rates* (R. N. Cooper et al., eds.). Cambridge, MA: Ballinger, 1981.

"The Use of SDRs to Supplement or Substitute for Other Means of Finance." In *International Money and Credit: The Policy Roles* (G. von Furstenberg, ed.). Washington, DC: International Monetary Fund, 1983.

"Improving the International Adjustment Process." In *World Money and National Policies*, Occasional Paper 12. New York: Group of Thirty, 1983.

"Prospects for Reform of the International Monetary System," *Journal of Development Planning* 14, 1984.

"Beyond Recovery: Challenges to U.S. Economic Policy in the 1980s," *The Global Repercussions of U.S. Monetary and Fiscal Policy* (S. A. Hewlett et al., eds.). Cambridge, MA: Ballinger, 1984.

"Macroeconomic Analysis and Policy: How the Closed Economy Was Opened." In *Handbook of International Economics*, Vol. II (R. W. Jones and P. B. Kenen, eds.). Amsterdam: North-Holland, 1985.

"Forward Rates, Interest Rates, and Expectations under Alternative Exchange-Rate Regimes," *Economic Record* 61, 1985.

"Measuring and Analyzing the Effects of Short-Term Volatility in Real Exchange Rates," *Review of Economics and Statistics* 68, May 1986 (with D. Rodrik).

"What Role for IMF Surveillance?" *World Development* 15, December 1987.

"Global Policy Optimization and the Choice of Exchange-Rate Regime," *Journal of Policy Modeling* 9, Spring 1987.

"Exchange Rate Management: What Role for Intervention?" *American Economic Review* 77, May 1987.

"International Money and Macroeconomics." In *World Economics Problems* (K. A. Elliott and J. Williamson, eds.). Washington, DC: Institute for International Economics, 1988.

"Reflections on the EMS Experience." In *The European Monetary System* (F. Giavazzi, S. Micossi, and M. Miller, eds.). Cambridge University Press, 1988.

"A Proposal for Reducing the Debt Burdens of Developing Countries." In *Changing Capital Markets and the Global Economy*

(D. B. H. Denoon, ed.). Philadelphia: Global Interdependence Center, 1988.

"The Use of IMF Credit." In *Pulling Together: The International Monetary Fund in a Multipolar World* (R. E. Feinberg and C. Gwin, eds.). Washington, DC: Overseas Development Council, 1989.

"Organizing Debt Relief: The Need for a New Institution," *Journal of Economic Perspectives* 4, Winter 1990.

"The Coordination of Macroeconomic Policies." In *International Policy Coordination and Exchange Rate Fluctuations* (W. H. Branson, J. A. Frenkel, and M. Goldstein, eds.). Chicago: University of Chicago Press, 1990.

"Debt Buybacks and Forgiveness in a Model with Voluntary Repudiation," *International Economic Journal* 5, Spring 1991.

"Transitional Arrangements for Trade and Payments among the CMEA Countries," *International Monetary Fund Staff Papers* 38, June 1991.

"Exchange Rates and Policy Co-ordination in an Asymmetric Model." In *International Economic Policy Co-ordination* (C. Carraro et al., eds.). Oxford: Blackwell, 1991.

"Exchange Rate Arrangements, Seigniorage, and the Provision of Public Goods." In *International Financial Policy: Essays in Honor of Jacques J. Polak* (J. A. Frenkel and M. Goldstein, eds.). Washington, DC: International Monetary Fund, 1991.

"What Have We Learned about the Adjustment Process?" In *International Adjustment and Financing: The Lessons of 1985–1991* (C. F. Bergsten, ed.). Washington, DC: Institute for International Economics, 1991.

"Coordinating Macroeconomic Policies." In *Change: Threat or Opportunity* (U. Kirdar, ed.). United Nations, 1992.

"Third World Debt." In *The New Palgrave Dictionary of Money and Finance* (P. Newman et al., eds.). New York: Stockton Press, 1992.

"The Bretton Woods System." In *The New Palgrave Dictionary of Money and Finance* (P. Newman et al., eds.). New York: Stockton Press, 1992.

"The European Central Bank and Monetary Policy in Stage III of EMU," *International Affairs* 68, 1992.

"Intramarginal Intervention in the EMS and the Target-Zone Model of Exchange-Rate Behavior," *European Economic Review* 36, December 1992 (with K. M. Dominguez).

"EMU, Exchange Rates, and the International Monetary System," *Recherches Economiques de Louvain* 59, Special Issue: Monetary Integration in Europe, January 1993.

"Financial Opening and the Exchange Rate Regime." In *Financial Opening in Developing Countries* (H. Reisen and B. Fischer, eds.). Paris: OECD Development Centre, 1993.

"How Useful Is an EC-wide Monetary Aggregate as an Intermediate Target for Europe?" *Review of International Economics* 1, October 1993 (with T. A. Bayoumi).

"Reforming the International Monetary System: An Agenda for the Developing Countries." In *The Pursuit of Reform* (J. J. Teunissen, ed.). The Hague: Forum on Debt and Development, 1993.

"Ways to Reform Exchange-Rate Arrangements." In *Bretton Woods: Looking to the Future*, Background Papers. Washington, DC: Bretton Woods Commission, 1994.

"Managing the World Economy under the Bretton Woods System: An Overview." In *Managing the World Economy: Fifty Years after Bretton Woods* (P. B. Kenen, ed.). Washington, DC: Institute for International Economics, 1994 (with B. Eichengreen).

"Floating Exchange Rates Reconsidered: The Influence of New Ideas, Priorities, and Problems." In *The International Monetary System: Essays in Memory of Rinaldo Ossola* (P. B. Kenen, F. Papadia, and F. Saccommani, eds.). Cambridge University Press, 1994.

"Capital Controls, the EMS and EMU," *Economic Journal* 105, January 1995.

"Agendas for the Bretton Woods Institutions." In *Fifty Years after Bretton Woods: The Future of the IMF and the World Bank* (J. M. Boughton and L. S. Sarwar Lateef, eds.). Washington, DC: International Monetary Fund and World Bank, 1995.

"What Have We Learned from the EMS Crises?" *Journal of Policy Modeling* 17, Special Issue on the International Monetary System, October 1995.

"The Feasibility of Taxing Foreign Exchange Transactions." In *The Tobin Tax: Coping with Financial Volatility* (M. ul Haq, I. Kaul, and I. Grunberg, eds.). New York and Oxford: Oxford University Press, 1996.

"How Can Future Currency Crises à la Mexico Be Prevented?" In *Can Currency Crises Be Prevented or Better Managed?* (J. J. Teunissen, ed.). Amsterdam: Forum on Debt and Development, 1996.

PART I
INTERNATIONAL TRADE THEORY

CHAPTER 2

Nature, capital, and trade: A second look

Patrick J. Conway

Peter Kenen has in recent years been better known for his analysis of international financial markets, but it is interesting to note that one of his first contributions to the economic literature was an article on trade theory. That article, modestly entitled "Nature, Capital, and Trade" (1965), illustrates a number of features of Kenen's research style. First was his preoccupation with real-world outcomes: his goal in that research effort was an explanation for the empirical observation of non-equalized factor prices and the Leontief paradox in the context of theoretical trade theory. Second was his reluctance to let international finance remain submerged, even in a model of international trade. Third was his willingness to shake the foundations of the theory to get at a restatement that fit the historical facts.

The fundamental proposition of the article (hereafter referred to as NCT) was that the empirical "irregularities" of factor price non-equalization and the Leontief paradox signaled a misspecification of the productive technology in theoretical models. Specifically, he posited that capital did not belong in the aggregate production function in the factor-proportions explanations (notably, the Heckscher–Ohlin [or HO] presentation) of trade theory, but rather entered production by improving the services offered by land and labor, the "natural" endowments. He laid out the logical implications of his conjecture in a mathematical model, and demonstrated that this alternative specification created an ingenious extension of the then-standard 2×2 HO trade model. His analytical results were promising, and the empirical evidence he offered indicated that this was indeed a possible explanation of the Leontief paradox. He then provided a more exhaustive statement of his theory in Kenen (1968).

Kenen's efforts in bringing the HO model into a more realistic and dynamic context are noted with respect by Samuelson (1965), Jones

31

(1971), and Findlay (1973), among others. The Kenen formulation of capital used to improve labor is an early description of human capital, introduced as well in 1965 by Becker's seminal *Human Capital* and Keesing (1965); although this has become a central concept in microeconomics, Kenen's proposition for an analogous treatment of capital in trade theory has remained peripheral. One reading of the profession's verdict on the contribution of NCT is provided by Smith (1984: 315), who stated in his summary to research in capital and trade theory that "Kenen's model seems not to have been productive of further work, perhaps because of its algebraic complexity." Current readers of academic journals can conclude only that Kenen was ahead of his time with this article.

Kenen was not alone in his efforts to extend the HO model to include additional factors of production. NCT considers capital as both traded and nontraded input to production, but gives pride of place to the nontraded case because of its consistency with observed factor–price non-equivalence. Others, however, followed the more tractable model for more than two goods proposed by Vanek (1968) to extend the theoretical structure to N goods and M factors. There have also been a number of efforts to test the HO model empirically based upon Vanek (1968) that point up its shortcomings in explaining trade patterns. When Kenen's conjecture is revisited in the light of this subsequent work, his formulation can be viewed as a set of testable restrictions on the $N \times M$ specification of HO theory. Imposition of these restrictions in empirical trade data provides a significant improvement to the explanatory power of recent econometric tests of the HO trade theory. It is satisfying, though not surprising, to find that the Kenen formulation more closely approximates reality – after all, that is what he set out to do!

I examine the issues raised by NCT in the following four sections. In the first section, Kenen's proposition on capital is examined and related to (much) earlier authors. In the second section the Kenen formulation is demonstrated to impose both restrictions and an extension on the traditional 3×3 model; Kenen's conclusions on factor–price equalization, pattern of trade, and the Leontief paradox are restated in this framework. In the third section the Kenen formulation is restated as a set of restrictions on the empirical estimation equations of Bowen, Leamer, and Sveikauskas (1987) and Trefler (1993, 1995). Examination of the data yields results supportive of these restrictions, and thus an affirmation of the Kenen formulation. The final section provides conclusions and suggestions for future research in this area.

What is capital's role in international trade?

NCT draws a fundamental distinction between "natural" factors of production and capital. Each economy is endowed by nature with labor and land stocks, and these provide services over time. Capital, by contrast, is a manufactured and depreciating factor of production. This should imply asymmetry in treatment of capital and "natural" endowments. As Kenen notes in NCT, "Because trade theory is concerned with long-run phenomena, it must treat capital as a stock of 'waiting,' not as a collection of tangible assets. It then proceeds, however, as though this disembodied stock were just like any other factor of production" (438).

The methodological solution that Kenen proposed was that land and labor be modeled as factors of production, whereas capital be viewed as "improving" the services of both these factors. The HO model of international trade is then defined in terms of these services. The natural endowments and capital do not enter the production function for final goods; rather, land and labor services do. These are in turn manufactured through use of the natural endowments and capital.

The notion that capital acts through improving the other factors can be found in earlier authors. Schumpeter (1966: 636–7) associates this notion of the primacy of land and labor with Ricardo, Senior, and James Mill, who spoke of "resolving" capital into hoarded labor and land. This view, however, was supplanted over time by the hypothesis of a triad of coequal factors, of which capital was one among three. Bohm-Bawerk rejected this specification in favor of one in which capital is an intermediate product, and provided a direct precursor to Kenen's formulation.[1] This rejection was not commonly accepted, though; the triad specification (or the triad plus entrepreneur of Marshall) became the commonplace for production, distribution, and international trade theory.[2] The subordinate role for capital is not, for example, found in the work of Heckscher and Ohlin; these two treat all factors as entering symmetrically into the production process.[3]

Kenen places the stock of capital in an idiosyncratic position in his model of production. It is not a part of "nature" (as are labor and land), nor does it enter directly into the production function. There is a three-step process in production:

(1) production of "improved" labor services and land services by application of capital to the natural endowments of labor and land;

(2) production of investment goods and commodity output from labor services and land services;

(3) augmentation of the stock of capital through accumulation of investment goods.

The capital stock augments the productivity of labor and land over time, although its effectiveness depreciates continuously.[4]

Capital is defined broadly in Kenen's formulation: as he puts it in NCT, "it can be employed with equal ease to build roads, drain swamps and train apprentices" (441). Capital will thus include not only the stock of machines and other physical assets, but the "stock" of human capital as well.

The Kenen formulation as a restriction on the 3 × 3 model

The Kenen formulation can be interpreted methodologically as an ingenious method to state a 3-factor, 3-good (3 × 3) HO trade model in two dimensions. The properties of this model have been documented in the years since 1965 (and are summarized nicely in Ethier 1984). A more recent restatement of these properties by Jones (1992) provides an attractive framework for expositing the Kenen formulation in this context.

Equilibrium in a general 3 × 3 model

There are three goods produced in each economy: x, y, and I. They are produced using factors labor (L), land (N) and capital (K) in constant-returns technologies. All factors and services are fully employed in each period. If all three goods are produced in equilibrium, the following equilibrium conditions can be specified.

$$AX = V \tag{2.1}$$

$$A^T W = P \tag{2.2}$$

V is the (3×1) vector of factor endowments, X is the (3×1) vector of outputs, and A is the (3×3) matrix of unit factor coefficients. Equation (2.1) states that the three full employment conditions hold with equality. Equation (2.2) indicates that the payment to productive factors just exhausts the revenue from sale of one unit of each good: W is the (3×1) vector of factor prices, while P is the (3×1) vector of commodity prices. Once commodity prices are defined in international trading equilibrium, both W and the elements of A are determined. For given endowments of factors, equation (2.1) determines the output of each good. Equation

(2.2) can be rewritten in a form conducive to diagrammatics through rowwise division by the elements of P. This becomes a system of three equations setting the sum of factor payment shares θ_{ij} equal to unity.

$$\Sigma_j \theta_{xj} = 1 \qquad j = K, N, L \tag{2.3a}$$

$$\Sigma_j \theta_{yj} = 1 \tag{2.3b}$$

$$\Sigma_j \theta_{lj} = 1 \tag{2.3c}$$

As Jones (1992) points out, following Leamer (1987), the productive equilibrium in this economy can be presented graphically. Given the trading prices of the final goods, the combination of factor payment shares for each production process can be represented as a point on a simplex that Jones calls the "Leamer triangle." With three goods (denoted x, y, and I) there will be three points – and these three define what Jones calls the "activity triangle" within the Leamer triangle. Figure 2.1 illustrates an activity triangle, and indicates for industry X the factor payment shares θ_{xj} received by factors L, N, and K. The total shares of income θ_j earned by the factor endowments of the economy are indicated by the point E_1 – since it lies within the activity triangle, the economy will produce all three goods in trading equilibrium.[5]

Jones (1992) illustrates the properties of the 3×3 model. Jones and Marjit (1991) derive conditions under which the Stolper–Samuelson Theorem will hold in this context, and relates those conditions to the earlier results of Chipman (1969) and Kemp and Wegge (1969) summarized in Ethier (1984). In Figure 2.1, the asymmetry of the activity triangle ensures that the Stolper–Samuelson result will not hold in strong form, as the Kemp–Wegge conditions are violated.

Given the world trading equilibrium (and the consequent prices of final goods), the shares of world income paid to the world endowments of the three factors can be indicated by a single point in the simplex – denoted E_w in Figure 2.1. With factor–price equalization across countries, the activity triangle will be the same for all countries. The country represented by E_1 can be shown to be land- and labor-scarce and capital-abundant (see Jones 1992). Goods x and y will be exported while good I is imported.

The 2×2 model is a degenerate example of this more general model. If land were not used in production, for example, and good I were not produced, then the activity triangle would degenerate to a line segment defined by x_0 and y_0 along the LK side of the simplex. The endowment would also be represented at some point along the LK side. If the endowment fell on the line segment defined by endpoints x_0 and y_0, then

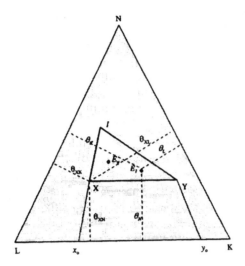

Figure 2.1. The general 3 × 3 model illustrated in a Leamer triangle.

the economy would produce both goods in trading equilibrium. With production of both goods using both factors, factor price equalization will occur as illustrated by Dixit and Norman (1980: 108–9).

It is important to note that both non-equalization of factor prices and a variant of the Leontief paradox are possible in this model. The first would occur for country 1 if its endowment point fell outside the activity triangle. At that point the economy would not produce all three goods in equilibrium, and domestic factor prices would diverge from world prices. The Leontief paradox can occur as well if only two factors are considered. Suppose that land were ignored in considering the trade pattern of country 1 represented in Figure 2.1. Country 1 is capital abundant relative to the world, but observed exports include x, the labor-intensive good. This is the rationale for the paradox put forward by Vanek (1963), Keesing (1965), and others, with various candidates in the role of "third factor." Kenen's contribution was distinct from this line of argument.

Equilibrium in the Kenen formulation

Kenen reshapes the 3 × 3 model to obtain his own model of production and trade. The first amendment concerns the factor endowments. Kenen asserts that in the long-run environment of international trade theory the stock of capital should not be taken as given. Rather, he defines a steady state in which the cost of loanable funds is set equal to the marginal return from investment in each country.[6] The second amendment is to the specification of the production technology: capital is removed from the production functions of the final goods.

In the context of equations (2.1) and (2.2), the endogenous stock of capital in the steady state implies that the return to capital in the W vector becomes exogenous to the production process (although it is endogenously determined by the product of propensities to save and the rate of depreciation of capital) while the capital element in the V vector and the other two elements of the W vector adjust to yield full employment equilibrium. In the Leamer triangle, the position of the activity triangle and the endowment point become functions of the characteristics of the loanable fund market and technological depreciation. Despite the existence of free trade in the three goods, factor prices and the production methods used in trading partners will not be identical if national financial markets are not integrated.

The Kenen specification of the production technology in addition imposes testable constraints upon the observed characteristics of the general 3×3 model. The (2×1) vector VS is defined as made up of land services (NS) and labor services (LS). These are produced with constant-returns technology from the fixed natural endowments (L, N) and capital, yielding the full-employment conditions in equation (2.4). Kenen posited a technology with unit factor coefficients g_{ij} in (2.4) and h_{ik} in the final-good production relation (2.5), with k the index for the use of improved factor services NS and LS.[7] The zero-profit conditions for final-good production are given in equation (2.6).

$$G\,VS = V$$

$$G = \begin{bmatrix} g_{LL} & 0 \\ 0 & g_{NN} \\ g_{LK} & g_{NK} \end{bmatrix} \tag{2.4}$$

$$H\,X = VS$$

$$H = \begin{bmatrix} h_{XL} & h_{YL} & h_{IL} \\ h_{XN} & h_{YN} & h_{IN} \end{bmatrix} \tag{2.5}$$

$$H^{\mathrm{T}}WS = P \tag{2.6}$$

The (2×1) vector WS represents the payments to the "improved" factor services included in the vector VS. As Kenen points out, this model will admit international trade in all three final goods (note that equations

(2.5) and (2.6) are five in number, with two factor prices and three outputs unknown); however, he chose to examine the case in which the investment good I is nontraded. Doing so brought him back comfortably into the Heckscher–Ohlin 2×2 framework, but with interesting twists.

With I nontraded, the full-employment and zero-profit conditions will still hold, but the price of investment goods p_I will not be given in international trade. The resulting system of equations is:

$$G\,VS = V \tag{2.4}$$

$$H^A X^A = VS - \begin{bmatrix} h_{IL} \\ h_{IN} \end{bmatrix} I, \quad H^A = \begin{bmatrix} h_{XL} & h_{YL} \\ h_{XN} & h_{YN} \end{bmatrix} \quad X^A = \begin{bmatrix} x \\ y \end{bmatrix} \tag{2.5a}$$

$$\left(H^A\right)^T WS = P^A \quad P^A = \begin{bmatrix} p_x \\ p_y \end{bmatrix} \tag{2.6a}$$

$$\begin{bmatrix} h_{IL} & h_{IN} \end{bmatrix} WS = p_I \tag{2.7}$$

Equations (2.5a) and (2.6a) represent a classic Samuelsonian Heckscher–Ohlin model of two traded goods in the abridged vector X^A, with unit factor coefficients in H^A and factor prices in WS defined in terms of the improved factor services LS and NS. Once commodity prices are determined by trade, factor prices are determined by (2.6a) and p_I is derived from equation (2.7). Equation (2.5a) provides the determination of commodity output x and y for given factor services, quantity invested, and factor prices. Equation (2.4) represents a Ricardo–Viner model of the production of factor services with specific factors L and N and mobile factor K.[8]

Kenen's conclusions about factor prices and trade become evident when the structure is recognized. The classical Heckscher–Ohlin structure in factor services leads to the classical theoretical results: factor price equalization in improved factor services, Stolper–Samuelson results in terms of commodity and improved factor service prices, and a definition of comparative advantage in terms of endowments in factor services. However, the Ricardo–Viner nature of the transformation of natural endowments to factor services implies that there will be no equalization of the payment to natural endowments in trading economies: we should not expect to see factor payments for "unimproved" labor and land, or for capital, equalized.

There is a further feature of the model that links the trading aspects of the model with the theory of capital. In equation (2.5a) the endowment

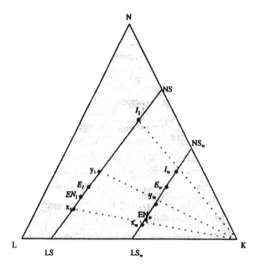

Figure 2.2. The Kenen formulation in the 3×3 model.

of factor services of importance to determination of output is not the *gross* supply of factor services, but the *net* supply after factor use to produce investment goods has been deducted. Two otherwise identical countries will have comparative advantages relative to one another if they choose to produce different quantities of the investment good. Differences in investment-good production have Rybczynski effects on output of the final goods; given identical and homothetic preferences of consumers, this will be sufficient to cause differing opportunity costs in autarky and the incentive to trade.

Why might two countries choose to produce different quantities of investment goods? Kenen attributes this in a world with nonintegrated national financial markets to different national propensities to save, leading to different interest rates on loanable funds and consequently different desired stocks of capital in the steady state. Investment in the steady state will be for replacement purposes only, but with a larger stock of capital there will be larger investment expenditures.

The Kenen formulation can be placed within the more general framework of the 3×3 model through use of the simplex in Figure 2.2. The first stage of production is the creation of improved factor services in equation (2.4). These are intermediate products or, in the terminology of Jones and Marjit (1991), "produced mobile factors." The technologies used to produce these are represented by the points *LS* and *NS* on the simplex. The second stage of production is the use of those services to manufacture the three final goods, as in equation (2.5a). The three activity points must then in this instance lie on the line segment connecting LS and NS.[9] The Kenen formulation is in this sense a tight restriction on technologies possible under Heckscher–Ohlin assumptions.

Kenen assumes that x is LS-intensive relative to both other goods. He assumes I to be NS-intensive with respect to the average of x and y production, but not necessarily with regard to y production alone. One consistent assignment of activity points is illustrated by x_1, y_1, and I_1 in Figure 2.2, with I_1 assumed NS-intensive relative to y_1. The economy's gross endowment of factor services in the steady state is indicated by the factor shares at point E_1. The gross endowment of services is not the defining factor for comparative advantage, as equation (2.5a) made clear. Kenen defines the net factor service ratio to correspond to the right-hand side of equation (2.5a); given the assumptions on factor intensities, this will be falling (i.e., becoming more labor-service abundant) as greater investment is undertaken.

Although there is no direct role of capital in final-good production, the graphical analysis here illustrates that the share of capital payments θ_K in the overall production process is well defined. These capital payments are a component of the payment for improved factor services; each factor receives a payment made up of both the "rent" due a scarce fixed factor (the natural endowment) and the return to capital used in improving the factor. In the simplex, the measure θ_K is the average return to capital in all production processes.

The pattern of international trade in the Kenen formulation

The pattern of international trade is introduced by describing the production processes of the rest of the world in this trading equilibrium. Unlike the general 3×3 model, the Kenen formulation is not characterized by identical technological choice in each country in terms of the natural endowments. I represent this by the rest-of-world activity points x_w, y_w, and I_w along the segment $LS_w–NS_w$.[10] The Heckscher–Ohlin nature of trade in goods x and y ensures that an identical technology will be chosen in production of those goods – the points x_1 and x_w will then be positioned an equal share down the $LS–NS$ segments, as will y_1 and y_w. Given the equalization of factor-service prices, the same condition will hold for I_1 and I_w. The share of total factor payments going to each natural endowment and capital in the rest of the world is illustrated at E_w. Observed factor service prices in two different countries will not be equalized, since there can be different amounts of capital embodied in the services, but the service "unit" will be priced identically.

The home country and the rest of the world have different activity points because of their different steady-state endowments of capital relative to the other factors.[11] As drawn, the rest of the world is the economy with larger steady-state relative stock of capital. The marginal return to capital is higher in the home country, perhaps because of a higher social discount rate, but the share of total income accruing to capital is higher in the rest of the world. In this sense, the Kenen formulation is an extension of the Heckscher–Ohlin model – the observed technologies when measured in "natural" units need not be identical in each country under trade.

Kenen derives carefully the aggregate evolution of capital from microeconomic behavior.[12] The result is a steady-state aggregate relationship between investment and desired capital that is similar to those used in macroeconomic models. In the steady state, capital depreciates (here, at rate δ) and is kept constant through replacement investment.

$$K_1 = (1 - \delta)K_1 + I_1 \tag{2.8}$$

or

$$I_1 = \delta K_1$$

The desired capital stock is itself a function of the interest rate in the market for loanable funds; as that rate rises, the desired capital stock falls.

The trade pattern is a function of this replacement investment, as noted earlier. As investment rises, the net endowment of factor services for X and Y production falls. Figure 2.2 illustrates an apparent reversal of comparative advantage. The gross factor-service endowments in the steady state are given by E_1 and E_w. The net factor-service endowments derived from equation (2.5a) are illustrated by EN_1 and EN_w. Given the greater replacement investment necessary in the rest of the world, the home country is labor-service abundant in gross terms but labor-service scarce in net terms. The country will then export good y to the rest of the world. The simplex is drawn for given commodity prices in the trading equilibrium, and thus it is difficult to illustrate the evolution from low to high capital stock. However, such an evolution could well lead to a reversal in comparative advantage due to the role played by investment goods.

As Kenen noted, there are a number of important implications of this equilibrium that make the model more consistent with observed international trade. First, the return to capital is not equalized across countries. This return is driven by the propensity to accumulate capital across countries, and without foreign investment such equalization will not occur. Second, the returns to land and labor services are equalized, but these are the prices of the "improved" factor. The returns accruing to the "natural" factors are not equalized, nor will the observed payment in different countries be – since their factors will be "improved" to different degrees. Third, this equilibrium can generate the Leontief paradox. Consider the equilibrium illustrated in Figure 2.2, and cast the United States in the role of the rest of the world. The United States is the capital-abundant country when measured in gross terms, but will export the labor-intensive good x. The source of the paradox is distinct from that of the general 3-factor model, however, and follows from the endogeneity of capital and investment in the trading partners.

Kenen did not remark at length upon the endogeneity of comparative advantage in his variant of the Heckscher–Ohlin model, perhaps because the notion of endogenous comparative advantage had not captured the imagination of mainstream international trade theory as it has done today. In the Heckscher–Ohlin formulation the comparative advantage of trading countries is exogenous and linked to endowment ratios. In the Kenen variant this is no longer the case – comparative advantage is an endogenous product of the economies' decision on the quantity of investment.[13] Missing is a rationale for manipulating comparative advantage.

Empirical testing of the Kenen formulation

Kenen's work was motivated in part by the divergence of observed trading behavior from that predicted by theory. Two major instances of this divergence were the non-equivalence of factor prices across countries and the Leontief paradox. Leontief's calculations within the 2×2 Heckscher–Ohlin model indicated that in 1947 the United States, widely considered capital-abundant relative to all other countries in international trade, was in fact exporting labor-intensive goods. Leontief (1953) attributed the differences to differing labor productivities across countries not captured in his input–output calculations. Vanek (1963) and Keesing (1965) provided explanations, each based upon a "missing factor" – land and skilled labor, respectively – from Leontief's calculations. NCT provided an explanation based upon the introduction of a third factor and then a specific restriction on the interaction of these in production, as noted above. His calculations, amending those of Leontief to allow for the contribution of capital to labor services, reversed the labor-intensity of imports for the United States. Kenen, in a perhaps too-optimistic note, indicated in NCT that "the paradox succumbs at last" (457).

Others kept the analysis of paradox alive. Vanek (1968) provided the multifactor framework within which subsequent groups of economists examined the question, and that Leamer and Levinsohn (1994) refers to as the Heckscher–Ohlin–Vanek (HOV) model.[14] The paradox seemed to weaken with age, and Stern and Maskus (1981) concluded that evidence of the paradox was absent from U.S. trade data by 1972. Most notable among recent empirical examinations of the HOV model are Bowen, Leamer, and Sveikauskas (1987) and Trefler (1993, 1995). Bowen, Leamer, and Sveikauskas (hereafter, BLS) provided an estimating structure for the multigood, multifactor version of the HOV model and tested it against a variety of alternative hypotheses. The results did not favor the HOV model, although there was indication of some factor-abundance-driven explanation for trade patterns. Trefler began with the BLS structure and then introduced the possibility that factor productivities differed across countries. This relaxation of the HOV structure led to results that were more consistent with the HOV predictions for international trading equilibrium.[15] There was little effort to provide a theoretical justification for this difference in productivities. All of these empirical analyses considered capital as a separate, and coequal, factor of production.

The BLS structure for empirical tests

The BLS test of the HOV model is based upon the full employment conditions in the economy. These can be presented in matrix form as in equation (2.1).

$$AX_k = V_k \tag{2.9}$$

Here the dimensions of the matrices are allowed to be more general. A is the $(M \times N)$ matrix of unit factor coefficients, X_k is the $(N \times 1)$ vector of output produced in country k, and V_k is the $(M \times 1)$ vector of factor endowments in that country.

The existence of international trade is introduced by creating a net export vector. Net exports are defined as the $(N \times 1)$ vector $T_k = X_k - C_k$, with C_k the $(N \times 1)$ vector of expenditure on goods. If C_k is premultiplied by A (to convert to factor equivalents) and subtracted from both sides:

$$AT_k = V_k - AC_k \tag{2.10}$$

The HOV (and Kenen) assumptions of identical and homothetic preferences, of competitive factor markets, and of the law of one price, are maintained. The technology embodied in A is assumed to be common to all countries, as in HOV.[16] World expenditure is equal to world production (XW), an ($N \times 1$) vector; each country's share in world expenditure is defined by $s_k = (Y_k - B_k)/YW$, where Y_k, B_k, and YW are scalars representing national income, trade surplus, and world income, respectively. This implies

$$AT_k = V_k - s_k A\,XW = V_k - s_k VW \qquad (2.11)$$

where the world full employment condition $A\,XW = VW$ has been used.

BLS uses equation (2.11) in a variety of guises to test the HOV model. In essence, the two sides of the vector equation generate values, and the HOV model indicates that the vectors should be equal. Stochastic elements can introduce inequality, but nonparametric tests can assess the degree to which the underlying equality is (or is not) evident. BLS does not find a strong correlation of the elements of these vectors.

Put differently, the right-hand side of equation (2.11) can be subtracted from the left-hand side to obtain a residual. This residual vector is denoted ε_k in equation (2.12).

$$AT_k - V_k + s_k VW = \varepsilon_k \qquad (2.12)$$

The HOV model predicts that the elements of this residual vector will be zero.

Trefler (1993) takes the $\varepsilon_k = 0$ prediction of the HOV model a step closer to the Kenen formulation. Following a suggestion of Leontief (1953), he rewrites the HOV equilibrium conditions as:

$$AT_k = \pi_k\left(V_k - s_k A\,XW\right) = \pi_k\left(V_k - s_k VW\right) \qquad (2.13)$$

$$\pi_k w_k = w^* \qquad (2.14)$$

The vectors w_k and w^* represent the factor returns at home and abroad, respectively. π_k is the vector of factor productivities in country k (with the foreign country productivity normalized at unity). The unit factor coefficients in A are then defined in terms of "effective" labor, with the norm for each factor j being $\pi_{kj} = 1$.

Trefler uses equation (2.13) to calculate the π vector for each country, and then uses that vector to examine the precision of (2.14). He finds substantial support for the HOV model as thus amended.

Kenen's formulation as an explanation of Trefler's results

The Kenen treatment of capital as an intermediate factor provides an important explanation for the results of BLS and Trefler (1993). If equation (2.9) is taken as the structure of the economy, then suppose that the first row of this $(M \times 1)$ vector equation represents full employment of capital. The Kenen hypothesis is that capital is fully employed, but only in "improving" the services offered by other factors of production. The vector of services is defined as the $((M - 1) \times 1)$ vector VS.[17] If the coefficient of improvement in other factors due to capital is denoted by the $((M - 1) \times 1)$ vector D, then the vector of factor services can be defined[18] (suppressing the country subscript)

$$VS = V_{2:M} + D V_1 \tag{2.15}$$

Substituting equation (2.15) into the last $(M - 1)$ rows of equation (2.11) yields:

$$A_{2:M}T + D V_1 = VS - sVW_{2:M} \tag{2.16}$$

$$A_{2:M}T + D\{A_1T + sVW_1\} = VS - sVW_{2:M}$$
$$\{A_{2:M} + DA_1\}T = VS - s\{VW_{2:M} + DVW_1\}$$

Define A^A as an $((M-1) \times N)$ matrix and VW^A as an $((M-1) \times 1)$ vector such that:

$$A^A = A_{2:M} + DA_1 \tag{2.17}$$

$$VW^A = VW_{2:M} + D VW_1 \tag{2.18}$$

Then the BLS equation can be rewritten:

$$A^A T = VS - sVW^A + \eta \tag{2.19}$$

over the $M - 1$ factors other than capital. This will be the appropriate specification of the HOV model under Kenen's hypothesis, with η the $(M - 1) \times 1$ vector of disturbances due to measurement error or other random event. The elements of A^A will be identical across countries from the equalization of prices of "improved" factors. Unfortunately, the variables of these matrices are not observed directly.

This relationship can be rewritten to illustrate its ability to explain the failure of the HOV model in BLS. Begin again with equation (2.16), written in a slightly different but equivalent way. Use the true relationship between variables defined by (2.19), and introduce as well the observed errors ε defined in (2.12):

$$\left\{ A_{2:M}T - V_{2:M} + sVW_{2:M} \right\} = \eta + D\left\{ V_1 - sVW_1 - A_1T \right\} \qquad (2.16')$$

$$\varepsilon_{2:M} = \eta - D\varepsilon_1 \qquad (2.20)$$

The left-hand side is the residual of the noncapital factors (i.e., 2 through M) in the BLS analysis. The right-hand side is the random error vector minus the residual from the capital equation (i.e., factor 1) multiplied by the capital coefficient vector D. Kenen's model will predict not that each element of ε will be zero, but that the $(M - 1)$ noncapital factors will generate residuals that are systematically and negatively correlated with those of the capital equation.

This prediction is directly related to, and provides a possible explanation for, Trefler's productivity calculations. Consider the second factor (labor, for example). The relevant row of equation (2.13) can be written:

$$A_2T = \pi_2\left\{ V_2 - sVW_2 \right\} \qquad (2.21)$$

In the Kenen formulation,

$$\begin{aligned} \pi_2 &= 1 + D_2\left\{ V_1 - sVW_1 - A_1 \right\}\big/\left[V_2 - sVW_2 \right] \\ &= 1 + \left\{ \left(\eta_2 - D_2\varepsilon_1 \right)\big/\left[V_2 - sVW_2 \right] \right\} \end{aligned} \qquad (2.22)$$

the productivity coefficient will differ from unity when the residual from the capital full-employment equation is nonzero. There will be a similar dependence in each factor's productivity upon the capital-market outcome.

Hypothesis testing

The Kenen formulation yields the testable prediction embodied in equation (2.20). I perform two calculations to examine this prediction. The first is based upon the implications for the Trefler productivity calculation in equation (2.22); the second is drawn directly from equation (2.20).

Trefler (1993) reports the productivity calculations in his paper for six categories of labor and two categories of land over 32 countries. As equation (2.22) illustrates, the Kenen hypothesis will have π_j for factor j negatively related to ε_1, other things equal. ε_1 will itself be declining in the stock of capital. Thus, the Kenen formulation hypothesizes that there will be a positive relationship between $\pi_{2:M}$ and V_1, the stock of capital. The null hypothesis – common to all empirical testing to date – is that the stock of capital will not have an independent effect on $\pi_{2:M}$.

Table 2.1 reports evidence on this hypothesis. The productivity parameters for 32 countries are reported in Trefler (1993). The capital stock levels were graciously provided by Professor Trefler in private correspondence. I posit a specification in which capital enters logarithmically, indicating a "decreasing returns" relationship of capital to noncapital factor productivity. The results indicate a significant positive relationship, as hypothesized, at the 95 percent level of confidence for all categories of labor. Interestingly, the same significant relationship is not observed in the categories of land. Thus, for labor, the null hypothesis can be rejected in favor of the Kenen alternative.

The second hypothesis test is derived directly from equation (2.20). The residuals ε_j are calculated for all factors and all countries. Separate data sets are formed for each factor, including all observed countries. The residual ε_j is regressed on ε_1. The null hypothesis is that these residuals will be uncorrelated. The alternative hypothesis is the Kenen formulation, since that builds in explicitly the cross-equation correlation of the specific form described here.

Using data provided by Professor Trefler, I was able to reconstruct the ε_j vectors calculated in Trefler (1993) for the 33 countries in his sample. Use of the specification of (2.20) on these data led to a resounding rejection of the Kenen formulation: for all noncapital factors j, ε_j, and ε_K were positively and significantly correlated. However, the results of Table 2.1 were also ratified: ε_j and K_j were positively and significantly correlated across the sample for all j, as Kenen's formulation would predict. Another paradox!

The paradox is resolved through the regression of ε_{Kj} on K_j:

$$\varepsilon_{Kj} = -1.08 + 1.64\,K_j$$

Both coefficients are significantly different from zero at the 99 percent level of confidence. This is the converse of what all HO-based theories would predict; it stems in the Trefler data set from the fact that consumption of capital (as measured by $s_j\,VW_K$) rises across countries more rapidly than does K_j, and can be attributed to the fact that Trefler (1993) calculates consumption shares through use of income shares unadjusted for purchasing-power parity.[19]

I recalculated the consumption shares based upon the purchasing-power-parity adjusted income levels reported in the Penn Tables for the 33 countries, and recalculated the residuals from equation (2.12). The regressions based upon equation (2.20) using the revised residuals are reported in Table 2.2. There is support, but only weak support, for the Kenen formulation – and this support is centered in the regressions on land. There is also evidence in the regression at the bottom of the table

Table 2.1. *The Kenen formulation in Trefler's productivity parameters*

Testing of the relationship of Trefler's productivity parameters (π) with the stock of capital. T-statistics in parentheses.

Productivity parameter for	c_0	c_1	R^2
	33 countries, as in Trefler (1993).		
Labor			
Professional and technical	0.14	0.10	0.22
	(2.24)	(2.95)	
Clerical	0.25	0.08	0.15
	(1.63)	(2.38)	
Sales	0.13	0.10	0.17
	(2.00)	(2.56)	
Services	0.07	0.13	0.29
	(2.88)	(3.56)	
Agriculture	0.18	0.07	0.16
	(2.17)	(2.42)	
Production/transport	0.09	0.11	0.28
	(2.91)	(3.52)	
Land			
Cropland	0.00	3.67	0.02
	(0.80)	(0.75)	
Pastureland	0.00	2.05	0.00
	(0.06)	(0.08)	
	When a 31-country sample is used (excluding Hong Kong and Singapore), the labor results are almost identical.		
Land			
Cropland	0.01	0.23	0.02
	(0.61)	(0.82)	
Pastureland	0.00	4.08	0.09
	(1.54)	(1.68)	

Model: $\pi_{ij} = \ln(c_0) + c_1 \cdot \ln(K_j)$, for factor i, country j
Critical values for 30 degrees of freedom: 90 percent confidence, 1.70; 95 percent confidence: 2.04.
Source: Author's calculations.

that the residuals have been purged of some, but not all, of the capital bias noted above.

Investigating the recalculated residuals yields an interesting regularity that I illustrate in Figure 2.3. The residuals for the professional labor equation are plotted against those for capital, and the pattern is one

Table 2.2. *The Kenen formulation and residuals from the BLS estimating equations: a revision* (33 countries, as in Trefler 1993; *T*-statistics in parentheses)

ε for	f_0	f_1	R^2
Labor			
Professional and technical	−1.31	−0.13	0.01
	(2.06)	(0.51)	
Clerical	−0.21	0.58	0.39
	(0.64)	(4.46)	
Sales	−0.94	−0.22	0.01
	(1.12)	(0.64)	
Services	−1.78	−0.59	0.08
	(1.96)	(1.61)	
Agriculture	−1.47	−0.62	0.08
	(1.52)	(1.59)	
Production/transport	−1.07	0.00	0.00
	(1.71)	(0.00)	
Land			
Cropland	−1.40	−0.85	0.12
	(1.38)	(2.08)	
Pastureland	−0.89	−0.74	0.10
	(0.94)	(1.91)	

The Kenen formulation predicts that the observed noncapital residual vector ε_j defined in equation (2.12) of the text will have a negative and significant relationship with the residual ε_{Kj} in that country. If the consumption vector is reformulated in terms of purchasing power parities, then the relations shown can be derived for the recalculated residuals ε_{ij}.

Model: $\hat{\varepsilon}_{ij} = f_0 + f_1 \cdot \hat{\varepsilon}_{Kj}$

The Kenen hypothesis is not rejected here, but there is insignificant negative coefficient in all cases. Reason: the correlation of ε_{jK} and K_j should be negative, but is in fact positive (though insignificant).

$\hat{\varepsilon}_{jK} = -0.71 + 0.72K_j \qquad R^2 = 0.04$
$\quad\;\;(1.46) \quad (1.26)$

Table 2.3. *The Kenen formulation and residuals from the BLS estimating equations: a truncated sample* (*T*-statistics in parentheses)

ε for	d_0	d_1	R^2
Labor			
Professional and technical	−2.08	−0.83	0.25
	(3.85)	(3.14)	
Clerical	−0.51	0.30	0.12
	(1.68)	(2.05)	
Sales	−1.71	−0.91	0.15
	(2.10)	(2.30)	
Services	−2.94	−1.63	0.40
	(3.89)	(4.43)	
Agriculture	−2.52	−1.57	0.31
	(2.89)	(3.70)	
Production/transport	−1.83	−0.68	0.19
	(3.42)	(2.62)	
Land			
Cropland	−2.30	−1.66	0.29
	(2.36)	(3.50)	
Pastureland	−0.87	−0.72	0.06
	(0.84)	(1.42)	

The Kenen formulation predicts that the observed residual vector ε_j defined in equation (2.12) of the text will have a negative and significant relationship with the residual ε_{Kj} in that country. If the consumption vector is reformulated in terms of purchasing power parities, then the relations shown can be derived. In this instance, evidence from the United States is excluded; 32 observations remain.

Model: $\hat{\varepsilon}_{ij} = d_0 + d_1 \cdot \hat{\varepsilon}_{Kj}$

Source: Author's calculations.

evident for the other factors as well. The scatter of observations lies within a generally downward-sloping grouping, as predicted by the Kenen formulation, but with a single outlier of paired large positive residuals. This pair, indicating a relative scarcity of both factors, is that of the United States. The United States is a similar outlier in all pairings of capital residuals with residuals of various labor categories. By excluding the United States from the data set I obtain results that strongly reject the null in favor of the Kenen formulation, as indicated in Table 2.3.

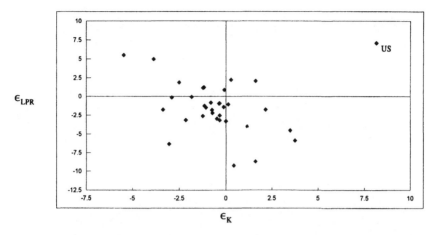

Figure 2.3. The Kenen formulation as evident in recalculated residuals. *Source*: Author's calculations.

Conclusions and suggestions for further research

Peter Kenen is not the timid type, and his modeling proposals in "Nature, Capital, and Trade" would have turned the theory of international trade inside out. As it happens, the impact has been much delayed. Dynamic analysis of the HO trade theory developed, beginning (in 1965 again!) with Oniki and Uzawa, but did not address the empirically important differences in interest rates across nations. Human-capital explanations for the Leontief paradox proliferated, but the implications of this for capital formation were left undeveloped. Only the recent explorations of endogenous-growth theories of international trade have brought the possibility of "improving" labor through investment to the core of intertemporal trade theory, and have demonstrated the power of such explanations for real-world phenomena like the divergence of growth rates across nations.

It is indicative of Kenen's research agenda that his conjectures on the role of capital lead to meaningful and empirically testable qualifications to the standard HO model. His research has consistently taken as goal the explanation of empirical regularities, and his work in "Nature, Capital, and Trade" is a strong example. As I demonstrate in this paper, current investigators of trading patterns will be well-served by revisiting his research.

The empirical results in this essay are derived from the careful work done by Bowen, Leamer, and Sveikauskas (1987) and Trefler (1993), but are suggestive of a relationship that could usefully be explored more extensively. Kenen suggested that investigators into trading patterns look more carefully to the asymmetric role of capital in production. Those doing research on endogenous growth in trading economies have taken this to heart, but in a limited way – the dynamic remains a simplistic one, based in the mechanistic application of an increasing-returns technology. Kenen's formulation will potentially be much richer, with the improving nature of capital available to many sectors and with a more complex "improvement" technology. Future researchers will find large dividends in paying close attention to this improvement process.

Peter Kenen will no doubt view the results with mixed emotions. There will be satisfaction in finding empirical support for his own proposals, but probably dismay as well: once again, as in the Leontief paradox, the United States is cast as the unexplainable outlier. Extensions of the model will certainly involve more careful empirical implementation of the assumption of identical preferences across countries. Future researchers will nevertheless have to contend, as Kenen did, with the asymmetric position of the U.S. economy.

NOTES

Thanks to Jerry Cohen, Arvind Panagariya, and participants at UNC Economics and Southeastern International Economics seminars for comments, to Bill Ethier and Ron Jones for helpful discussions, and to Daniel Trefler for access to his data on international trade and factor proportions.

1. Bohm-Bawerk's work is summarized in Schumpeter (1996: 901–9).
2. Marshall (1961: 788) nevertheless notes that "capital consists of those things which aid or support labor in production: or, as has been said more recently, it consists of those things without which production could not be carried on with equal efficiency, but which are not free gifts of nature." This is not inconsistent with the Kenen formulation.
3. See, for example, "The Effect of Foreign Trade on the Distribution of Income" by Heckscher and "The Theory of Trade" by Ohlin in Flam and Flanders (1991). Heckscher and Ohlin define the differences among factors largely in terms of factor mobility: land is immobile, capital somewhat mobile, and labor mobile.
4. Kenen distinguishes between firm-level and aggregate depreciation. He posits that the individual investment has undiminished productivity for v years, and then loses all productivity; if such investments are entered into continuously, the aggregate capital stock will have a constant rate of depreciation as well as a constant accumulation of investment goods.

5. This is the analogue for three factors of being inside the diversification cone; see Dixit and Norman (1980).

6. This marginal return from investment was assumed by Kenen to be decreasing in the capital stock; this will be a necessary consequence in the constant-returns production technology of the more general 3×3 HO model.

7. Note that equations (4) and (5) can be combined and compared with (1) to yield the equality $A = GH$. The specific structure Kenen imposes serves as a series of restrictions on the elements of A – restrictions nonexistent in the general model.

8. Jones (1971) provides a lucid exposition of this type of model, with special reference to NCT and to Temin (1966).

9. This line segment need not be parallel to the side LN. The distance from the activity point to that side measures the share of factor payments received by capital; given the Ricardo–Viner nature of the production of improved factor services, there is no reason for the share received by capital to be equalized. This is a generalization of NCT; in that paper, and associated erratum, Kenen assumes that capital shares in production of the two services were equal. Under this restrictive assumption, the line segments will be parallel to LN.

10. Given the Ricardo–Viner nature of production of factor services, there is no reason for LS_w–NS_w to be parallel to LS–NS.

11. This is a necessary, but not sufficient, condition. If the technologies for producing factor services were isoelastic in capital input, then the activity points would be the same although the steady-state capital stocks were different. The simplest example is the Cobb–Douglas technology – factor payment shares are constant for all quantities of factor use.

12. Kenen summarizes this derivation in the 1965 paper, and provides it in greater detail in Kenen (1968).

13. Consider the comparison between the Kenen and HO versions with labor and land services produced with the functions $LS = LK_L^\alpha$ and $NS = NK_N^\beta$. For Kenen the parameters α and β were positive and identical across countries, while for HO they would both be equal to zero. With two countries, numbered 1 and 2, and for allocations of capital to the two sectors that are proportional to the initial endowments of "natural" factors in each country, the condition under which country 1 exports the labor-service intensive good is $(L_1/N_1)^{1+\beta} > (L_2/N_2)^{1+\alpha}[(L_1K_1/N_2K_2)(K_2^*/K_1^*)]^{\beta-\alpha}$, with (K_2^*/K_1^*) the ratio of capital across countries implied by the size of the endowments of "natural" factors. For $\alpha = \beta = 0$, this becomes the HO definition of comparative advantage. For $\alpha \neq \beta$ and positive, both the endowments of capital and the technologies for production of factor services play a role. Specifically, for $\alpha < \beta$ a disproportionately large capital stock in economy 1 can reverse the pattern of comparative advantage predicted by the HO formulation. This outcome, further, is endogenous to the choice set of the economies.

14. Leamer has been a stalwart in the empirical testing of the HOV model in general as well as in the pursuit of the Leontief paradox. His contributions are summarized nicely in Leamer and Levinsohn (1994).
15. The title of Trefler's piece exclaims "Leontief was right!" This does not refer to the existence of the Leontief paradox, but rather to the explanation (based upon differing labor productivities across countries) that Leontief (1953) offered for the paradox.
16. The Kenen specification implies an analogous assumption over a restricted input–output table, as described below.
17. In what follows, if only rows q through r of a matrix W are to be considered, I use the notation $W_{q:r}$.
18. This is an exceedingly simple specification, but has the value of being linear. More appealing specifications will lead to nonlinear estimation.
19. Omitting the adjustment for purchasing power parity also helps to explain the anomalies that Trefler notes in terms of developing countries being abundant in almost all factors and developed countries being scarce in all factors. The United States is a good example of this phenomenon – it is calculated to be strongly scarce in capital and all categories of labor. This result is also found in *BLS*.

REFERENCES

Becker, Gary (1965). *Human Capital.* Chicago: University of Chicago Press.

Bowen, Harry, Edward Leamer, and Leo Sveikauskas (1987). "Multicountry, Multifactor Tests of the Factor Abundance Theory," *American Economic Review* 77(5) (December), 791–809.

Chipman, John (1969). "Factor Price Equalization and the Stolper-Samuelson Theorem," *International Economic Review* 10, 399–406.

Dixit, Avinash, and Victor Norman (1980). *Theory of International Trade.* Cambridge University Press.

Ethier, Wilfred (1984). "Higher Dimensional Issues in Trade Theory." In R. Jones and P. Kenen, eds., *Handbook of International Economics, Vol. 1*; chap. 3. Amsterdam: North-Holland.

Findlay, Ronald (1973). *International Trade and Development Theory.* New York: Columbia University Press.

Flam, Harry, and M. June Flanders, eds. (1991). *Heckscher–Ohlin Trade Theory.* Cambridge: MIT Press.

Jones, Ronald (1971). "A Three-Factor Model in Theory, Trade and History." In J. Bhagwati, R. Jones, R. Mundell, and J. Vanek, eds., *Trade, Balance of Payments and Growth*, chap. 1. Amsterdam: North-Holland.

Jones, Ronald (1992). "Factor Scarcity, Factor Abundance and Attitudes Towards Protection: The 3×3 Model," *Journal of International Economic Integration* 7(1) (Spring), 1–19.

Jones, Ronald, and Sugata Marjit (1991). "The Stolper–Samuelson Theorem, the Leamer Triangle, and the Produced Mobile Factor Structure." In Takayama,

Ohyama, and Ota, eds., *Trade, Policy and International Adjustments*. New York: Academic Press.

Keesing, Donald (1965). "Labor Skills and International Trade: Evaluating Many Trade Flows with a Single Measuring Device," *Review of Economics and Statistics* 47 (August), 287–94.

Kemp, Murray, and Leon Wegge (1969). "On the Relation between Commodity Prices and Factor Rewards," *International Economic Review* 10, 407–13.

Kenen, Peter (1965). "Nature, Capital, and Trade," *Journal of Political Economy* 73(5) (October), 437–60.

Kenen, Peter (1968). "Toward a More General Theory of Capital and Trade." In P. Kenen and R. Lawrence, *The Open Economy*. New York: Columbia University Press.

Leamer, Edward (1987). "Paths of Development in the Three-Factor N-Good General Equilibrium Model," *Journal of Political Economy* 95 (October), 961–99.

Leamer, Edward (1995). *The Heckscher–Ohlin Model in Theory and Practice*. Princeton Studies in International Finance 77, International Finance Section, Princeton University.

Leamer, Edward, and James Levinsohn (1994). "International Trade Theory: The Evidence." Discussion Paper 368, Institute of Public Policy Studies. University of Michigan, Ann Arbor, November.

Leontief, Wassily (1953). "Domestic Production and Foreign Trade: The American Capital Position Re-examined," *Proceedings of the American Philosophical Society* 97 (September), 332–49.

Marshall, Alfred (1965). *Principles of Economics*. New York: Macmillan, 1961.

Oniki, H., and H. Uzawa (1965). "Patterns of Trade and Investment in a Dynamic Model of International Trade," *Review of Economic Studies* 32, 15–38.

Samuelson, Paul (1965). "Equalization by Trade of the Interest Rate Along with the Real Wage." In R. Baldwin, R. Caves, H. Johnson, and P. Kenen, eds., *Trade, Growth, and the Balance of Payments*. Chicago: Rand McNally.

Schumpeter, Joseph (1966). *History of Economic Analysis*. New York: Oxford University Press.

Smith, Alasdair (1984). "Capital Theory and Trade Theory." In R. Jones and P. Kenen, eds., *Handbook of International Economics, Volume 1*, chap. 6. Amsterdam: North-Holland.

Stern, Robert, and Keith Maskus (1981). "Determinants of the Structure of U.S. Foreign Trade, 1958–1976," *Journal of International Economics* 11 (May), 207–24.

Temin, Peter (1966). "Labor Scarcity and the Problem of American Industrial Efficiency in the 1850s," *Journal of Economic History* 26/3 (September), 277–98.

Trefler, Daniel (1993). "International Factor Price Differences: Leontief Was Right!" *Journal of Political Economy* 101(6) (December), 961–87.

Trefler, Daniel (1995). "The Case of the Missing Trade and Other Mysteries," *American Economic Review* 85(5) (December), 1029–46.

Vanek, Jaroslav (1963). *The Natural Resource Content of United States Foreign Trade, 1870–1995*. Cambridge: MIT Press, 1963.

Vanek, Jaroslav (1968). "The Factor Proportions Theory: The N-Factor Case," *Kyklos* 21(4), 749–56.

CHAPTER 3

The Meade model of preferential trading: History, analytics, and policy implications

Arvind Panagariya

Though the theory of preferential trading had its birth in Jacob Viner's (1950) celebrated work for the Carnegie Endowment, *The Customs Union Issue*, the first complete general-equilibrium model of preferential trading was provided by James Meade (1955) in the de Vries Lectures, delivered at the Netherlands School of Economics while the Benelux union was in progress and published as *The Theory of Customs Unions*.[1] Remarkably, at a time when two-good models dominated the thinking of international trade theorists, Meade constructed a complete three-good, three-country model and even went on to extend it to a multicountry, multicommodity context. The model has proved as durable as Viner's concepts of trade creation and trade diversion with Lipsey (1958, chaps. 5–6, 1960), Mundell (1964), Vanek (1965, Appendix), Corden (1976), Collier (1979), McMillan and McCann (1981), and Lloyd (1982) making significant contributions to its further development.[2] Insights emerging out of the model have also shaped the policy debate on regional integration (see Bhagwati and Panagariya, 1996a).

Peter Kenen has much in common with Meade. Like Meade, he has the unusual distinction of having advanced both branches of international economics: pure trade and finance. Those of us who had the opportunity to sit through his lectures on international trade can also recall his clever use of geometry, as was done by Meade (1952) in *A Geometry of International Trade*. Indeed, Peter was once a student of Meade and, in the 1950s, alongside him, helped build the area of trade and welfare as we know it today (Kenen 1957 and 1959).

This essay honors Peter Kenen by bringing together the history, analytics, and policy implication of *The Theory of Customs Unions*. The essay is an appropriate tribute to Peter's scholarship not only because Meade was a major intellectual influence for him but also because he has himself made important contributions to the monetary theory of economic integration. Thus, whereas Meade (1955) gave us the first welfare theoretic analysis of customs unions in a general-equilibrium model, Peter Kenen (1969) pioneered the theory of optimum currency areas.

Though all contributors to the Meade model listed above, except Mundell (1964), used the term "customs unions" in their titles, only Viner (1950) and Vanek (1965) explicitly distinguished them as unions involving internal free trade and a *common* external tariff. Almost all other authors, including Meade himself, used the term more broadly for what is best described generically as a preferential trading area (PTA) involving only internal free trade and hence including free trade areas (FTAs). Thus, Lipsey explicitly defined the theory of customs unions as "the theory of geographically discriminatory reductions in tariffs." Meade and subsequent writers on "customs unions" almost never considered the implications of harmonization of external tariffs to a common level across member countries and generally focused on the effects of tariff preferences or free trade areas with external tariffs held at their original levels in each country.[3]

Because so much has been written on the Meade model during the past three decades, it may seem that there is little new to be added. Yet, there is a good deal to be gained by examining the original text, which has remained poorly understood in the literature. Thus, I will begin by establishing that the post-Meade literature on the Meade model has been in error in two important respects: (i) unlike the predominant impression in the literature, Meade evaluated preferential trading and free trade areas from the viewpoint of the world as a whole rather than the union or a union member, and (ii) unlike the modern versions of the "Meade Model," Meade himself did not assume fixed terms of trade between either union members or the union and the rest of the world.

I also provide a formal treatment of Meade's original analysis and unify it with the help of a few algebraic expressions. Among other things, this formalization will help us bring out clearly the importance Meade attached to tariffs in the outside country in evaluating the desirability of preferential trading arrangements. The subsequent literature has almost completely disregarded the importance of this factor. I also offer an analysis of the effects of preferential liberalization by a country on its welfare in the presence of flexible terms of trade.

A further contribution of this essay lies in providing a concise treatment of the small-union Meade model and offering some new results in this overcrowded field. In particular, I show that Lipsey's (1958) result that the larger the expenditure on home goods relative to that on the outside country's good the more likely that preferential liberalization will benefit a small country can be extended to the case of CES preferences. Lipsey had derived this result for Cobb–Douglas preferences.

Finally, I offer a detailed analysis of the implications of the Meade model for "natural trading partners" hypothesis, according to which the larger the initial volume of trade between union members the greater the likelihood that the union will be welfare improving. I conclude that the Meade model does not support this hypothesis.

In Section 1, I discuss *The Theory of Customs Unions* in detail. This discussion is divided into three subsections: history, analytics, and policy implications. In Section 2, I consider the small-union Meade model, extending the existing analysis. In particular, I derive an expression for the second-best optimum tariff that is far more transparent and intuitive than that in the existing literature. In Section 3, the issue of "natural trading partners" is examined critically in the context of the Meade model. Here I generalize Lipsey's result as mentioned above and discuss briefly the implications of fully flexible terms of trade for it. I conclude the essay in Section 4.

3.1 James Meade's theory of customs unions

There are eight chapters and two appendices in *The Theory of Customs Unions*. Chapter 1 discusses policies to maintain full employment and balance of payments within the context of a customs union. This chapter is not central to the analysis of customs unions but perhaps reflects the general preoccupation of economists with balances of payments and full employment issues at the time. In Chapter 2, Meade provides a formal interpretation and critique of Viner's theory of customs unions. He takes the view that Viner's (1950) analysis is based on a model characterized by infinite supply elasticities and zero demand elasticities in all countries.[4]

In Chapter 3, he introduces his basic model, which has three goods and three countries. Taking the opposite extreme of his formulation of the Viner model, Meade postulates zero supply elasticities and positive demand elasticities. These properties are obtained by restricting the analysis to the pure exchange model and by assuming that demands behave in the normal fashion. Some of Meade's key conclusions are stated in this chapter. In Chapter 4, Meade extends his model to many commodities and allows all commodities to be produced in all countries. The key contribution of this chapter is to develop a measure of a change in the world welfare due to a policy change. In Chapter 5, he applies this measure to preferential liberalization by a union member and offers a rich analysis under alternative assumptions of substitutability and complementarity between the liberalized and other goods.

To proceed in steps, Meade limits the analysis in Chapter 5 to the effects that accompany a reduction in the price of the liberalized good in the country granting the preference and an increase in the price of the same good in the country receiving the preference. Noting that these effects leave imbalances in the countries' trade accounts, in Chapter 6, Meade turns to the effects on welfare that will arise from policies aimed at restoring trade balance in each country. Here, in the spirit of Chapter 1, he launches into a discussion of monetary and exchange-rate policies to restore trade balance. In my view, this is the least satisfactory chapter in the book, for two reasons. First, as we will see explicitly below, the welfare measure used by Meade requires equality of income and expenditure or, equivalently, balance in trade for each country. What is left out of balance in Chapter 5 is not the trade accounts of different countries but of world markets in goods. Meade's technique involves deriving the changes in imports and exports due to certain price changes, assumed to have been induced by preferential liberalization by one of the countries, and then evaluating the effects of these changes on world welfare. But because the price changes are themselves not fully endogenized, there is no guarantee that the changes in exports and imports of different countries will be just right to clear the world markets. Second, the natural instrument to restore full equilibrium in pure trade models is not macroeconomic policies, to which Mcadc rcsortcd, but the terms of trade.

In Chapter 7, Meade discusses the limitation of his analysis. Interestingly, here he provides an important result, in the presence of quantitative restrictions, that has been identified incorrectly by Baldwin and Venables (1995) as what has come to be known as the Kemp–Wan theorem. In Chapter 8, Meade summarizes his main conclusions. Appendix 1 offers the rules of the game for the balance of payments of an economic union that partner countries may wish to adopt, and Appendix 2 derives an expression for the change in welfare in a closed economy. Apart from Appendix 2, the entire book is written in straight prose with no diagrams or equations.

3.1.1 *History: some common confusions*

Economists familiar with post-Meade (1955) writings on the Meade model but not *The Theory of Customs Unions* will be surprised to know that the latter said little about the impact of preferential trading on union members themselves. With rare exceptions, the focus of Meade's original text was exclusively on the impact of preferential trading on world welfare.[5] He set the stage for his analysis on the second page of Chapter 1 thus,

> The problem which I want to discuss in these lectures is whether this removal of barriers to trade between the two partner countries is likely to lead to a more or less economic use of the world's economic resources. It is not my intention to inquire into the possible effects of the formation of the union upon the level of economic activity within the various parts of the world.

Throughout the book, unless otherwise noted, whenever Meade uses the term "welfare effects" or "effects on standards," he means world welfare. In Chapter 7, which is devoted primarily to a discussion of the limitations to his analysis, Meade notes,

> A third important way in which my analysis has been restricted up to this point is that it has made no allowance for the effects of the customs union upon the distribution of income between the trading countries concerned. (94)

Despite these clear statements, the post-Meade literature has attributed to Meade results derived for an individual union member or the union as a whole.[6]

A related confusion in the literature concerns the treatment of the terms of trade. Though Meade did not explicitly solve his model for changes in the terms of trade, nowhere in the book did he assume that the terms of trade are fixed. Indeed, his analysis explicitly considers the effects of the change in the international price of the product on which the tariff preference is granted. Nevertheless, the Meade model, as we know it today, assumes that union members are price takers in the world market (Lloyd 1982, table 1). As far as I am able to trace, the switch was made by Lipsey (1958, chaps. 5 and 6) without explicit recognition and adopted by virtually all subsequent analysts of the model.[7] Unlike Meade (1955), the small-union model focuses naturally on the welfare of the union or individual union members rather than the world.

Why has this confusion persisted in the literature? We will see below that the results obtained by Meade *for world welfare under flexible terms of trade* are qualitatively similar to those obtained for *the union or an individual union member under fixed terms of trade*. In the spirit of two negatives turning into a positive, the *double switch* in assumptions – one making the union or a union member the object of analysis and the other fixing the terms of trade – leads to no change in results. It is this fact that perhaps led Lipsey (1958, 1960) and others to equate erroneously their model and results to those of Meade.[8] But, of course, each switch in assumptions by itself is important. Thus, if Lipsey had made only one switch by focusing on the welfare of a union member but retaining the assumption of fully flexible terms of trade, his results would have been drastically different from those of Meade.

3.1.2 *Analytics and main results*

Let us set up the problem in the most general form as Meade would have ideally liked and, indeed, implicitly did in Chapter 4 of his book.[9] Assume there are n goods indexed by i and m countries indexed by j. We use a subscript to identify a commodity and superscript to distinguish a country. Denote by p_i^* the international price of good i, p_i^j the (domestic) price of good i in country j and t_i^j the corresponding *ad valorem* trade tax. Per-unit trade tax on good i in country j is $t_i^j \cdot p_i^* \equiv p_i^j - p_i^*$ in the case of an importable and $t_i^j \cdot p_i^* \equiv p_i^* - p_i^j$ in the case of an exportable. If trade tax on a commodity is zero, its domestic price equals the international price.

For any country j, the expenditure–income equality implies

$$e^j\left(p_1^j, p_2^j, \ldots, p_n^j; u^j\right) = r^j\left(p_1^j, p_2^j, \ldots, p_n^j\right)$$
$$+ \sum_i\left(p_i^j - p_i^*\right)\left(e_i^j - r_i^j\right) \quad j = 1, \ldots m \quad (3.1)$$

where $e^j(\cdot)$ and $r^j(\cdot)$ are, respectively, the standard expenditure and revenue functions for country j. In addition, $e_i^j \equiv \partial e^j/\partial p_i^j$ and $r_i^j \equiv \partial r^j/\partial p_i^j$. Defining $m^j(p_1^j, p_2^j, \ldots, p_n^j; u^j) \equiv e^j(\cdot) - r^j(\cdot)$, we can rewrite (3.1) as

$$m^j\left(p_1^j, p_2^j, \ldots, p_n^j; u^j\right) = \sum_i{}^i\left(p_i^j - p_1^*\right)m_i^j(\cdot) \quad (3.1')$$

where $m_i^j \equiv \partial m^j/\partial p_i^j$ is the compensated import-demand function for good i in country j. The market-clearing condition for good i requires

$$\Sigma_j m_i^j = 0, \quad i = 1, \ldots n \quad (3.2)$$

The relationship between the domestic and international prices may be written

$$t_i^j p_i^* \equiv p_i^j - p_i^* \quad \text{if } m_i^j > 0 \text{ and}$$
$$t_i^j p_i^* \equiv p_i^* - p_i^j \quad \text{if } m_i^j < 0 \quad i = 1, \ldots n; \quad j = 1, \ldots m \quad (3.3)$$

Note that m_i^j is positive or negative as country j imports or exports good i. In (3.1'), (3.2), and (3.3), we have $m + n + mn$ equations in m utilities, n international prices, and mn domestic prices. We can choose one international price arbitrarily by the choice of a numeraire and drop one of the corresponding market-clearing conditions in (3.2). The remaining system defines an equilibrium in the world economy of the kind envisioned by Meade.

To obtain the key expression that serves as the basis of all of Meade's analysis, let us suppose that there is a small change in the tariff rates of various goods in different countries. Later, we will focus on the change in just one tariff rate, but that is not necessary at this stage. Differentiating (3.1) totally, we can obtain

$$e_u^j du^j = -\sum_i m_i^j dp_i^* + \sum_i \left(p_i^j - p_i^* \right) dm_i^j \quad i = 1, \ldots n; \quad j = 1, \ldots m \qquad (3.4)$$

where $e_u^j \equiv \partial e^j / \partial u^j$ and we make use of the fact that $r^j(\cdot)$ does not depend on u. Because e_u^j is the reciprocal of the marginal utility of income, the left-hand side of (3.4) represents the change in utility in terms of the numeraire good and may be thought of as the change in the real income of country j. Looking at the right-hand side, the change in the real income equals the import-weighted sum of the change in the terms of trade plus the change in tariff revenue valued at the initial tariff rates. This is now a standard result in trade models.

Because Meade assesses the desirability of preferential trading from the viewpoint of the world, we need to develop an expression for the world welfare. This Meade did by summing the changes in real incomes across countries. Thus, letting w stand for the world welfare,

$$dw = \sum_j e_u^j du^j = -\sum_j \sum_i m_i^j dp_i^* + \sum_j \sum_i \left(p_i^j - p_i^* \right) dm_i^j$$
$$i = 1, \ldots n; \quad i = 1, \ldots m$$
$$= -\sum_i dp_i^* \sum_j m_i^j + \sum_j \sum_i \left(p_i^j - p_i^* \right) dm_i^j \qquad (3.5)$$

Recalling, however, that $\Sigma_j m_i^j = 0$ by the market-clearing condition (3.2), we obtain[10]

$$dw = \sum_j \sum_i \left(p_i^j - p_i^* \right) dm_i^j \quad i = 1, \ldots n; \quad j = 1, \ldots m \qquad (3.6)$$

If we assume that there are no export taxes in any of the countries, the second equality in (3.3) yields $p_i^* = p_i^j$, where p_i^j is the price of good j in the country exporting that product. Similarly, for an importable, using the first equation in (3.3), we have $p_i^j - p_i^* \equiv t_i^j p_i^*$. We can rewrite equation (3.6) as

$$dw = \sum_j \sum_i t_i^j \cdot p_i^* dm_i^j \quad i = 1, \ldots n; \quad j = 1, \ldots m \qquad (3.6')$$

where p_i^* is the supply price of good i in the exporting country. Equation (3.6') constitutes the key to all of Meade's results. Though

Meade does not derive it explicitly in the book, he states it in precise terms as follows:

> What we need to do, therefore, is to take all the changes in international trade which are due directly or indirectly to the reduction in the Dutch duty on Belgian beer; value each change at its supply price in the exporting country and weight it by the *ad valorem* rate of duty in the exporting country; add up the resulting items for all increases of trade and do the same for all decreases of trade; if the resulting sum for the increases of trade is greater than that for the decreases of trade, then there is an increase in welfare; and vice versa. (66)

A key point to note is that the changes in real incomes of individual countries arising out of shifts in the terms of trade play no role in the determination of the change in the real income of the world. Being redistributive in nature, the welfare effects due to changes in the terms of trade cancel one another entirely when summed across countries. By focusing on the world welfare, Meade is able to work with a model with fully flexible terms of trade without having to deal with the complications arising out of such changes. According to (3.6'), irrespective of how the terms of trade change, an expansion of imports of good i in country j increases world welfare if such imports are restricted initially by a tariff.

This is not to suggest that the changes in the terms of trade do not matter. If we were to carry equation (3.6') any further by decomposing the total change in the $m_i^j(\cdot)$ into those arising from changes in the various arguments of the latter – tariffs, terms of trade, and utility – the terms of trade effects will come back to haunt us. The terms of trade determine (and are determined by) how exactly the $m_i^j(\cdot)$ change.

Equation (3.4), which underlies equation (3.6'), requires that the income-expenditure equality, shown in (3.1) or (3.1'), holds at all times. This equality is, of course, equivalent to the trade balance condition for country j.[11] If (3.6') is to be used as a measure of the change in welfare, trade balance is required in each country. Therefore, Meade is in error when he begins Chapter 6 under the premise that the changes discussed in Chapter 5 leave the countries out of trade balance. What are left out of balance are goods markets. For, in deriving (3.6'), we do not require that the goods market be cleared in the postpreference equilibrium, that is, we do not impose the condition $\Sigma_j dm_i^j = 0$ ($i = 1, 2, 3$).[12]

The conclusion quoted following equation (3.6') is stated by Meade in Chapter 4 in the context of a multicountry, multicommodity model. But prior to considering this general model, he discusses, in Chapter 3, the special case of a three-country, three-commodity model. It is useful to consider that model in detail here. Meade assumes that each country is

Table 3.1. *Domestic prices in the Meade model, Chapter 3 (good 1 is exported by Country A, 2 by B, and 3 by C)*

	Good 1	Good 2	Good 3
Country A	$p_1^A \equiv p_1^*$	$p_2^A \equiv p_2^*(1 + t_2^A)$	$p_3^A \equiv p_3^*(1 + t_3^A)$
Country B	$p_1^B \equiv p_1^*(1 + t_1^B)$	$p_2^B \equiv p_2^*$	$p_3^B \equiv p_3^*(1 + t_3^A)$
Country C	$p_1^C \equiv p_1^*(1 + t_1^C)$	$p_2^C \equiv p_2^*(1 + t_2^A)$	$p_3^C \equiv p_3^*$

specialized completely in the production of its export good and imports the other two goods. His objective is to focus on the effects arising out of shifts in demand, in contrast to Viner, who had focused on shifts in supply.

Denote the three countries by A, B, and C and the commodities produced and exported by them by 1, 2, and 3, respectively. Each country exports the good it produces to the other two and imports the goods produced by them. Because each country levies tariffs but no export taxes, the pattern of domestic prices takes the form shown in Table 3.1. In this setting, assuming that goods are substitutes, Meade offers the following conclusions at the end of Chapter 3:

> We can conclude that from the point of view of our present simple model where the advantages of trade consist solely in satisfying demands better out of given fixed supplies, a customs union is more likely to raise standards: (i) the higher are the initial duties of the countries forming the union, (ii) the lower are the duties in the outside countries, (iii) the more substitutable for each other are the products of the countries forming the union, and (iv) the less substitutable are the products of the outside world with the products of the countries forming the union. We can add to these conclusions the observation that the first stages of mutual tariff reduction on the Dutch–Belgian trade are likely to do more good (or less harm) than the later stages. (52)

To see how and under what conditions these results emerge, let us rewrite equation (3.6′) for the present three-good model. Remembering that countries A, B, and C export goods 1, 2, and 3, respectively, and do not produce imported goods, (3.6′) reduces to

$$dw = \sum_{i=2,3} t_i^A p_i^* de_i^A + \sum_{i=1,3} t_i^B p_i^* de_i^B + \sum_{i=1,2} t_i^C p_i^* de_i^C \qquad (3.7)$$

where e_i^j is the demand for commodity i in country j.

A complete analysis of this model requires us to solve for the changes in the terms of trade and utility and use these, in turn, to solve for the de_i^j.

Meade does not undertake this complicated exercise but instead bases his results on the following observations:

(i)   Mutual tariff preferences by countries A and B will expand their imports from each other; that is, de_2^A, $de_1^B > 0$. In Vinerian terms, these changes represent trade creation.

(ii)   Countries A and B will import less from country C; that is, de_3^A, $de_3^B < 0$. These changes constitute trade diversion.

(iii) Country C will import less from A and B; that is, de_1^C, $de_2^C < 0$. These changes can also be called trade diversion.[13]

A tariff preference by each member country lowers the domestic price of the good imported from the partner relative to those of other goods, giving rise to observation (i). Given substitutability, a reduction in the relative price of the partner's good reduces the demand for the outside country's good, leading to observation (ii). Finally, because the supplies of 1 and 2 are redirected toward A and B due to preferences, these goods become more expensive to C, which gives rise to observation (iii).[14]

Given observations (i)–(iii), the results appearing in the quotation following equation (3.6') are straightforward. The more substitutable are goods 1 and 2 for each other and the less substitutable are these goods for good 3, the larger will be the changes in (i) relative to those in (ii) and (iii) in absolute terms. The presumption then is that the first two terms in (3.6') are positive while the third one is negative. *Given this result*, the higher the initial tariffs in A and B relative to those in C, the more likely that the right-hand side of the equation will be positive.

Suppose now that the initial tariffs in all countries are nondiscriminatory. Then, if the effects in (i) are large relative to those in (ii) and (iii), the initial tariff preference will raise world welfare. Moreover, the larger the tariffs in A and B relative to that in C, the larger will be the gain. As further tariff preferences are granted, however, the t_i^j multiplying the changes in demands in (i) will decline while those multiplying the changes in demands in (ii) and (iii) will remain unchanged; that is, as more and more preferences are granted, the weights on the positive terms in (3.7) become smaller relative to those on the negative terms. As stated in the last sentence of Meade's statement quoted above, the gains are likely to be smaller or losses larger on the later stages of tariff preferences.

We can conclude this subsection with an interesting result that appears in Chapter 7 almost as a "throw away." Noting that an important limitation of his analysis in the preceding chapters is the exclusion of quantitative restrictions (96–9), Meade deals briefly with the implications of these restrictions and offers the following result:

> We can, therefore, conclude that if all trade barriers take the form of fixed and unchanged quantitative restrictions, then a customs union must increase economic welfare. The primary expansion of trade between the partner countries will, as we have seen, invariably increase welfare, and there can be no secondary or tertiary changes in trade except in markets in which either there are no quota restrictions or existing quota restrictions have become ineffective. In either case the secondary and tertiary changes have no effect upon economic welfare. (98)

This result, stated with respect to world welfare, can be derived from equation (3.6′). With quotas in place, the t_i^j must now be interpreted as implicit *ad valorem* quota rents. For products subject to an effective import quota, this quota rent is positive. A relaxation of effective import quotas between union members expands trade between them but has no effect on trade in other products subject to effective quotas. It is then immediate that such a change improves world welfare. Intuitively, the relaxation of quota generates a positive, trade-creation effect in the sector subject to the change but, because imports of other products subject to effective quotas do not decline, there is no trade diversion. In sum, freeing up of trade between members in the presence of quantitative restrictions gives rise to the effects in (i) above but not those in (ii) and (iii).

This result must be distinguished from another important result in the literature, stated originally by Kemp (1964), proved formally by Ohyama (1972) and Kemp and Wan (1976), and known in the literature as the Kemp–Wan theorem.[15] Because, in their recent important survey of the literature on regional integration, Baldwin and Venables (1995) have identified the two results as essentially the same, it is worthwhile to consider the distinction between them in some detail. It is best to begin by quoting Kemp's original statement of the result:

> Thus, suppose that the union sets its common external tariffs at levels calculated to achieve the same volume and composition of trade with the rest of the world as occurred before the union was formed. The improved productive and distributive efficiency of the union ensures that the union and, after compensation if necessary, all member countries are better off after the union than before. And, obviously, the nonmember countries are not worse off. It follows that the world as a whole is better off. (1964: 176)

Next, let us quote Baldwin and Venables:[16]

> Inspection of eq. (2.2) reveals that internal trade is the optimal policy for the RIA if, as its internal trade policy is changed, the external trade of the RIA remains constant (i.e., $dm_{31} = dm_{32} = 0$). This is the Meade–

> Ohyama–Kemp–Wan theorem. Meade (1955, p. 98) showed that if all external trade barriers are "fixed and unchanging" quantitative restrictions, then the RIA must increase the sum of the economic welfare of member nations. Ohyama (1972), and Kemp and Wan (1976) rediscovered and extended Meade's result by showing that a sufficiently intricate change in the CU's external tariffs could be used to freeze external trade, so that standard gains from trade arguments could be applied to trade within the RIA. (1995: 1605)

In my view, this statement is in error for both understating and overstating Meade's contribution. It understates Meade's contribution by suggesting that his result requires freezing the rest of the world's trade vector and, hence, its terms of trade. As we have already seen, Meade required no such assumption. The statement overstates Meade's contribution by suggesting that he showed that "if all external trade barriers are 'fixed and unchanging' quantitative restrictions, then an RIA must increase the sum of the economic welfare of member nations." Meade neither showed nor claimed to have shown an improvement in the welfare of the union; his analysis and claim were confined to an improvement in the welfare of the world as a whole. Indeed, to guarantee Kemp's result of an improvement in the welfare of the union with no change in the welfare of the rest of the world, it is not sufficient to assume that all external trade *barriers* are fixed and unchanging as *stated* by Baldwin and Venables in the third sentence of the above excerpt; instead, the result requires that all external *trade* be fixed and unchanging as actually *assumed* by them in the first sentence. The distinction is important because Meade makes only the former assumption: although all trade barriers must take the form of quantitative restrictions, they need not apply to all trade. As is clear from the second half of the excerpt from Meade (1955) reproduced above, he explicitly allows for changes in the rest of the world's trade in the products that are either free from trade barriers or become free because the formation of the union renders the restrictions on them redundant.

Under Meade's assumption, following a regional integration agreement, trade in some products with the rest of the world can change, which, in turn, implies that the terms of trade between the union and the rest of the world can change. And because we cannot rule out the possibility that the terms of trade can turn against the union, an improvement in its welfare cannot be guaranteed even though an improvement in global welfare is guaranteed.[17]

But this is not all. There is another subtle difference between the results of Meade and Kemp. The Kemp result deals specifically with a customs union in which all external barriers are replaced by a *common* external tariff. There is no such requirement in Meade's result. Thus, Meade's result, focusing as it does exclusively on world welfare, does not require the union members to adopt an (implicit) common external tariff by turning the initial country-specific quotas on the rest of the world into union-wide quotas in the post-union equilibrium. Each member's quotas on trade with outside countries are kept *individually* at their original levels and, therefore, tariffs implied by those quotas can be different. For example, take Meade's three-country, three-commodity model with complete specialization. Suppose countries A and B have import quotas on each other's goods initially, B has a quota on imports from C, and A does not restrict imports from C. If A and B now form a free trade area, eliminating import quotas on each other, the implicit tariff on C's product will be zero in A but positive in B. This is entirely consistent with Meade's general approach, which focused on FTAs rather than customs unions.

It is tempting to think that if all of A's and B's imports from C are subject to quotas in the initial equilibrium and if, upon the formation of the union, the quotas are unified at the union level to hold total commodity-wise imports from C fixed, the Meade result will coincide with the Kemp result. But even this correspondence will fail to obtain in a multicommodity world, since there is no guarantee that this will leave *commodity-wise* exports to the rest of the world unchanged.[18] Free trade within the union will, in general, lead to changes in exports to the rest of the world even if the union's *import* vector is unchanged. Note that Kemp fixes the entire trade vector, including exports.

Though the Kemp result is, thus, distinct from the Meade result, the latter does anticipate a different result in the literature on piecemeal trade reform. According to this latter result, established formally by Corden and Falvey (1985), the relaxation of an effective import quota by a small open economy is necessarily welfare improving. The mechanism underlying this result is the same as that underlying Meade's result: the relaxation of quota generates a direct welfare gain but brings no losses due to a contraction of imports of other products subject to positive quota rent. And within a small country, there are no terms-of-trade effects.

3.1.3 *Policy implications: further results*

Is preferential trading or an FTA likely to improve or worsen world welfare? In Chapter 3, Meade sidesteps this question by confining himself to stating the conditions under which the change is welfare improving and not taking a position on whether these conditions are likely to be met. After generalizing the model to many commodities and production of all goods in all countries in Chapter 4, he takes up this question in Chapter 5. He first presents a relatively complete taxonomy of possible effects of an infinitesimally small tariff preference by one of the member countries and then offers his judgment on which of the various effects are more likely in practice.

Suppose that country A gives a small tariff preference to country B on good 2. As already noted, Meade does not solve the model fully. Instead, he focuses on the effects that arise from the changes in the price of the product subject to the tariff preference. The preference lowers p_2^A and raises p_2^B and increases imports of good 2 into A from B. Meade calls this expansion of trade between A and B the *primary effect* of the tariff preference. The change is necessarily beneficial.

The primary effect is accompanied by what Meade calls *secondary effects*: the changes in international trade in products that, in A or B, are close substitutes for or close complements to good 2. He distinguishes eight cases, four involving substitutability and four complementarity.

Case 1. In A, good 2 exhibits substitutability with good 3, which is imported from C. The decline in p_2^A in this case diverts A's demand away from good 3; that is, there is a *secondary contraction of A's imports* from C, which is harmful.

Case 2. In A, good 2 is a close substitute for its own exportable, good 1. In this case, the decline in p_2^A lowers the demand for good 1 and releases it for exports. There is a *secondary expansion of A's exports* which is beneficial.

Case 3. In B, good 2 exhibits substitutability with a product exported to C. The rise in p_2^B leads to a contraction of this product and reduces B's exports to the latter. This is a harmful *secondary contraction of B's exports*.

Case 4. In B, good 2 exhibits substitutability with a good imported by B. Then a rise in p_2^B leads to a beneficial *secondary expansion of imports* into B.

Corresponding to each of these cases, Meade notes a case involving complementarity and, therefore, giving rise to the opposite welfare effect. For instance, corresponding to case (i), suppose that in country A, good 2 exhibits complementarity with a good imported from C. This could happen if good 2 (e.g., beer) is consumed jointly with the good imported from C (e.g., beer bottles). In this case, the reduction in p_2^A leads to a beneficial *secondary expansion of imports* into A. Other cases of complementarity can be constructed similarly.

From a policy standpoint, the critical issue is which of these cases are most plausible. Meade takes the following view:

> Then two cases which may perhaps most commonly occur are those in which the primary commodity is a close substitute with other imports in the country of imports (Case 1 above) and with other exports in the country of exports (Case 3 above). (1955: 73)

Meade provides a detailed analysis of why these two cases are important in practice. Space constraints do not permit me to reproduce this most interesting discussion, though I recommend it strongly to the reader. It is worthwhile, however, to reproduce one other paragraph summarizing the implications of Cases 1 and 2:

> If we allow for the possibility that there is trade diversion on the demand side in the importing country and on the supply side in the exporting country it is clear that the removal of the duties on imports from one country might do very considerable damage. The Netherlands removes its duties on imports from Belgium. The Netherlands may now purchase from Belgium the sort of things which it previously purchased from elsewhere, and at the same time Belgium may now sell to the Netherlands the sort of things which she was previously selling elsewhere. If there is any presumption that any country's imports are likely to be highly competitive with each other, since the country is likely to import the same class of products, and that any country's exports are likely to be highly competitive with each other, because it is likely to export the same general class of products, – then this is the sort of result which we should expect. The Netherlands will import from Belgium instead of from outside countries and Belgium will sell to the Netherlands rather than to outside countries. The losses from the combined trade diversion of Dutch imports and of Belgian exports may well much outweigh the advantages to be gained from the net trade expansion between the Netherlands and Belgium. (Meade 1955: 77–8)

This discussion suggests that Meade is skeptical of trade preferences or FTAs leading to net benefits for the world as a whole. It must be noted, however, that his skepticism is not as unequivocal as that of Viner.[19] Meade's arguments for why a tariff preference might do "very considerable damage," and suggestions on how Viner "might still further have strengthened his case against customs unions" are invariably followed by qualifications and examples in which trade diversion effects may not occur. But, at a minimum, we can safely conclude that he does not attempt to make a persuasive case in favor of preferential trading and that, on balance, his analysis is unfavorable to FTAs as an instrument of enhancing world welfare.

3.2 The small-union model

Let me now turn to what is popularly known as the "Meade Model." The main results are due to Lipsey (1958, chaps. 5 and 6) with McMillan and McCann (1981) reformulating the model in terms of compensated demands. I first derive the results derived by Lipsey (1958) in chapter 5 (conclusions #1–#4, Lipsey 1970: 38) and then consider McMillan and McCann's formulation. In chapter 6, Lipsey provides a further important result relating welfare results to expenditure shares on domestic and outside country's goods. This result, its possible generalizations, and its limitations are discussed in Section 3 below.

Assume that there are three countries, A, B, and C, and three goods, 1, 2, and 3. Countries A and B are completely specialized in 1 and 2, respectively, whereas C produces all three commodities. Countries A and B are potential union members and are small in relation to C. Assuming that there are no trade taxes in C, border prices facing A and B coincide with those prevailing in C. The structure of prices in the three countries is summarized in Table 3.2.

An obvious but important point to note is that in any model with union members specialized completely in the export commodity and all border prices determined outside the union, a union member will be affected by its own policy changes only and not by policy changes in the partner country. Thus, in the small-union Meade model outlined in the previous paragraph, preferential liberalization by country A will affect itself but not country B. The reason for this property is that domestic prices which guide economic activity in each country are determined by the border price plus the country's own tariff, and the border price is entirely unaffected by policy changes in the partner country. In order for preferential liberalization by A to affect B, its policy changes must have an influence on the latter's internal prices.[20]

Given that each country is unaffected by changes in tariffs in the partner country, we can analyze the effects of a preferential trading agreement in exactly the same way as we analyze (unilateral) trade reform by a small open economy in isolation. Moreover, because of the symmetry between union members, it suffices to analyze the effects of preferential trading by one union member. The effects on the other member and the union as a whole can be inferred by symmetry. The rest

Table 3.2. *Domestic Prices in the small-union Meade model (good 1 is exported by Country A, 2 by B, and 3 by C; prices in C are fixed)*

	Good 1	Good 2	Good 3
Country A	$p_1^A = p_1^*$	$p_2^A \equiv p_2^*(1 + t_2^A)$	$p_3^A \equiv p_3^*(1 + t_3^A)$
Country B	$p_1^B \equiv p_1^*(1 + t_1^B)$	$p_2^B = p_2^*$	$p_3^B \equiv p_3^*(1 + t_3^A)$
Country C	p_1^*	p_2^*	p_3^*

of the world is, of course, unaffected due to the fact that the union is too small to affect the prices there.

Let us consider country A. Because the only relevant variables other than world prices are those relating to country A, we drop the country superscript and distinguish world prices by an asterisk. The equilibrium in country A is given by

$$e\left(p_1^*, \left(1+t_2\right)p_2^*, \left(1+t_3\right)p_3^*; u\right) = p_1^* \tilde{q}_1 + t_2 p_2^* e_2(\cdot) + t_3 p_3^* e_3(\cdot) \qquad (3.8)$$

where $\tilde{q}_1$ is the quantity of good 1 produced. Because of complete specialization, this quantity is fixed. As before, $e_i(\cdot)$ $(i = 1, 2, 3)$ is the partial derivative of $e(\cdot)$ with respect to the ith argument and p_i^* is the international price (i.e., the price in country C) of good i and is constant.

We are now interested in the effect of a small reduction by A in the tariff on the good imported from B. Differentiate equation (3.8) with respect to t_2, and we have

$$e_u du = t_2 p_2^* de_2(\cdot) + t_3 p_3^* de_3(\cdot) \qquad (3.9)$$

This equation is analogous to equation (3.7) for the world welfare in the presence of endogenous terms of trade. Thus, the equation obtained for a single country under the small-country assumption matches closely that obtained for the world as a whole under flexible terms of trade. This will not be true if we assumed A to be large, as is verified readily by comparing (3.7) to (3.4).

Equation (3.9) immediately yields Lipsey's (1970: 38) result #4: a sufficient (but not necessary) condition for a preferential liberalization to improve a country's welfare is that it increase the quantity of all imports. Intuitively, tariffs restrict imports below the optimal level. Any change which increases imports is a move toward the optimum.

Next, observe that the trade balance condition implies $\Sigma_i p_i^* e_i = p_1^* \tilde{q}_1$. Given fixed terms of trade, total differentiation of this condition yields

$$p_3^* de_3 = -\left(p_1^* de_1 + p_2^* de_2\right) \tag{3.10}$$

Substituting (10) into (9), we obtain,

$$e_u du = -\left(t_3 - t_2\right)p_2^* de_2(\cdot) - t_3 p_1^* de_1(\cdot) \tag{3.11}$$

Because $t_3 - t_2 \geq 0$ by assumption and a reduction in t_2 increases the imports of good 2, the first term on the right-hand side is nonpositive. This gives us Lipsey's (1970: 38) result #3: a necessary condition for preferential liberalization to improve a country's welfare is that it lowers the country's expenditure on its domestic good, thereby increasing the volume of imports, both measured at world prices. Intuitively, suppose the expenditure on the domestic good and, hence, the total volume of imports, at world prices, is unchanged. Then the expansion in the imports of good 2 is exactly offset by the contraction of imports of good 3. With $t_3 \geq t_2$, the beneficial effect of the former change is at most as large as the harmful effect of the latter.

From (3.11), starting with a nondiscriminatory tariff, we have $t_3 = t_2$ initially. Therefore, for the initial tariff preference, a reduction in the expenditure on the domestic good, measured at the world price, is necessary and sufficient for an improvement in country A's welfare. Assuming gross substitutability, a reduction in t_2 increases the imports of good 2 and reduces those of good 3. Therefore, it follows from (3.9) that, ceteris paribus, for each subsequent reduction in t_2, the lower is t_2, the less likely that the reduction will improve welfare. Under gross substitutability, once t_2 reaches a certain level, further tariff reductions will be associated with welfare deterioration. As Lipsey (1970: 36) noted, this value of the tariff can be called the *second-best optimum tariff*. We now have Lipsey's (1970: 38) result #1: a union that reduces the tariff on the partner country's good is more likely to be beneficial than the one which removes the tariff entirely.

Finally, suppose we assume that the initial level of tariff on the partner country exceeds that on the outside country. Then it is straightforward from (3.11) that a decline in the expenditure on the domestic good, measured at the world price, is no longer necessary for welfare improvement. For example, a reduction in t_2 improves welfare even if it leaves the expenditure on the domestic good unchanged. This is the main result derived by Corden (1976).

Alternatively, ceteris paribus, the gain from initial tariff reductions will be larger the higher the initial tariff on the partner in relation to that on the outside country. Moreover, the higher t_2 is in relation to t_3 initially, the more tariff reductions it will take before we get to the point where

the reductions begin to yield welfare losses. These facts give rise to
Lipsey's (1970: 38) result #2: an FTA is more likely to raise welfare the
higher is the level of tariff on the partner initially in relation to that on
the outside country.

So far, we have derived the results in terms of ex post responses of
expenditures in country A. But we can push the analysis one step further
by solving the model in terms of ex ante responses imbedded in the
expenditure function.[21] Thus, since $de_2 = e_{22}p_2^*dt_2 + e_{2u}du$ and $de_3 = e_{32}p_2^*dt_2 + e_{3u}du$, we can rewrite equation (3.9) as

$$S.du = p_2^*\left(t_2 p_2^* e_{22} + t_3 p_3^* e_{32}\right)dt_2 \tag{3.12}$$

where $S \equiv e_u - t_2 p_2^* e_{2u} - t_3 p_3^* e_{3u}$. Because e_u is linear homogeneous in
domestic prices, we have $e_u = p_1^* e_{u1} + (1+t_2)p_2^* e_{u2} + (1+t_3)p_3^* e_{u3}$ and, hence,
$S = p_1^* e_{u1} + p_2^* e_{u2} + p_3^* e_{u3}$. Assuming all goods to be normal in consumption,
$S > 0$ and the sign of du corresponds to the sign of the right-hand side of
(3.12). Because $e_{22} < 0$ by concavity of the expenditure function, a sufficient condition for a reduction in t_2 to improve welfare is that goods 2 and
3 be independent or net complements in country A's demand (i.e., $e_{32} \leq$
0). This result is similar to Lipsey's result #4, noted above, and can be
found in McMillan and McCann (1981).

We can derive results similar to Lipsey's results #1–3 in terms of net
substitutability. But I will leave this task to the reader and focus, instead,
on the role of the *relative* degree of substitutability between good 2
on the one hand and 1 and 3 on the other. To study this relationship,
it is useful to transform (3.12) further. Remembering that $e_2(\cdot)$ is
homogeneous of degree zero in domestic prices, we have

$$p_1^* e_{21} + \left(1+t_2\right)p_2^* e_{22} + \left(1+t_3\right)p_3^* e_{23} = 0 \tag{3.13}$$

Solving this equation for e_{22}, substituting the resulting value into (3.12),
and simplifying, we obtain

$$S.du = -\frac{p_2^*}{1+t_2}\left[t_2 p_1^* e_{21} + \left(t_2 - t_3\right)p_3^* e_{32}\right]dt_2 \tag{3.14}$$

Denote by $\eta_{2i} \equiv (p_i/e_2)e_{2i}$ $(i = 1, 3)$ the compensated cross-price elasticity
of demand for good 2 with respect to the (domestic) price of good i
in country A where $p_1 = p_1^*$ and $p_3 = (1 + t_3)p_3^*$. We can rewrite (3.14)
as

$$S.du = -p_2^* e_2\left[\frac{t_2}{1+t_2}\eta_{21} + \left(\frac{t_2}{1+t_2} - \frac{t_3}{1+t_3}\right)\eta_{23}\right]dt_2 \tag{3.14'}$$

If good 2 exhibits substitutability with both 1 and 3, the η_{2i} are positive. Assuming further that $t_3 \geq t_2$, the first term in brackets on the right-hand side is positive and the second one is negative. In the spirit of Meade's results for the world welfare, we see that the more substitutable is B's good for A's and the less substitutable it is for C's, the more likely that an increase in tariff preference will improve welfare. Also, ceteris paribus, as t_2 is reduced relative to t_3, the gain is smaller and smaller until it becomes negative. The second-best optimum tariff where this switch takes place can be obtained by setting $du = 0$ in (3.14′). Denoting this tariff by t^{opt}, we have[22]

$$\frac{t_2^{opt}}{1+t_2^{opt}} = \frac{t_3}{1+t_3} \cdot \frac{1}{1+\dfrac{\eta_{21}}{\eta_{23}}} \tag{3.15}$$

Not surprisingly, the optimum tariff is related positively to the tariff on the outside country. The higher the latter, the greater the loss from trade diversion caused by preferential liberalization. Moreover, the greater the degree of substitutability between the two importables relative to that between the partner's good and the home good, the higher the second-best optimum tariff.

So far, we have assumed that countries A and B are completely specialized in their export goods. We may ask whether the model can be generalized to allow for the production of imported goods in A and B. On the face of it, this seems simple enough and Lloyd (1982: 54), indeed, notes that the "results carry over if one allows production of all commodities and replaces the net substitution or independence in demand relations with net substitution or independence in excess demand."

Yet, the generalization is tricky on account of a point made by Richardson (1994). Suppose A and B produce all goods, including good 3. Suppose further that the tariff on good 3 is higher in A than in B, yielding $p_3^A > p_3^B$ where $p_3^j = (1 + t_3^j)p_3^C$ $(j = A, B)$. If A and B form an FTA, however, producer prices in the two countries must necessarily equalize. There are no restrictions on the movement of goods *produced* within an FTA. This means that producers of good 3 in country B will want to sell all their output in country A and buyers there will have to import everything they consume from C. The producer price for good 3 will become p_3^A throughout the union while consumers in B will be subject to p_3^B.[23]

This complication arises whenever a good imported from outside the union is also produced by the union member with the lower external tariff on it.[24] In particular, the analysis in Meade's Chapters 4 and 5 can be subject to this critique. The implicit assumption that validates the analysis when all goods are produced in all locations is that the goods imported from the outside country remain subject to a nondiscriminatory tariff.[25] Thus, the generalization suggested by Lloyd will be valid only if it is assumed that A and B subject each other to the same tariff on good 3 that they impose on C. A weaker restriction is that the level of preference on good 3 by a union member does not exceed the other union member's tariff on that good. Alternatively, we can assume that good 3 is not produced in the country with the lower tariff on that good on the outside country.

3.3 "Natural trading partners" and the Meade model

Wonnacott and Lutz (1989), Krugman (1991), and Summers (1991) have argued that countries that trade disproportionately large amounts with each other are "natural trading partners" and FTAs between them are likely to be welfare improving. For example, Krugman asserts,

> To reemphasize why this matters: if a disproportionate share of world trade would take place within trading blocs even in the absence of any preferential trading arrangement, then the gains from trade creation within blocs are likely to outweigh any possible losses from external trade diversion. (29)

In a similar vein, Summers argues,

> Are trading blocs likely to divert large amounts of trade? In answering this question, the issue of natural trading blocs is crucial because to the extent that blocs are created between countries that already trade disproportionately, the risk of large amounts of trade diversion is reduced. (297)

Bhagwati (1993), Panagariya (1996a), and Bhagwati and Panagariya (1996a) have subjected this view to a systematic critique. The main issue in the present context is whether we can find support for the natural trading partners hypothesis in the Meade model. There are two references in the literature that may appear to offer an affirmative answer and, therefore, deserve a careful scrutiny. The first reference is in Meade's Chapter 8 and the second in Lipsey (1960). In Chapter 8, summarizing his conclusions, Meade notes:

> Fourth, a customs union between two countries will be the more likely to raise economic welfare, if each is the principal supplier to the other of the products which it exports to the other and if each is the principal market for the other of the products which it imports from the other. Thus if the Netherlands makes up the main external market for Bel-

> gium for the sort of things *which she imports from Belgium*, there is less *scope for* the diversion of Belgian exports from other markets to the Dutch market. Similarly, if Belgium makes up the main external source for the Netherlands of the sort of things *which she exports to the Netherlands*, there is *less scope* for the diversion of Dutch imports from other countries' products onto Belgian products. (1955: 108–9; emphasis added)

Two points can be made against any possible support for the natural trading partners hypothesis in this paragraph. First, it does not relate the extent of *total* intraregional trade to the likelihood of welfare improvement from preferential trading. The member countries may trade very little with each other and yet they may be principal sources of and destinations for the products *which they trade with each other* and vice versa. Second, if the partner is the major source of the types of products it supplies a member, there is less *scope for* trade diversion. But the actual trade diversion depends, not on the *scope for* trade diversion, but on the degree of substitutability between the partner's goods and those of outside countries. And there is no hint anywhere in the book that the degree of substitutability depends on the extent of intraregional trade in the products traded by member countries with each other. The same point applies to the criterion that if a partner is the main destination for the types of products exported by a member, there is less scope for trade diversion.

The second reference bearing on natural trading partners hypotheses appears in Lipsey (1960), who, drawing on Lipsey (1958), notes:

> This argument gives rise to two general conclusions. . . . The first is that *given a country's volume of international trade*, a customs union is more likely to raise welfare the higher is the proportion of trade with the country's union partner and the lower the proportion with the outside world. The second is that a customs union is more likely to raise welfare the lower is the total volume of foreign trade, for the lower is foreign trade, the lower must be purchases from the outside world relative to purchases of domestic commodities. (emphasis in the original)

Several points must be noted with respect to these two conclusions. First, though Lipsey (1960) states them as general conclusions without any qualifications whatsoever, they are actually derived, in Lipsey (1958, chapter 6), under two highly restrictive conditions: (i) the country is specialized completely in the export good, and (ii) preferences are Cobb–Douglas. I show at the end of this section that the conclusions can be generalized to CES preferences, but that, too, is highly restrictive, especially when taken in conjunction with the complete specialization assumption.

Recall that the general criterion for welfare improvement from a tariff preference, emerging from equation (3.14′), is based on substitutability: the more substitutable are home goods for imports from the partner relative to the substitutability between the two types of imports, the more likely that preferential liberalization will improve welfare. In the context of the North American Free Trade Agreement (NAFTA), the more substitutable are U.S. goods for Mexican goods relative to those coming from outside countries, the more likely that Mexico will benefit from preferential liberalization. But, as Meade himself argued, the relative substitutability is likely to go the other way: the U.S. goods are likely to be better substitutes for outside countries' goods than those of Mexico.

Second, these conclusions also require the small-country assumption. But, in general, preferential liberalization by a country is likely to worsen its terms of trade vis-à-vis the union partner. This is particularly true when the initial degree of openness in the member countries is highly uneven. In such a situation, the more open member of the union undertakes far less preferential liberalization than the less open partner. For example, prior to NAFTA, the United States had much lower external tariffs than Mexico. Therefore, NAFTA involves far more preferential liberalization by Mexico than the United States and is likely to result in a deterioration of the former's terms of trade vis-à-vis the latter. And when the terms of trade deteriorate, the larger the initial volume of imports from the partner, the larger the loss. This point will also be developed formally below.

Finally, as Bhagwati (1993) noted in his original critique of the natural trading partners hypothesis, even if we swallow Lipsey's (1958) highly restrictive assumptions, his conclusions point to a small expenditure on the outside country's good relative to that on *home goods* as the key criterion for welfare improvement rather than a low expenditure on the partner country's goods relative to the *outside country's goods*. Thus, a country buying 20 percent of its total imports from the outside country but devoting only 10 percent of its expenditure to home goods will likely fail the Lipsey test, whereas a country buying 80 percent of its imports from the outside country but devoting 80 percent of its expenditure to home goods will likely pass it.

The inevitable conclusion is that the Meade model provides no support for natural trading partners hypothesis. In the remainder of this section, I generalize Lipsey's result to CES utility function and indicate briefly the implications of endogenous terms of trade for natural trading partners hypothesis.

Let the utility function be

$$u\big(c_1,\, c_2,\, c_3\big) = \left[\sum_{i=1}^{3} a_i c_i^{\alpha}\right]^{\frac{1}{\alpha}} \tag{3.16}$$

where c_i is the consumption of good i ($i = 1, 2, 3$) and a_i and α are constants such that $a_i > 0$ and $-\infty < \alpha < 1$. The expenditure function associated with this utility function is

$$e\big(p_1,\, p_2,\, p_3;\, u\big) = \left[\sum_{i=1}^{3} a_i^{\sigma} p_i^{1-\sigma}\right]^{\frac{1}{1-\sigma}} u \tag{3.17}$$

where $\sigma \equiv 1/(1 - \alpha)$ is the elasticity of substitution between any pair of goods. Given (3.17), simple manipulations allow us to obtain

$$\eta_{2k} \equiv \frac{p_k}{e_2} \frac{\partial e_2}{\partial p_k} = \sigma\left(\frac{p_k e_k}{e}\right) \equiv \beta_k \qquad k = 1,\, 3 \tag{3.18}$$

where β_k is the proportion of total expenditure devoted to product k. Substituting from (3.18) into (3.15), the second-best optimum tariff in the present CES case becomes

$$\frac{t_2^{\text{opt}}}{1+t_2^{\text{opt}}} = \frac{t_3}{1+t_3} \cdot \frac{1}{1+\dfrac{\beta_1}{\beta_3}} \tag{3.19}$$

It is immediately clear from this equation that the larger the share of expenditure devoted to the home good relative to that to the outside country's good, the smaller is the second-best optimum tariff on the partner and hence the more likely that an FTA between countries A and B will be beneficial to A. Lipsey (1958) established this result for the special case of Cobb–Douglas preferences, that is, $\sigma = 1$.

Finally, let us consider the large-union case.[26] Focus, once again, on country A. Set $p_1^* \equiv 1$ by the choice of numeraire. Differentiating (3.8) totally, allowing t_2 and the terms of trade to change, we have

$$\begin{aligned}
S.du = {} & -e_2 dp_2^* - e_3 dp_3^* \\
& + \Big[t_2 p_2^* e_{22} + t_3 p_3^* e_{32}\Big]\big(1+t_2\big)dp_2^* \\
& + \Big[t_2 p_2^* e_{23} + t_3 p_3^* e_{33}\Big]\big(1+t_3\big)dp_3^* \\
& + \Big[t_2 p_2^* e_{22} + t_3 p_3^* e_{32}\Big]p_2^* dt_2
\end{aligned} \tag{3.20}$$

Note that, as we saw in equation (3.12) under the small-union assumption, we obtain only the last term of equation (3.20). This term is the sole source of the results considered so far in the present section. But with intra-union as well as extra-union terms of trade variable, we have four additional terms. The first two terms, shown in the top row of equation (3.20), capture the direct effects of changes in the intra- and extra-union terms of trade, respectively.[27] The magnitude of these effects depends on the initial volume of imports times the change in the relevant price. Mundell (1964) shows that preferential liberalization by a country worsens its intra-union terms of trade, that is, a reduction in t_2 by A leads to a rise in p_2^*. Mundell also shows that the effect of preferential liberalization on the country's extra-union terms of trade is ambiguous in general, but the presumption is in favor of an improvement in them: the diversion of demand toward the partner's good and away from the outside country's good is likely to lower p_3^*. Evidently, the larger the initial imports from the partner, the greater the loss to A from the deterioration in its intra-union terms of trade (i.e., the rise in p_2^*). Moreover, since this loss accrues on the entire quantity of imports, even if the rise in p_2^* accounts for half of the reduction in t_2, the loss to A can be large in relation to any gain that will accrue on account of the last term in (3.20), on which Lipsey's results rest.[28] Thus, ceteris paribus, a large volume of trade with the partner is associated with a welfare loss, not gain, from preferential liberalization. According to the second term in (3.20), accepting Mundell's presumption that country A's extra-union terms of trade improve, the smaller the initial volume of trade with the outside country, the smaller the gain on this account.

What can we say about the terms in the last three rows in equation (3.20)? The terms in the second and third rows represent the effects on tariff revenue attributable to *changes in imports* resulting from shifts in the terms of trade. The term in the last row, analyzed by Lipsey, Lloyd, and others, represents the change in tariff revenue resulting from the change in imports attributable to the change in t_2, holding all terms of trade constant. To find out the signs of these terms, we need to use the zero-degree homogeneity of e_2 shown in equation (3.13) and a similar property for e_3. Recall that, using (3.13), we were able to transform the term in parentheses in equation (3.12) as shown in (3.14). This same transformation for the second and fourth rows and an analogous transformation, using zero-degree homogeneity of e_3, for the third row allows us to rewrite (3.20) as

$$S.du = -e_2 dp_2^* - e_3 dp_3^*$$
$$- \left[t_2 p_1^* e_{12} + (t_2 - t_3) p_3^* e_{32} \right] dp_2^*$$
$$- \left[t_3 p_1^* e_{13} + (t_3 - t_2) p_2^* e_{23} \right] dp_3^*$$
$$- \left[t_2 p_1^* e_{12} + (t_2 - t_3) p_3^* e_{32} \right] p_2^* dt_2 \qquad (3.20')$$

Assuming goods 1 and 2 are net substitutes, at $t_2 = t_3$, the term in the second row is negative. Thus, the effect of the change in terms of trade with respect to the partner country is unambiguously negative. The rise in p_2^* by itself reduces imports and hence tariff revenue. Assuming that p_3^* falls, the third row is positive. The reduction in p_3^* leads to increased imports from country C, which is unambiguously beneficial. Finally, given $dt_2 < 0$ by assumption, the last term is positive at $t_2 = t_3$, but ambiguous in general.

It may be noted that I have considered here the effect of a reduction in the tariff by A only. To the extent that B lowers its tariff on A's good, the latter's terms of trade with the former may not deteriorate. But in situations such as NAFTA, where the extent of preferential liberalization is asymmetric, the effects discussed above will predict the results correctly.

3.4 Concluding remarks

Rather than restate the results of the essay, which have already been summarized in the introduction, I conclude with suggestions for future research. Though much has been written on the Meade model, there is clearly need for further work. Despite Mundell's (1964) seminal contribution, little has been written on the welfare implications of the model for union members in the presence of endogenous terms of trade. This essay has made a beginning but fallen short of solving the problem completely. The problem of the world welfare can also be analyzed further by solving the model in terms of the expenditure function rather than ex post, total changes as in equation (3.6). Finally, because the assumption of complete specialization is arbitrary, it may be worthwhile to formulate the model in terms of the Dixit–Stiglitz–Krugman model of monopolistic competition. These are some of the directions in which my current research is moving.

NOTES

I am grateful to Jagdish Bhagwati for his generous comments which, in particular, helped sharpen the distinction between one of Meade's results and the

Kemp–Wan theorem. Thanks are also due to Jerry Cohen and Dani Rodrik for comments on an earlier draft.

1. Sadly, James E. Meade passed away on December 22, 1995, while this essay was still in progress.
2. Also see the more general treatment of the theory of the second best in Lipsey and Lancaster (1956–57). Lipsey (1958), the author's Ph.D. thesis, was subsequently published under its original title, with minor corrections, as Lipsey (1970). To keep the chronology of the development of the Meade model straight, I have referred to this key contribution as Lipsey (1958) in most of this essay, but, where page numbers had to be specified due to a lack of availability of the thesis, I have used Lipsey (1970). By doing so, I have avoided the error made by Collier (1979) in identifying Lipsey (1970) as a post-Lipsey (1960) development.
3. Bhagwati (1995) has urged, and Bhagwati and Panagariya (1996a, 1996b) have adopted, the use of the term PTA to include *both* customs unions and FTAs.
4. This interpretation has subsequently become synonymous with the "Viner model." There has been a controversy in the literature on whether or not Viner actually assumed infinite supply elasticities and zero demand elasticities (Bhagwati 1971, 1973; Johnson 1974; Kirman 1973). In a letter to Max Corden dated March 13, 1965, and published subsequently in the *Journal of International Economics*, Viner (1965) himself disagreed vehemently with Meade's interpretation of his model. Michaely (1976) provides a fuller account of the controversy. On zero demand elasticities, which essentially amount to ignoring consumption effects, Michaely rejects Johnson's (1974) contention that these effects were incorporated by Viner in his trade creation effect and essentially agrees with Bhagwati's (1973) view that Viner had simply "not thought through the question completely." On the supply side, Michaely concludes that though Viner explicitly assumed increasing costs and, hence, finite supply elasticities, his conclusion that, in any one industry, preferential liberalization leads to either trade creation or trade diversion, but not both, does require infinite supply elasticities.
5. On pages 46 and 48, Meade does refer to welfare effects of preferential trading on the member countries' welfare. But such references are rare.
6. Thus, see Lloyd (1982: 52). There also exists some ambiguity concerning the object of welfare analysis in Lipsey's (1960) discussion of Meade. Lipsey introduces a figure 3 to explain Meade's welfare analysis. In discussing this figure, he does not make explicit whether it is the welfare of the world or of the union that is being considered. From the context of the paper, a casual reader is likely to be misled into thinking that the discussion applies to the union's welfare, though it actually applies to world welfare.

   In print, I have been able to find only Corden (1965: 55) as explicitly recognizing that Meade's analysis applies to global rather than the union's welfare. Interestingly, Corden sees this fact as the "principal limitation" of Meade's work.

7. The sole exception is the important but neglected paper by Mundell (1964), which focuses directly on the terms of trade effects of preferential liberalization. Though Lipsey (1958) also deals with flexible terms of trade in chapters 7 and 8, there he switches to a two-good model.

8. Interestingly, in footnote 8, Lloyd (1982) notes, "Meade did not make the small country assumption." But, in the text, he attributes results based on the small-country model to Meade. From an individual member's viewpoint, these results cannot obtain in a model with flexible terms of trade and, therefore, could not have been obtained by Meade.

9. Thus, in the concluding paragraph of Chapter 4, describing the problem in terms of a union between Netherlands and Belgium, with Germany representing the rest of the world, Meade notes, "We need, therefore, to consider the direct and indirect effect of a small reduction in the Dutch duty on Belgian beer upon all trades in all products between the Netherlands, Belgium and Germany. Now at this point one should, perhaps, try to build a complicated model in which every economic quantity in the world is made to depend upon every other quantity. . . . I am not able to handle the mathematics which would be necessary for such an analysis. We shall have to be content with a more rough and ready method." (1955: 66)

10. This expression is also derived by Kowalczyk (1990) in passing.

11. Because $m^j(\cdot)$ is linear homogeneous in the goods prices, we have $m^j = \Sigma_i p_i^j m_i^j$. Making use of this equality, (3.1') reduces to $\Sigma_i p_i^* m_i^j = 0$, which is the trade balance condition.

12. Of course, we do require that goods markets be cleared in the *initial* equilibrium. Recall that we do use equation (3.2) in deriving (3.6').

13. Though the post-Meade literature has generally focused on the effects of preferential trading on union members, there has been some revival of interest in studying the effects of this change on the rest of the world. Thus, see Bliss (1994), Srinivasan (1996), and Winters (1995).

14. Although observations (i)–(iii) are plausible, they are not infallible. Income effects due to shifts in the terms of trade could easily reverse some of these results. Meade himself does not represent these results as the only possibility. Moreover, in Chapter 5, where he analyzes the multicountry, multi-commodity model, he offers a wide array of possibilities.

15. Vanek (1965, chap. 7) also states this result, along with a proof, for the special case of a three-country, two-commodity model. There is no reference to Kemp (1964) in Vanek (1965) or vice versa.

16. In the following quotation, RIA stands for regional integration agreement.

17. For instance, if the products on which union members remove quotas against each other exhibit complementarity with those imported from the rest of the world freely, the terms of trade can turn against the union.

18. Recall here that throughout the book, Meade works only with import restrictions. Indeed, Meade himself did not even think in terms of a union-wide quota or quantitative restrictions on all imports from the rest of the world.

On pp. 96–9, nowhere does Meade indicate that union members adopt a union-wide quota in the post-union equilibrium. Furthermore, as a careful reading of the passage quoted in the text of this paper will reveal, Meade's result requires only that "all trade barriers take the form of fixed and unchanged quantitative restrictions" rather than that all trade be subject to quantitative restrictions.

19. In the concluding paragraph of his book, Viner offered the following verdict on the role of customs unions as a solution to the existing problems in the field of international economics: "Whether used as a mere incantation against the evils resulting from present-day economic policy or vigorously prosecuted, it will in either case be unlikely to prove a practical and suitable remedy for today's economic ills, and it will almost inevitably operate as a psychological barrier to the realization of the more desirable but less desired objective of the Havana chapter – the balanced multilateral reduction of trade barriers on a nondiscriminatory basis."

20. Mundell (1964), Berglas (1979), and Riezman (1979), as well as Meade (1955) allow for endogenous terms of trade. As a result, in these models, policy changes in one country do affect other countries. Berglas works with what appears to be a small-union model but manages to link the price of one of the commodities in a member country to that in the partner country by assuming that the former cannot trade this commodity with the rest of the world.

21. McMillan and McCann (1981) also analyze the small-union Meade model in terms of net substitutability, but do not make many of the points made below.

22. McMillan and McCann (1981) also derive this second-best optimum tariff, but their expression is more complex and does not lend itself to as clear an interpretation as that in equation (3.15).

23. This outcome assumes that A continues to import some of good 3 from country C. It is possible that B will eliminate C as a supplier, in which case both the consumer and producer prices in A will fall below $(1 + t_3^A)p_3^C$.

24. The problem arises whenever the tariff on a good in a member country is smaller than the margin of preference given by the partner country. Thus let A have the higher external tariff on good 3 than B. Denote by t_3^A A's tariff on C and by τ_3^A its tariff on country B with $t_3^A - \tau_3^A$ representing the tariff preference. The net price received by B's producers in A equals $(1 + t_3^A - \tau_3^A)p_3^C$. If this price exceeds $(1 + t_3^B)p_3^C$, that is, if the tariff preference in A exceeds the tariff preference in B, all supplies of good 3 in B will be diverted to A. Thus, for $t_3^A - \tau_3^A = t_3^B$, our calculus method will break down.

25. Strictly speaking, we must also assume that each good exported by a union member to the partner is also exported to the outside country.

26. Here I draw on Panagariya (1996b).

27. From country A's viewpoint, a rise in p_2^* and p_3^* is equivalent to a deterioration in the intra- and extra-union terms of trade, respectively.

28. This point is emphasized in Bhagwati and Panagariya (1996a).

REFERENCES

Baldwin, Richard, and Anthony Venables (1995), "Regional Economic Integration." In Gene Grossman and Ken Rogoff, *Handbook of International Economics*, Vol. III, pp. 1597–1644. Amsterdam: North Holland.

Berglas, Eitan (1979). "Preferential Trading: The *n* Commodity Case," *Journal of Political Economy* 87(21), 315–31.

Bhagwati, Jagdish (1971). "Trade-Diverting Customs Unions and Welfare Improvement: A Clarification," *Economic Journal* 81, 580–7.

Bhagwati, Jagdish (1973). "A Reply to Professor Kirman," *Economic Journal* 83, 895–7.

Bhagwati, Jagdish (1993). "Regionalism and Multilateralism: An Overview." In Melo and Panagariya, 1993, pp. 22–51.

Bhagwati, Jagdish (1995). "U.S. Trade Policy: The Infatuation with Free Trade Areas." In J. Bhagwati and Anne O. Krueger, eds., *The Dangerous Drift to Preferential Trade Agreements*, pp. 1–18. Washington, DC: American Enterprise Institute for Public Policy Research.

Bhagwati, Jagdish, and Arvind Panagariya (1996a). "Preferential Trading Areas and Multilateralism: Strangers, Friends or Foes?" In Jagdish Bhagwati and Arvind Panagariya, eds., *The Economics of Preferential Trade Agreements*, Washington, DC: AEI Press, pp. 1–78.

Bhagwati, Jagdish, and Arvind Panagariya (1996b). "The Theory of Preferential Trade Agreements: Historical Evolution and Current Trends." *American Economic Review: Papers and Proceedings* 86(2) (May), 82–7.

Bliss, Christopher (1994). *Economic Theory and Policy for Trading Blocks*, Manchester, V. K., and New York: Manchester University Press.

Collier, Paul (1979). "The Welfare Effects of Customs Union: An Anatomy," *Economic Journal* 89 (March), 84–95.

Corden, W. M. (1965). *Recent Developments in the Theory of International Trade.* Special Papers in International Economics 7, International Finance Section, Princeton University, March.

Corden, Max (1976). "Customs Unions Theory and the Nonuniformity of Tariffs," *Journal of International Economics* 6, 99–106.

Corden, Max, and Rodney Falvey (1985). "Quotas and the Second Best," *Economics Letters*, 18, 67–70.

Johnson, H. G. (1974). "Trade Diverting Customs Union: A Comment," *Economic Journal* 84, 618–21.

Kemp, Murray, C. (1964). *The Pure Theory of International Trade.* Englewood Cliffs, NJ: Prentice-Hall, 176–7.

Kemp, Murray C., and Henry Wan (1976). "An Elementary Proposition Concerning the Formation of Customs Unions," *Journal of International Economics* 6 (February), 95–8.

Kenen, Peter B. (1957). "On the Geometry of Welfare Economics," *Quarterly Journal of Economics* 71(3) 426–47.

Kenen, Peter B. (1959). "Distribution, Demand and Equilibrium in International Trade: A Diagrammatic Analysis," *Kyklos* 12(4), 629–38.

Kenen, Peter B. (1969). "The Theory of Optimum Currency Areas: An Eclectic View." In R. A. Mundell and A. K. Swaboda, eds., *Monetary Problems of the International Economy*, pp. 41–60. Chicago: Chicago University Press, 1969.

Kirman, A. P. (1973). "Trade Diverting Customs Unions and Welfare Improvement: A Comment," *Economic Journal* 83, 890–4.

Kowalczyk, Carsten (1990). "Welfare and Customs Unions," NBER Working Paper No. 3476, October.

Krugman, P. (1991). "The Move to Free Trade Zones." In *Policy Implications of Trade and Currency Zones*, pp. 7–41. Symposium Sponsored by the Federal Reserve Bank of Kansas City.

Lipsey, Richard (1958). "The Theory of Customs Unions: A General Equilibrium Analysis," Ph.D. thesis, University of London.

Lipsey, Richard (1960). "The Theory of Customs Unions: A General Survey," *Economic Journal* 70, 498–513.

Lipsey, Richard (1970). *The Theory of Customs Unions: A General Equilibrium Analysis*, LSE Research Monographs 7. London: London School of Economics and Political Science.

Lipsey, Richard, and Kelvin Lancaster (1956–57). "The General Theory of Second Best," *Review of Economic Studies* 24, 11–32.

Lloyd, Peter J. (1982). "3 × 3 Theory of Customs Unions," *Journal of International Economics* 12, 41–63.

McMillan, John, and Ewen McCann (1981). "Welfare Effects in Customs Union," *Economic Journal* 91 (September), 697–703.

Meade, James E. (1952). *A Geometry of International Trade*. London: Allen and Unwin.

Meade, James E. (1955). *The Theory of Customs Unions*. Amsterdam: North-Holland.

Melo, Jaime de, and Arvind Panagariya, ed. (1993). *New Dimensions in Regional Integration*. Cambridge University Press.

Michaely, Michael (1976). "The Assumptions of Jacob Viner's Theory of Customs Unions," *Journal of International Economics* 6, 75–93.

Mundell, Robert A. (1964). "Tariff Preferences and the Terms of Trade," *Manchester School of Economic and Social Studies*, 1–13.

Ohyama, M. (1972). "Trade and Welfare in General Equilibrium," *Keio Economic Studies* 9, 37–73.

Panagariya, Arvind (1996a). "The Free Trade Area of the Americas: Good for Latin America?" *World Economy* 19(5) (September), 485–515.

Panagariya, Arvind (1996b). "Preferential Trading and the Myth of Natural Trading Partners," Working Paper No. 200. New York University: Center for Japan–U.S. Business and Economic Studies, Stern School of Business.

Richardson, M. (1994). "Why a Free Trade Area? The Tariff Also Rises," *Economics and Politics* 6(1) (March), 79–95.

Riezman, Raymond (1979). "A 3 × 3 Model of Customs Unions," *Journal of International Economics* 9, 341–54.

Srinivasan, T. N. (1996). "Common External Tariffs of a Customs Union: Alternative Approaches," New York University: Working Paper No. 200. Center for Japan–U.S. Business and Economic Studies, Stern School of Business.

Summers, Lawrence (1991). "Regionalism and the World Trading System," In *Policy Implications of Trade and Currency Zones*, pp. 295–301. Symposium Sponsored by the Federal Reserve Bank of Kansas City.

Vanek, Jaroslav (1965). *General Equilibrium of International Discrimination. The Case of Customs Unions.* Cambridge: Harvard University Press.

Viner, Jacob (1950). *The Customs Union Issue.* New York: Carnegie Endowment for International Peace.

Viner, Jacob (1965). "A Letter to W. M. Corden," published in *Journal of International Economics* (1976) 6(1), 107–8.

Winters, L. A. (1995). "European Integration and Economic Welfare in the Rest of the World," mimeo., The World Bank.

Wonnacott, Paul, and Mark Lutz (1989). "Is There a Case for Free Trade Areas?" In Jeffrey Schott, ed., *Free Trade Areas and U.S. Trade Policy*, pp. 59–84. Washington, DC: Institute for International Economics.

CHAPTER 4

International trade and big government

Dani Rodrik

I Introduction

What sets international economics apart as a separate field of study within economics? That is the question with which Peter Kenen would start his lectures on international trade at Princeton. His answer remains vivid in this author's mind after fifteen years: what is special about international economics is that it deals with economic transactions between *sovereign* entities.

As Kenen explained, sovereignty has a number of important implications for the study of economics. The most obvious is that governments impose restrictions on the mobility of goods, services, and factors of production across their national borders. Countries also differ in their tax/trade/regulatory regimes, so that such restrictions operate asymmetrically. Moreover, these policies are *endogenous* to the nature of international economic interactions faced by sovereign entities. Governments respond to the opportunities, pressures, and challenges posed by international economic integration. Indeed, the study of this interdependence between policy and resource allocation constitutes the core of international economics.[1]

This essay documents one little-known but significant way in which governments have apparently responded to international integration: exposure to foreign trade is strongly and positively correlated with the size of government (as a share of GDP). Governments in more open economies tend to consume, transfer, and invest a higher share of national income. This relationship holds both for the OECD countries and a larger sample of countries exceeding 100 in number. Moreover, openness in the early 1960s is a statistically significant predictor of the *expansion* of the government sector over the following three decades. The correlation between openness and size of government is robust in the sense that it is unaffected by the inclusion of other variables in the regression equation, including regional dummies; it holds for both the low- and high-income subsamples; and it exists in all the available data sets, including Summers–Heston data on government consumption, World Bank data on broader spending, IMF data on tax revenues, and UNESCO data on public spending on education. The components of government spending closely associated with openness are economically meaningful items such as education, subsidies, social security, and welfare, and public investment (and not defense, interest payments, and "other" expenditures). Preliminary work on estimating a system of equations that treats both government spending and openness as endogenous suggests that the causality runs directly from openness to spending.

This is an empirical regularity that should be counterintuitive and puzzling to many economists. The degree of openness to trade is partly a function of policy (through tariff and nontariff barriers to trade) and partly a consequence of history and geography (related to the size of the economy, proximity to trading partners, etc.). Treating openness as a policy decision, the expectation would be that governments that allow free trade to prevail would be the ones philosophically least inclined to build large public sectors. Treating openness as determined by geography and history, on the other hand, the expectation would be that greater openness undercuts the effectiveness of government intervention and correspondingly reduces the useful scope of government spending. Hence, on a priori grounds one might have expected the relationship between openness and government spending to be negative, rather than positive.

This is not the first essay to suggest that more open economies have larger governments. In a paper published in 1978 and which is well known in political science (but not in economics), David Cameron (1978) showed that the best single predictor of the increase in an OECD government's size between 1960 and 1975 was the economy's openness in 1960, with a correlation coefficient of 0.78. Cameron proxied the size of the public sector by the share of government revenue in GDP and openness by the share of trade (exports plus imports) in GDP. Cameron's study was limited to 18 OECD countries. The problem with such a small sample is that it raises doubts about the generality of the finding. Perhaps more importantly, it does not allow for an adequate test for omitted variables, preventing the analyst from discriminating among alternative hypotheses. For example, it is impossible to distinguish Cameron's hypothesis from one that relates the scope of government to a third variable, country size. Small countries like the Netherlands, Norway, and Belgium trade more and tend to have larger governments. Openness and country size are too collinear in the OECD sample to determine which one of the two is the driving force behind the expansion of the public sector.

The current study goes beyond Cameron's not only in looking at a much larger group of countries, but also along other dimensions. The larger sample allows me to experiment with a broader set of potential omitted variables, and to check the robustness of the openness coefficient with respect to them. As mentioned above, I look at measures of the public sector drawn from different data sets. I analyze the relationship between openness and different components of government spending and tax revenue individually. I instrument for openness to remove possible simultaneous-equation bias.

Taking the statistical relationship between openness and public spending as given, the important question is why it exists. After dismissing other potential explanations, I conclude, tentatively, that a large public sector serves a sheltering role in economies that are very open and consequently exposed to significant amounts of external risk. In other words, the public sector insulates society to some degree from the vagaries of the global market place, and the demand for such insulation is greatest in societies that are most exposed to the rest of the world. The clearest piece of evidence in favor of this conclusion is that, as I will show below, the positive relationship between openness and the scope of government is stronger in countries with more unstable external terms of trade. A separate work (Rodrik 1996) provides more detail and evidence on this interpretation.

That government expenditure plays this stabilizing role was also the conclusion of Cameron (1978) in his study of OECD countries. Cameron argued that more open economies have higher rates of industrial concentration, which tends to foster higher unionization, greater scope for collective bargaining, and stronger labor confederations. These in turn result in larger demands for government transfers – social security, pensions, unemployment insurance, job training, etc. – which mitigate external risk. Cameron's specific arguments are probably too specialized to be relevant to our 100-plus country sample. In particular, it is not plausible to attach such importance to the role of labor organizations in most developing countries. And, in any case, the empirical relationship between openness and government spending holds at the level of government *consumption* as well (and not just for transfers). But the evidence is consistent with the central idea that public spending is a risk-reducing instrument on which there is greater reliance in more open economies.[2]

II A first look at the evidence

In this section we take a first look at the data, focussing on the simple relationship between openness and government spending without controlling for other variables.

Figure 4.1 shows the relationship for 23 OECD countries. The vertical axis represents total government spending as a share of GDP, excluding interest payments, averaged over the 1990–2 period. Along the horizontal axis is shown the share of exports plus imports in GDP, averaged over the decade 1980–9. Note that our measure of openness is calculated over the decade prior to the dates for government spending since the causality is assumed to go from openness to size of government. This is the convention I follow throughout the paper. But since openness changes generally slowly, the results would be unaffected had we looked at contemporaneous measures of openness. (Data are from the World Bank's *World Data 1995* for government spending, and from *Penn World Tables* 5.6 for openness.)

The figure reveals an unmistakable positive association between openness and size of government. A semilogarithmic regression equation fits the data extremely well, explaining 44 percent of the cross-country variance in government expenditures. At one end of the distribution we have the United States and Japan, which have the lowest trade shares in GDP and (along with Turkey and Canada) the lowest shares of government spending. At the other end we have Luxembourg, Belgium, and the Netherlands, with very high degrees of openness and large government. Aside from the Cameron (1978) paper already mentioned, earlier studies that have found a correlation between openness and the size of the public economy for the OECD countries include Schmidt (1983) and OECD (1985). Figure 4.1 shows that the correlation continued to hold as of the early 1990s.

Most economists would react to the above finding by expressing suspicion that the association between openness and the scope of government is a spurious one. Indeed, the OECD evidence is fragile against alternative hypotheses, such as: (a) small countries have larger government shares and are at the same time more open; or (b) European countries have large government sectors and are also more open due to the presence of a common market among members of the European Union. However, the relationship holds also for a much larger sample of countries, as Figure 4.2 shows. This figure includes observations for all countries included in the *Penn World Tables* for which government spending data were available from the World Bank for at least one of the years 1990–2. This leaves 76 countries, including the 23 OECD ones. The

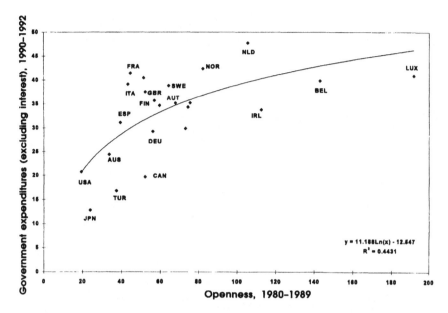

Figure 4.1. Relationship between openness and public expenditures.

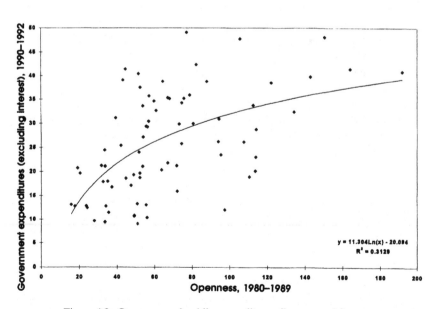

Figure 4.2. Openness and public expenditures (large sample).

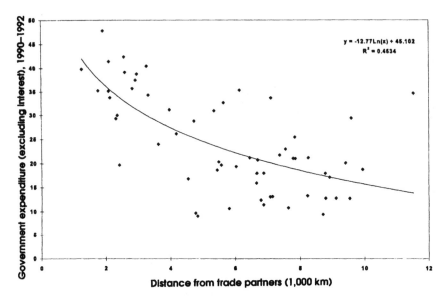

Figure 4.3. Distance from trade partners and public expenditures.

fit of a semilogarithmic equation is almost as good for this larger sample, with an R^2 of 0.31. (Incidentally, excluding the OECD countries from this larger sample actually improves the fit of the regression.) The positive association between openness and the size of government is obviously not an exclusively rich-country phenomenon.

Figure 4.3 shows that there is a striking negative association between the *geographical distance* of a country's trade partners and the size of that country's government sector. The distance variable used here is the average distance for each country to the capitals of the world's 20 major exporters, weighted by the value of bilateral imports (as calculated by Barro and Lee 1994). The figure includes all countries (59) for which the Barro–Lee data set has a distance observation and the World Bank reports government spending for at least one of the years 1990–2. The R^2 for the semilogarithmic regression is 0.45. Moreover, regression analysis reveals that distance remains a statistically significant predictor of government spending (at the 5 percent level or better) when additional variables are included, such as country size (population or total income), per capita income, and regional dummies. It is hard to think of any reason why distance should matter to an economy other than the obvious fact that the extent of a country's integration with the world economy is, everything else being equal, an inverse function of the geographical distance separating it from potential trade partners. Hence Figure 4.3 is rather compelling evidence that the size of government increases with international integration.

III Regression analysis

In this section I undertake a more formal regression analysis of the relation between openness and government spending, and also consider different measures of government spending.

One shortcoming of the World Bank measure of government spending is that it does not correct for cross-country differences in the relative price of government purchases. Two countries with identical levels of *real* government purchases may appear to have very different shares of government in GDP if the price index for such purchases relative to the GDP deflator differs. So we start the regression analysis with the *Penn World Tables* data (version 5.6a) on government consumption. These data are in principle free of this problem, based as they are on purchasing-power adjusted expenditures. They have the added advantage of being available in electronic form for a larger group of countries than the World Bank data are for the early 1990s. The disadvantage is that his measure of government includes only consumption, and excludes government transfers and public investment. I report regression results using World Bank data in the next section.[3]

Previous studies on the determinants of government spending in large cross-sections of countries have focused on income levels (the so-called Wagner's law), demographic variables, and structural conditions. See for example Tait and Heller (1982), Ram (1987), and Heller and Diamond (1990).[4] In light of these studies, our benchmark regression includes the following explanatory variables in addition to openness: *GDPSH5xx*: the Heston–Summers measure of per-capita GDP in year *19xx*; *DEPENDxx*: the dependency ratio in the population in year *19xx*; *URBANxx*: the urbanization rate in year *19xx*; SOC: a dummy for socialist countries; and OECD: a dummy for OECD members. These variables were selected after some experimentation to achieve the best overall fit for the regression, within the constraints of data availability. The income variable was generally insignificant (contrary to Wagner's law), but I have retained it in the benchmark specification because it is such an important variable to control for. The regressions also include *OPENAVGxxyy*, which is the ratio of trade (sum of imports and exports) to GDP, averaged over the prior decade. The sources for all variables used in this paper are listed in the appendix.

The dependent variable in these regressions is a three- or five-year average of real government consumption (as a share of GDP) expressed in international prices (*CGAVGxxyy*). The sample consists of all countries included in the *Penn World Tables* for which the requisite data exist. I have arbitrarily (but reasonably) decided to exclude observations for which the openness ratio exceeds 200 percent. This cutoff has very little significance for the actual results as it is binding in only two instances: Hong Kong in the case of *OPENAVG8089* and Singapore in the case of *OPENAVG7079*. Including these observations has no qualitative effect on the statistical significance of the coefficients on openness. This gives us between 103 and 125 countries, depending on the time period.

Table 4.1 displays the benchmark results for 1990–2 as well as for successive five-year periods going back to the early 1970s. The fit of the regressions is generally good for the 1980s and early 1990s. The dependency ratio enters positively as a determinant of government consumption and is statistically significant at the 1 percent level since the early 1980s. Urbanization enters negatively and is significant at the 5 percent level for the last two periods. The dummy for socialist countries has generally a positive coefficient, but is significant only in 1990–2. As mentioned previously, the income variable does not have a statistically significant effect in any period, and neither does the OECD dummy.

We are mainly interested in the coefficient on *OPENAVGxxyy*, which comes out positive and significant at the 5 percent level for 1990–2, positive and significant at the 1 percent level for 1985–9 and 1980–4, and positive but insignificant for 1975–9 and 1970–4. The estimated coefficient for the post-1980 period suggests that an increase in the (long-run) import/GDP ratio of 10 percentage points – which corresponds to an increase in $(X + M)$/GDP of 20 percentage points in the long run – is associated with an increase in the share of government consumption of 1–1.2 percentage points. A sense of the quantitative significance of this can be obtained by noting that the median shares of government consumption in GDP in the current sample are around 17–19 percent (depending on the period). The insignificance of the openness coefficient for the 1970s suggests that the positive association between exposure to trade and government consumption is a relatively recent phenomenon.

The last point can be brought into sharper relief with the help of the regressions shown in Table 4.2. These regressions look at the relationship between the *increase* in government consumption since the early 1960s and openness at the beginning of the period. The dependent variable – denoted *DGOV6090* or *DGOV6085* – is *CGAVG9092* (or *CGAVG8589*) divided by *CGAVG6064*, and indicates the multiple by which government consumption (as a share of GDP) has increased in the

Table 4.1. *Relationship between government consumption and openness, by subperiods*

| Independent variables | Dependent variable: Real government consumption (%of GDP) | | | | |
	CGAVG9092 1990–92 (1)	CGAVG8589 1985–89 (2)	CGAVG8084 1980–84 (3)	CGAVG7579 1975–79 (4)	CGAVG7074 1970–74 (5)
Constant	7.046 (5.805)	9.062*** (5.271)	8.153 (5.142)	30.722* (6.629)	31.706* (5.863)
GDPSH5xx (at beginning of period)	−1.16E−05 (0.000)	−0.000 (0.000)	−0.000 (0.000)	−0.000 (0.000)	−0.000 (0.000)
DEPENDxx	18.163* (5.715)	16.549* (5.130)	17.176* (5.043)	−6.843 (6.722)	−10.750*** (5.973)
URBANxx	−0.096** (0.043)	−0.085** (0.041)	−0.055 (0.044)	−0.087 (0.054)	−0.066*** (0.048)
SOC	6.054** (2.532)	3.271 (2.195)	1.326 (2.128)	0.646 (2.733)	−0.483 (2.426)
OECD	1.684 (3.367)	1.619 (2.901)	3.248 (2.952)	−1.458 (3.798)	−3.635 (3.362)
OPENAVGxxyy (avg for previous decade)	0.050** (0.020)	0.053* (0.019)	0.059* (0.020)	0.025 (0.025)	0.011 (0.023)
n	103	125	121	117	116
Adjusted R^2	0.352	0.339	0.332	0.171	0.148

Notes: See appendix for variable definitions. Standard errors are reported in parentheses: * significant at 1% level; ** significant at 5% level; *** significant at 10% level.

Table 4.2. *Relationship between increase in government consumption and openness*

Independent variables	Dependent variable: Increase in Real Government Consumption (% of GDP) in:	
	DGOV6090 1960–90 (1)	*DGOV6085* 1960–85 (2)
Constant	2.652*	2.279*
	(0.648)	(0.553)
CGAVG6064	–0.091*	–0.083*
	(0.011)	(0.009)
GDPSH560	1.86E–05	2.77E–05
	(5.44E–05)	(4.95E–05)
DEPEND70	0.546	0.79
	(0.595)	(0.510)
URBAN70	–0.011**	–0.009**
	(0.005)	(0.004)
SOC	0.958*	0.790*
	(0.268)	(0.206)
OECD	–0.320	–0.380
	(0.292)	(0.267)
LAAM	–0.235	–0.239
	(0.201)	(0.170)
ASIAE	–0.583**	–0.518**
	(0.238)	(0.221)
OPENAVG6064	0.006*	0.005*
	(0.002)	(0.002)
n	98	114
Adjusted R^2	0.532	0.535

Notes: See appendix for variable definitions. Standard errors are reported in parentheses:
* significant at 1% level; ** significant at 5% level; *** significant at 10% level.

intervening period. The median number in our sample for *DGOV6090* (*DGOV6085*) is 1.38 (1.44), so that half of the countries have experienced since the early 1960s increases in the share of government consumption of more than 38 percent. The explanatory variables in our regressions now include, on top of our earlier variables, the initial share of government consumption (*CGAVG6064*) and additional dummies for Latin American (*LAAM*) and East Asian (*ASIAE*) countries. The presence of *CGAVG6064* on the right-hand side of the equation allows for a

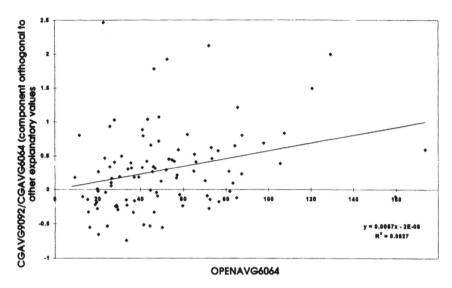

Figure 4.4. Partial relation between openness and increase in government consumption, 1960–1992.

"convergence" effect in government consumption, and indeed the coefficient on this variable is negative and highly significant (with a t-statistic exceeding 8). The fit of the regression equation is rather good, with an adjusted R^2 of 0.53 in both cases.

The initial level of openness in the early 1960s ($OPENAVG6064$) has a positive coefficient and is also statistically significant at the 1 percent level in both regressions. The quantitative significance of the association is not overwhelming, as can also be seen from Figure 4.4. But it is still remarkable that average openness during 1960–4 has such a tight relationship to the growth in government consumption over the subsequent three decades, especially in view of the diversity of the 100-plus countries in our sample.

We next check the robustness of the benchmark specification displayed in Table 4.1. Table 4.3 reports the results for the 1985–9 period. We focus on 1985–9 because we have the largest number of observations (125) for this period; the 1990–2 and 1980–4 regressions yield the same conclusions. Since we are interested in the coefficients for only $OPENAVG7584$ and newly added variables, the table suppresses information on the coefficients for other variables included in the benchmark regression. Column 1 of the table reproduces the benchmark result from Table 4.1.

Table 4.3. *Robustness*

Independent variables		(1)	(2)	(3)	(4)	(5)	(6)	(7)	(8)	(9)	(10)	(11)	(12)
		Dependent variable: Real government consumption as % of GDP (CGAVG8589)											
OPENAVG7584		0.053*	0.065**	0.063*	0.059*	0.057*	0.049**	0.048**	0.065*	0.055*	0.064*	0.059*	0.059*
		(0.019)	(0.031)	(0.022)	(0.019)	(0.020)	(0.022)	(0.021)	(0.022)	(0.019)	(0.024)	(0.019)	(0.019)
LAAM					-4.087***								
					(2.106)								
ASIAE					-6.514**								
					(2.860)								
SAFRICA					-3.848***								
					(2.069)								
POP90						3.87E–09							
						(5.68E–09)							
AREA							8.40E–05						
							(0.000)						
GDPTOT85								-6.54E–11					
								(1.76E–09)					
MANEXP85									-1.653				
									(3.320)				
POPGR90										0.990			
										(0.927)			
DETGNP85											0.021***		
											(0.014)		
GRAVG7085												-41.207	
												(33.237)	
DEMOC6													-3.207
													(3.305)
n		125	64	61	125	123	115	120	107	124	89	120	124
Adjusted R^2		0.339	0.160	0.384	0.363	0.323	0.347	0.337	0.294	0.341	0.337	0.344	0.335

Notes: See appendix for variable definitions. Standard errors are reported in parentheses: * significant at 1% level; ** significant at 5% level; *** significant at 10% level.

Other regressors not shown in this table: *GDPSH585, DEPEND90, URBAN90, SOC,* and *OECD.*

Column (2): GDP Per Capita < $2,500.

Column (3): GDP Per Capita > $2,500.

The next two columns of the table show the results of splitting the sample into two subsamples according to level of income, using $2,500 in 1985 dollars as the cutoff. The coefficient on *OPENAVG7584* is virtually identical for the two income groups, with the only change being that the estimate for the lower-income group is statistically significant at the 5 percent (rather than 1 percent) level. The basic strategy in the remaining columns is to check whether the coefficient on openness is stable and remains statistically significant when additional candidate explanatory variables are included in the regression. Column 4 includes in the regression regional dummies for Latin America (*LAAM*), East Asia (*ASIAE*), and sub-Saharan Africa (*SAFRICA*). With these dummies added, the estimated coefficient on openness increases and its *t*-statistic also rises. Columns 5, 6, and 7 experiment with three different measures of country size: population, land area, and GDP. The idea behind including these variables is to test whether the observed correlation between openness and government size is due to the following possibility: Assume that the provision of public services is subject to significant indivisibilities – e.g., every country, regardless of size, needs one parliament. Then government size as a share of GDP will be negatively correlated, ceteris paribus, with country size. Since openness is negatively correlated with country size as well, the observed association between openness and government spending could be spurious and due to the omission of a size variable.[5] However, there is no evidence that something like this is at work here. None of our size variables enters with a coefficient close to statistical significance, while openness remains statistically significant in each case.

The rest of the columns report the results when the following variables are included individually: the manufactures share in total exports (*MANEXP85*); population growth rate (*POPGR90*); the debt-to-GNP ratio (*DETGNP85*); output growth rate per capita, 1970–85 (*GRAVG7085*); democracy (*DEMOC6*). The use of each of these variables was suggested by a specific story as to why the association between openness and government spending may have been spurious. But none of them turns out to be statistically significant, and the coefficient on *OPENAVG7584* is robust to their inclusion.

To sum up, I have shown in this section that there is a robust empirical association between openness to trade and the Heston–Summers measure of government consumption (as a share of GDP) in a large cross-section of countries. In the sample on which we have focused here, the correlation exists starting from the early 1980s (and not in the 1970s). Openness in the early 1960s is positively correlated with subsequent increase in government consumption (as a share of GDP) during the following three decades.

IV Disaggregating government spending

The Heston–Summers measure of government consumption used in the previous section is a narrow indicator of government activity as it excludes transfers (e.g., social security) and government investment. We return in this section to the World Bank data on total government expenditures (used in Section II) to undertake an analysis of *disaggregated* government expenditures, which these data allow. The main purpose of the exercise is to see which categories of expenditure are the driving force behind the result. Such information may also provide clues as to the reason(s) behind the association.

Table 4.4 displays the results for government spending (1990–2), both in aggregate and disaggregated by economic category. The first column is the regression for aggregate government spending (excluding interest payments, *GEXP9NOINT*). The coefficient on openness is about three times as large as that obtained with government consumption (indicating that the impact of openness goes beyond current spending on goods and services), with a *t*-statistic exceeding 6! The dependent variables in the other columns are as follows; current expenditure on goods and services (Column 2); current expenditure on interest payments (Column 3); current expenditure on subsidies (Column 4); current expenditure on transfers to other levels of government (Column 5); and capital expenditures (Column 6). The only regressions in which openness is not statistically significant are those for interest payments (Column 3) and for transfers to other levels of government (Column 5). Government investment and government subsidies both increase with exposure to trade. Note also that the coefficient in the regression for current expenditure on goods and services (Column 2) is of the same order of magnitude as that we previously obtained with the Heston–Summers measure of government consumption, which is reassuring.

Table 4.5 repeats the exercise with *functional* categories of government expenditure: general public services; defense; education; health; social security and welfare; housing and community amenities; recreation, culture, and religion; economic affairs and services; and other purposes. We find that openness exhibits a positive and statistically significant relationship with all of these categories of public spending, except for defense spending and "other" expenditures.

Finally, we take advantage of the presence of data for a larger group of countries on two specific items of public spending in the Barro and Lee (1994) data set, education and public investment, albeit for the earlier 1980–4 period. The original sources for these data are UNESCO (for education) and the World Bank (for public investment). Table 4.6

Table 4.4. *Government expenditures by economic category, 1990–1992 (World Bank Data)*

Independent variables	Dependent variable					
	GEXP9NOINT (1)	GURGDSER9 (2)	CURINT9 (3)	CURSUB9 (4)	CURTRFOTH9 (5)	CAPEXP9 (6)
Constant	10.374	−1.746	6.048***	8.044	6.798	3.901
	(8.872)	(5.184)	(3.622)	(7.022)	(4.301)	(3.224)
GDPSH589	−3.11E−04	7.76E−05	−3.13E−04**	−7.66E−05	−4.39E−04***	−3.2E−0.4**
	(3.61E−04)	(2.11E−04)	(1.47E−04)	(2.85E−04)	(2.57E−04)	(1.36E−04)
DEPEND90	7.600	16.439*	−2.043	−9.434	−6.318	1.020
	(8.705)	(5.086)	(3.554)	(6.890)	(4.702)	(3.250)
URBAN90	0.014	−0.045	0.016	0.07	0.034	−7.40E−03
	(0.061)	(0.036)	(0.025)	(0.048)	(0.031)	(0.023)
SOC	16.062*	5.858***	0.756	13.546*	2.293	−3.465***
	(5.235)	(3.059)	(2.137)	(4.143)	(3.099)	(1.983)
OECD	10.792*	0.195	2.413***	10.551*	6.184**	0.133
	(3.442)	(2.011)	(1.405)	(2.724)	(2.329)	(1.300)
LAAM	−7.773**	−3.361***	−0.847	−1.774	−0.868	−2.349**
	(3.040)	(1.776)	(1.241)	(2.406)	(1.679)	(1.134)
ASIAE	−7.550**	−1.681	−1.028	−4.272	0.017	−1.469
	(3.499)	(2.045)	(1.429)	(2.770)	(1.677)	(1.299)
SAFRICA	−5.469***	−3.952**	−1.295	−2.379	0.852	1.186
	(2.836)	(1.657)	(1.158)	(2.244)	(1.773)	(1.058)
OPENAVG8089	0.161*	0.072*	−1.35E−03	0.047**	−8.89E−03	0.038*
	(0.026)	(0.015)	(0.010)	(0.020)	(0.012)	(9.54E−03)
n	73	73	73	73	44	74
Adjusted R^2	0.584	0.429	−0.004	0.680	0.309	0.446

Notes: See appendix for variable definitions. Standard errors are reported in parentheses:
* significant at 1% level; ** significant at 5% level; *** significant at 10% level.

Table 4.5. *Government expenditure by functional category, 1990–1992*

Independent variables	Dependent variable								
	PUBSERV9 (1)	DEF9 (2)	EDUC9 (3)	HEALTH9 (4)	SOCSEC9 (5)	HOUSE9 (6)	CULTURE9 (7)	ECON9 (8)	EXPOTH9 (9)
OPENAVG8089	0.019* (5.55E–03)	5.08E–03 (7.87E–03)	0.034* (5.62E–03)	0.018** (7.10E–03)	0.042** (0.016)	0.014* (3.59E–03)	2.79E–03*** (1.59E–03)	0.044* (7.76E–03)	–5.59E–03 (0.014)
n	61	59	61	61	58	60	56	61	61
Adjusted R^2	0.169	0.428	0.476	0.193	0.642	0.277	0.181	0.452	–0.003

Notes: See appendix for variable definitions. Standard errors are reported in parentheses:
* significant at 1% level; ** significant at 5% level; *** significant at 10% level.
Other regressors not shown in the table: *GDPSH589, DEPEND90, URBAN90, SOC, OECD, LAAM, ASIAE,* and *SAFRICA*.

Table 4.6. *Public spending on education and public investment, 1980–1984*

Independent variables	Dependent variable	
	GEETOT5 (1)	INVPUB5 (2)
Constant	−0.875	5.265
	(1.360)	(3.792)
GDPSH580	2.6E–04*	−3.95E–04***
	(7.51E–05)	(2.10E–04)
DEPEND70	3.922*	6.484***
	(1.320)	(3.791)
URBAN70	−2.61E–03	−0.024
	(0.012)	(0.033)
SOC	0.174	2.414
	(0.638)	(1.558)
LAAM	−0.858***	−2.926**
	(0.452)	(1.338)
ASIAE	−1.270**	−2.440
	(0.639)	(1.769)
SAFRICA	−0.173	−3.379**
	(0.488)	(1.291)
OPENAVG7079	0.023*	0.040*
	(4.53E–03)	(0.013)
n	102	108
Adjusted R^2	0.360	0.232

Notes: See appendix for variable definitions. Standard errors are reported in parentheses:
* significant at 1% level; ** significant at 5% level; *** significant at 10% level.

reruns regressions of the previous kind using these indicators as the dependent variable, and the earlier results are spectacularly confirmed for this larger sample. The *t*-statistic on the openness coefficient is 5 in the regression on education spending, and 3 in the regression on public investment.

V Openness and government revenue

The fact that openness and government spending are highly correlated suggests that a similar correlation should exist between openness and

Table 4.7. *Tax revenue and openness*

Independent variables	Dependent variable					
	TOTAL8688 (1)	INCOME8688 (2)	INDIV8688 (3)	CORP8688 (4)	DOMGS8688 (5)	GSVAT8688 (6)
Constant	21.579* (4.604)	3.801 (3.295)	3.824** (1.540)	−1.187 (2.883)	11.267* (2.552)	6.605* (2.078)
GDPSH585	0 (0.000)	0 (0.000)	0 (0.000)	4.24E−04 (2.89E−04)	9.46E−05 (0.000)	−3.05E−05 (0.000)
DEPEND90	−15.885* (4.362)	−1.979 (3.122)	−3.773** (1.457)	2.754 (2.741)	−8.820* (2.418)	−5.712* (1.959)
URBAN90	−0.026 (0.036)	−0.026 (0.025)	−0.008 (0.012)	−0.014 (0.022)	−0.016 (0.020)	−0.021 (0.016)
DETGNP85	0.033* (0.011)	0.005 (0.008)	0.003 (0.004)	0.002 (0.007)	0.029* (0.006)	0.017* (0.005)
SOC	7.197* (2.552)	4.060** (1.826)	3.015* (0.917)	2.152 (1.741)	3.641** (1.415)	0.959 (1.157)
OPENAVG7584	0.102* (0.018)	0.044* (0.013)	0.021* (0.006)	0.022** (0.011)	−0.016 (0.010)	0.000 (0.008)
n	69	69	64	65	69	70
Adjusted R^2	0.551	0.224	0.317	0.076	0.384	0.219

Notes: See appendix for variable definitions. Standard errors are reported in parentheses:
* significant at 1% level; ** significant at 5% level; *** significant at 10% level.

government *revenues* as well. That is indeed what we find. In this section I make use of a data set put together at the Fiscal Affairs Division of the IMF (and kindly made available by Vito Tanzi) to ask what type of revenue is most sensitive to openness. This data set includes developing countries only, so the following regressions (unlike the previous ones) exclude high-income countries.

The benchmark specification used to explain cross-country variation in tax–GDP ratios includes the same variables used before (per-capita GDP, dependency ratio, urbanization, socialist dummy, and openness) as well as the debt–GNP ratio, which was found to be significant in previous work by Tanzi (1992). The OECD dummy is now excluded from the benchmark specification since the sample includes developing countries only. The first column of Table 4.7 displays the results for total tax revenue during 1986–8 (the latest three years available to me) for the 69 countries for which data were available. The explanatory power of the regression is decent, with an adjusted R^2 of 0.55. The dependency ratio, debt–GNP ratio, and socialist dummy enter significantly. Openness itself is highly significant, with a coefficient of 0.10 and a *t*-statistic of 5.6.

Table 4.7. *(cont.)*

	Dependent variable					
EXCISE8688 (7)	INTL8688 (8)	IMPORT8688 (9)	EXPORT8688 (10)	SS8688 (11)	WEALTH8688 (12)	OTHER8688 (13)
4.673*	3.233	2.769	0.618	2.753	0.542	−0.131
(1.468)	(2.343)	(2.201)	(0.767)	(1.665)	(0.377)	(0.886)
−2.96E−05	−9.99E−04*	−9.76E−04*	−2.21E−05	3.08E−04***	1.81E−05	1.27E−04
(0.000)	(2.40E−04)	(2.26E−04)	(7.90E−05)	(1.71E−04)	(3.87E−05)	(9.09E−05)
−3.109**	−0.339	−0.823	0.483	−4.108**	−0.418	−0.061
(1.391)	(2.220)	(2.085)	(0.724)	(1.570)	(0.357)	(0.840)
0.003	0.009	0.015	−0.008	0.011	0.001	−0.004
(0.011)	(0.018)	(0.017)	(0.006)	(0.013)	(0.003)	(0.007)
0.009*	−0.015*	−0.018*	0.001	0.008**	8.25E−05	0.007*
(0.003)	(0.005)	(0.005)	(0.002)	(0.004)	(0.001)	(0.002)
2.888*	−0.476	−0.097	−0.199	−0.133	0.030	0.026
(0.814)	(1.300)	(1.220)	(0.427)	(0.928)	(0.209)	(0.491)
−0.17*	0.075*	0.077*	−0.003	−0.001	0.000	0.000
(0.006)	(0.009)	(0.009)	(0.003)	(0.007)	(0.001)	(0.004)
69	69	69	70	70	69	68
0.299	0.506	0.537	0.018	0.298	−0.024	0.118

The other columns of Table 4.7 display the relationship between openness and disaggregated categories of tax revenue. We find a strong positive association between openness and import tax revenues, which is at first sight counterintuitive. Why should governments in countries that are more open, and by implication have fewer trade restrictions, earn more revenue from import taxes? The apparent paradox can be resolved by considering a combination of two possibilities: (a) more open economies tend to rely more on import taxes and less on quantitative restrictions (such as import quotas which do not raise revenue); and (b) import demand elasticities tend to exceed unity, so that tariff reductions generally generate a sufficiently large increase in import volumes to enhance revenues from (lower) tariffs (a Laffer curve for import tariff revenues). From our current perspective, what is particularly important, however, is that there is also a strong positive association between openness and the intake from *income* taxes as well. The latter appears to come about on account of both individual income taxes and (less significantly) corporate income taxes. It is harder to explain why there should be a positive correlation between income taxes and openness, except of course for the idea that governments resort to income taxes to finance the additional expenditures required – for one reason or another – by increased openness.

As regards other sources of tax revenue, there is either no relationship with openness, or the relationship is actually negative. Revenue from VAT, export taxes, social security contributions, wealth taxes, and other taxes have coefficients that are not statistically significant, whereas the coefficient on excise taxes is, somewhat puzzlingly, negative and statistically significant at the 1 percent level. This exception notwithstanding, the overall correlation between openness and tax revenue is strongly positive, as indicated above.

VI Joint dependence between openness and government spending?

The maintained hypothesis so far has been that the direction of causality goes from openness to government expenditures, and not vice versa. This is reflected in my use in the regressions of an openness measure averaged over the decade predating the spending variable. A strong hint regarding the direction of causality is also provided by the results in Table 4.2, which show that openness in 1960–4 predicts *subsequent* expansion of government spending. Another strong hint is the evidence previously shown in Figure 4.3, namely that government spending is negatively related to geographic distance from trade partners – the latter variable being as exogenous as one can get. Nonetheless, openness itself is certainly an endogenous variable and it is entirely possible that taking proper account of that could alter the results.

An adequate systems estimation that treats both openness and government spending as endogenous is hampered by a number of factors. In particular, since we do not have a good theory of government spending, nor of why openness should matter to it, a certain amount of ad-hoc-ery is inevitable. Therefore, the following should be treated as no more than preliminary.

The structural specification we use is the following:

$$GEXP9NOINT = \alpha + \beta DEPEND90 + \gamma URBAN90 + \delta SOC$$
$$+ \zeta OPENAVG9092 + \varepsilon_1$$

$$OPENAVG9092 = \eta + \theta GDPSH589 + \kappa DIST + \lambda AREA$$
$$+ \mu GDPTOT85 + \xi BMB6L$$
$$+ \rho GEXP9NOINT + \varepsilon_2$$

Openness is taken to be a function of per-capita income ($GDPSH589$), distance from trade partners ($DIST$), size (as measured by land area,

Table 4.8. *System estimation: Openness and government spending*

	OLS Dependent variable		2SLS Dependent variable		3SLS Dependent variable	
Independent variables	GEXP9NOINT (1)	OPENAVG9092 (2)	GEXP9NOINT (3)	OPENAVG9092 (4)	GEXP9NOINT (5)	OPENAVG9092 (6)
Constant	12.052 (8.571)	0.493** (0.237)	1.237 (11.472)	0.406 (0.551)	2.745 (6.857)	0.402 (0.490)
DEPEND90	2.036 (8.785)		5.807 (10.952)		2.396 (5.307)	
URBAN90	0.034 (0.061)		-0.010 (0.078)		0.027 (0.044)	
SOC	10.870 (6.895)		9.327 (8.533)		7.901 (7.394)	
OPENAVG9092	0.111* (0.030)		0.256* (0.070)		0.249* (0.063)	
GDPSH589		2.45E-05 (1.706E-05)		2.23E-05 (2.12E-05)		1.57E-05 (1.36E-05)
GEXP9NOINT		1.202*** (0.655)		1.529 (1.986)		1.673 (1.742)
DIST		-0.016 (0.021)		-0.013 (0.025)		-0.018 (0.017)
AREA		-1.99E-05 (2.40E-05)		-1.67E-05 (3.01E-05)		-2.04E-05 (1.98E-05)
GDPTOT85		-1.25E-10 (9.54E-11)		-1.13E-10 (1.18E-10)		-8.79E-11 (7.68E-11)
BMP6L		-0.108 (0.092)		-0.101 (0.100)		-0.069 (0.062)
n	53	53	53	53	53	53
Adjusted R^2	0.601	0.271	0.393	0.267	0.408	0.255

Notes: See appendix for variable definitions. Standard errors are reported in parentheses:
* significant at 1% level; ** significant at 5% level; *** significant at 10% level.
Other regressors not shown in the table: OECD, LAAM, ASIAE, and SAFRICA.

AREA, and *GDP*, *GDPTOT85*), policy distortions (proxied by the black-market premium for foreign currency, *BMP6L*), and government expenditure.[6] Note that government spending and openness are contemporaneous in this specification, both being averages for 1990–2. A set of regional and OECD dummies is also included in each equation, but not shown above. We have the required data for only 53 countries, which is another unsatisfactory aspect of the exercise. The results in OLS, 2SLS, and 3SLS are shown in Table 4.8.

The first two columns of the table report the OLS estimates of the two equations above (for the 53-country sample with the requisite data for systems estimation). The OLS estimates of ζ and ρ are both positive and statistically significant, albeit the latter only at the 10 percent level. The next two columns display the 2SLS results. We note that the 2SLS estimate of ζ remains significant (at the 1 percent level) and is now more than twice as large as the OLS estimate. The 2SLS estimate of ρ meanwhile is no longer statistically significant. The same pattern is repeated in the 3SLS estimation. Hence the systems estimation gives us little reason to believe that our basic approach so far has been mis-specified. Causality is apparently unidirectional, from openness to scope of government.

VII But why?

I hope to have convinced the reader by this point that the statistical association between openness and government spending is a genuine one. It is not a spurious relationship generated by omitted variables. Nor is it an artifact of the sample of countries selected or of a specific data source. The question is why this relationship exists.

We have eliminated some potential explanations along the way: one possibility is that small country size is responsible for both openness and large government spending (relative to GDP). This is ruled out because controlling for country size (population, land area, or GDP) does not alter the result. Another possibility is that open economies have higher prices for nontradables (and hence government services) relative to tradables and, therefore, for unchanged levels of real government consumption, a higher share of government spending in GDP. This is ruled out because the Heston–Summers data on government consumption are in real terms (i.e., adjusted for purchasing-power differences across countries). A third possibility is that larger spending is enabled by higher import tax revenues in open economies, assuming that the price elasticities of import demand are generally larger than unity (in absolute value). There is support for this hypothesis in our findings (cf. Table 4.7), but it is clearly not the whole story, since income tax revenues increase with openness as well. Fourth, perhaps a larger tradable sector (in open economies) enlarges the effectively taxable share of the economy, allowing the government to spend more. But if so, why is it that indirect taxes (excise and VAT) either bear no relationship to openness or are actually negatively correlated with it? A final possibility is that governments in more open economies can borrow larger amounts from international capital markets – since the credit ceiling is higher for countries with larger export-GDP ratios. But controlling for the debt–GNP ratio does not affect the correlation between openness and government spending (cf. Table 4.3).

The explanation for which some evidence does exist is the one offered in the introduction. More open economies have greater exposure to the risks emanating from turbulence in world markets. We can view larger government spending in such economies as performing an insulation function, insofar as the government sector is the "safe" sector (in terms of employment and purchases from the rest of the economy) relative to other activities and especially compared to tradables. Hence, in countries significantly affected by external shocks, the government can mitigate risk by taking command of a larger share of the economy's resources. More precisely, a larger government sector can reduce instability in economies that would otherwise experience higher levels of aggregate volatility due to exposure to external risk. Whether government consumption can play such a role or not is, of course, an empirical matter. Elsewhere, I have provided some direct evidence (Rodrik 1996) that suggests the answer is positive for the vast majority of countries.

In principle, external risk should be diversifiable for small countries through participation in international capital markets. In practice, this does not prove possible, either because full capital market openness conflicts with other objectives of government policy or because incentive and sovereign-risk problems restrict the range and extent of financial instruments available to countries. One might also object that the government's risk-reducing role could be best played through the establishment of a safety net, in which case it would show up only in government spending on social security and welfare, and not at all in government *consumption*. However, social security systems are difficult to set up even in the most advanced countries, and it stands to reason that the developing countries that predominate in our cross-section would rely on a broader set of instrumentalities to achieve risk reduction.

The idea that greater openness to foreign trade increases the risk to which residents are exposed also deserves comment. It is generally not the case that the world economy as a whole is more volatile than the economy of any single country. In fact, we would expect the world market to be less risky than any of its constituent parts. But note that openness to trade generally implies *specialization* in production through the forces of comparative advantage. Hence, all else being equal, we would expect the production structure to be less diversified in more open economies. And in an economy that cannot purchase insurance from the rest of the world, what matters is not the stability of the world economy as a whole, but the stability of the stream of earnings from *domestic* production. Consequently, it is not implausible that greater openness translates into greater risk for domestic residents. For evidence that greater exposure to external risk results in increases in aggregate income and consumption risk see Rodrik (1996).

A test of these ideas is to check whether the relationship between openness and government spending is stronger in economies that are likely to be exposed to greater external risk, holding the ratio of trade to GDP itself constant. A reasonable hypothesis is that among countries that are equally open, the ones that are subject to the greatest amounts of external risk would be those that: (a) have a low share of manufactured products in total exports; and (b) have greater variability in their external terms of trade. The reason why the manufactures share of exports should matter is that the markets for manufactures tend to be more stable than those for primary commodities. The reason why terms-of-trade variability should matter is obvious. Note that if all markets were to clear through price adjustments and there were no domestic unemployment, a measure of risk based on the forecast errors of the stream of income gains/losses generated by the path of the terms of trade would be the appropriate summary statistic for external risk. That indeed will be a measure I will use below. But when some markets clear through quantity adjustments, the variability in the terms of trade will give at best a partial picture. For example, a reduction in foreign demand can generate domestic unemployment without necessarily reducing the price of exports. For this reason, I use the manufactures share of exports as an additional indicator of exposure to external risk.

The basic strategy in the next set of regressions, then, is to interact (a) the manufactured share of exports and (b) terms-of-trade variability with openness to see whether the inclusion of these additional variables results in statistically significant coefficients and improves the fit of the regressions. The first column of Table 4.9 shows the benchmark regression for government consumption, with the sample now restricted to the 97 countries for which data on manufactured share of exports and terms of trade are available. The purpose of this first column is to facilitate comparison with the new regressions in the rest of the table.

Table 4.9. *The importance of manufactured exports and terms-of-trade variability*

Independent variables	Dependent variable: Real government consumption as % of GDP (*CGAVG9092*)						
	(1)	(2)	(3)	(4)	(5)	(6)	(7)
OPENAVG8089	0.072*	0.148*	0.136*	−0.100***	−0.125***	−0.010	
	(0.024)	(0.035)	(0.035)	(0.056)	(0.071)	(0.101)	
MANEXP90		14.033**	20.644*			6.297	6.842
		(5.850)	(7.002)			(7.237)	(4.964)
OPENMAN9		−0.240*	−0.351*			−0.117	−0.126**
		(0.080)	(0.103)			(0.109)	(0.061)
OPENINC9			1.22E−05***		3.39E−06		
			(7.28E−06)		(6.01E−06)		
TOTDLOGSTD				−69.141*	−73.181*	−50.891***	−48.342*
				(22.062)	(23.273)	(28.388)	(14.245)
OPENTOTDLOGSTD				1.143*	1.219*	0.785	0.739*
				(0.340)	(0.367)	(0.474)	(0.162)
n	97	97	97	97	97	97	97
Adjusted R^2	0.326	0.376	0.388	0.390	0.385	0.384	0.391

Notes: See appendix for variable definitions. Standard errors are reported in parentheses:
* significant at 1% level; ** significant at 5% level; *** significant at 10% level.
Other regressors not shown in the table: *GDPSH589, DEPEND90, URBAN90, SOC*, and *OECD*.

Column 2 of the table displays the results when the manufactured share of exports is added to regression, both individually (*MANEXP90*) and interacted with openness (*OPENMAN9*). As predicted by the risk-mitigating hypothesis discussed above, the coefficient on *OPENMAN9* is negative and statistically significant (at the 1 percent level). Hence, the effect of openness on government consumption is strongest in countries with low manufactures shares in total exports. Note also that the coefficient on openness (*OPENAVG8089*) doubles and remains significant at the 1 percent level. The coefficient on *MANEXP90* is also positive and statistically significant. The fit of the regression is improved, with the adjusted R^2 rising from 0.33 to 0.38.

Since *MANEXP90* is highly correlated with per-capita income (richer countries have higher shares of manufactured exports), could it be that the results in Column 2 are reflecting the fact that openness exerts a stronger influence on government consumption in *poorer* countries? Column 3 of Table 4.9 allows for this possibility by adding to the regression in Column 2 the interaction of openness with per-capita GDP (*OPENINC9*). The coefficient on *OPENINC9* is statistically significant only at the 10 percent level, whereas *MANEXP90* and *OPENMAN9* remain significant at the 1 percent level (and now have higher estimated coefficients). This strongly suggests that it is not the income level per se, but the composition of exports that is the intermediary variable between openness and government consumption.

Column 4 is analogous to Column 2, but now the additional two variables included in the regression relate to uncertainty vis-à-vis the terms of trade. The first of these is the standard deviation of the log-differences in the annual terms of trade over the period 1971–90 (*TOTDLOGSTD*). This is an appropriate measure of uncertainty, since the log-differences in the terms of trade tend to be stationary for most countries. The second variable is *TOTDLOGSTD* multiplied by *OPENAVG8089* (*OPENTOTDLOGSTD*), and constitutes the appropriate measure of risk referred to above, namely the standard deviation of the forecast errors of the stream of income gains/losses (as a share of GDP) generated by the path of the terms of trade.[7] We indeed find that the coefficient on this measure of risk is positive and statistically significant at the 1 percent level. *Openness matters to government consumption most in countries with the greatest variability in their terms of trade.* The measure of terms-of-trade uncertainty alone (*TOTDLOGSTD*) also enters significantly, but with a negative sign. And the coefficient on openness also turns *negative*, and is statistically significant at the 10 percent level. The adjusted R^2 has jumped to 0.39.

Column 5 checks and confirms, as before, that these results reflect the contribution of the terms of trade proper and not of the income level, with which terms-of-trade instability is strongly correlated. The coefficient on *OPENINC9* in Column 5 is not significant even at the 10 percent level.

The remaining two columns in Table 4.9 add the variables relating to manufactured exports and terms-of-trade instability jointly. Both sets of variables appear to have separate explanatory power, and it is not possible to say much about which performs better.

One way to summarize what we have learned from Table 4.9 is to use the estimated coefficients to ask how much openness matters to government consumption in countries at different points along the distribution of terms-of-trade instability. Estimates in Column 4 suggest that an increase in the share of total trade (exports plus imports) in GDP of 10 percentage points would increase government consumption by 0.7 percentage points of GDP in a country located at the mean of the cross-country distribution of terms of trade instability (*TOTDLOGSTD*). The same increase in openness would lead to an increase in government consumption of 1.6 percentage points of GDP in a country that experiences terms-of-trade instability one standard deviation above the mean. For a country with terms-of-trade instability one standard deviation *below* the mean, the impact on government consumption would be virtually nil.

I have shown elsewhere that the same kind of results are obtained with a measure of external risk based on the product concentration of a country's exports (Rodrik 1996). This is further confirmation of the central hypothesis in this paper.

VIII Concluding comments

That international trade is a friend of big government is one of those delicious ironies that the real world occasionally turns up for the unsuspecting economists. It is one that perhaps will not surprise Peter Kenen, a scholar whose research has never strayed too far from the real world. Indeed, upon some reflection, the idea that societies develop defense mechanisms to cope with the insecurities generated by participation in the world market, and that the scope of the public sector is one such mechanism, should not sound outlandish.

This is a conclusion reminiscent of one of the major themes in Karl Polanyi's well known book *The Great Transformation* (1944). What is perhaps most distinctive about the world market, as compared to national markets, is that there exists no central political authority to regulate it. As Polanyi pointed out long ago in connection with the expansion of the global economy in the nineteenth century, this is an anomaly in the context of human history:

> A self-regulating market demands nothing less than the institutional separation of society into an economic and political sphere. . . . It might be argued that the separateness of the two spheres obtains in every type of society at all times. Such an inference, however, would be based on a fallacy. True, no society can exist without a system of some kind which ensures order in the production and distribution of goods. But that does not imply the existence of separate economic institutions; *normally, the economic order is merely a function of the social, in which it is contained.* Neither under tribal, nor feudal, nor mercantile conditions was there, as we have shown, a separate economic system in society. Nineteenth century society, in which economic activity was isolated and imputed to a distinctive economic motive, was, indeed a singular departure. (1944: 71, emphasis added)

Writing during the Second World War, Polanyi interpreted the social history of his age – the emergence of mass social movements, the rise of Fascism and Nazism, the revolutions in central and eastern Europe, the collapse of the gold standard, the rise of central planning in Soviet Russia – as a process of market expansion accompanied by efforts to mitigate its social consequences:

> While on the one hand markets spread all over the face of the globe and the amounts of goods involved grew to unbelievable proportions, on the other hand a network of measures and policies was integrated into powerful institutions designed to check the action of the market relative to labor, land, and money. While the organization of world commodity markets, world capital markets, and world currency markets under the aegis of the gold standard gave an unparalleled momentum to the mechanism of markets, a deep-seated movement sprang into being to resist the pernicious effects of a market-controlled economy. Society protected itself against the perils inherent in a self-regulating market system – this was the one comprehensive feature in the history of the age. (76)

Hence Polanyi traced the reasons behind the collapse of the major nineteenth-century institutions – the balance-of-power system, the international gold standard, the liberal state, and free trade – ultimately to the contradictions between the demands of a "self-regulating market" and those of societal stability.

The postwar period, with more than five decades of continued economic growth based on (more or less) open markets and accompanied by social stability in at least the major capitalist societies, would appear to have proved Polanyi wrong. However, as convincingly argued by John Ruggie (1982), the international economic liberalism of this period, far from shunting aside the role of government policy, gave it a central role. Ruggie has called this "the compromise of embedded liberalism":

> The task of postwar institutional reconstruction . . . was to . . . devise a framework which would safeguard and even aid the quest for domestic stability without, at the same time, triggering the mutually destructive external consequences that had plagued the interwar period. This was the essence of the embedded liberalism compromise: unlike the economic nationalism of the thirties, it would be multilateral in character; unlike the liberalism of the gold standard and free trade, *its multilateralism would be predicated upon domestic interventionism.* (1982: 393, emphasis added)

According to Ruggie, the objective of stabilizing domestic employment and output was never meant to be sacrificed at the altar of free trade. Consequently, the apparent derogations vis-à-vis the liberal norm that we have since witnessed – for example, the exclusion of agriculture from the multilateral free trade regime, the spread of voluntary export restraints, or the rise of regionalism – are to be viewed less as deviations from the original conception and more as diverse manifestations of a liberalism embedded within social order.

The results of this essay provide concrete, and perhaps unexpected, support for the arguments of Polanyi and Ruggie. Societies have demanded and received a larger government role when faced with greater exposure to external market risk. In practice, government and the market have been complements, and not substitutes, for each other.

This last conclusion opens interesting new avenues for research. First, to the extent that the hypothesis advanced in this essay (and in Rodrik 1996 in greater detail) is correct, we need to understand better the channels – political economy or otherwise – through which governments have been forced to respond to increased openness. Second, and far more importantly, we need to do some forward thinking about the role of government in today's global economy: if the conclusions of this essay are correct and governments have traditionally been the handmaiden of international economic integration, there will exist serious difficulties in sustaining globalization in an era where governments and the welfare state have gone out of fashion.

APPENDIX

List of Variables and Sources

Variable	Definition	Source
AREA	Land area	Barro & Lee 1994
ASIAE	Dummy for East Asian countries	Barro & Lee 1994
BMP6L	Log of black-market premium, 1985–9	WD
CAPEXP9	Government capital expenditures	PWT 5.6
CGAVGXXYY	Real government consumption as a percent of GDP	FAD
CORP8688	Corporate income tax revenue	WD
CULTURE9	Government expenditure on culture & recreation	WD
CURINT9	Government expenditure on interest	WD
CURSUB9	Government expenditure on subsidies	WD
CURTRFOTH9	Government expenditure on transfers to other levels of government	WD
DEF9	Government defense expenditures	WD
DEMOC6	Index of democracy	Barro & Lee 1994
DEPENDXX	Dependency ratio	WD
DETGNP85	Debt–GNP ratio, 1985	WD
DGOVXXYY	*CGAVGXX* divided by *CGAVGYY*	PWT 5.6
DIST	Geographic distance from 20 major world exporters	Barro & Lee 1994
DOMGS8688	Tax revenue on domestic goods and services	FAD
ECON9	Government expenditure on economic affairs & services	WD
EDUC9	Government education expenditures	WD
EXCISE8688	Tax revenue from excise taxes	FAD
EXPORT8688	Export tax revenue	FAD
EXPOTH9	Other government expenditures	WD
GDPSH5XX	Per-capita GDP	Barro & Lee 1994
GDPTOT85	GDP, 1985	PWT 5.6
GEETOT5	Government expenditure on education, 1980–4	Barro & Lee 1994
GEXP9NOINT	Government expenditure net of interest payments	WD

Variable	Description	Source
GRAVG7085	Average per-capita GDP growth, 1970–85	Barro & Lee 1994
GSVAT8688	Tax revenue from sales taxes and VAT	FAD
GURGDSER9	Government current expenditure on goods & services	WD
HEALTH9	Government education on health	WD
HOUSE9	Government expenditure on housing and community affairs	WD
IMPORT8688	Import tax revenue	FAD
INCOME8688	Income tax revenue	FAD
INDIV8688	Individual income tax revenue	FAD
INTL8688	Taxes on international trade	FAD
INVPUB5	Public investment, 1980–4	Barro & Lee 1994
LAAM	Dummy for Latin American countries	
MANEXPXX	Share of manufactures in total exports	WD
OECD	Dummy for OECD countries	
OPENAVGXXYY	Exports plus imports divided by GDP	PWT5.6
OPENINC9	*OPENAVG8089* times *GDPSH589*	
OPENMAN9	*OPENAVG8089* times *MANEXP90*	
OPENTOTDLOGSTD	*OPENAVG8089* times *TOTDLOGSTD*	
OTHER8688	Other tax revenue	FAD
POP90	Population in 1990	WD
POPGR90	Population growth rate, 1990	WD
PUBSERV9	Government expenditure on public services	WD
SAFRICA	Dummy for sub-Saharan African countries	
SOC	Dummy for socialist countries	Sachs & Warner 1995
SOCSEC9	Government expenditure on social security and welfare	WD
SS8688	Social security contributions	FAD
TOTAL8688	Total tax revenue	FAD
TOTDLOGSTD	Standard deviation of log-differences in terms of trade, 71–90	WD
URBANXX	Urbanization rate	WD
WEALTH8688	Wealth tax revenue	FAD

Notes: "XX" refers to year 19XX, whereas "XXYY" refers to an average during 19XX–19YY (unless specified otherwise). All government expenditure and revenue data are expressed as a percent of GDP or GNP. "PWT 5.6" stands for *Penn World Tables 5.6*; "WD" for World Data 1995 (World Bank), "FAD" for Fiscal Affairs Department of IMF.

NOTES

I thank Jerry Cohen, Patrick Conway, and Arvind Panagariya for helpful comments, and Chi Yin for excellent research assistance.

1. Kenen discusses these issues in his textbook (Kenen 1994: 5–11).
2. A related idea has been developed by Bates, Brock, and Tiefenthaler (1991). These authors argue that greater terms-of-trade risk increases the likelihood that a country will raise trade barriers. In addition, they suggest that the availability of social insurance programs reduces this likelihood.
3. It turns out that including the Summers–Heston relative price index for government consumption in the regressions using nominal World Bank data on government spending does not affect the results.
4. The share of foreign trade in GDP was one of the variables included in the Heller and Diamond (1990) study, but the authors do not report their results because they apparently found the coefficient on this variable to be statistically insignificant.
5. This was the most frequently advanced hypothesis when I asked fellow economists to come up with reasons why openness may be correlated with the size of government.
6. Instrumenting for openness in this fashion should also take care of possible biases arising from the presence of a Keynesian correlation between increased government spending and increased imports and hence openness (assuming trade imbalances persist for long time periods). I thank Patrick Conway for bringing this possibility to my attention.
7. More formally, let x, m, and y stand for volumes of exports, imports, and GDP, respectively. Let p be the price of exports relative to imports (the terms of trade). Let the (log) of the terms of trade follow a random walk, possibly with drift (a hypothesis that cannot be rejected for most countries). The unanticipated component of the income effects of the terms-of-trade shock can then be expressed as a percentage of GDP as $\frac{1}{2}[(x + m)/y][dlogp - \alpha]$, where α is the trend growth rate of the terms of trade. The standard deviation of this is $\frac{1}{2}[(x + m)/y]$st.dev. ($dlogp$), which is $\frac{1}{2}$ times $OPENTOTDLOGSTD$.

REFERENCES

Barro, Robert J., and Jong-Wha Lee (1994). "Data Set for a Panel of 138 Countries," unpublished manuscript, Harvard University, January.

Bates, Robert H., Philip Brock, and Jill Tiefenthaler (1991). "Risk and Trade Regimes: Another Exploration," *International Organization* 45(1) (Winter), 1–18.

Cameron, David R. (1978). "The Expansion of the Public Economy," *American Political Science Review* 72, 1243–61.

Heller, Peter S., and Jack Diamond (1990). *International Comparisons of Government Expenditure Revisited: The Developing Countries, 1975–86*, IMF Occasional Paper 69. Washington, DC: International Monetary Fund.

Kenen, Peter B. (1994). *The International Economy*, 3rd ed. Cambridge University Press.

OECD (1985). "The Role of the Public Sector: Causes and Consequences of the Growth of Government," *OECD Economic Studies* 4 (Spring).

Polanyi, Karl (1944). *The Great Transformation: The Political and Economic Origins of Our Time.* Boston: Beacon Press.

Ram, Rati (1987). "Wagner's Hypothesis in Time-Series and Cross-Section Perspectives: Evidence from 'Real' Data for 115 Countries," *Review of Economics and Statistics*, 194–204.

Rodrik, Dani (1996). "Why Do More Open Economies Have Bigger Governments?" NBER Working Paper 5537 April.

Ruggie, John Gerard (1982). "International Regimes, Transactions, and Change: Embedded Liberalism in the Postwar Economic Order," *International Organization* 36(2) (Spring), 379–415.

Sachs, Jeffrey, and Andrew Warner (1995). "Economic Reform and the Process of Global Integration," *Brookings Papers on Economic Activity* 1, 1–95.

Schmidt, Manfred G. (1983). "The Growth of the Tax State: The Industrial Democracies, 1950–1978." In Charles Lewis Taylor, ed., *Why Governments Grow: Measuring Public Sector Size*, pp. 261–85. Beverly Hills and London: Sage.

Tait, Alan A., and Peter S. Heller (1982). *International Comparisons of Government Spending*, IMF Occasional Paper 10. Washington, DC: International Monetary Fund, April.

Tanzi, Vito (1992). "Structural Factors and Tax Revenue in Developing Countries: A Decade of Evidence." In Ian Goldin and L. Alan Winters, eds., *Open Economies: Structural Adjustment and Agriculture*, pp. 267–85. Cambridge University Press.

PART II
INTERNATIONAL MONETARY THEORY

CHAPTER 5

Exchange rate regimes and international trade

Reuven Glick and Clas G. Wihlborg

5.1 Introduction

Empirical applications of the theory of exchange rate regime choice and optimal currency areas typically have involved estimating the effects of exchange rate risk on international trade flows. A finding that a measure of greater exchange rate risk or variability dampens the volume of international trade is interpreted as evidence against the desirability of adopting a floating rate regime (Cushman 1983, 1986; Akhtar and Hilton 1984; Kenen and Rodrik 1986). In actuality, it has proven difficult to establish empirically an unambiguous relation between exchange rate risk measures and trade flows, or a clear correspondence between a country's exchange rate regime and the level of risk.

There are several reasons why research has failed to establish clear relations among risk, exchange rate regimes, and trade flows. First, the relation between exchange rate variability and risk exposure under different exchange rate regimes is tenuous. If, for example, exchange rate fluctuations work to stabilize output in a country subject to aggregate demand shocks, a firm's overall uncertainty about macroeconomic shocks may decrease rather than increase with increased exchange rate variability. Thus, greater exchange rate variability does not necessarily imply greater exposure to risk. Second, the time variation in the subjective evaluation of risk is hard to capture with empirical proxies. This difficulty is particularly acute under pegged exchange rates when exchange rates change infrequently, but uncertainty exists about continued maintenance of the peg.

To overcome these difficulties, in this essay we analyze the empirical relation across countries between exchange rate risk, exchange rate regimes, and international trade, using a measure we call "exchange rate flexibility" to characterize each country's exchange rate regime. Rather

125

than reflect only exchange rate volatility per se, this exchange rate flexibility-measure scales actual exchange rate variability by the total pressure put by macroeconomic shocks on the exchange rate. Thus, it reflects the share of exchange market pressure that is not offset by (unsterilized) intervention, but is allowed to be transmitted into actual exchange rate changes. This measure better captures the risk characteristics associated with a country's exchange rate regime.[1]

We utilize this measure in estimates of price and income elasticities of export and import volumes *across* countries and exchange rate regimes. We argue that there is less ambiguity about the relation between exchange rate risk and trade *elasticities* than about the relation between exchange rate risk and trade volume *levels*. The cross-country approach obviates the need to construct time-dependent country-specific measures of risk and regime that have been shown as difficult to capture by empirical proxies. Moreover, since we expect more variation in both risk and regime across countries than across time for any individual country, the cross-country approach potentially provides greater power in empirical tests.

The plan of the essay is as follows. Section 5.2 discusses the relation between exchange rate risk, exchange rate regimes, and trade volume elasticities. It also motivates the specification of our empirical tests. Section 5.3 describes our data and our estimation procedure involving pooled cross-section times-series equations for U.S. bilateral export and import volumes vis-à-vis its thirty largest trading partners over the period 1980 to 1993. In these pooled regressions we utilize a measure of bilateral exchange rate flexibility for each country relative to the United States over the period. Section 5.4 presents the results, including tests of whether cross-country variations in income and price elasticities depend on cross-country differences in the degree of exchange rate flexibility. In Section 5.5 we discuss how factors other than exchange rate regime-related risk may influence the relation between exchange rate regimes and trade volume elasticities. Conclusions follow in Section 5.6.

5.2 Exchange rate regime, risk, and trade flows

5.2.1 *Empirical literature*

The literature on the relation between exchange rate volatility and international trade typically argues that exchange rate volatility imposes costs on risk-averse firms who generally respond by favoring domestic over foreign trade at the margin. Hooper and Kohlhagen (1978), for example, formulate a model of exporting and importing firms who are risk-averse to variations in nominal profits, and find it costly to fully hedge exposure to exchange rate risk. In this model, an increase in exchange rate volatility increases the risk facing traders and shifts both export supply and import demand curves back, resulting in a decrease in the equilibrium quantity of traded goods.

The hypothesis that exchange rate volatility has a negative influence on international trade flows has been subject to empirical testing in numerous studies.[2] However, these empirical analyses have in general been unable to establish a significantly negative relationship between measured exchange rate volatility and the volume of international trade in time-series regressions. Hooper and Kohlhagen (1978), estimating effects on bilateral U.S. trade flows, rejected the hypothesis that exchange risk discourages the volume of trade. This was supported by an International Monetary Fund survey (1984) of work in the early 1980s. Cushman (1983) estimated 16 bilateral trade equations and found evidence that exchange risk had a significantly negative effect on trade in six cases and a significantly positive effect in two cases. In a later study (1986), he analyzed the effect of exchange rate risk for U.S. bilateral exports to its six major trading partners, while controlling for risk associated with third-country currencies. Across various specifications and sample periods, less than half of the coefficients on exchange rate risk were ever significantly negative. The evidence from gravity models of bilateral trade flows is more mixed. Thursby and Thursby (1987) find some support for the hypothesis that exchange rate flexibility discourages the volume of trade; however, Brada and Mendez (1988) reject the hypothesis.

Some have argued that by focusing on multilateral rather than bilateral trade flows, misspecification problems arising from not including relative prices involving third country importers and exporters can be avoided. However, studies using multilateral trade flows have provided no more conclusive evidence. Ahktar and Hilton (1984) reported significantly negative effects of exchange rate risk on U.S. and German multilateral exports and German multilateral imports, while Gotur (1985), after updating their work, found a significant negative effect for German imports only, and significantly positive effects on multilateral U.S. exports and Japanese imports. Kenen and Rodrik (1986) analyzed multilateral manufacturing imports for eleven industrial countries and found a significantly negative effect in only four cases.[3] Bailey, Tavlas, and Ulan (1986, 1987) found no significant effect of exchange rate volatility on multilateral exports of industrial countries.

Some have suggested the need to disaggregate trade by goods sectors in order to avoid the aggregation problems that arise when sectors are exposed to exchange risk to different degrees. Maskus (1986), for example, examined real exchange risk effects on U.S. bilateral trade with four countries, disaggregated into nine industry sectors. Of his 64 estimated equations, only 26 had significantly (at a 10 percent level) negative coefficients on exchange rate risk. Klein (1990) analyzed the effects of real exchange rate variability on the proportions of U.S. bilateral exports to seven major trading partners, disaggregated into nine goods categories. In contrast to the results of Maskus, he found that in five of nine categories the volatility of the real exchange rate significantly and positively affected the value of exports; this effect was significantly negative only in one category.

Others have argued that the empirical trade effects of exchange rate risk are sensitive to the statistical techniques employed and have suggested alternative methodologies. However, these results are nonrobust as well. For example, Koray and Lastrapes (1989) and Lastrapes and Koray (1990) estimate vector autoregressions of trade levels and their determinants; they find little or no effect of exchange rate volatility on trade. Utilization of time series techniques that take into account that international trade and its determinants may be nonstationary integrated variables has not provided unambiguous results either. For example, Asseery and Peel (1991) and Arize (1995) estimate error correction models with co-integrating long-run relationships between trade, output, and relative prices. In the former paper, exchange rate risk was found to have a positive effect on exports, whereas in the latter the effect was found to be negative. Gagnon (1993) parameterizes a theoretical model of trade under uncertainty and demonstrates that exchange rate variability of the magnitude typical among industrial countries during the floating rate period has an insignificant effect on the level of international trade.

Our brief review of the empirical literature indicates that time-series analyses have not been successful in establishing a robust relation between exchange rate risk and international trade. As noted in Section 5.1, there are several reasons for the lack of an unambiguous relationship between the exchange rate regime, exchange rate risk, and trade. First, an increase in (nominal or real) exchange rate risk need not be associated necessarily with an increase in uncertainty about macroeconomic conditions. For example, an increase in exchange rate variability associated with the shift to a more flexible exchange rate regime may be accompanied by a reduction in other kinds of risk in the form of lower inflation, interest rate, or output variability. Conversely, although exchange rate variability may be low under a fixed exchange rate regime, uncertainty about inflation, interest rates, or aggregate demand may be relatively higher instead. Thus, overall uncertainty about macroeconomic conditions is reflected in different variables under different regimes, and is not necessarily correlated with (unconditional or conditional) exchange rate variability.[4] The problem of properly measuring exchange rate regime-related risk is compounded by difficulties in constructing a time-series measure of exchange rate risk, since expectations are inherently difficult to measure.

We seek to overcome these difficulties by analyzing cross-country variations in trade flow responsiveness under different exchange rate regimes, and by utilizing a continuous measure of the degree of bilateral exchange rate "flexibility" over long time periods for individual countries, rather than focusing on exchange rate variability alone. With this flexibility measure, we hope to obtain an improved proxy for the exchange rate regime-related risk faced by firms in international trade. Another difference between our approach and the surveyed literature is that we investigate how trade flow elasticities, rather than trade flow levels, are affected by the exchange rate regime.

5.2.2 Empirical specification and hypotheses

To motivate our empirical specification and hypotheses tests, consider the following basic equations from a partial equilibrium model for real U.S. exports (X) to, and U.S. imports (M) from, country j in period t (lagged variables are omitted for simplicity):

$$X_{jt} = x_{cj} + x_{pj}P_{jt} + x_{yj}Y_{jt} + \varepsilon_{xjt} \tag{5.1a}$$

$$M_{jt} = m_{cj} + m_{pj}P_{jt} + m_{yj}Y_{USt} + \varepsilon_{mjt} \tag{5.1b}$$

where P_j denotes the relative price of traded goods between the United States and country j, and is synonymously referred to as the real exchange rate (with a rise in P corresponding to real appreciation of currency j against the dollar); Y denotes real GDP in the importing country; $\varepsilon_{xjt}, \varepsilon_{mjt}$ are error terms; and x_{ij} and $m_{ij}, i = c, y, p$, are coefficients. All variables are in log form, implying that the coefficients can be interpreted as elasticities. The coefficients are subscripted by country j as well as by time t because exchange risk and other regime characteristics are assumed to vary across countries.[5] In order to focus on the determinants of elasticities, we abstract here from third-country relative prices and nonprice factors, which may also affect trade flow volumes.[6] We focus on the cross-country determinants of the x_{ij} and m_{ij} coefficients, and do not include a time-varying measure of exchange risk, for reasons discussed above. It is assumed that each of these coefficients can be decomposed into a component that is common across countries and a country-specific component that depends on the risk regime and other characteristics of country j, captured by a vector Z_j:[7]

$$x_{ij} = x_{io} + x_{izj}Z_j, \quad i = c, p, y \tag{5.2a}$$

$$m_{ij} = m_{io} + m_{izj}Z_j, \quad i = c, p, y \tag{5.2b}$$

The x_{io}, m_{io}-coefficients, for $i = p, y$, reflect the "usual" trade elasticities for relative price and income changes. For each country j, it is hypothesized that an increase in the real price of the country's currency increases U.S. bilateral exports to the country ($x_{po} > 0$) and decreases U.S. bilateral imports from the country ($m_{po} < 0$), while an increase in the importing country's income increases its bilateral imports (x_{yo}, $m_{yo} > 0$).

The coefficients x_{iz}, m_{iz}, $i = c, p, y$, reflect the effects of country-specific risk and other exchange rate regime-related characteristics. (Where possible, we suppress reference to the "j" subscript from now on.) The typical presumption that the *level* of trade flows decreases with the degree of exchange rate risk because of, for example, greater transaction or other costs, implies that the intercept terms depend negatively on Z, that is, x_{cz}, $m_{cz} < 0$.[8] However, as is well-known, uncertainty about influences on product demand and supply may have a positive impact on a firm's desired capital stock and, therefore, on supply: Because profits tend to be multiplicative in factors shifting demand and supply functions, the expected value of future profits can depend positively on the variance of these factors.[9] For this reason the effect of uncertainty about exchange rates and other factors influencing export supply and import demand is ambiguous on theoretical grounds.

In our analysis, we emphasize the cross-country effects of exchange rate regime-related risk on price and income elasticities as well: that is, x_{pz}, m_{pz}, x_{yz}, $m_{yz} \neq 0$. Supply elasticities with respect to price, P, and income, Y, should be relatively sensitive to country characteristics associated with risk and exchange rate regimes because supply decisions generally require investments in capital and other resources necessary for expanding capacity, adapting products to foreign markets, and developing marketing and distribution networks, particularly for manufactures. Because these investment costs are usually irreversible, risk considerations about future prices are particularly important in supply decisions. Since demand decisions occur without any significant commitment of resources over time, risk considerations are of lesser importance for demand responses.

This discussion implies that the variation in the x_{iz}, m_{iz}, $i = p, y$, elasticities across countries is attributable primarily to variations in exporters' supply elasticities. In other words, in the U.S. export equation (5.2a) the cross-country variation in the Z_j-dependent part of the x_p, x_y-coefficients can be associated primarily with the variation in U.S. exporters' supply responses to changes in P_j and Y_j across destination countries with different exchange rate regimes. In the U.S. import equation (5.2b), the variation in the m_{pz}, m_{yz}-coefficients can be associated largely with the variation across countries in foreign exporters' supply responses to changes in P_j and Y_{US}.

Specific hypotheses about the signs of the x_{iz}, m_{iz}, $i = p, y$, coefficients in (5.2a) and (5.2b) require further discussion of the relation between export supply elasticities with respect to P and Y and risk under different exchange rate regimes. Because product supply decisions generally require capital investments, this relation can be better understood by considering how risk affects the elasticity of the desired export-geared capital stock with respect to changes in expected return. Assume, for example, that changes in P_j and Y_j affect the expected relative return (R_j) on the capital stock K_j held by U.S. firms that is geared to exports to country j, and that the riskiness of this return can be attributed to country-specific factors Z_j.

The irreversibility of investment provides one argument why the return elasticity of investment $(dK_j/dR_j)(R_j/K_j)$ and hence the price elasticity of export supply declines with greater uncertainty about the returns to exporting. If investment is irreversible, there is an "option" value of waiting that renders firms cautious about exiting and giving up on investments in foreign markets or investing in entering new markets. With greater uncertainty about the exchange rate and other determinants of investment and supply, the option value of not acting increases. The increased reluctance of firms to deviate from the status quo implies in the aggregate a decline in the elasticity of the capital stock and export supply with respect to the real exchange rate (P_j) and the importing country's GDP (Y_j).[10]

A second argument for reduced elasticities is obtained if one interprets the determination of the capital stock K_j as a portfolio decision. The determination of the desired level of K_j and hence exports to country j then can be interpreted as similar to a portfolio decision by U.S. investors about how many shares of capital, K_j, to hold.[11] Clearly, if risk related to exchange rate regimes were irrelevant for U.S. investors, then the capital associated with exporting to different markets would be perfect substitutes and the desired K_j would be infinitely elastic with respect to R_j; that is, $(dK_j/dR_j)(R_j/K_j)$ would tend toward infinity. If the capital stocks associated with exporting to different markets are not perfect substitutes, then the higher the country-specific risk associated with country j, the less substitutable is K_j for capital geared to exports to other countries, and $(dK_j/dR_j)(R_j/K_j)$ declines.

These arguments imply that, across U.S. exports to countries with different risk and exchange rate regimes, the export elasticity coefficients in (5.2a) will *decrease* as country-related risk, Z_j, increases; that is, $x_{iz} < 0$, $i = p, y$. Analogous arguments can be made for U.S. imports. Therefore, we expect the export supply response to *decrease* (in absolute value) as country-related risk, Z_j, rises; that is, $|m_{pz}| < 0$ and $m_{yz} < 0$.

Beyond risk considerations, other differences across countries, such as in wage–price rigidities, market structure, and so forth, might also affect foreign exporters' supply responses. Only with the assumption that these factors are independent of exchange rate regime and risk can we unambiguously hypothesize that the elasticities m_{pz}, m_{yz} are decreasing in exchange rate regime-related risk. This is our working hypothesis, but, to the extent that price and wage rigidities vary across countries, U.S. bilateral imports provide a less clear test of the relation between elasticities and exchange rate regime-related risk. For this reason, U.S. bilateral exports rather than imports are more likely to reflect variations in elasticities associated with regime-related risk. We return to this issue in Section 5.5.

The relation between risk and exchange rate regimes remains to be discussed. In the empirical analysis we employ two measures of cross-country risk: a traditional measure of exchange rate variability calculated from the variance of exchange rate changes, and an alternative, exchange rate "flexibility" measure. The option value of waiting and portfolio substitutability arguments suggest that a ceteris paribus increase in exchange rate variability that raises risk should decrease the sensitivity of international trade flows to changes in relative prices and income. However, as suggested in Section 5.2.1, from an overall macroeconomic perspective, greater exchange rate variability may imply less, rather than more, risk for firms in international trade. If, for example, exchange rate fluctuations work as an automatic stabilizer of aggregate real demand shocks, overall uncertainty about macroeconomic shocks may decline. Conversely, with lower exchange rate variability the overall risk facing firms in international trade may rise as it shows up more in fluctuations in variables other than the exchange rate. Consequently, overall risk could decline with our exchange rate flexibility measure.

We conclude this section with the specification of our estimating equations and statement of hypotheses based on the discussion above. Substituting (5.2a) and (5.2b) into (5.1a) and (5.1b), respectively, gives the following U.S. bilateral export and import equations:

$$X_{jt} = x_{co} + x_{czj}Z_j + x_{po}P_{jt} + x_{pzj}P_{jt}Z_j + x_{yo}Y_{jt} + x_{yzj}Y_{jt}Z_j + \varepsilon_{xjt} \quad (5.3a)$$

$$M_{jt} = m_{co} + m_{czj}Z_j + m_{po}P_{jt} + m_{pzj}P_{jt}Z_j + m_{yo}Y_{USt} + m_{yzj}Y_{USt}Z_j + \varepsilon_{mjt}$$
$$(5.3b)$$

In our empirical analysis we also consider other variables, but our interest is focused on the coefficients in (5.3a) and (5.3b). Recalling that P_j denotes the real dollar price of currency j, Y_j denotes income, and Z_j refers to country j's exchange rate risk, exchange rate regime, and other country characteristics, the hypotheses are:

Hypothesis 1. $x_{po} > 0$ and $m_{po} < 0$; i.e., U.S. exports to (imports from) country j increase (decrease) when the currency j appreciates in real terms, relative to the dollar.

Hypothesis 2. $x_{yo} > 0$ and $m_{yo} > 0$; i.e., U.S. exports (imports) increase with an increase in income in country j (United States).

If exchange rate variability is positively associated with risk facing exporters, for Z denoting exchange rate variability, we test the following hypotheses:

Hypothesis 3a. $x_{pz} < 0$ and $x_{yz} < 0$; i.e., the higher the exchange rate variability facing U.S. exporters, the *lower* is the U.S. export elasticity with respect to both the real exchange rate and foreign income.

Hypothesis 4a. $|m_{pz}| < 0$ and $m_{yz} < 0$; i.e., the higher the exchange rate variability facing foreign exporters, the *lower* is the U.S. import elasticity (in absolute value) with respect to both the real exchange rate and U.S. income.

Because of the suggested inverse relation between exchange rate flexibility and the overall risk facing exporters, for Z representing the degree of exchange rate flexibility, we test the following hypotheses:

Hypothesis 3b. $x_{pz} > 0$ and $x_{yz} > 0$; i.e., the greater the degree of exchange rate flexibility facing U.S. exporters, the *higher* is the U.S. export elasticity with respect to the real exchange rate and foreign income.

Hypothesis 4b. $|m_{pz}| > 0$ and $m_{yz} > 0$; i.e., the greater the degree of exchange rate flexibility facing foreign exporters, the *higher* is the U.S. import elasticity (in absolute value) with respect to the real exchange rate and U.S. income.

We do not specify a hypothesis with respect to the effects of risk and regime on the trade volume levels (x_{cz} and m_{cz}). In our empirical analysis, by defining each variable X_j, M_j, P_j, and Y_j for country j as deviations from its mean for that country, we remove country-specific influences, including the effects of risk, on the average level of trade during the estimation period. (This is equivalent to including country-specific intercept dummies.) Because our measures of exchange rate risk vary only across countries and not across time, this precludes testing hypotheses about x_{cz} and m_{cz}. As noted above, however, we do not have unambiguous hypotheses for these coefficients.

5.3 Data and estimation procedure

Our empirical work focuses on quarterly U.S. bilateral trade flows from 1980 through 1993. We restrict our analysis to manufactures trade flows to strip away the effects of trade in agricultural goods and raw materials. Trade in agricultural goods, for example, has typically been more subject to restrictive import quotas or government procurement arrangements than other commodities.

Table 5.1 lists the 30 largest trading partners of the United States that constitute our sample. They are reported in descending order by their share of the summed dollar value of U.S. manufacturing exports, averaged over the period 1990–2. The table also reports their shares of U.S. manufacturing imports. These countries constitute roughly 83 percent of total U.S. manufacturing exports and 80 percent of U.S. manufacturing imports.[12]

The dependent variables of our analysis are the real volumes of manufacturing exports and imports. The real volume of U.S. bilateral exports (X) is defined as the dollar value of bilateral exports deflated by a bilateral export deflator constructed as the weighted dollar price of U.S. exports of capital goods, airplanes, and other durable manufactures, with time-varying quarterly weights given by the foreign country's share of each category in its total manufacturing imports from the United States. The real volume of U.S. bilateral imports (M) is defined as the dollar value of bilateral imports deflated by the product of the foreign wholesale price and the dollar price of foreign exchange. A detailed description of the sources and construction of data is contained in the Appendix.

Among our explanatory variables, the relative price variable P (i.e., the real exchange rate) used in both the export and import bilateral trade equations is defined as the nominal spot rate (quoted as dollars per foreign currency of country j) times the ratio of country j's wholesale price index to the U.S. wholesale price index. Y is the real income in the importing country, defined as nominal GDP deflated by the implicit GDP deflator; Y_{US} is U.S. real GDP. Limitations on the

Table 5.1. *U.S. bilateral manufactured trade, share of total manufacturing trade (percent)*

	Country	Exports	Imports
1	Canada	27.36	18.40
2	Japan	10.74	31.64
3	Mexico	9.73	7.70
4	United Kingdom	7.40	4.58
5	Germany	6.84	7.91
6	France	4.87	3.45
7	Netherlands	3.26	0.84
8	Korea	3.23	5.68
9	Singapore	2.93	3.55
10	Australia	2.73	0.29
11	Belgium	2.53	0.60
12	Italy	2.32	3.19
13	Brazil	1.69	1.26
14	Switzerland	1.57	1.38
15	Malaysia	1.52	2.17
16	Spain	1.39	0.57
17	Venezuela	1.31	0.06
18	Sweden	1.15	1.38
19	Thailand	1.08	1.67
20	Ireland	0.95	0.48
21	Israel	0.82	0.62
22	Philippines	0.69	1.15
23	Argentina	0.66	0.09
24	Colombia	0.66	0.14
25	Chile	0.62	0.04
26	Indonesia	0.52	0.63
27	Norway	0.47	0.11
28	Denmark	0.45	0.32
29	New Zealand	0.32	0.04
30	Greece	0.22	0.05

Note: Calculations are averages for 1990–2.

availability of some variables restricted the data range for some countries.[13]

We have also constructed measures of cross-country characteristics (represented by the variable Z in our notation above) that may potentially influence the volume and elasticities of trade. These included two exchange rate risk measures – the variance of bilateral exchange rate changes (*XRVAR*) and the degree of bilateral exchange rate "flexibility" (*XRFLEX*) – and a measure of each country's openness (*OPEN*). The definition and construction of these variables is defined below. Table 5.2 presents the values of these variables as constructed for the sample period indicated for each country.[14]

The variance of the exchange rate (*XRVAR*) is measured conditionally from the residuals of a regression of percent monthly (log) changes in the nominal exchange rate (expressed as domestic currency per U.S. dollar) on 12 months of lagged changes, together with 11 seasonal dummies. As is usually the case, it makes little quantitative difference whether anticipated or unanticipated, or nominal or real, exchange rates are used instead.[15]

Our measure of exchange rate flexibility, *XRFLEX*, is intended to capture the variance of the actual exchange rate change relative to the variance of the change that would have occurred in the absence of foreign exchange market intervention. *XRFLEX* is defined as

$$XRFLEX_j = \frac{XRVAR_j}{XRVAR_j + RESVAR_j} \tag{5.4}$$

where $RESVAR_j$ denotes the variance of changes of foreign exchange reserves in domestic currency terms, measured as a fraction of the lagged monetary base in country j. Analogously to *XRVAR*, *RESVAR* is constructed from the residuals of the actual monthly change (divided by the lagged base) regressed on 12 lags of the dependent variable, together with seasonals. The denominator in (5.4) can be interpreted as a measure of the variance of the "total" pressure put by macroeconomic shocks on the exchange rate, given by the sum of actual as well as "incipient" exchange rate variability. $RESVAR_j$ captures the "incipient" change in the exchange rate that is prevented from occurring as a result of foreign exchange market intervention by country j. The change in foreign exchange reserves (in domestic currency terms) is scaled by the monetary base because of the assumption that (unsterilized) foreign exchange market intervention amounting to a 1-percent rise (fall) in the monetary base prevents a 1-percent domestic currency appreciation (depreciation).[16] *XRFLEX* thus measures the proportion of the pressure on the exchange rate caused by macroeconomic shocks that is allowed on average over the period to translate into actual exchange rate changes. The exchange rate is perfectly flexible, that is, *XRFLEX* = 1, if there are no unanticipated reserve changes (*RESVAR* = 0). The exchange rate is perfectly fixed, that is, *XRFLEX* = 0, if there are no unanticipated changes in the exchange rate (*XRVAR* = 0) or if the variance of reserve changes is very large (*RESVAR* = ∞).

Table 5.2. *Cross-country regime characteristics*

Country	Abbreviation	Sample	Range	XRVAR	XRFLEX	OPEN
Canada	can	80:1	93:12	0.15	0.08	0.46
Japan	jap	80:1	93:12	1.00	0.94	0.19
Mexico	mex	80:1	93:12	3.69	0.28	0.21
United Kingdom	gbr	80:1	93:12	1.23	0.53	0.40
Germany	deu	80:9	93:12	1.11	0.51	0.48
France	fra	80:1	93:12	1.12	0.48	0.36
Netherlands	nld	80:1	93:12	1.14	0.37	0.95
Korea	kor	80:1	93:12	0.21	0.08	0.58
Singapore	sin	80:1	93:12	0.16	0.04	2.97
Australia	aus	80:1	93:12	0.84	0.27	0.27
Belgium	blx	80:1	92:12	1.17	0.33	1.23
Italy	ita	80:1	93:9	1.01	0.78	0.34
Brazil	bra	80:1	92:12	3.31	0.30	0.16
Switzerland	che	80:1	93:3	1.32	0.60	0.57
Malaysia	mal	80:1	93:12	0.15	0.02	1.05
Spain	esp	80:1	93:12	1.10	0.68	0.28
Venezuela	ven	80:1	93:12	9.13	0.46	0.42
Sweden	swe	80:1	93:12	1.02	0.12	0.29
Thailand	tha	80:1	92:12	0.24	0.10	0.49
Ireland	irl	80:1	93:12	1.08	0.10	0.98
Israel	isr	80:1	93:9	1.10	0.47	0.56
Philippines	phi	80:1	93:12	0.98	0.17	0.40
Argentina	arg	80:1	90:12	41.52	0.79	0.12
Colombia	col	80:1	93.9	0.01	0.00	0.25
Chile	chi	80:1	93:12	0.88	0.52	0.42
Indonesia	idn	80:1	93:12	1.35	0.26	0.39
Norway	nor	80:1	93:12	0.87	0.04	0.56
Denmark	dnk	80:1	93:12	1.06	0.04	0.53
New Zealand	nzl	80:1	93:12	1.12	0.01	0.43
Greece	grc	80:1	91:3	1.01	0.56	0.37

Note: *XRVAR*, *XRFLEX*, and *OPEN* denote the variance of exchange rate changes, the degree of exchange rate flexibility, and multilateral openness, respectively, calculated over the sample range indicated. See the Data Appendix for details of calculation. *XRVAR* figures are multiplied by 1,000.

Figure 5.1 shows a scatter plot of the log of the exchange rate variance against the degree of exchange rate flexibility for each country calculated over the sample period (the abbreviations used for individual countries are presented in Table 5.2). The variances are logged to reduce the extreme spread of the unlogged values. Observe that there is very little cross-country variation in the amount of exchange rate volatility against the dollar. This can be attributed largely to the fact that almost half of the countries in the sample, particularly those participating in the European

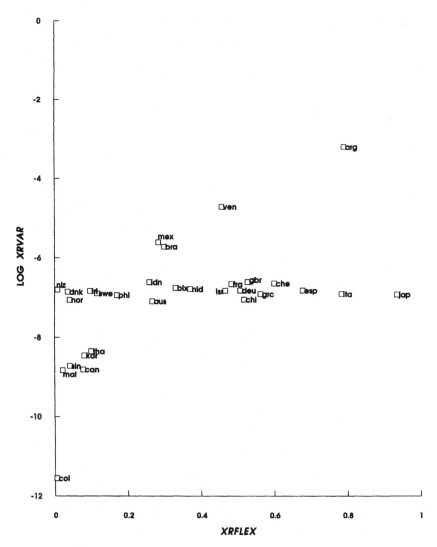

Figure 5.1. Variance of the exchange rate ($XRVAR$) and the degree of exchange rate flexibility ($XRFLEX$).

Exchange Rate Mechanism, limit exchange rate changes against each other much more than against the dollar. The lack of variation in *XRVAR* limits its usefulness in cross-country estimation because of multicollinearity problems it introduces between this variable and the magnitude of real exchange rate changes across countries. In contrast,

XRFLEX is distributed over its full range, reflecting cross-country variations in intervention policy.[17]

The lack of cross-country variation in *XRVAR* implies, from inspec-
tion of the definition of *XRFLEX* (equation (5.4)), that the cross-
country variation in *XRFLEX* is dominated by variation in *RESVAR*,
capturing differences in individual countries' average inclination to intervene against pressures on the exchange rate. In other words, because
there is little variation across countries in *XRVAR*, *XRFLEX* decreases
the more that foreign exchange market pressures are absorbed by
changes in foreign exchange reserves. Thus, to the extent that the total
risk faced by exporting firms rises with foreign exchange market pressure
from macroeconomic shocks, an increase in exchange rate flexibility,
XRFLEX, may be interpreted as a *fall* in total risk. This is in accordance
with our Hypotheses (3b) and (4b).

A measure of each country's multilateral openness to international
trade over the sample period, *OPEN*, is also reported in Table 5.2.
OPEN is defined as the sum of a country's total (nominal) exports and
imports relative to (nominal) GDP. This variable is intended to capture
factors influencing trade flows, such as the degree of foreign competition
in a country's markets, as well as to control for non-risk-related country
characteristics that might affect trade flows and trade flow elasticities.

Our specification follows equations (5.3a) and (5.3b), augmented with
seven lags of the real exchange rate *P*; income *Y* enters only contem-
poraneously. Interactive terms involving the degree of exchange rate
flexibility (*XRFLEX*) and openness (*OPEN*) are included with the same
number of lags as the associated variable. Seasonal dummies and a time
trend are included as well. The time trend is intended to capture possible
exogenous worldwide growth in trade volumes. In one set of regressions,
exporting countries' GDP is included as well in order to control for other
supply effects and check the robustness of results.

The regressions for U.S. bilateral exports and imports were estimated
using a pooled times-series cross-section analysis with fixed effects. This
procedure produces more efficient coefficient estimates than a two-stage
procedure to explain the cross-country variation in the elasticity coefficients for relative prices and income. To control for country-specific
autocorrelation and cross-country heteroscedasticity we used the following estimation procedure: (i) for each individual country, an estimate of
the first-order serial-correlation coefficient (ρ_j) was obtained from the
residuals of an OLS log-linear regression of exports (or imports) on 0 to
7 lags of *P*, contemporaneous *Y* or Y_{US}, and seasonal dummies[18]; (ii)
quasi-differencing the data for each country with ρ_j, that is, forming $X_{jt} -
\rho_j X_{jt-1}$ for the dependent and explanatory variables, in order to control

for serial correlation later in the pooled regression; (iii) repeating OLS for each country on its quasi-differenced data, obtaining the standard error equation estimate (SEE_j), and then scaling the quasi-differenced data for each country by this value, SEE_j, to control for heteroscedasticity across country equations; (iv) then taking the deviation from the mean of each transformed data series for the period, in order to control for fixed country effects; (v) for each variable, stacking all of the individual country data into pooled time-series vectors; and (vi) with these pooled vectors, obtaining OLS estimates of the regression specification described above. This procedure provides a consistent estimate of coefficients (see Kmenta 1986).[19] The sample range of observations for individual countries in the stacked dependent-variable vectors is indicated in Table 5.2; the explanatory variable vectors are augmented by the appropriate number of lags.

Note that the transformation of data into deviations from the mean is equivalent to including country intercept dummies in the pooled regressions.[20] In this way we control for differences in trade flow levels across countries due to such time-invariant factors as distance from the United States.

5.4 Empirical results

Tables 5.3 and 5.4 report the results of our pooled regressions. The coefficient estimates for the real exchange rate, the importing country's GNP, the interactive term ($P \cdot XRFLEX$), and the time trend are given in column (1). In column (2), a second interactive term ($Y \cdot XRFLEX$) is added. In column (3) the openness variable, $OPEN$, is added interactively with both of the time-varying variables. Column (4) augments this regression with the contemporaneous (transformed) level of exporting countries' GDP. The coefficient reported for the real exchange rate when entered alone and interactively is the sum of the coefficients for lags 0 through 7. We report results for all 30 countries in the sample, and for the 17 OECD countries alone in columns (5)–(8).[21] Results for OECD countries alone are included because the OECD countries can be expected to be more homogeneous with respect to various factors influencing trade flows that are not captured in the regressions. The reported standard errors are based on White's (1980) heteroscedasticity-consistent covariance matrix.[22] Plots of the residuals of the export and import regressions indicate that the residuals are of similar magnitudes across countries, with only a few outliers.[23]

Table 5.3 shows that the export volume elasticities with respect to the real exchange rate and foreign GDP have the expected positive sign and

Table 5.3. *Pooled bilateral U.S. manufactures exports*

Explanatory variables	All countries				OECD countries			
	(1)	(2)	(3)	(4)	(5)	(6)	(7)	(8)
P	0.61 (0.10)***	0.66 (0.10)***	0.70 (0.13)***	0.36 (0.12)***	0.84 (0.13)***	0.98 (0.14)***	1.18 (0.23)***	1.10 (0.21)***
Y	1.45 (0.07)***	1.38 (0.07)***	1.28 (0.09)***	1.15 (0.09)***	1.83 (0.16)***	1.56 (0.21)***	1.25 (0.27)***	0.30 (0.23)
$P \cdot XRFLEX$	0.79 (0.19)***	0.52 (0.20)**	0.44 (0.22)**	1.10 (0.21)***	0.30 (0.22)	−0.05 (0.25)	−0.18 (0.27)	−0.02 (0.25)
$Y \cdot XRFLEX$		0.69 (0.18)***	0.82 (0.20)***	0.35 (0.19)*		0.70 (0.29)**	0.91 (0.31)***	1.09 (0.25)***
$P \cdot OPEN$			0.02 (0.11)	0.14 (0.10)			−0.30 (0.27)	−0.35 (0.24)
$Y \cdot OPEN$			0.09 (0.05)*	0.09 (0.04)*			0.77 (0.41)*	0.91 (0.30)***
$TREND$	0.03 (0.00)***	0.03 (0.00)***	0.03 (0.00)***	−0.00 (0.01)	0.03 (0.01)***	0.03 (0.01)***	0.02 (0.01)***	−0.02 (0.01)**
Y_{US}				1.34 (0.17)***				2.00 (0.21)***
$\bar{R}^2$	0.71	0.71	0.72	0.75	0.74	0.74	0.74	0.79
$D.W.$	1.75	1.78	1.78	1.56	1.84	1.84	1.84	1.73
SEE	1.23	1.23	1.23	1.29	1.22	1.22	1.22	1.22

Notes: The dependent variable is (logged) real bilateral manufactured exports X. P, Y, and Y_{US} denote the (logged) real dollar price of foreign exchange, foreign GDP, and U.S. GDP, respectively. $XRFLEX$ and $OPEN$ denote the degree of exchange rate flexibility and multilateral openness, respectively. Details of the estimation procedure are described in the text. Heteroscedastic-adjusted standard errors in parentheses; * denotes significance at the 0.10 level; ** denotes significance at the 0.05 level; *** denotes significance at the 0.01 level.

Table 5.4. *Pooled bilateral U.S. manufactures imports*

Explanatory variables	All countries				OECD countries			
	(1)	(2)	(3)	(4)	(5)	(6)	(7)	(8)
P	-1.14	-1.23	-1.33	-1.82	-0.92	-1.01	-1.41	-1.48
	(0.11)***	(0.12)***	(0.17)***	(0.13)***	(0.13)***	(0.15)***	(0.26)***	(0.20)***
Y_{US}	2.53	2.92	2.69	3.80	2.77	3.05	2.60	2.13
	(0.12)***	(0.19)***	(0.24)***	(0.26)***	(0.15)***	(0.23)***	(0.33)***	(0.30)***
$P{\cdot}XRFLEX$	-0.25	0.00	0.03	0.50	-0.45	-0.26	-0.01	0.08
	(0.19)	(0.21)	(0.23)	(0.20)**	(0.21)**	(0.26)	(0.30)	(0.25)
$Y_{US}{\cdot}XRFLEX$		-0.83	-0.67	-2.23		-0.53	-0.27	-0.61
		(0.28)***	(0.31)**	(0.30)***		(0.32)*	(0.34)	(0.30)**
$P{\cdot}OPEN$			0.22	0.17			0.70	0.42
			(0.17)	(0.12)			(0.31)**	(0.19)**
$Y_{US}{\cdot}OPEN$			0.39	-0.36			1.23	1.35
			(0.18)**	(0.16)**			(0.45)***	(0.30)***
$TREND$	0.04	0.04	0.04	0.01	0.01	0.01	0.00	-0.00
	(0.00)***	(0.00)***	(0.00)***	(0.01)*	(0.01)*	(0.01)	(0.01)	(0.01)
Y				1.00				0.75
				(0.15)***				(0.13)***
$\bar{R}^2$	0.64	0.64	0.64	0.78	0.65	0.65	0.66	0.72
$D.W.$	1.76	1.77	1.77	1.30	1.84	1.84	1.88	1.60
SEE	1.36	1.36	1.36	1.75	1.32	1.32	1.31	1.35

Notes: The dependent variable is (logged) real bilateral manufactured imports M. P, Y_{US}, and Y denote the (logged) real dollar price of foreign exchange, U.S. GDP, and foreign GDP, respectively. *XRFLEX* and *OPEN* denote the degree of exchange rate flexibility and multilateral openness, respectively. Denmark is excluded from all regressions. Details of the estimation procedure are described in the text. Heteroscedastic-adjusted standard errors in parentheses; * denotes significance at the 0.10 level; ** denotes significance at the 0.05 level; *** denotes significance at the 0.01 level.

are strongly significant in all specifications, as is consistent with Hypotheses 1 and 2. For the full sample of countries, both of the interactive terms involving the degree of flexibility ($XRFLEX$) are positive and significant across specifications without and with the openness interaction terms (though including Y_{US} does lower the significance level for the interactive term with foreign GDP). Thus, both the real exchange rate elasticity of U.S. exports as well as the elasticity of U.S. exports with regard to foreign GDP *increase* (in absolute value) as the degree of exchange rate flexibility rises, as Hypotheses (3b) and (4b) imply when greater flexibility is associated with lower risk. For OECD countries alone, the interactive term with the degree of exchange rate flexibility is significant and positive only in its effect on the elasticity with regard to foreign GDP. The finding of a positive effect of exchange rate flexibility on U.S. exports and the interpretation that greater exchange rate flexibility is associated with lower risk is supported by the observation in Section 5.3 that most of the variation in our exchange rate flexibility measure is attributable to differences in incipient exchange rate changes offset by central bank intervention, rather than to differences in exchange rate variability per se.

Regressions with exchange rate variability, $XRVAR$, substituted for exchange rate flexibility, $XRFLEX$, are not presented here, but the main results are easily summarized. Both of the interactive terms, $P \cdot XRVAR$ and $Y \cdot XRVAR$, are far from significant in all specifications. As noted, this insignificance can be attributed to the small variation in exchange rate variability across countries.

To enhance our understanding of the relation between exchange rate flexibility and U.S. export elasticities, Figure 5.2 presents a scatter plot of individual country export elasticities with respect to the real exchange rate (x_{pz}) against our measure of exchange rate flexibility, $XRFLEX$. The price elasticities for each country are estimated from an OLS log-linear regression using the quasi-differenced and SEE-scaled data following the general export equation specification. The elasticity and exchange rate flexibility observations for each country are weighted by the standard deviation of its (quasi-differenced and scaled) real exchange rate. This weighting procedure is analogous to the weight given each country's observations in the pooled regressions and gives the more uncertain estimates less weight.[24] The scatter plot shows a positive relation between the export elasticities and the degree of exchange rate flexibility, consistent with the positive sign on the corresponding interaction term in the pooled regression; the positive relation is robust with respect to removal of outliers from the sample of countries.[25]

Table 5.4 reports the results for U.S. bilateral manufacturing imports

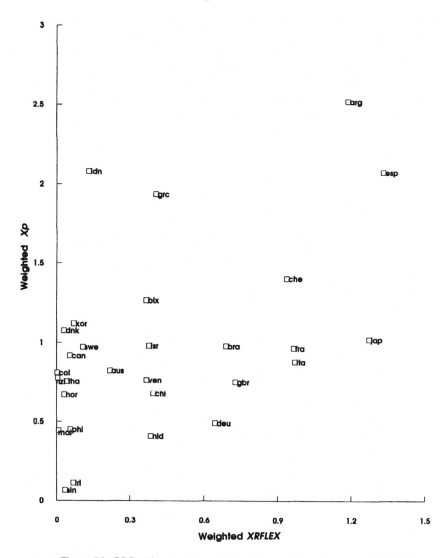

Figure 5.2. OLS estimates of export elasticity against exchange rate flexibility.

from all countries and for OECD countries.[26] Import volume elasticities with respect to the real exchange rate and U.S. GDP have the signs consistent with Hypotheses 1 and 2 (negative and positive, respectively) and are strongly significant in all specifications. In the full sample, the interactive term involving P and $XRFLEX$ is positive and significant only for the case reported in column (4), where exporters' GDPs are included. The positive sign implies that the absolute value of the real exchange rate elasticity declines, contrary to Hypothesis (4b). The interaction term with Y_{US} is negative and significant (mostly at better than 1 percent), indicating that the elasticity with respect to U.S. GDP *falls* as exchange rate flexibility increases. This is contrary to Hypothesis (4b) as well. The latter effect is robust to the inclusion of interaction terms with the openness variable, as well as exporters' GDPs. For the smaller OECD sample, the two interaction terms involving *XRFLEX* are both significantly negative when entered individually; but when both are included, only the term with Y_{US} is significant (though only at 10 percent). The negative effect is especially strong when both openness and exporters' GDP are included. Again the results are contrary to Hypothesis (4b).

The import equations were also estimated, with *XRVAR* substituted for *XRFLEX*. As with the export equations, the interactive term *P·XRVAR* was insignificant in all specifications. However, the term $Y_{US}·XRVAR$ was generally positive and significant at the 5 or 10 percent level. The positive sign suggests that the import income elasticity increases with exchange rate variability.

We noted in Section 5.2 that the import equations are less suitable for testing our hypotheses, because foreign exporters' supply responses may depend on other country characteristics not considered here. In particular, the import equation results could be influenced by the cross-country correlation between the exchange rate regime, exchange rate variability, and wage and price rigidities.[27] We return to a discussion of the import equation results in Section 5.5.

Turning finally to the interaction variables involving openness, reported in columns (3), (4), (7), and (8) of Tables 5.3 and 5.4, we find that for both U.S. exports and imports the elasticities with respect to importers' GDP generally increase with foreign country openness (the exception is when foreign GDP is added to the U.S. import equation). In other words, the more open are foreign economies, the greater the response of U.S. exporters to foreign income demand shifts, as well as the response of foreign exporters to U.S. income demand shifts.

The interaction of openness with the real exchange rate is not significant in the case of exports. In the case of U.S. imports, particularly for the OECD sample, there is some indication that the elasticity with respect to the real exchange rate falls (in absolute terms, since the algebraic coefficient for *P·OPEN* is positive) with greater openness abroad. We abstain from speculating about explanations for this result.

We conclude this section by briefly comparing the results presented

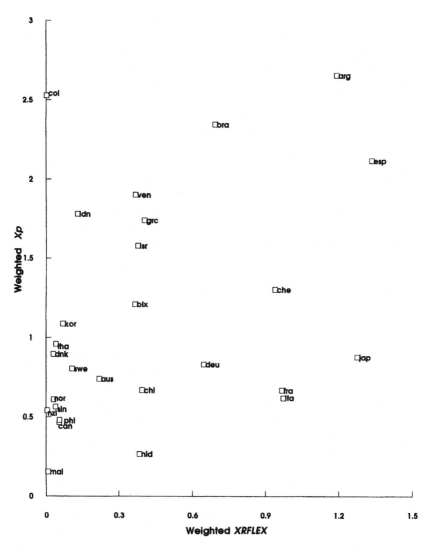

Figure 5.3. Johansen estimates of export elasticity against exchange rate flexibility.

here for pooled cross-section, time-series analysis with results using alternative procedures. In particular, the Johansen procedure for estimating long-run export elasticities in an error-correction model was implemented.[28] The scatter plot in Figure 5.3 reveals that the relation between the (weighted) real exchange rate elasticity for U.S. bilateral exports and the (weighted) degree of exchange rate elasticity using the Johansen procedure is similar to the relation between the same two variables in Figure 5.2, where individual country elasticities were OLS-estimated.[29] Thus the relation between bilateral export elasticities and our measure of exchange rate flexibility appears robust to estimation procedure.

5.5 Exchange rate regime and elasticities: Additional considerations

Although we found that U.S. bilateral export elasticities *increase* with the degree of bilateral exchange rate flexibility of the importing country, the U.S. bilateral import regression results showed that increasing exchange rate flexibility in the exporting country is associated with a *decreasing* elasticity of country j exports (in absolute terms) with respect to changes in U.S. GDP. If higher values of our exchange rate flexibility measure reflected increased risk for exporters, then this result would be in accordance with conventional hypothesis, but we have argued that increasing flexibility is associated with less risk.

In Section 5.2 we suggested that the U.S. import regressions provide a weaker test of the relation between elasticities and exchange rate regime-related risk than do the export regressions. The reason is that the variation in export supply elasticities across countries affecting U.S. import elasticities is most likely to be strongly influenced by country-specific factors abroad, such as factor market and price flexibility. It is possible that the variation in these factors and the endogenous choice of exchange rate regimes play a role in our import results.

To explore this possibility further, we refer to the optimum currency area literature concerning the criteria for exchange rate regime choice.[30] A central tenet of the OCA literature is that exchange rate adjustment may substitute for nominal wage flexibility and/or labor mobility in response to aggregate demand or supply shocks. Thus, the benefits of flexible exchange rates rise with increasing rigidity of wages and labor supply. It follows that if the responsiveness of a foreign country's export supply decreases with a country's degree of labor market rigidity, and if countries choose their exchange rate regime taking into account labor market rigidities, then lower export supply elasticities would tend to be associated with greater exchange rate flexibility. As a result, in a cross-section of U.S. import elasticities with respect to U.S. GDP, the endogeneity of exchange rate regimes with respect to foreign supply elasticities would explain the observation that elasticities decrease (in absolute value) as bilateral exchange rate flexibility increases.

In another strand of the OCA literature, openness plays a major role for the relative benefits and costs of exchange rate regimes. McKinnon (1963) argued that the inflationary (deflationary) impact of a depreciation (appreciation) is larger in an open economy than in a closed economy. The explanation is that a large share of goods in the price index is affected by an exchange rate change immediately or, at least within a short time. If so, the supply response to an exchange rate change will be relatively small, even if the exchange rate change initially is real, because of expectations that the exchange rate change is likely to be reversed in the near future. Under these circumstances, the export supply elasticity with respect to a contemporaneous exchange rate change will be low in a relatively open economy. The positive sign for openness when interacting with the (negative) real exchange rate elasticity in U.S. imports, as reported in Table 5.4, is consistent with this reasoning.

5.6 Conclusions

In this essay we have reexamined the existing evidence on the trade volume effects of exchange rate risk and exchange rate regime choice. Our analysis involved estimating the effects of cross-country differences in exchange rate regime on export and import elasticities using a continuous measure of the degree of exchange rate flexibility. We have argued that risk for firms involved in international trade tends to decrease with greater exchange rate flexibility. In formulating our hypotheses we argued that the cross-country variation in U.S. export elasticities with respect to the real exchange rate and foreign GDPs is primarily attributable to the cross-country variation in bilateral exchange rate regime-related risk. The cross-country variation in U.S. import elasticities, on the other hand, may depend on additional factors influencing supply conditions in exporting countries.

The empirical results showed that U.S. export elasticity *increases* with the degree of bilateral exchange rate flexibility of the importing country. We interpreted this result as an indication that the total macroeconomic risk exporters face decreases with the degree of exchange rate flexibility in accordance with our hypotheses. This interpretation is supported by the observation that increasing exchange rate flexibility across our sample of countries is correlated with decreasing variability in foreign exchange market pressures. Thus, our empirical evidence lends no support to the conventional presumption that firms face more risk under floating exchange rates, and that exchange rate flexibility reduces international trade.

The results for U.S. bilateral imports showed that the elasticity with respect to U.S. GDP *decreases* with higher exchange rate flexibility. The optimum currency area literature provides an explanation for this result under the presumption that countries with substantial labor market rigidities, and therefore low export elasticities, are more likely to choose a high degree of exchange rate flexibility to facilitate price adjustment.

The analysis of this paper can be extended in several directions. One possibility is to take account of industrial composition effects. To the extent that export supply elasticities vary across industries, the effects of cross-country differences in exchange rate regimes and risk on international trade flows may depend on the industrial composition of exports to destination markets. This would involve working with disaggregated manufacturing data and pooling both across countries and across industries, while also adding variables to control for industry-specific characteristics that reflect differential exposure to risk. Another avenue for future research is to take account of how the nature of underlying shocks – for example, domestic or foreign, real or nominal, permanent or temporary – influences adjustment behavior across exchange rate regimes. This would require a more formal analysis of the joint determination of international investment, production, and trade flow decisions in a general equilibrium stochastic framework. Such a framework would yield testable hypotheses about how international trade behavior depends on the underlying sources of exchange rate variability.

DATA APPENDIX

Quarterly data for the period 1978:I to 1993:IV for the dollar value of bilateral manufactured exports and imports were obtained from the Department of Commerce, Bureau of Economic Analysis Trade Database. Manufactured trade flows are defined as the sum of trade in capital goods (except automobiles), automotive vehicles, manufactured consumer nondurable goods, and manufactured consumer durable goods.

The real volume of U.S. bilateral exports (X) is defined as the dollar value of bilateral exports deflated by a bilateral export deflator constructed as the weighted dollar price of U.S. exports of capital goods (except automotive), automotive vehicles, and consumer manufactures, with time-varying quarterly weights given by the foreign country's share of each goods category in its total bilateral manufacturing imports from the U.S. The price data for U.S. manufactured export categories were obtained from the Department of Commerce, Bureau of Economic Analysis, *Survey of Current Business*. Since the price index for exports of capital goods (excluding automotive) was unavailable before 1982:I, we backfilled missing observations by assuming that they grew at the same rate as available data on "other" capital goods that excluded airplane and computer equipment.

The real volume of U.S. bilateral imports (M) is defined as the dollar value of bilateral imports deflated by the product of the foreign wholesale price and the (period average) dollar price of domestic currency. The bilateral exchange rate and wholesale price data were obtained from the International Monetary Fund *International Financial Statistics* (lines rh and 63, respectively). Due to the unavailability of quarterly wholesale price numbers for France and Malaysia, the consumer price index (line 64) was used instead for these countries.

The relative price variable (P), that is, the real exchange rate, is defined as the (period average) dollar price of the domestic currency times the domestic wholesale price index divided by the U.S. wholesale price index. (A rise in P corresponds to a real appreciation of the domestic currency against the dollar.)

Real gross domestic product (Y) data were obtained from *IFS* line 99 b.r. Where only annual real gross domestic product numbers were available (Belgium, Brazil, Chile, Colombia, Denmark, Indonesia, Ireland, Malaysia, Mexico, New Zealand, Philippines, Thailand, Venezuela, and Singapore), the annual observations were interpolated to obtain quarterly observations, using a distribution procedure provided by the econometric software package RATS.

The measures of exchange rate variability ($XRVAR$) and flexibility ($XRFLEX$) were constructed for each country from monthly data, also obtained from the *IFS* (the sample periods for these measures are given in Table 5.2). The bilateral exchange rate was measured by the end-of-month domestic currency per dollar rate (line ae). The monetary base ("reserve money") and foreign exchange reserves ("total reserves, excluding gold") were obtained from line 14 and line 11.d, respectively; the latter series was converted into domestic currency units using the end-of-month exchange rate. Since the base series for Colombia had missing values for 1983.1–1982.2, 1983.4–1983.5, 1985.7–1985.8, 1985.11, 1986.1, 1986.7, 1986.10–1986.11, 1987.1–1987.2, 1987.4–1987.5, they were interpolated using the RATS distribution procedure. In addition, in the case of the United Kingdom, a consistent monthly series for the base was not available prior to 1986.9 because of a change in definition (with the Building Societies Act of 1986) that began treating deposits of building societies as part of reserves. We used the average of the ratio of observations from the old definition and the new definition for two overlapping quarters (1986:III and 1986:IV) to scale up quarterly numbers available for the old definition to match the new definition for the period prior to 1986.9. These scaled-up new quarterly numbers were then interpolated to obtain monthly observations using the RATS distribution procedure as above.

The variance of the exchange rate ($XRVAR$) is measured conditionally from the residuals of a regression of percent monthly (log) changes in the (end-of-period) nominal exchange rate on 12 months of lagged changes, together with 11 seasonal dummies. $XRFLEX$ was defined as by equation (5.4) with $RESVAR$ constructed from the residuals of the actual monthly change in reserves (divided by the lagged base) regressed on 12 lags of the dependent variable, together with seasonals.

The openness variable ($OPEN$) was constructed as the sum of a country's total nominal exports and imports in domestic currency (lines 70 and 71.v, respectively) divided by nominal GDP (line 99b.c). Due to the unavailability of multilateral exports and imports in local currency for Argentina, Brazil, Chile, Colombia, Indonesia, and Venezuela, multilateral exports and imports in U.S. dollars (lines 70..d and 71.vd) were converted to local currency using the period average exchange rate (line rf) for these countries.

NOTES

Research assistance by Barbara Rizzi is gratefully acknowledged. We thank Tamim Bayoumi, Benjamin Cohen, Linda Goldberg, and Richard Sweeney for helpful comments. The views presented in this paper are those of the authors alone and do not reflect those of the Federal Reserve Bank of San Francisco or the Board of Governors of the Federal Reserve System.

1. Related measures of exchange rate flexibility have been developed by Holden, Holden, and Suss (1979) to test optimum currency hypotheses, and by Glick, Kretzmer, and Wihlborg (1995) to explain cross-regime differences in the real effects of monetary shocks.
2. Edison and Melvin (1990) provide a critical survey of the empirical literature on exchange rate volatility and international trade.
3. Nevertheless, Kenen and Rodrik interpreted their findings as evidence in support of arguments for greater exchange rate fixity.
4. Oxelheim and Wihlborg (1987) explore the corporate finance implications of this view.
5. The standard partial equilibrium model assumes two countries, each producing a single tradable good that is an imperfect substitute for the good produced in the other country. If, as is often assumed in the empirical estimation of international trade equations, supply elasticities are infinite, then the estimated coefficients depend only on demand elasticities in the importing country. However, below we assume that supply elasticities are less than infinite, but that supply effects show up primarily in the cross-country variation in sensitivity to exchange-rate regime-related risk.
6. In our empirical analysis we report results for regressions augmented by the GDP of the exporting country to control for supply effects not otherwise captured. Hooper and Marquez (1995) survey the large number of empirical studies, using a wide variety of theoretical models and estimation techniques, that have estimated price and income elasticities of international trade.
7. We discuss these country-specific characteristics more fully in the following section.
8. It is generally recognized in the corporate finance field that a project's "own" variance increases the cost of capital even when shareholders can diversify project-specific risk. Another argument for a negative effect of risk on the capital stock involves viewing the firm as having an option as long as investment in sunk costs has not taken place. The value of this option increases with uncertainty.
9. See, for example, Giovannini (1988) and Aizenman (1992). Brada and

Mendez (1988) suggest that a positive relation between exchange rate variability and trade flows may arise because of an association of fixed exchange rates with restrictive commercial policies.

10. See, for example, Dixit (1989a, 1989b) and Baldwin and Krugman (1989); a particularly accessible variation of this argument can be found in Krugman (1989, chap. 2). Aizenman (1992), Goldberg and Kolstad (1995), and Goldberg (this volume) explore the international direct investment implications of variable exchange rates more formally. Aizenman (1992) formulates an open economy model in which risk-neutral producers engage in foreign investment in order to achieve ex post production flexibility and higher profits in response to real and nominal shocks. He characterizes how the association between investment and exchange rate variability depends on the nature of the underlying shocks. Goldberg and Kolstad (1995) show how investment decisions depend on the degree of risk aversion. For risk-neutral producers, foreign investment decisions do not depend on volatility in their framework. However, for risk-averse producers seeking to diversify risk, the share (though not necessarily the level) of foreign investment increases as exchange rate variability rises.

11. In general, the theory of investment assumes lags in the adjustment to the desired capital stock; we abstract from these considerations here. In the empirical analysis we implicitly take account of possible investment lags by including lags of the explanatory variables.

12. South Africa is excluded, even though it is among the top 30 largest U.S. trading partners, because of the world trade embargo in effect for most of the sample period.

13. Quarterly data for some variables, notably real GDP, were interpolated for some countries from annual data as described in the appendix.

14. The sample periods indicated in Table 5.2 allow for seven lags for each country in the pooled estimation of equations (5.3a) and (5.3b).

15. Various (nominal and real) exchange rate risk measures have been employed in international trade analyses. These include the absolute difference between current spot rates and corresponding earlier forward rates (Hooper and Kohlhagen 1978; Maskus 1986; Cushman 1988), the absolute value of current and/or lagged changes in the exchange rate (Bailey, Tavlas, and Ulan 1986), moving-sample standard deviations of past exchange rate changes (Ahktar and Hilton 1984; Gotur 1985; Kenen and Rodrik 1986; Cushman 1983, 1986, 1988; Bailey, Tavlas, and Ulan 1987; Koray and Lastrapes 1989; Klein 1990; Lastrapes and Koray 1990; Chowdhury 1993), and deviations of exchange rate changes from trend or other estimated processes (Cushman 1988; Peree and Steinherr 1989; Asseery and Peel 1991). Others have employed conditional variance measures based on ARCH models (Arize 1995; Kroner and Lastrapes 1993; Caporale and Doroodian 1994).

16. This assumption can be motivated by a monetary approach model to the balance of payments. See, for example, Girton and Roper (1977), who construct an exchange rate pressure variable with an incipient component defined similarly to ours. Note also that our definition abstracts from any

intervention by the United States against currency j. This is a reasonable characterization of U.S. exchange rate policy.

17. Our *XRFLEX* variable remains quite stable for almost all countries when constructed over various five-year subperiods within the overall sample range, indicating that the exchange rate regime for individual countries does not change much over the sample.

18. We do not allow individual time trends in these individual country regressions. In the pooled regressions the time trend variable is constrained implicitly to be identical across countries. The results with respect to our hypotheses are not affected if the trend term is omitted from the pooled regression.

19. As with most other empirical analyses of international trade flows, it is assumed that the real exchange rate and income are predetermined with respect to trade flows. Possible simultaneity bias with our OLS estimates should be less important for analyzing the effects of risk on trade flows than for estimating the magnitude of trade elasticities. At the end of Section 5.4 we check the sensitivity of our results to estimating elasticities from cointegrating relationships.

20. Because the variables in Z_j are time-invariant by definition, the product of Z_j and the demeaned variables P_j and Y_j are also demeaned.

21. Mexico, a recent member of the OECD, is excluded from the OECD sample.

22. This was implemented with RATS' ROBUSTERRORS option.

23. These plots are available upon request.

24. This scatter gives only a suggestive understanding of the relation between the export elasticities and the degree of export flexibility because it ignores possible correlations among these variables and other variables in the general export regression. Countries with wrong signs are omitted.

25. A line fitted to the points in Figure 5.2 is significantly positive at better than 1 percent.

26. Denmark is removed from both samples, because with a high export elasticity (in absolute terms) and a very low degree of exchange risk flexibility, it appeared to be an extreme outlier. Removing it from the samples improved the significance of the results, without affecting signs.

27. We do not show a scatter plot for import elasticities and *XRFLEX* analogous to Figure 5.2 because of the problems of interpreting the import results.

28. The procedure was implemented with RATS' CATS procedure, with the DRIFT option (implying a random walk trend in the data space), for a three-variable system consisting of the (logged) real exchange rate, importing country GDP, and real trade flow, as well as seasonal dummies. The income variable was assumed to be weakly exogenous. For each country, enough lags were included to reduce the significance of any first-order serial correlation in the system's residuals to less than 5 percent. The reported elasticities were taken from normalization of the cointegrating relation. Countries with wrong signs for either the relative price or income variable are omitted.

29. A line fitted to the points in Figure 5.3 is significant at 8 percent.

30. For a review of the OCA literature a classic reference is Tower and Willett (1976). An updated review can be found in Wihlborg and Willett (1991). The classic references are Mundell (1961), McKinnon (1963), and Kenen (1969). Bayoumi and Eichengreen (this volume) present empirical tests of the predictions of this theory.

REFERENCES

Aizenman, Joshua (1992). "Exchange Rate Flexibility, Volatility, and the Patterns of Domestic and Foreign Direct Investment," IMF *Staff Papers* 39, 890–922.

Akhtar, Ahkbar, and R. Spence Hilton (1984). "Effects of Exchange Rate Uncertainty on German and U.S. Trade," Federal Reserve Bank of New York *Quarterly Review* (Spring), 7–16.

Arize, Augustine (1995). "The Effects of Exchange-Rate Volatility on U.S. Exports: An Empirical Investigation," *Southern Economic Journal* 62, 34–43.

Asseery, A., and D. Peel (1991). "The Effects of Exchange Rate Volatility on Exports: Some New Estimates," *Economic Letters* 37 (October), 173–7.

Bailey, Martin, George Tavlas, and Michael Ulan (1986). "Exchange Rate Variability and Trade Performance: Evidence for the Big Seven Industrial Countries," *Weltwirtschaftliches Archiv* 126, 466–77.

Bailey, Martin, George Tavlas, and Michael Ulan (1987). "The Impact of Exchange-Rate Volatility on Export Growth," *Journal of Policy Modeling* 9 (Spring), 225–43.

Baldwin, Richard, and Paul Krugman (1989). "Persistent Trade Effects of Large Exchange Rate Shocks," *Quarterly Journal of Economics* 104, 635–54.

Brada, Josef, and José Méndez (1988). "Exchange Rate Risk, Exchange Rate Regime and the Volume of International Trade," *Kyklos* 41, 263–80.

Caporale, Tony, and Khosrow Doroodian (1994). "Exchange Rate Variability and the Flow of International Trade," *Economic Letters* 46, 49–54.

Chowdhury, A. (1993). "Does Exchange Rate Volatility Depress Trade Flows? Evidence from Error-Correction Model," *Review of Economics and Statistics*, 700–6.

Cushman, David (1983). "The Effects of Real Exchange Rate Risk on International Trade," *Journal of International Economics* 15 (August), 45–63.

Cushman, David (1986). "Has Exchange Rate Risk Depressed International Trade? The Impact of Third-Country Exchange Risk," *Journal of International Money and Finance* 5, 361–79.

Cushman, David (1988). "U.S. Bilateral Trade Flows and Exchange Risk During the Floating Period," *Journal of International Economics* 24, 317–30.

Dixit, Avinash (1989a). "Entry and Exit of Firms under Uncertainty," *Journal of Political Economy* 97, 620–38.

Dixit, Avinash (1989b). "Hysteresis, Import Penetration, and Exchange-Rate Pass Through," *Quarterly Journal of Economics* 104, 205–28.

Edison, Hali, and Michael Melvin (1990). "The Determinants and Implications of the Choice of an Exchange Rate System." In W. Haraf and T. Willett, eds.,

Monetary Policy for a Volatile Global Economy, pp. 1–44. Washington, DC: American Enterprise Institute.

Gagnon, Joseph (1993). "Exchange Rate Variability and the Level of International Trade," *Journal of International Economics* 34, 269–87.

Giovannini, Alberto (1988). "Exchange Rates and Traded Goods Prices," *Journal of International Economics* 24 (February), 45–68.

Girton, Lance, and Donald Roper (1977). "A Monetary Model of Exchange Rate Pressure Applied to the Postwar Canadian Experience," *American Economic Review* 67, 537–48.

Glick, Reuven, Peter Kretzmer, and Clas Wihlborg (1995). "Real Exchange Rate Effects of Monetary Disturbances under Different Degrees of Exchange Rate Flexibility: An Empirical Analysis," *Journal of International Economics* 38 (May), 249–73.

Goldberg, Linda, and C. Kolstad (1995). "Foreign Direct Investment, Exchange Rate Variability, and Demand Uncertainty," *International Economic Review* 36, 855–73.

Gotur, P. (1985). "Effects of Exchange Rate Volatility on Trade: Some Further Results," IMF *Staff Papers* 32, 475–512.

Holden, P., M. Holden, and E. Suss (1979). "The Determinants of Exchange Rate Flexibility: An Empirical Investigation," *Review of Economics and Statistics* 61, 327–33.

Hooper, Peter, and Steven Kohlhagen (1978). "The Effect of Exchange Rate Uncertainty on the Prices and Volume of International Trade," *Journal of International Economics* 8, 483–511.

Hooper, Peter, and Jaime Marquez (1995). "Exchange Rates, Prices, and External Adjustment in the U.S. and Japan." In Peter Kenen, ed., *Understanding Interdependence: The Macroeconomics of the Open Economy*, pp. 107–168. Princeton, NJ: Princeton University Press.

International Monetary Fund (1984). *Exchange Rate Volatility and World Trade*, Occasional Paper No. 28. Washington, DC: IMF.

Kenen, Peter (1969). "The Theory of Optimum Currency Areas: An Eclectic View." In Robert Mundell and Alexander Swoboda, eds., *Monetary Problems of the International Economy*, pp. 41–60. Chicago: University of Chicago Press.

Kenen, Peter, and Dani Rodrik (1986). "Measuring and Analyzing the Effects of Short-Term Volatility in Real Exchange Rates," *Review of Economics and Statistics* 68 (May), 311–15.

Klein, Michael (1990). "Sectoral Effects of Exchange Rate Volatility on United States Exports," *Journal of International Money and Finance* 9, 299–308.

Kmenta, Jan (1986). *Elements of Econometrics*, 2nd ed. New York: Macmillan.

Koray, Faik, and William Lastrapes (1989). "Real Exchange Rate Volatility and U.S. Bilateral Trade: A VAR Approach," *Review of Economics and Statistics* 71 (November), 708–12.

Kroner, Kenneth, and William Lastrapes (1993). "The Impact of Exchange Rate Volatility on International Trade: Reduced-Form Estimates Using the

GARCH-in-Mean Model," *Journal of International Money and Finance* 12 (June), 298–318.

Krugman, Paul (1989). *Exchange-Rate Instability*. Cambridge, MA: MIT Press.

Lastrapes, William, and Faik Koray (1990). "Exchange Rate Volatility and U.S. Multilateral Trade Flows," *Journal of Macroeconomics* 12, 341–62.

McKinnon, Ronald (1963). "Optimal Currency Areas," *American Economic Review* 53 (September), 717–25.

Maskus, Keith (1986). "Exchange Rate Risk and U.S. Trade: A Sectoral Analysis," Federal Reserve Bank of Kansas City, *Economic Review* 71 (March), 16–28.

Mundell, Robert (1961). "A Theory of Optimum Currency Areas," *American Economic Reivew* 51 (September), 657–65.

Oxelheim, Lars, and Clas Wihlborg (1987). *Macroeconomic Uncertainty: International Risks and Opportunities for the Corporation*. Chichester, U.K.: John Wiley.

Peree, Eric, and Alfred Steinherr (1989). "Exchange Rate Uncertainty and Foreign Trade," *European Economic Review* 33 (July), 1241–64.

Thursby, Marie, and Jerry Thursby (1987). "Bilateral Trade Flows, the Linder Hypothesis, and Exchange Risk," *Review of Economics and Statistics* 69 (August), 488–95.

Tower, Edward, and Thomas Willett (1976). *The Theory of Optimal Currency Areas and Exchange Rate Flexibility*. Special Papers in International Economics 11, International Finance Section, Princeton University.

White, Halbert (1980). "A Heteroskedasticity-consistent Covariance Matrix Estimator and a Direct Test for Heteroskedasticity," *Econometrica* 48, 817–38.

Wihlborg, Clas, and Thomas Willett (1991). "Optimum Currency Areas Revisited in the Transition to a Monetary Union," in C. Wihlborg, M. Fratianni, and T. D. Willett, eds., *Financial Regulation and Monetary Arrangements after 1992*. Amsterdam: North-Holland.

CHAPTER 6

Exchange rates and investment response in Latin America

Linda S. Goldberg

I Introduction

The idea that countries should limit the movements of nominal or real exchange rates is a theme that arises in policy discussions for both industrialized and developing economies. One channel for exchange rate effects is via changes in producer profitability, which also can drive real investment activity. Endogeneity of sectoral investments has clear and potentially strong implications for overall sectoral growth and aggregate GDP.

The potential implications of nominal and real exchange rates for investment has been a theme often considered in the thoughtful work of Peter Kenen. In the mid-1990s, Kenen (1994) restated his concerns about exchange rate and investment linkages, arguing that "uncertainty about future exchange rates has probably affected capital formation in ways that reduce economic efficiency, and that same uncertainty may also explain why trade balances have adjusted sluggishly to exchange rate changes." Although Kenen's contributions are oriented mainly toward industrialized countries, there clearly are strong developing country parallels. Fluctuations and cycles in real exchange rates often are observed, and these steep movements in exchange rates can likewise slow capital formation and reduce economic efficiency.

In the present essay I focus on the link between real exchange rate movements and investment activity in Latin America.[1] For individual producers, investment responds to exchange rates by altering the expected marginal profitability of capital (Campa and Goldberg, 1996). Three main factors influence the size and direction of profitability response to an exchange rate depreciation (appreciation): (i) higher producer export shares raise profitability; (ii) higher reliance on imported inputs into production effectively imply exchange-rate induced cost

157

shocks and lower profitability; and (iii) sectoral exchange rate pass-through elasticities have mixed effects depending on whether they pertain to domestic sales, export sales, or imported input costs.

Investment theory shows that profit endogeneity with respect to exchange rates is an important determinant of the sign of investment response, but not necessarily of the degree of this response. Ultimately this response also depends on: the discount factor weighing expected future producer profits in investment decisions; the rate of depreciation of capital stocks; and the cost of adjusting the rate of capital accumulation in an economy. Exogenous to the model are other factors that can shield or offset producer exposures to movements in exchange-rate induced profitability. These factors may include dollarization of the economy, the sophistication and horizon of the financial sector, and internationalization of production activity.

The movements in real exchange rates and the aggregate terms of trade for six Latin American countries (Argentina, Brazil, Chile, Colombia, Mexico, and Venezuela) are documented in Section III.[2] The exposition also emphasizes the potential for country exposure to exchange rates through exports and imported productive inputs. I detail the main export sectors of each economy, and consider the likelihood that producers in these sectors have any ability to influence world market prices for their goods. Likewise, I examine the mix of imports into each economy and posit the extent of producer reliance on imported inputs. Given this trade and industrial organization background of each country, in Section IV I examine the empirical linkage between exchange rates and investment activity. Ideally one would want to conduct this examination using detailed time-series investment data by firm or by sector. However, since this type of data either is unavailable or incomplete for most Latin American economies, I use aggregate real investment data for the analysis. Based on these data, I estimate investment rate elasticities and quantify for each country the importance of the different channels of exposure to exchange rates.

In Section V of the essay I provide a perspective on the theoretical and empirical results. The central theme of this discussion concerns exchange rate movements in relation to economic development strategies. Generally, development strategists contend that countries should diversify production so that individual shocks would have milder aggregate implications. While I concur with this view, in the present essay I find it useful to consider whether such diversification of exports is appropriate when the main stimuli against which producers should diversify are exchange rate movements.

Unlike commodity price movements, exchange rate movements are common to all traded-goods sectors. In this context, it is possible that diversification of production activity is not the best approach. Instead, the impact of the shock might be lessened if producers have balanced exposure through revenue and cost channels. In other words, it is theoretically possible that diversification of exchange rate risk may be accomplished by offsetting export exposures with imported input exposures. The extent to which this offset is required would depend on the industrial organization of respective sectors. Specifically, the theory of investment under imperfectly competitive markets (spelled out in Section II) shows that producers that are large in international markets for their export good may have some price-setting ability. This price-setting ability partially insulates revenues from exchange-rate movements, and in principle should reduce the impact of exchange rates on investment activity.

For Latin American countries, the extent of the linkage between exchange rates and investment under different patterns of production activity is an empirical issue. Do these producers have enough international market power so that concentrated production and export activity helps insulate them from exchange rate changes and international shocks? Or is the concentrated production accomplishing only an intensification of aggregate economic exposure? The empirical results of Section IV show that the revenue elasticities of exchange rate effects is smallest for Mexico and Argentina among our sample of Latin American countries. The revenue elasticities are strongest for Chile and Venezuela, the two countries in the group with the least diversified export activity. We infer that these countries do not appear to have shielded domestic export revenues from exchange rate fluctuations, despite having relatively more potential for exerting market power.

However, the fact that revenues fluctuate with movements in exchange rates does not necessarily imply exposed profits. In the 1990s, for example, Chile and Venezuela also have had the largest shares of imported inputs into production, and these costs fluctuate with movements in exchange rates. The net consequences for profitability and investment of exchange rate movements vary by country. The reliance on imported inputs in Chile and Venezuela serves to dampen but not outweigh the overall positive (negative) revenue and investment effects from depreciation (appreciation). Indeed, when one accounts for imported input reliance, real depreciation may actually slow investment in Colombia and Mexico.

II Real exchange rates, the terms of trade, and investment

The importance of investment for output growth in Latin America is a well-documented and sensible finding (de Gregorio 1992). Exchange rate patterns have been shown to contribute to this lower growth (Edwards 1991). Latin American regional growth rates fall well below rates achieved in industrialized countries. Low investment rates in plant and equipment (and in human capital) have significant explanatory power for low overall growth. Recent research by the Inter-American Development Bank (1995) attributes much of this slow growth to patterns in exchange rates, the terms of trade, and policy tools. Although their analysis explicitly considers volatility of these series (and not actual levels of the series), the volatility results are instructive for thinking about the first-order effects of movements in these series.

The IDB finds that, controlling for monetary and fiscal policy volatility (which together reduce Latin American growth by 0.424 percent), terms-of-trade volatility reduced growth rates by 0.411 percent on average and real exchange rate volatility by another 0.228 percent. More detailed computations, reproduced in Table 6.1, show that particular Latin American countries have different reasons for low growth over the past 30 years. For all countries, real exchange rates volatility reduced growth significantly. For Chile and Argentina this effect was more important terms-of-trade volatility or explicit volatility of monetary and fiscal policy. By contrast, in Brazil the real exchange rate did not have a large depressing effect overall.[3]

The objective of the present essay is to explore more carefully the conditions under which real exchange rate movements influence investment. I argue that the form of producer and country exposures to exchange rates are key. The export share of aggregate production is also key, as is the share of imported inputs into production. Ultimately, both the level of external trade and the ability of producers to influence world market prices for their product are important.

A model of exchange rates and investment

Following the approach of Campa and Goldberg (1996), investment is modeled using a neoclassical approach with explicit dynamics, whereby a producer maximizes the present discounted stream of future profits. Investments are made up until the point where the marginal profitability of capital equals its cost. Quadratic adjustment costs to the capital accumulation rate are assumed, and there is a one period time-to-build lag on investments. The exchange rate influences investment by altering the

Table 6.1. *Contributions of alternative forms of volatility to Latin American growth rates, relative to industrialized country averages 1960– 85 (percent)*

	Effect of terms-of trade volatility	Effect of real exchange rate volatility	Effect of fiscal and monetary policy volatility	Total effects on country growth
Chile	−0.28	−0.57	−0.30	−1.16
Brazil	−0.25	−0.17	−0.43	−0.85
Argentina	−0.10	−0.92	−0.68	−1.70
Venezuela	−2.78	−0.25	−0.19	−3.22
Mexico	−0.23	−0.28	−0.31	−0.82
Colombia	−0.54	−0.09	−0.02	−0.62

Source: IDB 1995, Table 6: Estimated impact of macroeconomic volatility on GDP growth – Latin America.

marginal profitability of capital. The marginal profitability of capital responds in accordance with exchange rate exposures of the revenue and cost side of the producer balance sheet.

A firm chooses investment I_t to maximize its value V_t, equal to the expected present value of future profits (equation 6.1). The maximization is subject to a traditional capital accumulation equation and costly adjustment of the capital stock (equations 6.2 and 6.3):

$$V_t\left(K_t,\ e_t\right) = \max E_t \sum_{j=0}^{\infty} \beta^j \left[\pi_{t+j}\left(K_{t+j},\ e_{t+j}\right) - c\left(I_{t+j},\ K_{t+j}\right)\right] \quad (6.1)$$

$$K_{t+1} = \left(1 - \delta\right)K_t + I_t \quad (6.2)$$

$$c\left(I_t,\ K_t\right) = \frac{\psi}{2} K_t \left(\frac{I_t}{K_t} - \mu\right)^2 \quad (6.3)$$

where $\pi_t(K_t, e_t)$ represents the maximized value of net cash flow (profits) at time t, β is the discount rate, K_t is the current capital stock of the firm, δ is the depreciation rate of capital, E_t is the expectations operator, and e_t is the exchange rate, expressed in terms of domestic currency per unit of foreign exchange. $c(I_t, K_t)$ represents the cost of adjustment to changes in the capital stock, where ψ and μ are constant parameters representing the scope of adjustment costs and desired capital accumulation rates, respectively.

The first-order condition from the maximization problem is:

$$\frac{I_t}{K_t} = \mu + \frac{\beta}{\psi} E_t V_K \tag{6.4}$$

where $V_k = \partial V_{t+1}(\cdot)/\partial K_{t+1}$ is the marginal value of capital. The first-order condition states that investment increases relative to the capital stock of the industry when the expected marginal value of capital rises. The expected marginal value of capital is an increasing function of the marginal profitability of capital.

Producer profits gross of investment are the sum of receipts on domestic and foreign sales receipts, net of operating costs, and are optimized with respect to production volumes and input quantities:

$$\pi(K_t:e_t) = \max_{y,L,L^*} p(q_t,\ e_t:Q_w)q_t + e_t p^*(q_t^*,\ e_t:Q_w)q_t^* - w_t L_t - e_t w_t^* L_t^* \tag{6.5}$$

Quantities q_t and q_t^*, with $y_t = q_t + q_t^*$, represent domestic and foreign sales, whereas Q_w represents world market conditions or the overall terms-of-trade changes. The domestic and foreign demand functions and the local currency goods prices depend on the quantities supplied to respective markets and on the exchange rate. The exchange rate is introduced to potentially shift the demand schedule for domestically produced goods, especially if import competition exists for these products.

By differentiating the profit function with respect to capital we derive an expression for the marginal profitability of capital:

$$\pi_{K,t} \equiv \frac{\partial \pi_t}{\partial K_t} = \frac{1}{K_t}\left(MKUP_t^{-1} p_t q_t + MKUP_t^{*-1} e_t p_t^* q_t^* - \left(w_t L_t + e_t w_t^* L_t^* \right) \right) \tag{6.6}$$

where

$$MKUP = \frac{1}{\left(1+\eta^{-1}\right)}, \ MKUP^* = \frac{1}{\left(1+\eta^{*-1}\right)},$$

and η and η^* represent price elasticities of demand in respective markets.[4] To determine the sensitivity of investment to exchange rates, we differentiate the investment equation (6.4) and the marginal profitability of capital (6.5) with respect to exchange rates.[5] For a given industry, differentiation of the components of equation (6.5) with respect to the exchange rate yields equation (6.7). This partial derivative is central to understanding industry and aggregate investment responsiveness to movements of the real exchange rate, given a partial equilibrium world and neoclassical model of investment:

$$\frac{\partial I_t}{TR_t} = \frac{\beta}{\psi\left(1 - \beta(1 - \delta)\right)} \cdot E_t \left[\frac{1}{AMKUP_t} \left(\begin{array}{c} \left(\eta_{p,e} - \eta^i_{MKUP,e}\right)\left(1 - X_t\right) \\ + \left(1 + \eta_{p^*,e} - \eta^i_{MKUP^*,e}\right)X_t \\ - \left(1 + \eta_{w^*,e}\right)\alpha_t \end{array} \right) \cdot \frac{\partial e_t}{e_t} \right]$$

(6.7)

where $\eta_{p,e}$ and $\eta_{p^*,e}$ are "exchange-rate pass-through" elasticities in domestic and foreign markets; $\eta_{MKUP,e}$ and $\eta_{MKUP^*,e}$ are markup elasticities with respect to exchange rate changes; and $AMKUP_t$ is the average price-over-cost markup across domestic and foreign sales.[6] X_t represents the share of total revenues TR_t associated with export sales; $(1 - X_t)$ is the share associated with domestic sales; and α_t, the share of imported inputs in total production costs, is multiplied by the elasticity of these input costs with respect to exchange rates, $(1 + \eta_{n^*,e})$. $\eta_{w^*,e}$ reflects the degree to which domestic exchange rate changes influence the world market price of the imported input. The discount rate β is assumed independent of the real exchange rate.

Equation (6.7) contains the main theoretical relationship between the exchange rate and investment. Each line inside the brackets on its right-hand side represents one of the three channels through which exchange rates influence the expected marginal profitability of capital. The first line states that revenues from domestic sales (weight $1 - X_t$ in total revenues) respond if domestic prices and price-over-cost markups are responsive to exchange rate changes. The endogeneity of these prices depends on the competitive structure of the home markets. Markets that are closer to perfect or monopolistic competition will have exchange-rate pass-through elasticities near zero; markets best described as Cournot will have $\eta_{p,e} > 0$.[7]

The second line in equation (6.7) indicates export revenues' response to exchange rates. A depreciation immediately raises the value of exports one to one, but some of this revenue increase may be offset (or smoothed) if the producer lowers the price charged in international markets on the export goods (i.e., if $\eta_{p^*,e} < 0$). The ability of domestic exporters to influence world market prices on their goods is greatest when these exporters control a significant proportion of the world market supply of the export good. Thus, the revenue effect of a depreciation is smaller for monopolistic exporters than for exporters who are small in terms of world markets for particular commodities or product groups. In other words, fluctuations in exchange rates translate into larger net revenue fluctuations for small exporters.

In addition to these revenue implications of exchange rates, the third line of equation (6.7) shows that exchange rates influence profitability through the elasticity of production costs. A depreciation is expected to raise imported input costs one for one. However, some of this cost increase can be mitigated if the depreciation reduces the world market price of the imported inputs. As discussed in Section III, this type of market power is unlikely in the developing country context, so we expect $\eta_{w^*,e} \approx 0$.[8]

Although the three aforementioned forces indicate the endogeneity of the marginal profitability of capital, the overall investment response also depends on $\beta/[\psi(1 - \beta(1 - \delta))]$ and by $AMKUP^{-1}$, which multiply the right-hand side of equation (6.7). These terms moderate the scale of investment changes following a change in the marginal profitability of capital. Investment response is low: if the costs of adjusting the capital accumulation rate are high (high ψ); if capital depreciates rapidly (high δ); if producers have a high rate of time preference (low β). Also, if price-over-cost markups are high, producers will be able to absorb some changes in profitability before altering investment choices. High average markups can reduce investment responsiveness to exchange-rate induced changes in the average profitability of capital.

Equation (6.7) provides a basic framework for interpreting correlations between exchange rate movements and changing patterns of investment. The main shortcoming of this approach in our present context is that the theory is developed from the vantage point of a particular producer, not necessarily for an aggregate economy. To link these results to our aggregate data, we need to have a sense of whether the export sectors of an economy represent a narrow or diverse group of industries. Given these industries, we also need to discern whether producers in the export sectors are likely to be able to influence world market prices for the exported goods. Thus, export composition and export industry world market conditions will provide insights into whether $\eta_{p^*,e} < 0$ is significantly large (in absolute terms) or expected to be near zero for an economy overall. Before turning to the investment regression results and their interpretation (Section IV), in Section III I provide background on the external exposures in Latin America.

III Real exchange rates and trade composition of Latin American countries

This section provides an overview of the real exchange rate patterns and trade and production structures in six Latin American economies: Argentina, Brazil, Chile, Colombia, Mexico, and Venezuela. The real exchange rate movements are provided to emphasize that in each country this relative price has moved considerably over the past two decades, experiencing both real appreciation and depreciation intervals. The trade composition details are intended to provide intuition about which countries may contain exporters with some latitude in adjusting export prices to absorb real exchange rate movements.

A *Real exchange rate movements*

The real exchange rate changes have been large and prevalent throughout Latin America, especially in the context of stabilization episodes. Figures 6.1a through 6.1f show the real exchange rates for Argentina, Brazil, Chile, Colombia, Mexico, and Venezuela for the mid-1970s into the mid-1990s. Very distinct gradual real appreciation/sharp depreciation patterns emerge for each of the respective currencies. As documented in Table 6.2, most of these countries experienced four or five peak–trough cycles during this interval. Since the early 1980s, Chile, Colombia, Mexico, and Venezuela have experienced a longer-term trend real depreciation of their currencies. The table shows the range of movements of the real exchange rates and the normalized standard deviation of real exchange rates within each exchange rate cycle. The intent of this exposition is to show the depth of exchange rate changes and relative variance of these movements.

Argentina has experienced five distinct real exchange rate cycles since 1975. Over the course of each of these cycles, which have spanned between two and four years, the standard deviation of the real exchange rate has been on the order of one quarter of the mean level of the real exchange rate. In Brazil, the real exchange rate cycles have been more regular, generally occurring over intervals of approximately four years. Compared with Argentina, the normalized standard deviations of the Brazilian real exchange rates are significantly less. The Chilean currency has experienced fewer sharp swings in its real value. The peso experienced a sharp real appreciation in the first half of the 1980s, followed by a correction that persisted into the late 1980s. Since that time, the real value of the Chilean peso has steadily increased with relatively little overall volatility.

Argentina, Mexico, and Venezuela have had very turbulent real exchange rates, characterized by gradual real appreciation and sharp nominal and real depreciation of the currency value. For example, in a number of real appreciation/real depreciation cycles, the Mexican peso and Venezuelan Bolivares have altered their values by more than 50 percent. For all three countries, the monthly standard deviations of these

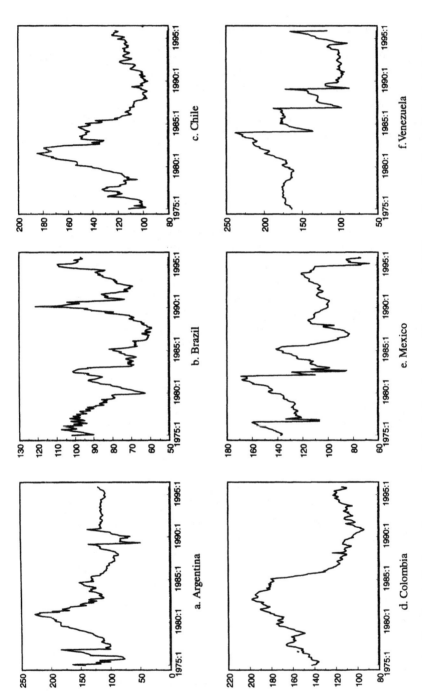

Figure 6.1. Broad real effective exchange rates for six Latin American countries. *Source:* J. P. Morgan Securities, Inc. An increase in the index reflects a real appreciation of the domestic currency.

Table 6.2. *Measures of real exchange rate range and volatility over currency cycles, monthly data 1975:1–1995:12*

	Number of cycles (trough, peak, trough)	Within-cycle real exchange rate range	Mean real exchange rate level in cycle	Average normalized standard deviation of RER in cycle
Chile	3	34.50	114.67	0.09
		80.20	148.78	0.16
		55.30	119.27	0.16
Brazil	4	45.00	92.49	0.10
		38.70	81.35	0.14
		22.60	67.55	0.09
		61.90	79.41	0.18
Argentina	5	88.10	117.16	0.20
		107.70	120.79	0.27
		124.40	155.30	0.23
		66.10	116.26	0.14
		87.10	100.48	0.21
		88.50	107.61	0.14
Venezuela	4	102.80	194.92	0.12
		90.10	167.44	0.10
		84.50	127.75	0.14
		77.80	108.91	0.14
Mexico	5	52.50	142.83	0.11
		83.90	136.33	0.13
		58.40	113.01	0.15
		33.00	102.95	0.09
		54.30	107.87	0.10
Colombia	2	104.10	150.62	0.23

Source: Author's calculations using real exchange rate indices (RERs) compiled by J. P. Morgan securities. An increase in the index reflects a real appreciation of a currency value.

rates have been on the order of 15 percent of mean real exchange rate levels.

B *Main production and trade exposures of six Latin American countries*

The implications of exchange rate movements for producer profitability depend on the export, import, and expenditure patterns and composition of each country, described in the series of tables that follows. Table 6.3 presents the largest export sectors of each country (relative to total exports) and their evolution over time. Total exports relative to GDP are presented to better depict the overall importance of the foreign relative to domestic sales.

Exports remain heavily concentrated in some Latin American economies. In 1991 ten leading export products accounted for approximately 90 percent of Venezuela's exports, 70 percent of Chile and Colombia's exports, and 45 percent of the exports of Brazil, Argentina, and Mexico. This concentration of exports and production is especially prevalent in Chile, which remains a big copper producer – both relative to all other exports and relative to GDP – and Venezuela, in which 80 percent of exports were directly related to crude petroleum. Petroleum also continues to play a large role in Colombian and Mexican exports (30 percent in 1991), although for Mexico the share of petroleum in exports is half of its 1980 level and in Colombia petroleum exports have boomed in the past decade.

Table 6.4 provides summary information on the main markets for the exports of each country, detailing whether these markets are industrialized countries or developing countries. From these data we can consider whether it is theoretically possible that a country has pricing power in its export markets. The concentration of export activity suggests that Chile could potentially move the world market price of copper. Colombia may influence the world market for coffee. Although both Mexico and (especially) Venezuela are large producers of crude petroleum, the specifics of the petroleum market and the structure of contracts reduce the likelihood that exchange rate changes in these countries would affect petroleum world market prices.

Consider the implications of these observations for the effects of exchange rate movements on the marginal revenues on country exports. The exchange rate depreciation may have less of an expansionary effect on revenues of countries with market power in their export industries. In other words, Venezuela and Chile may be able to offset some real exchange rate movements by passing a portion through to foreign prices. If so, they would have marginal revenues from exports that are relatively less responsive to exchange rate movements than Argentina, Brazil, and Mexico. If all else were equal, including exposure on the imported input cost side, investment responsiveness of these countries would behave in a qualitatively similar fashion.

Of course, all else is not equal. Countries significantly differ in the structure and content of their imports. Table 6.5 provides information on the types of imported goods entering each country and the evolution of

Table 6.3. *Largest export sectors within total exports, and total exports to GDP (as percentage of total exports)*

		1980	1990
Chile	Copper and related products	46.8	46.5
	Exports of 10 leading products	70.0	67.5
	Total exports as % GDP	23.0	27.5
Brazil	Iron ore and concentrates	7.7	7.7
	Oil seed cake and related	7.5	5.3
	Coffee, green or roasted	12.4	3.5
	Exports of 10 leading products	45.0	40.2
	Total exports as % GDP	9.0	7.1
Argentina	Oil seed cake and related	3.7	9.2
	Wheat and meslin, unmilled	10.2	7.1
	Soya beans	7.5	5.6
	Exports of 10 leading products	49.8	44.7
	Total exports as % GDP	7.0	8.7
Venezuela	Crude petroleum and products	62.6	80.5
	Aluminum	2.0	5.0
	Exports of 10 leading products	97.5	88.3
	Total exports as % GDP	31.0	36.0
Mexico	Crude petroleum	60.9	29.8
	Passenger motor cars and parts	1.3	7.3
	Coffee, green or roasted	2.9	2.4
	Exports of 10 leading products	79.7	53.0
	Total exports as % GDP	11.0	11.2
Colombia	Crude petroleum	—	22.8
	Coffee, green or roasted	59.9	20.9
	Coal	—	7.9
	Exports of 10 leading products	78.5	71.5
	Total exports as % GDP	17.0	16.8

Sources: *Statistical Yearbook for Latin America and the Caribbean*, 1992 edition, and *Handbook of International Trade and Development Statistics*, United Nations Conference on Trade and Development, 1993 edition; *International Financial Statistics*, 1990.

Table 6.4. *Destination countries of exports of Latin American economies, 1980 and 1990*

	Exports (as % total exports)		
	1980	1990	Details on export destination
Chile			
Industrialized	63.1	72.9	Mainly United States, Japan, and Germany
Developing	33.9	25.9	Largest shares: Brazil and Argentina
Brazil			
Industrialized	57.3	68.1	Mainly United States, Netherlands, Japan, and Germany
Developing	38.4	30.4	Largest share Argentina
Argentina			
Industrialized	43.1	49.7	Mainly United States, Netherlands, and Germany
Developing	34.9	48.9	Largest share: Brazil
Venezuela			
Industrialized	58.3	64.2	Mainly United States
Developing	40.3	32.3	Mixed across Latin America
Mexico			
Industrialized	85.4	90.0	Mainly United States
Developing	12.6	9.1	Largest share: Brazil
Colombia			
Industrialized	90.7	78.5	Mainly United States and Germany
Developing	9.3	19.5	Largest share: Venezuela

Source: IMF *Direction of Trade Statistics.*

these imports over time. The breakdown presented is between food products, agricultural raw materials, ores and metals, manufactured goods with a subgrouping of machinery and equipment, and fuels. Each of these is presented relative to total imports of a country in each year. Also provided in the table are data on total imports as a fraction of GDP.

There are striking similarities across Latin American economies in the pattern of imports. First, the majority of imports are manufactured goods, which in 1990 comprised approximately 75 percent of import

Table 6.5. *Main import categories, as percent of total imports*

Country	Year	Food	Agricultural raw materials	Fuels	Ores and metal	Manufactured goods	% of which are machinery and equipment	Imports/GDP*
Argentina	1980	5.7	3.7	10.3	2.9	77.3	40.2	4.5
	1990	4.0	4.0	8.1	5.8	73.7	31.0	2.6
Brazil	1980	9.6	1.3	43.1	5.1	40.8	19.5	9.7
	1990	9.4	2.6	26.8	4.6	56.7	27.6	4.7
Colombia	1980	11.7	2.8	12.2	3.2	69.4	37.6	20.6
	1990	7.1	3.5	6.0	3.5	76.6	36.8	32.0
Chile	1980	15.0	1.8	18.4	1.7	59.6	33.4	12.1
	1990	4.4	2.2	15.7	1.2	75.3	43.4	9.3
Mexico	1980	16.1	3.0	2.0	4.0	74.9	43.1	9.5
	1990	15.7	4.0	4.1	3.3	71.5	36.1	14.4
Venezuela	1980	14.5	2.7	1.6	2.1	79.1	42.8	18.0
	1990	11.6	3.9	2.9	4.9	76.0	39.3	14.4

Source: United Nations Conference on Trade and Development (UNCTAD); * International Financial Statistics (IFS).

expenditures in all countries but Brazil, where this ratio was closer to 60 percent. Roughly half of these manufactured good imports are machinery and equipment, that is, mainly inputs into the production process. Agricultural raw materials, and ores and metals, are not major imports of this region. The import dependence on food and fuels varies strikingly across countries, and reveals patterns consistent with those shown in the export share tables. Argentina and Chile are not big food importers, but do import fuels. Brazil imports both food and fuels, but has a lower share of manufactured good imports. Venezuela and Mexico import larger proportions of food, but do not import significant quantities of fuel. In Chile and Venezuela, the import tab exceeds a quarter of their GDP.

Table 6.6, on the source countries of Latin American imports, provides further insight into the importance of the Latin American destinations relative to the overall production of the source country. For Chile, Brazil, and Argentina, industrialized countries are the source of roughly 60 percent of imported goods, whereas developing countries account for the remaining 40 percent. For Venezuela, Mexico, and Colombia, the imports from industrialized countries represent much higher shares, almost 75 percent for Colombia and more than 90 percent for Mexico. The lion's share of this trade is with the United States, with Germany and then Japan as the secondary source countries. It is reasonable to assume that individual Latin American countries constitute a relatively small part of the overall market for the products of these exporting countries. Thus, it is reasonable to expect that conditions in Latin American countries have (at best) second-order effects on the world market prices of the goods that they import. In terms of equation (6.7), this suggests that $\eta_{w^*,e} = 0$.

In the unlikely event that considerable market power exists in import prices for Latin American products, this pricing power might show up in the machinery and equipment area. The extent of this power would be of similar magnitudes across countries. It also is theoretically possible that Brazil could influence the price of their imports of fuel.

Overall, our expectations are that exchange rate changes in Latin American countries will pass through one-for-one into the domestic currency prices of these imports. In terms of our testing equation on investment, this implies that import prices rise in proportion to real depreciation of the domestic currencies; and the coefficient on investment of exchange rates interacted with imported input shares would be negative and significant.

As a rough proxy for net exposures of these six Latin American

Table 6.6. *Source country for imports of Latin American economies, 1980 and 1990*

	Imports by source (as % total imports)		
	1980	1990	Details
Chile			
Industrialized	68.1	57.6	Mainly United States, Japan, and Germany
Developing	36.2	38.4	Largest shares: Brazil and Argentina
Brazil			
Industrialized	46.6	55.0	Mainly United States, Japan, and Germany
Developing	52.7	44.5	Largest share: Argentina
Argentina			
Industrialized	68.2	58.9	Mainly United States and Germany
Developing	30.4	41.1	Largest share Brazil
Venezuela			
Industrialized	86.3	82.4	Mainly United States, then Germany
Developing	13.0	17.4	Largest shares: Brazil and Colombia
Mexico			
Industrialized	85.8	91.3	Mainly United States, then Germany and Japan
Developing	5.9	8.2	Largest share: Brazil
Colombia			
Industrialized	56.8	73.8	Mainly United States, then Germany
Developing	42.2	25.4	Largest share: Venezuela

Source: IMF, *Direction of Trade Statistics.*

countries to real exchange rate movements, consider the difference between export share and imported-input share, where the latter is proxied by the sum of fuel and machinery and equipment imports relative to GDP. These numbers are presented below for 1990. In net and rough terms, observe that Chile, Venezuela, and Colombia have large net producer exposure to movements in exchange rates.

	1990 exports (percent of GDP)	1990 imported inputs (percent of GDP)	1990 net exposure
Chile	27.5	13.7	13.8
Brazil	7.1	2.6	4.5
Argentina	8.7	1.0	7.7
Venezuela	36.0	6.1	29.9
Mexico	11.2	4.2	7.0
Colombia	16.8	4.4	12.4

Finally, the net effect of exchange-rate induced changes in profitability also depends on a range of other features that determine the links between profitability and investment. For example, the cost of adjusting the capital accumulation rate is expected to differ across industries and across countries. It may be more costly to make this adjustment in capital intensive production sectors, so that investment response to changes in profitability in Chile (copper), Venezuela (petroleum), and Mexico (petroleum) may be more limited. This suggests that the interacted coefficient on export share with the exchange rate in the investment equations may be lower for Chile, Venezuela, and Mexico than for Argentina, Brazil, and possibly Colombia. I examine the empirical validity of this supposition in the regression results of Section IV.

IV Exchange rates and investment in Latin America

Based on equation (6.7), pooled time-series data from the six Latin American countries are used in the following investment equation:

$$\log \frac{I_t^i}{I_{t-1}^i} = \lambda^i + \left(\beta_0 + \beta_1^i \chi_t^i + \beta_2 \alpha_t^i\right) \log \frac{\partial e_t^i}{e_{t-1}^i} + \beta_3 \log \frac{\partial y_t^i}{y_{t-1}^i} + \beta_4^i \log \frac{\partial TOT_t^i}{TOT_{t-1}^i} + \mu_t$$

(6.8)

where i is a country index y_t^i is real GDP, and TOT_t^i is the terms of trade.[9] In these regressions and in contrast to the way exchange rates were defined in Figure 6.1 and Table 6.2, an increase in the exchange rate represents a real depreciation of the domestic currency.

In general, the annual aggregate data for each country span 1970 through 1994, and include: real gross fixed capital formation (source: DRI); real GDP (source: IFS); the ratio of total exports to GDP (constructed from IFS data); the imported input share as the sum of machinery and equipment plus fuel imports to GDP (constructed from UNCTAD and IFS data); the real exchange rate (source: J. P. Morgan) and terms-of-trade series (source: InterAmerican Development Bank) are trade-weighted measures.[10]

The timing of data in the regressions incorporates the concept of agents being forward looking in assessing the future marginal profitability of capital, which would suggest using expected values of $t + 1$ data as the right-hand-side variables. However, since we also want to account for a one year time to build lag, this means that period t data instead of period $t + 1$ data are the appropriate series to include in the investment regressions.

Equation (6.8) posits that investment growth relative to GDP has a country-specific average. This average is influenced by movements in real exchange rates, in output growth, and the country's terms of trade. The effects of real exchange rate movements are posited to depend on country export shares and imported input usage in production. From equation (6.7), recall that the size of the respective coefficients on exchange rate terms introduced in this regression depends on various domestic and export market price elasticities. The coefficient on the exchange rate terms may differ across countries if there are relevant differences in institutional features of each country or in the pass-through elasticities on the goods sold by different countries. For example, all else equal, we expect countries with market power on exports to have a larger negative $\eta_{p^*,e}$ and consequently a smaller positive coefficient on the interacted export-share term in the regressions.

Various regression specifications are reported in Table 6.7. Some regression specifications for the pooled sample of Latin American countries allow for country dummy in the intercepts and/or in the exchange rate term that interacts with export share. Venezuelan investment growth levels and elasticities are the base against which the other five countries are compared. Intercept country dummies are intended to capture fixed country effects on average investment growth. The country dummies (DUM preceded by the first two letters of the country name) that interact with exchange rates are intended to proxy for differences in investment responsiveness to exchange rate movements. These latter differences may be due to different sensitivities of revenues to exchange rates and/or to investment to changes in profitability.[11]

The first lesson from the regression is that coefficients on the export share and imported input share terms, interacted with exchange rates, have the sign patterns predicted by the theory. These coefficients

Table 6.7. *Real gross fixed capital formation and exchange rates, pooled cross-country results for Latin America*

$$\log \frac{I_t^i}{I_{t-1}} = \lambda^i + (\beta_0 + \beta_1^i \chi_t + \beta_2 \alpha_t) \log \frac{\partial e_t^i}{e_{t-1}^i} + \beta_3 \log \frac{\partial y_t^i}{y_{t-1}^i} + \beta_4^i \log \frac{\partial TOT_t^i}{TOT_{t-1}^i} + \mu_t$$

	(1)	(2)	(3)	(4)	(5)	(6)
Constant	-0.068***	-0.070***	-0.072***	-0.067***	-0.070***	-0.072***
	(0.013)	(0.013)	(0.013)	(0.013)	(0.013)	(0.013)
Exchange rate	-0.445**	0.038	-0.219	-0.435***	0.108	-0.0198
	(0.190)	(0.463)	(0.199)	(0.191)	(0.465)	(0.201)
χ_i.exchange rate	3.212**	3.710**	3.980***	3.165*	3.670**	4.002**
	(1.648)	(1.887)	(1.621)	(1.727)	(1.943)	(1.692)
χ_i.ARDUM exchange rate		-2.574			-3.042	
		(4.144)			(4.163)	
χ_i.BRDUM exchange rate		-0.627			-1.028	
		(3.797)			(3.807)	
χ_i.CHDUM exchange rate		4.950***	5.211***		5.213***	5.520***
		(1.858)	(1.765)		(1.895)	(1.799)
χ_i.CODUM exchange rate		-2.353			-2.588	

	(1)	(2)	(3)	(4)	(5)	(6)
χ_i.MEDUM exchange rate		(2.935)			(2.940)	
		-2.133			-2.368	
		(2.639)			(2.680)	
α_i exchange rate	-0.220	-11.094*	-9.366*	-0.170	-11.922*	-9.834*
	(4.589)	(6.076)	(5.427)	(4.713)	(6.222)	(5.539)
GDP	2.736***	2.823**	2.855***	2.769***	2.869***	2.910***
	(0.229)	(0.233)	(0.226)	(0.239)	(0.244)	(0.236)
Terms of trade	-0.187***	-0.178***	-0.171***	-0.184***	-0.174***	-0.168***
	(0.063)	(0.062)	(0.061)	(0.064)	(0.063)	(0.062)
Lagged investment				0.007	0.012	0.002
				(0.065)	(0.064)	(0.063)
Number of observations	133	133	133	127	127	127
adjR2	0.526	0.543	0.553	0.533	0.553	0.563
D.W.	2.242	2.199	2.228	2.164	2.143	2.159

***, **, and * indicate statistical significance at the 1, 5, and 10 percent levels. Standard errors in parentheses. χ_i = export share; α_i = imported input share.

Comments: Although regressions results were generated for fixed effects entering through country-specific means of investment growth rates, these were not statistically significant and are excluded from the reported regressions. Ideally GDP growth should be replaced by an appropriate instrument. Efforts at finding this instrument have not yet been successful. Lagged GDP growth is a poor instrument and, generally, its inclusion in regressions instead or GDP growth removes the significance of the exchange rate and terms-of-trade variables.

also are statistically significant. Namely, the higher the export share, the greater the stimuli to investment of a real exchange rate depreciation. The higher the imported input share in production, the more that a depreciation depresses overall domestic investment activity. The elasticity of overall investment with respect to higher imported input costs is larger than the elasticity of response to pure revenue changes.

Cross-country differences exist in the interacted coefficients regarding export revenue implications. The results do not support the hypothesis that Latin American countries with concentrated production are relatively more insulated from exchange rate movements. In fact, the results show that investments in countries with more concentrated export activity have higher sensitivity to exchange rate movements, even after one controls for the level of a country's exports at any point in time. Chile, with its important role in the copper market, and Venezuela, with its major petroleum exports, are the two countries with the largest estimated parameters for the interacted export share/exchange rate terms in the investment equation.

To consider the overall partial equilibrium correlation between increased depreciation rates and investment rates, we sum the coefficient on the noninteracted exchange with the coefficients on the interacted export share (adjusted for country dummies) and imported input share terms, where each of these interacted coefficients is multiplied by country-specific information on export and imported input shares. For our exposition we use the parameters from regression (2) reported in Table 6.7 and the share data for 1990 for each country.

According to these numbers, a 10 percent increase in the real rate of depreciation will raise the investment rate by 9 percent in Chile and by approximately 7 percent in Venezuela.[12] If imported input use had been zero in these countries, the respective effects would have been 24 percent and 14 percent respectively. For Argentina and Brazil, the net effect of the depreciation on investment appears to be negligible. For Colombia and Mexico, the negative effect of a real depreciation through the imported input channels actually appears to outweigh the positive revenue effect of the depreciation. In these countries, an increase in the real depreciation rate slows the rate of investment by about 2.5 percent.

Finally, it is worth pointing out that the regressions indicate strong accelerator forces driving investment rates in Latin America. Given that exchange rate changes also are introduced into the regressions, terms-of-trade improvements have a residual and statistically significant negative effect on investment activity.

V Concluding remarks

Real exchange rate movements can have important implications for export revenues in any country. These implications may be magnified for developing countries that are unable to pass some of these exchange rate changes through to prices in their export markets. Implications for net marginal profitability and investment also depend on the cost side of the producer balance sheet. In Latin America, although production and export activity are often concentrated, this concentration is frequently accompanied by relatively high imported input use. This implies that cost and revenue exposure to exchange rates provide some offset of exchange rate risk, and can mitigate some of the tendency for real exchange rate movements to contribute to investment and output volatility. This form of diversified exposure could be quite important for those Latin American countries that experience deep and repeated cycles in real exchange rates. Without diversification on the producer balance sheet, real exchange rate cycles would be associated with even greater cycles in real investment activity.

We observe that real depreciations stimulate investment in relation to export market exposure, with the effects strongest for Chile and Venezuela, and depress investment in relation to imported input reliance. If the investment data were available for specific industrial sectors, the magnitude and distributional consequences would be much more pronounced. These developing country findings concur with results for industrialized countries, and most specifically with Japan and the United States (Campa and Goldberg 1996). For industrialized countries the effects of exchange rates are magnified for low markup sectors, that is, ones that rely more heavily on cash flow and retained earnings than external loans for financing investment spending. For developing countries, which on balance rely more uniformly on retained earnings, the magnified effects of exchange rate movements may be manifested across the board.

The arguments put forth in this essay are part of a rich area for future research that has its early roots in work by Peter Kenen on exchange rate volatility and trade.[13] When thinking about exchange rate policy and the choice of an exchange rate regime, we need a better understanding of why and how much exchange rates matter for real economic activity. The theme of the present essay[14] is part of a research agenda with this intent.

In both international and development economics there are many useful ways to apply microeconomic insights to macroeconomic issues. Investment and employment decisions depend, presumably, on optimizing the behavior of producers. Different markets have differing degrees of market power in sales and in purchasing inputs. This degree of market power colors responses to international stimuli to producers, regardless of whether these stimuli are from exchange rates, tariffs, aggregate demand changes, or commodity price movements. As a consequence, there will be distinct cross-country as well as intracountry sectoral effects of the stimuli. Future research may start from this vantage point to document empirically the significant real implications of exchange rates and other macroeconomic variables. With such evidence in hand, policy decisions for developing and industrialized countries may be better informed.

APPENDIX

Exchange rate pass-through elasticities under alternative modes of competition

The predicted exchange rate pass-through elasticities depend on the competitive structure of the home and foreign markets for the good, which determine $\eta_{p,e}$ and $\eta_{p^*,e}$ and the market for the imported input good, which determines $\eta_{ew^*,e} > 0$.[15] Under Dixit–Stiglitz monopolistic competition, markups are constant and independent of exchange rate changes. Assuming inputs into production are domestically supplied at exogenous domestic currency wages, domestic prices and quantities supplied by domestic producers are unchanged by a depreciation, i.e., $\eta_{p,e} = 0$. The domestic currency price of exports also remains unchanged, so the foreign currency price falls to offset the domestic currency depreciation, i.e., $\eta_{p^*,e} = -1$.

If the monopolistic competitor faces variable marginal costs, the exchange-rate pass-through elasticities depend on the effects on marginal costs of changes in the total production for domestic and foreign markets. If imported input costs rise with depreciation, i.e., if $\eta_{ew^*,e} > 0$, then both domestic and export price elasticities rise accordingly.

Under static Cournot competition, markups on exported goods rise when the domestic currency depreciates. The domestic producer can undercut foreign competition abroad by lowering the sale price in foreign currency terms at the same time that the domestic currency price of the export has risen. The markup increase is negatively related to the degree of foreign competition in the export market. In domestic markets the pass-through coefficient depends on the pricing behavior of foreign suppliers and on local import competition.

Static models	$\eta_{p,e}$	$\eta_{p^*,e}$	$\eta_{ew^*,e}$
Perfect competition	0	0	0
Monopolistic competition	0	−1	$0 < \eta_{ew^*} < 1$
Cournot	$0 < \eta_{p,e} < 1$	$-1 < \eta_{p^*,e} < 0$	$0 < \eta_{ew^*,e} < 1$

NOTES

1. Earlier studies of investment and growth in Latin America include Cardosa (1991) and Corbo and Rojas (1995).
2. My analysis examines only these six countries because of their size and the availability of appropriate data.
3. The IADB study attempts to identify that portion of exchange rate volatility that influences growth, even after one controls for the effects on growth of monetary and fiscal policy volatility. This approach does not fully isolate "exogenous" exchange rate volatility, since measured volatility may be induced by forward-looking agents who anticipate future changes in fiscal and monetary policy. In this sense, movements in real exchange rates may be picking up expected inflation or fiscal expenditures. The depressing effect of exchange rate volatility per se, i.e., exogenous to policy volatility, may be overstated.
4. $\eta_t = p_t/p_t'q_t$ and $\eta_t^* = p_t^*/p_t^{*'}q_t^*$. The markups in each market are equal to price over marginal cost.
5. The parameters of the investment cost function are assumed to be independent of the real exchange rate.
6. Since we will not be able to observe distinct markups for sales in domestic and foreign markets, I assume these markups are identical to the average markup in deriving this final expression.
7. See theoretical derivations by Dornbusch (1987) and Marston (1990, 1996). The size of this price elasticity is presented in the Appendix; this coefficient will be greatest under conditions of Cournot competition in domestic markets.
8. Total expenditure on domestically supplied inputs, mainly labor, is treated as insensitive to exchange rate movements.
9. Ideally, real interest rates also should be included in this regression. For Latin American countries this inclusion is stymied by data limitations.
10. The terms-of-trade series are defined as the ratio of the export unit value index to the import unit value index. The terms of trade need not be closely related to real exchange rate movements. Indeed, annual data show that changes in these series are negatively correlated for Argentina, Chile, and Mexico, positively correlated for Brazil and Venezuela, and near zero for Colombia. In all cases, none of the correlation coefficients exceed 0.40 in absolute value. Due to data limitations, we run our regressions for the full sample without the interest rate measures, which in general are not consistently available prior to the mid-1980s.
11. I also ran supplementary regressions with individual country data only, rather than the stacked group of countries. These latter regression results (not reported) give a qualitatively similar set of results on exchange rate implications for investment. However, these latter regressions have very few degrees of freedom since the data sample is relatively short (at most 24 years of annual data).
12. My results for Chile contrast with those in Solimano's (1992) study of the

determinants of quarterly aggregate investment in Chile between 1977 and 1987. He concluded that investment is sensitive to the estimated average profitability of capital. The profitability of capital, however, is estimated to be negatively and significantly correlated with real depreciation of the Chilean currency.

13. See, for example, Kenen (1979) and Kenen and Rodrik (1986).

14. The present essay is part of a series of papers by the author on quantifying these real implications. See Goldberg (1993), Campa and Goldberg (1995, 1996, 1997), and Goldberg and Kolstad (1995).

15. See Dornbusch (1987) and Marston (1990, 1996). This exposition is based on Campa and Goldberg (1996a).

REFERENCES

Campa, J., and L. Goldberg (1995). "Investment, Exchange Rates and External Exposure," *Journal of International Economics* 38 (May), 297–320.

Campa, J., and L. Goldberg (1996). "Investment, Pass-through, and Exchange Rates: A Cross Country Comparison" Federal Reserve Bank of New York Staff Repor #14.

Campa J., and L. Goldberg (1997). "The Evolving External Orientation of Manufacturing Industries: Evidence from Four Countries," Federal Reserve Bank of New York, *Economic Policy Review*.

Cardosa, E. (1991). "Capital Formation in Latin America." NBER working paper #3616 (Cambridge, MA).

Corbo, Vittorio, and Patricio Rojas (1995). "Exchange Rate Volatility, Investment, and Growth: Some New Evidence," unpublished manuscript (September).

deGregorio, Jose (1992). "Economic Growth in Latin America," *Journal of Development Economics* 39, 59–84.

Dornbusch, R. (1987). "Exchange Rates and Prices," *American Economic Review* 77 (March), 93–106.

Edwards, S. (1991). "Trade Orientation, Distortions, and Growth in Developing Countries." NBER working paper #3716 (Cambridge, MA).

Goldberg, L. (1993). "Exchange Rates and Investment in United States Industry "*Review of Economics and Statistics* 75(4) (November), pp. 575–88.

Goldberg, L., and C. Kolstad (1995). "Foreign Direct Investment, Exchange Rate Variability, and Demand Uncertainty," *International Economic Review* 36(4) (May).

Inter-American Development Bank (1995). *Macroeconomic Volatility in Latin America: Causes, Consequences and Policies to Assure Stability*. Washington, DC: Inter-American Bank.

Kenen, P. B. (1994). "Ways to Reform Exchange-Rate Arrangements." In *Bretton Woods: Looking to the Future*, pp. c-13 to c-20. Washington, DC: Bretton Woods Commission.

Kenen P. B. (1979). "Exchange Rate Instability: Measurement and Implications," International Finance Section, Research Memorandum, Princeton University.

Kenen, P. B., and Dani Rodrik (1986). "Measuring and Analyzing the Effects of Short-Term Volatility in Real Exchange Rates," *Review of Economics and Statistic*, 311–15.

Marston, R. (1990). "Pricing to Market in Japanese Manufacturing," *Journal of International Economics* 29 (November), 217–236.

Marston, R. (1996). "The Effects of Industry Structure on Economic Exposure." NBER working paper #5518 (March). (Cambrige, MA).

Solimano, A. (1992). "How Private Investment Reacts to Changing Macroeconomic Conditions: The Case of Chile in the 1980s." In A. Chhibber, M. Dailami, and N. Shafik eds., *Reviving Private Investment in Developing Countries*. Amsterdam: North-Holland.

CHAPTER 7

Optimum currency areas and exchange rate volatility: Theory and evidence compared

Tamim Bayoumi and Barry Eichengreen

I Introduction

One of the limitations of the literature on optimum currency areas, a topic to which Peter Kenen so importantly contributed, has always been the difficulty of confronting theory with evidence. We have at best limited information on the symmetry of shocks, the sectoral distribution of employment, the mobility of labor, the volume of interregional trade, and the other variables assumed to drive the decision of whether to form a monetary union (Mundell 1961; McKinnon 1963; Kenen 1969). Precisely because they are monetary unions, few national states gather data with which to test the predictions of optimum currency area (OCA) theory. It is not hard to see why: one can imagine the political problems that would arise were it discovered, for example, that New York runs a trade deficit with the rest of the United States.

If the theory of optimum currency areas does in fact possess significant explanatory power, then the same factors that influence monetary arrangements within countries should also govern arrangements between them. In the same way that two regions should form a monetary union if they experience similar disturbances, factors of production flow freely between them, and they trade heavily with one another, we should expect to see two countries that maintain separate currencies follow different exchange-rate-management practices depending on whether these conditions are or are not met. The closer two countries are to satisfying the criteria for an optimum currency area, in other words, the more likely they are to have limited currency fluctuations with one another. Indeed, one of the motivations of the early contributors to the literature on optimum currency areas was a contemporary debate (viz. Friedman 1953) about appropriate exchange rate arrangements for different types of countries.

184

It is surprising, therefore, that few scholars have systematically applied the OCA literature to the question of countries' choice of exchange rate regime. Two exceptions are Tower and Willett (1976) and Wickham (1985). But although these authors discuss the implications of OCA theory for the choice of exchange rate regime, they do not apply it in a systematic, econometric manner.[1] Still, it is fair to say that most empirical work on this subject, especially recent studies, take their cue from very different considerations, such as the susceptibility of countries to inflationary pressures, the depth of their financial markets, and their exposure to international capital flows.[2]

Our goal in this essay is to weave together these separate strands of literature. We start by asking whether the variables to which the theory of optimum currency areas directs attention help to explain the behavior of the real and nominal exchange rates. We then extend our treatment to incorporate variables suggested by other approaches and ask whether the explanatory power of the OCA approach survives this generalization.

According to Goodhart, "evidence . . . suggests that the theory of optimum currency areas has relatively little predictive power" (1995, p. 452). Goodhart points to countries that based on their size, openness, and the correlation of their business cycles with those of their neighbors might be predicted to share a common currency, but do not. His can fairly be regarded as the consensus view. Most observers would dismiss OCA theory when attempting to explain countries' choice of exchange rate regime.[3]

In the analysis that follows we suggest that this dismissal of the empirical implications of the theory of optimal currency areas is too quick. In fact, the variables to which it points have economically important and statistically significant effects on exchange rate behavior when they are analyzed in a framework that incorporates systemic factors – from a perspective that acknowledges that the behavior of the exchange rate can involve groups of governments and that it is influenced by the structure and incentives provided by the broader international system. In other words, the choice of exchange rate regime cannot be understood as a unilateral decision.

Our analysis has several features that distinguish it from most of the previous literature, in addition to its emphasis on the theory of optimum currency areas. First, instead of basing our analysis on the relatively judgmental categorization of exchange rate arrangements utilized in most previous studies, we analyze the determinants of real and nominal exchange rate variability.[4] The variability of real and nominal exchange rates is itself the outcome of the choice of exchange rate regime and as such should contain information about the decision of what arrangement to adopt. Actual exchange rate behavior may in fact convey more information about underlying economic determinants than the putative exchange rate regime. Countries not only have to adopt an exchange rate regime; they also have to maintain it. To put it another way, the limited-dependent variable on which most previous investigators focus does not make use of all the information available in the variability of the exchange rate.

Second, we employ data for the industrial countries rather than the developing world. Since the developing countries are more heterogeneous, the assumption of a common structure linking country characteristics to exchange rate variability is more problematic. Moreover, the industrial countries have tended to maintain more liberal external regimes and have thus been more dependent on market forces in determining their international economic policies. Finally, the choice of exchange rate regime has gained new urgency in the industrial world in the wake of the crisis in the European Monetary System and the debate over European monetary unification. Any light that can be shed on the desirability of different European countries pegging their exchange rates and joining their neighbors in a monetary union would be particularly valuable at this juncture.

Third, as already alluded to, we examine countries' choice of exchange rate regime in a framework that allows us to consider systemic as well as country-specific factors. Previous work on this issue has proceeded country by country, ignoring changes in the structure of the international system and the implications of policy in neighboring countries. For example, in the Bretton Woods period when the major currencies were pegged, it made little difference from the point of view of an individual country whether to peg to one reserve currency or another, since the rates between them varied so little. But once the dollar and DM began to float against one another, pegging to the DM meant floating against the dollar, and vice versa, complicating efforts to stabilize exchange rates. In contrast to previous work, we take into account the entire network of bilateral exchange rate arrangements and not just individual country conditions when modeling the choice of exchange rate regime.

Fourth, as anticipated by the previous point, we adopt a historical perspective on the choice of exchange rate regime. We compare exchange rate behavior under Bretton Woods, during the transition to generalized floating in the 1970s, and in the 1980s and 1990s when that transition was largely complete. The behavior of real and nominal exchange rates turns out to be related to our explanatory variables differently in these different historical periods, suggesting that the evolution of the broader system has been critically important for decision making at the country level. This observation reinforces the implications of our analysis of systemic factors. It suggests that countries have been moving toward greater exchange rate flexibility not just because of the increasing difficulty of defending pegged rates (as emphasized by Kenen 1988, Crockett 1994, and Eichengreen 1995, among others) but also because fluctuations between the anchor currencies have diminished the attractiveness of any peg. Collectively, these individual decisions, made in the national self-interest in response to the greater flexibility of exchange rates elsewhere in the world, have accelerated the evolution of the international monetary system in the direction of generalized floating.

II The literature on choice of exchange rate regime

The empirical literature on the choice of exchange rate regime is relatively limited. In part this reflects the difficulty of measuring regime type and modeling a choice between discrete alternatives. The International Monetary Fund distinguishes countries that peg to an individual currency, countries that peg to the SDR or to another currency composite, and countries whose currencies exhibit limited flexibility vis-à-vis another individual currency, as well as cooperative arrangements, like the European Monetary System, that involve elements of both pegging and floating, currencies that are adjusted according to an explicit set of indicators, countries with managed floating rates, and countries with independent floating currencies (see Table 7.1). These are the data on which most previous studies are based.

This classification is problematic on several counts. The category "pegged to a single currency" includes pegs to currencies as disparate as the U.S. dollar, the French franc, and the Russian ruble, reference currencies that hardly offer the same combinations of stability and flexibility to governments deciding whether to peg or to float. It is not clear whether intermediate arrangements have more in common with pegged or floating rates. And it is not always clear what criteria are used to place countries in particular categories.

Even if one is prepared to accept these data, analyzing them is not straightforward. Weil (1983) and Bosco (1987) collapse the IMF data into two categories: pegged- and floating-rate regimes. Other authors distinguish countries pegging to a single currency, those pegging to a basket, and those with a flexible exchange rate, but model the choice between each pair using binomial techniques. This will be inappropriate insofar as countries choose simultaneously between the three options.

Table 7.1 *Exchange rate arrangements, 1978–1995*

	1978	1984	1995
Pegged	*94*	*93*	*67*
U.S. dollar	40	34	23
French franc	14	13	14
Other currency	8	5	3
SDR	12	11	3
Other composite	20	30	20
Limited flexibility	*6*	*15*	*14*
Versus a single currency	n.a.	7	4
Cooperative arrangement	6	8	10
More flexible	*30*[a]	*38*	*98*
Adjusted by indicators	5	6	3
Managed float	n.a.	21	36
Independent float	n.a.	11	59
Total	130	146	179

[a] Includes limited flexibility against another currency.
Source: 1MF, *International Financial Statistics*, various issues.

Some authors (e.g., Savvides 1990, 1993) have followed Dreyer's (1978) and Melvin's (1985) tripartite categorization but argue that the selection of an exchange rate regime should be thought of not as a discrete choice between three options but rather as a two-stage decision process: a first decision of whether to peg or adopt a more flexible exchange-rate arrangement, and, if the choice is made to peg rather than float, the choice between pegging to a single currency or a basket. Clearly, there is no single correct way to model what is potentially a hierarchy of choices. These problems lead us to analyze instead the determinants of what can be thought of as the reduced-form outcome of this process, namely the level of exchange rate variability.

One thing for which it is impossible to criticize these studies is restricting their attention to a limited range of explanatory variables.[5] In a sense, the problem posed by the literature is the opposite: that the range of independent variables is so broad as to make it difficult to distill empirical implications. Most studies have considered country size, while offering a variety of different justifications for its inclusion. Heller (1978) and Weil (1983), for example, predict that large countries will be more inclined to float on the grounds that they are not forced to take the world market prices of traded goods as given. Other authors follow Kenen in emphasizing the diversity of large-country employment portfolios. Holden, Holden, and Suss (1979) and Savvides (1993) consider the level of economic development, arguing that less-developed countries will shun flexible rates because of the unavailability of domestic substitutes for imported goods, which leaves only limited scope for substituting domestic and foreign goods. They consider the geographical concentration of exports and imports, arguing that countries whose trade is concentrated with a relatively small number of partners will have a particularly strong incentive to peg. Dreyer (1978) emphasizes the commodity diversification of exports, providing some evidence that high export diversification is associated with policies to limit exchange rate flexibility. McKinnon (1979) argues that links between domestic and foreign financial markets enhance the attractiveness of floating – a country with exchange controls and restrictions on international payments will be inclined to limit currency fluctuations – whereas Heller argues the opposite: that countries with highly integrated capital markets will prefer to peg.[6] Corden (1972) and Melvin (1985) emphasize differences in inflation rates, arguing that countries that prefer different positions on the Phillips Curve will tend to float. Melvin argues further that the larger are domestic monetary shocks, the greater the incentive for a country to peg its currency. All of these authors consider openness, with all of them but Savvides (1990) arguing that it strengthens the desire to peg.

The problem for interpretation is similar to that identified by Levine and Renelt (1992) in their analysis of cross-country growth regressions: given multicolinearity among variables and the sensitivity of estimates to specification, there may exist few robust correlations. The nearest approximation to their study in the exchange-rate-regime context is Honkapohja and Pikkarainen (1992): these authors conclude that country size and export diversification, à la Kenen, are two of the few robust predictors of regime choice.

In a sense, the problem for interpretation is that few authors explicitly link theory to evidence. Theories of the choice of exchange rate regime, if adequately elaborated, may point to explanatory variables that matter as a group but whose individual significance is disguised by multicollinearity. A few useful efforts have been made to derive empirical implications from theory. Thus, Savvides links his econometric specification to the literature on optimum currency areas. Melvin builds on the Mundell–Fleming model, deriving a specification with two sets of variables: measures of foreign price disturbances (which make exchange rate flexibility more attractive) and measures of domestic monetary disturbances (which encourage pegging). Branson and Katseli (1981) argue that modern models of international finance yield two testable hypotheses: the more open the goods markets in an economy the less likely it is that floating will be attractive, while the more extensive the integration of domestic and foreign capital markets the greater the benefits of a floating rate. Sachs (1995), drawing on the recent literature on inflation stabilization, argues that pegged exchange rates will be valued as a nominal anchor by countries with histories of high inflation but that most other economies will wish to float in order to retain the freedom to intervene in domestic financial markets. Eichengreen (1995) suggests extending to exchange-rate behavior political-economy models linking governmental instability and inflation, and with Simmons provides some evidence on the relationship for an earlier period of floating (Eichengreen and Simmons 1995).

We now attempt to operationalize these concepts, taking as our point of departure the theory of optimum currency areas.

III A preliminary look at the data

As explained above, we depart from previous studies by focusing on the variability of real and nominal exchange rates rather than analyzing taxonomies of the exchange-rate regime. Some properties of the data we analyze are summarized in Tables 7.2–7.4. These display the variability of nominal bilateral exchange rates for the countries in our sample separately for three decades: 1963–72, 1973–82, and 1983–92.[7] Exchange rate variability is defined as the standard deviation of the change in the logarithm of the nominal year-end bilateral exchange rate.[8] To facilitate comparison, entries have been shaded to highlight periods and areas of high volatility. Heavily shaded observations indicate exchange rate variability in excess of 8 percent per annum, while lightly shaded entries indicate moderate volatility (in the 4 to 8 percent range), and unshaded entries are for volatility of less than 4 percent.

At one level, the patterns are familiar: the increase in exchange rate variability between the 1960s and 1970s is one of the best-known facts in the literature on open-economy macroeconomics. By comparison, differences in the behavior of different bilateral rates have been less thoroughly considered and are less well understood. It is this combination of differences in exchange rate behavior over time and across countries that provides the variation needed to identify both country-specific and systemic factors in the choice of exchange rate regime. It is worth starting, therefore, by reviewing the pattern of bilateral exchange rate variability in our different historical periods.

Table 7.2. *The Variability of Nominal Exchange Rates in the 1960s*

	US	JA	GR	FR	IT	UK	CA	AS	AU	BE	DE	FI	GC	IR	NT	NZ	NO	PO	SP	SW
US	0.046																			
JA	0.036	0.030																		
GR	0.042	0.027	0.047																	
FR	0.019	0.027	0.025	0.028																
IT	0.046	0.054	0.047	0.059	0.045															
UK	0.016	0.042	0.025	0.045	0.020	0.045														
CA	0.016	0.030	0.026	0.030	0.004	0.044	0.017													
AS	0.026	0.022	0.023	0.027	0.011	0.045	0.022	0.012												
AU	0.034	0.012	0.025	0.024	0.015	0.048	0.032	0.018	0.012											
BE	0.034	0.032	0.030	0.039	0.024	0.023	0.032	0.025	0.024	0.025										
DE	0.034	0.032	0.030	0.039	0.024	0.023	0.032	0.032	0.024	0.025	0.025									
FI	0.065	0.071	0.063	0.077	0.064	0.024	0.063	0.063	0.025	0.066	0.034	0.043								
GC	0.000	0.036	0.036	0.042	0.019	0.046	0.016	0.016	0.026	0.034	0.034	0.065	0.046							
IR	0.046	0.054	0.047	0.059	0.045	0.000	0.045	0.044	0.045	0.048	0.023	0.059	0.024	0.046						
NT	0.029	0.023	0.025	0.025	0.011	0.046	0.026	0.013	0.006	0.006	0.024	0.064	0.029	0.029	0.046					
NZ	0.066	0.065	0.061	0.072	0.062	0.020	0.064	0.062	0.061	0.062	0.038	0.020	0.066	0.020	0.020	0.061				
NO	0.022	0.024	0.024	0.027	0.002	0.045	0.021	0.006	0.009	0.013	0.023	0.064	0.022	0.044	0.008	0.062	0.061			
PO	0.015	0.031	0.026	0.031	0.005	0.044	0.016	0.001	0.012	0.019	0.025	0.063	0.015	0.044	0.014	0.023	0.002	0.007		
SP	0.050	0.042	0.041	0.052	0.041	0.018	0.047	0.042	0.040	0.039	0.018	0.030	0.050	0.018	0.039	0.023	0.040	0.002	0.009	
SW	0.023	0.023	0.024	0.027	0.004	0.045	0.023	0.007	0.007	0.011	0.024	0.064	0.023	0.045	0.008	0.061	0.061	0.002	0.016	0.040
SZ	0.029	0.024	0.024	0.029	0.016	0.045	0.023	0.016	0.005	0.016	0.026	0.064	0.029	0.045	0.010	0.061	0.061	0.014	0.016	0.041

Key: US = United States; JA = Japan; GR = Germany; FR = France; IT = Italy; UK = United Kingdom; CA = Canada; AS = Australia; AU = Austria; BE = Belgium; DE = Denmark; FI = Finland; GC = Greece; IR = Ireland; NT = The Netherlands; NZ = New Zealand; NO = Norway; PO = Portugal; SP = Spain; SW = Sweden; SZ = Switzerland.

Table 7.3. The Variability of Nominal Exchange Rates in the 1970s

	US	JA	GR	FR	IT	UK	CA	AS	AU	BE	DE	FI	GC	IR	NT	NZ	NO	PO	SP	SW
US	0.106																			
JA	0.114	0.112																		
GR	0.129	0.126	0.056																	
FR	0.114	0.123	0.058	0.049																
IT	0.108	0.123	0.096	0.095	0.058															
UK	0.035	0.129	0.127	0.143	0.133	0.125														
CA	0.087	0.103	0.114	0.125	0.121	0.111	0.087													
AS	0.108	0.114	0.052	0.047	0.052	0.090	0.097	0.111												
AU	0.128	0.115	0.014	0.052	0.063	0.121	0.111	0.125	0.040											
BE	0.113	0.112	0.041	0.047	0.065	0.097	0.141	0.111	0.030	0.038										
DE	0.111	0.111	0.029	0.047	0.071	0.105	0.125	0.111	0.062	0.080	0.067									
FI	0.073	0.123	0.071	0.075	0.069	0.082	0.076	0.032	0.039	0.054	0.043	0.064								
GC	0.095	0.107	0.040	0.077	0.036	0.094	0.109	0.107	0.062	0.075	0.080	0.077	0.068							
IR	0.109	0.120	0.066	0.078	0.051	0.040	0.127	0.119	0.009	0.043	0.033	0.066	0.037	0.060						
NT	0.109	0.115	0.015	0.056	0.093	0.091	0.123	0.116	0.084	0.099	0.092	0.086	0.075	0.083	0.086					
NZ	0.103	0.100	0.084	0.112	0.068	0.068	0.115	0.065	0.044	0.062	0.048	0.030	0.048	0.079	0.050	0.079				
NO	0.084	0.114	0.054	0.064	0.091	0.091	0.091	0.036	0.101	0.113	0.097	0.066	0.110	0.124	0.108	0.108	0.069			
PO	0.114	0.150	0.109	0.097	0.123	0.123	0.108	0.083	0.069	0.081	0.065	0.065	0.072	0.079	0.071	0.065	0.100	0.088		
SP	0.123	0.151	0.072	0.071	0.070	0.094	0.128	0.112	0.069	0.081	0.065	0.065	0.072	0.079	0.071	0.065	0.035	0.071	0.065	
SW	0.100	0.122	0.067	0.054	0.071	0.093	0.105	0.100	0.059	0.057	0.053	0.040	0.065	0.065	0.087	0.065	0.100	0.068	0.071	0.093
SZ	0.125	0.102	0.057	0.072	0.080	0.116	0.140	0.125	0.061	0.069	0.054	0.100	0.073	0.088	0.059	0.106	0.087	0.123	0.097	0.093

Key: US = United States; JA = Japan; GR = Germany; FR = France; IT = Italy; UK = United Kingdom; CA = Canada; AS = Australia; AU = Austria; BE = Belgium; DE = Denmark; FI = Finland; GC = Greece; IR = Ireland; NT = The Netherlands; NZ = New Zealand; NO = Norway; PO = Portugal; SP = Spain; SW = Sweden; SZ = Switzerland.

Table 7.4. The variability of nominal exchange rates in the 1980s

	US	JA	GR	FR	IT	UK	CA	AS	AU	BE	DE	FI	GC	IR	NT	NZ	NO	PO	SP	SW
US																				
JA	0.121																			
GR	0.132	0.094																		
FR	0.133	0.111	0.033																	
IT	0.126	0.103	0.025	0.028																
UK	0.099	0.098	0.066	0.058	0.057															
CA	0.045	0.126	0.134	0.136	0.124	0.092														
AS	0.092	0.138	0.145	0.145	0.132	0.103	0.065													
AU	0.132	0.094	0.001	0.033	0.026	0.066	0.134	0.145												
BE	0.136	0.106	0.021	0.015	0.022	0.061	0.137	0.146	0.021											
DE	0.131	0.104	0.018	0.019	0.025	0.059	0.133	0.145	0.018	0.010										
FI	0.114	0.109	0.067	0.065	0.055	0.054	0.106	0.116	0.067	0.064	0.064									
GC	0.112	0.127	0.076	0.062	0.062	0.045	0.102	0.100	0.076	0.067	0.067	0.073								
IR	0.123	0.106	0.038	0.017	0.031	0.049	0.125	0.137	0.038	0.027	0.025	0.067	0.059							
NT	0.135	0.096	0.006	0.029	0.024	0.065	0.136	0.146	0.005	0.017	0.015	0.025	0.063	0.074						
NZ	0.101	0.098	0.090	0.094	0.082	0.046	0.077	0.078	0.090	0.092	0.090	0.073	0.067	0.063	0.036					
NO	0.093	0.098	0.053	0.045	0.044	0.030	0.094	0.105	0.053	0.049	0.046	0.058	0.039	0.074	0.088	0.062				
PO	0.159	0.150	0.094	0.069	0.080	0.083	0.154	0.148	0.094	0.078	0.083	0.109	0.061	0.065	0.090	0.111	0.079			
SP	0.136	0.133	0.079	0.054	0.061	0.058	0.131	0.126	0.078	0.062	0.068	0.061	0.052	0.055	0.075	0.090	0.057	0.058		
SW	0.110	0.102	0.061	0.044	0.050	0.040	0.112	0.114	0.061	0.050	0.053	0.054	0.049	0.042	0.060	0.076	0.033	0.072	0.038	
SZ	0.140	0.096	0.020	0.048	0.038	0.075	0.140	0.152	0.020	0.035	0.031	0.071	0.089	0.051	0.023	0.096	0.067	0.109	0.091	0.1

Key: US = United States; JA = Japan; GR = Germany; FR = France; IT = Italy; UK = United Kingdom; CA = Canada; AS = Australia; AU = Austria; BE = Belgium; DE = Denmark; FI = Finland; GC = Greece; IR = Ireland; NT = The Netherlands; NZ = New Zealand; NO = Norway; PO = Portugal; SP = Spain; SW = Sweden; SZ = Switzerland.

In the 1960s (Table 7.2) there are no heavily shaded entries, all of the bilateral rates in our sample displaying nominal volatility of less than 8 percent per annum. Indeed, most are below 4 percent, reflecting the success with which the Bretton Woods system delivered exchange rate stability. The main exceptions are the United Kingdom, which experienced repeated exchange-market difficulties before being forced to devalue in 1967, and certain countries whose economies were linked to it, such as Ireland and New Zealand.[9] The tendency for these countries to follow the U.K. in financial affairs is evident in the low variability of exchange rates within the group.

That the 1970s were different is evident from Table 7.3. In this period, the United Kingdom, the United States, Japan, Canada, Australia, and New Zealand have highly variable exchange rates against virtually every country in the sample; in comparison, the exchange rates of the Continental European countries are relatively stable against one another. Exceptions are Ireland and Portugal, the first of which behaves "Continentally," the second of which behaves more like the United Kingdom than a Continental European country.

These patterns suggest that the transitional exchange rate arrangement of the 1970s, the European Snake, had a noticeable impact on currency volatility. The founding members of the Snake (Belgium, France, Germany, Italy, Luxembourg, the Netherlands) display lower-than-average variability vis-à-vis one another. (Denmark and the United Kingdom, with Ireland as part of the U.K. currency area, joined less than a week after the creation of the Snake; Norway followed within a month.) That the United Kingdom and Italy are exceptions to the rule of exchange rate stability among Snake members is not surprising in light of the fact that the former withdrew after less than a month and the latter followed after fewer than ten months of participation. Portugal, of course, was never a member of the Snake, and Ireland followed sterling out of the system. Still, the decision of whether to participate in the Snake provides a less-than-complete explanation for exchange-rate variability in this period (in addition to begging the question of why countries chose to participate). Among the patterns that are not so easily explained by this institutional arrangement are that Germany had lower exchange rate variability vis-à-vis her immediate neighbors Austria, Denmark, and Holland than against the rest of Continental Europe, and that the same is true of France vis-à-vis Belgium, Denmark, and Italy.

In the 1980s (Table 7.4), the non-Europeans continue to display high levels of currency variability. In contrast, the core members of the Exchange Rate Mechanism (ERM) of the European Monetary System – Germany, France, Italy, Belgium, Denmark, Ireland, and the Netherlands – display low volatility not just against one another but also vis-à-vis the rest of the world. Austria and Switzerland, neither of which belonged to the European Community nor participated in the ERM but which maintained close economic relations with its core members, display similarly low levels of currency volatility. The other European countries in the sample, including the United Kingdom, occupy middling positions with respect to both the European "core" and one another.

Overall, Tables 7.2–7.4 convey an impression of movement from a system of pegged exchange rates characterized by uniform behavior across countries through a transitional period in the 1970s to a new system characterized by floating between the major reserve currencies but a stable European core in the 1980s. This European core is similar to, but not indentical with, the EC. It includes Switzerland and Austria, neither of which joined the EC during the sample period, but excludes the United Kingdom and Spain.

Sophisticated inferences cannot be drawn from simple correlations. Still, the contrasts in Tables 7.2 through 7.4 suggest that global and regional monetary arrangements (the Bretton Woods System, the Snake, and the European Monetary System) and not merely individual country characteristics have had important implications for individual countries' choice of exchange rate regime. A country-by-country analysis of the choice of regime may be misleading insofar as it neglects their role.

The implications for the theory of optimum currency areas are less clear. One the one hand, the pronounced changes in the pattern of exchange rate volatility in Tables 7.2 through 7.4 are difficult to reconcile with a theory that attributes the choice of regime to economic characteristics that change only gradually. On the other hand, the fact that some countries (the United Kingdom, for example) display consistently high volatility while others (like Germany) are at the opposite end of the spectrum may be explicable in part by the slowly evolving structural variables to which this theory points.

IV Optimum currency area theory and exchange rate behavior

The theory of optimum currency areas focuses on characteristics which make a currency union either more or less desirable across regions or countries.[10] The most important of these characteristics are the relative importance of asymmetric disturbances to real output, the level of trade linkages, the usefulness of money for domestic transactions, the degree of labor mobility, and the level of automatic stabilizers provided by federal governments. Although the last two characteristics are clearly important for behavior across regions within a country, they have not been important factors in responding to shocks across different countries, at least over our historical period. As a result, our empirical work focuses on capturing the first three factors.

We measure asymmetric output disturbances as the standard deviation of the change in the log of relative output in the two countries. Thus, for countries in which business cycles are symmetric and national outputs move together, the value of this measure will be small.[11] The dissimilarity of the commodity composition of the exports of the two countries is included as another proxy for the asymmetry of shocks on the grounds that industry-specific shocks will be more symmetric when two countries have a revealed comparative advantage in the same export industries. To construct this variable we collected data on the shares of manufactured goods, food, and minerals in total merchandise trade for each country.[12] The dissimilarity of the commodity composition of two countries' exports was then defined as the sum of the absolute values of the differences in each share (with higher values indicating less similarity in the composition of commodity exports between the two countries).

We measure the importance of trade linkages by using data in bilateral trade. Since our dependent variables are bilateral exchange rates, our independent variables are defined for country pairs. In this case, we used the average value of exports to the partner country, scaled by GDP, for the two countries concerned. The costs of a common currency, in terms of macroeconomic policy independence forgone, should be balanced against the benefits, which will be greatest for small economies where there is least scope for utilizing a separate national currency in transactions. That is, small countries should benefit the most from the unit of account, means of payment, and store of value services provided by a common currency. We measure the benefits from a more stable currency by including the arithmetic average of (the log of) real GDP in U.S. dollars of the two countries as a measure of country size. An alternative, suggested by McKinnon (1963), is to use openness to international trade as a measure of the benefits from stabilizing the exchange rate. However, economic size would appear to be a better measure of the benefits from a stable currency, as a comparison between the benefits provided by the national currencies of Germany (a large and relatively open economy) and Spain (a smaller and more closed economy) should make clear. To ensure that the exclusion of openness from the regression is not an important factor in the empirical results, we included openness in an extended regression discussed further below.

The estimating equation was therefore:

$$SD(e_{ij}) = \alpha + \beta_1 SD(\Delta y_i - \Delta y_j) + \beta_2 DISSIM_{ij} + \beta_3 TRADE_{ij} + \beta_4 SIZE_{ij},$$

where $SD(e_{ij})$ is the standard deviation of the change in the logarithm of the end-year bilateral exchange rate between countries i and j, $SD(\Delta y_i - \Delta y_j)$ is the standard deviation of the difference in the logarithm of real output between i and j, $DISSIM_{ij}$ is the sum of the absolute differences in the shares of agricultural, mineral, and manufacturing trade in total merchandise trade, $TRADE_{ij}$ is the mean of the ratio of bilateral exports to domestic GDP for the two countries, and $SIZE_{ij}$ is the mean of the logarithm of the two GDPs measured in U.S. dollars.[13] In each case, the independent variables are measured as average values over the entire data period (1963–72, 1973–82, or 1983–92).

This equation seeks to explain observed exchange rate variability. It should be recognized, however, that optimum currency area criterion can affect exchange rate behavior in two ways, either by reducing under-lying pressures in the market for foreign exchange or by raising the incentives for the government to intervene in this market. To the extent that economies experience similar disturbances or are closely linked by bilateral trade, smaller bilateral exchange rate movements will be needed in response to disturbances, implying smaller underlying ex-change rate pressures. Factors such as the greater usefulness of money as a means of transactions, on the other hand, will tend to make policy makers in large economies less concerned about exchange rate fluctuations than those in small economies, and hence less likely to use policy measures to limit exchange rate volatility. In future work we hope to differentiate the impact of these factors on underlying pressures and intervention.[14]

Table 7.5 reports the results of estimating the coefficients on these four optimum currency area variables for our three decades. We focus on the results for nominal exchange rate variability, although those for the real exchange rate are in fact quite similar. Remarkably, all 12 OCA coefficients enter with their anticipated signs, and 11 of the 12 differ from zero at standard confidence levels (the exception being country size in the 1960s). A notable feature of these results is the increase over time in the size and significance of the coefficients on these four OCA variables. They are largest in the 1980s, when they all enter with t-ratios in excess of three.[15] They explain over half of cross-section differences in bilateral exchange rate variability in the most recent decade, up from about 15 percent in the 1960s.

The greater ability of the OCA variables to explain exchange rate behavior over time reflects the greater diversity of exchange rate rela-tionships available as the period progressed. In the 1960s, when virtually all industrial countries pegged within 1 percent bands as required by the provisions of the IMF Articles of Agreement, there was little cross-

Table 7.5. *Results for all countries using optimum currency areas variables*

	1960s		1970s		1980s	
	Nominal	Real	Nominal	Real	Nominal	Real
Variability of output	0.50 (0.13)**	0.45 (0.11)**	0.49 (0.19)**	0.53 (0.17)**	1.46 (0.21)**	1.41 (0.19)**
Trade ratio ($\times10^{-2}$)	-0.13 (0.05)*	-0.14 (0.04)**	-0.46 (0.06)**	-0.37 (0.05)**	-0.54 (0.07)**	-0.46 (0.06)**
Size of economy ($\times10^{-2}$)	0.13 (0.14)	0.11 (0.11)	1.70 (0.19)**	1.68 (0.17)**	2.50 (0.23)**	2.53 (0.21)**
Dissimilarity of exports ($\times10^{-2}$)	1.03 (0.31)**	0.81 (0.26)**	1.89 (0.54)**	1.93 (0.48)**	2.24 (0.62)**	2.80 (0.58)**
Number of observations	210	210	210	210	210	210
R^2	0.15	0.17	0.40	0.41	0.51	0.54

Notes: Standard errors are reported in parentheses. One and two asterisks indicate that the coefficient is significant at the 5 and 1 percent probability level, respectively. See the text for an explanation of the variables.

section variation in bilateral rates to be explained. By the 1970s, although the transition to floating was under way, some industrial countries sought to continue pegging. But the inability of many of them to maintain durable pegs in this turbulent environment makes it difficult to account for their behavior using equilibrium models. By the 1980s, countries had begun to settle into equilibrium relationships, and the coexistence of cooperative exchange rate arrangements and more freely floating rates provided the variation in the dependent variable necessary to identify the influence of the four optimum currency area variables. There is an irony, then, that the variables identified by Mundell, McKinnon, and Kenen have the least explanatory power for the decade in which these authors wrote.

An econometric issue is whether these correlations reflect causality running from exchange rate variability to trade and output as well as in the other direction. Although this possibility is suggested by the literature on the effects of exchange rate variability, the results from this literature are mixed, and most observers have concluded that the impact of exchange rate instability on trade and growth is probably small.[16] In any case, the independent variables in our analysis are not growth but rather the standard deviation of the difference in the growth rates of the two partner countries, and not the volume of trade but rather the volume of bilateral trade. Given these variable definitions, the force of the reverse-causality argument should be considerably reduced.

We now add four variables suggested by the broader literature on choice of exchange arrangements and one measure of the international regime. To test McKinnon's hypothesis that countries lacking linkages between domestic and international financial markets will prefer to float against Heller's conjecture that countries whose financial markets are integrated internationally will be inclined to peg, we include an indicator of the presence of capital controls (constructed from tabulations of restrictions on capital-account transactions published in the International Monetary Fund's *Exchange and Trade Restrictions* volumes).[17] As a measure of financial development we include the ratio of broad money to GDP (constructed as the average of the two countries' money/GDP ratios). To capture the idea that more open economies will be more inclined to employ an external anchor, we include the average trade-to-GDP ratio (where trade equals exports plus imports) for the two countries.[18] Finally, as a measure of the magnitude of asymmetric monetary disturbances, we include the average difference in the absolute change in the log of the money supply.

Our measure of the international regime is the arithmetic average of the variability of the U.S. dollar exchange rates of each country pair. This is designed to capture the idea that in periods when the dollar was pegged, governments were not forced to trade off stability vis-à-vis third currencies against stability vis-à-vis the dollar, which should have increased the attractions of pegging to third countries. This variable takes on a value of zero when the United States is one of the two partner countries.[19]

The results of estimating the extended model are shown in Table 7.6. The coefficients on the four OCA variables analyzed in Table 7.5 are little changed. They are generally significant and rise in absolute value over time, as does their joint significance (measured by the relevant F-statistic), although these trends are more pronounced when the new variables are not included. Thus, the four variables we take as representing the empirical implications of the theory of optimum currency areas are robustly related to observed exchange rate behavior even when the model is extended to include the influence of other factors.

F-tests for the significance of the four additional variables (that is, variables other than the four OCA variables and our measure of the international regime, which is considered separately below) indicate that as a group they had significant effects on observed exchange rate variability (whether measured by the variability of real or nominal rates) in the 1960s; the evidence for the 1970s is more mixed, with these four variables significantly adding to our ability to account for the variability of nominal but not real rates. In the 1980s, however, they are better at explaining real rates.

The economic importance and statistical significance of the individual variables is also varied. The ratio of money to GDP is negative and significant in the 1960s, suggesting that countries with deeper financial markets are better able to sustain real and nominal stability, but positive (and generally insignificant) in the 1970s and 1980s. Capital controls are associated with lower exchange rate variability – particularly when the real exchange rate is considered – consistent with McKinnon's thesis and inconsistent with Heller's; it would appear that capital controls give countries significant insulation from speculative pressures and room to maneuver to defend currency pegs. This coefficient is insignificant in the 1960s and 1970s, however, perhaps reflecting the near universality of controls. The other variables have generally small and insignificant coefficients. In particular, we find little evidence for the industrial countries that more open economies are more inclined to peg; this is consistent with the finding of Honkapohja and Pikkarainen (1992) for developing countries, that size rather than openness is the more robust predictor of choice of regime.

Overall, then, the results of estimating the extended model point in

Table 7.6. *Results for all countries from the general model*

	1960s		1970s		1980s	
	Nominal	Real	Nominal	Real	Nominal	Real
OCA variables						
Variability of output	0.40 (0.13)**	0.42 (0.11)**	0.30 (0.20)	0.50 (0.18)**	1.28 (0.22)**	1.04 (0.19)**
Trade ratio ($\times 10^{-2}$)	-0.16 (0.05)**	-0.14 (0.04)**	-0.45 (0.06)**	-0.39 (0.06)**	-0.39 (0.07)**	-0.50 (0.06)**
Size of economy ($\times 10^{-2}$)	0.34 (0.15)*	-0.11 (0.13)	1.57 (0.26)**	1.49 (0.24)**	1.88 (0.32)**	1.48 (0.29)**
Dissimilarity of exports ($\times 10^{-2}$)	0.57 (0.29)	0.51 (0.26)*	2.57 (0.57)**	2.14 (0.52)**	2.29 (0.64)**	2.40 (0.56)**
Other explanatory variables						
Capital controls ($\times 10^{-2}$)	-0.03 (0.16)	0.00 (0.15)	-0.08 (0.20)	-0.33 (0.18)	-0.23 (0.30)	-1.19 (0.26)**
Money ratio ($\times 10^{-1}$)	-0.33 (0.09)**	-0.20 (0.08)*	0.24 (0.15)	-0.15 (0.14)	0.32 (0.15)*	-0.03 (0.13)
Openness ($\times 10^{-1}$)	0.04 (0.27)	-0.03 (0.24)	0.29 (0.28)	0.29 (0.25)	0.68 (0.33)*	0.38 (0.29)
Relative growth of money ($\times 10^{-1}$)	0.93 (0.62)	1.67 (0.54)**	2.50 (0.89)**	0.12 (0.82)	0.59 (0.57)	0.60 (0.50)
Variability of U.S. dollar exchange rate	0.40 (0.08)**	0.11 (0.07)	-0.11 (0.06)	-0.05 (0.05)	-0.25 (0.06)**	-0.28 (0.06)**
Number of observations	210	210	210	210	210	210
R^2	0.34	0.29	0.45	0.44	0.56	0.63
F test of OCA variables $F_{4,200}$	6.6**	6.9**	25.5**	25.6*	35.6**	37.6**
F text of other variables $F_{4,200}$	5.1**	6.5**	3.8*	1.9	2.4*	7.2**

Notes: Standard errors are reported in parentheses. One and two asterisks indicate that the coefficient is significant at the 5 and 1 percent probability level, respectively. See the text for an explanation of the variables.

the same direction as the simple OCA specification. Determinants of the choice of exchange-rate regime have more explanatory power in the 1960s and 1980s than in the 1970s, as if the intermediate decade was one in which exchange arrangements were "out of equilibrium," countries not yet having adapted to changes in economic circumstances. But whereas the OCA variables have the most explanatory power in the 1980s, the other determinants of choice of exchange-rate regime, such as relative size and financial depth, have their most powerful effects in the 1960s.

Finally, our proxy for the global exchange-rate regime confirms that the structure of the international system matters for countries' choice of monetary arrangement. The variability of the dollar rate enters positively in the 1960s, insignificantly in the 1970s, and negatively in the 1980s.[20] These shifts in sign and significance can be interpreted as follows. Under the Bretton Woods system of pegged-but-adjustable rates, stabilization against the dollar was consistent with stabilization against other currencies; since countries with more stable dollar rates also had more stable rates vis-à-vis other currencies, the coefficient on the "system" variable is positive. In the 1980s, the emergence of Germany as an alternative center of monetary gravity to which other industrial countries, especially in Europe, might peg forced them to choose between stability against the dollar and stability against the mark. Because the U.S. and German currencies fluctuated widely against one another, stabilizing the exchange rate against one anchor currency meant accepting greater variability against the other. Hence, the coefficient on our "system" variable is significantly negative. For the 1970s we cannot reject the null hypothesis that the coefficient on this variable is zero. During these years of transition from pegged to floating rates, in other words, there was no stable tradeoff between stability vis-à-vis the dollar and stability against other currencies. This is evidence, then, that not just country characteristics but also the structure of the international system matters for countries' choice of exchange rate regime.

Our interpretation of this last variable in terms of the emergence of Germany as an alternative center of monetary gravity can be tested more directly using European data. Indeed, the explanatory power of OCA theory is a question of particular immediacy in the European context. We therefore turn to the European case.

V Evidence for Europe

In Tables 7.7 and 7.8 we report the results of estimating the same models on the European subsample. In Table 7.7 the coefficients on each of the

Table 7.7. *Results for European countries using optimum currency area variables*

	1960s		1970s		1980s	
	Nominal	Real	Nominal	Real	Nominal	Real
Variability of output	0.36 (0.16)*	0.37 (0.11)**	0.53 (0.24)*	0.69 (0.21)**	0.75 (0.20)**	0.97 (0.16)**
Trade ratio ($\times 10^{-2}$)	−0.18 (0.06)**	−0.17 (0.04)**	−0.20 (0.07)**	−0.14 (0.06)*	−0.26 (0.06)**	−0.19 (0.05)**
Size of economy ($\times 10^{-2}$)	0.37 (0.22)	0.23 (0.16)	0.32 (0.33)	0.65 (0.29)*	0.31 (0.31)	0.71 (0.25)**
Dissimilarity of exports ($\times 10^{-2}$)	1.17 (0.50)*	0.91 (0.36)*	−2.01 (1.10)	−0.39 (0.95)	−1.30 (0.79)	−1.36 (0.62)*
Number of observations	120	120	120	120	120	120
R^2	0.15	0.22	0.15	0.15	0.27	0.35

Notes: Standard errors are reported in parentheses. One the two asterisks indicate that the coefficient is significant at the 5 and 1 percent probability level, respectively. See the text for an explanation of the variables.

Table 7.8. *Results for European countries from the general model*

	1960s		1970s		1980s	
	Nominal	Real	Nominal	Real	Nominal	Real
OCA variables						
Variability of output	0.53 (0.18)**	0.30 (0.14)*	0.24 (0.19)	0.47 (0.21)*	0.77 (0.22)**	0.70 (0.18)**
Trade ratio ($\times 10^{-2}$)	-0.17 (0.06)**	-0.14 (0.05)**	-0.16 (0.06)*	-0.13 (0.07)	-0.12 (0.06)	-0.10 (0.05)
Size of economy ($\times 10^{-2}$)	0.53 (0.22)*	0.22 (0.17)	0.82 (0.30)**	0.86 (0.32)**	0.52 (0.33)**	0.65 (0.29)*
Dissimilarity of exports ($\times 10^{-2}$)	1.16 (0.48)*	0.62 (0.37)	0.79 (0.94)	0.77 (0.98)	-0.86 (0.77)	-0.51 (0.64)
Other explanatory variables						
Capital controls ($\times 10^{-2}$)	-0.76 (0.33)*	0.06 (0.27)	-0.18 (0.21)	-0.30 (0.23)	0.81 (0.32)**	-0.23 (0.24)
Money ratio ($\times 10^{-1}$)	-0.53 (0.14)**	-0.14 (0.11)	-0.09 (0.17)	-0.11 (0.18)	0.64 (0.16)**	0.16 (0.13)
Openness ($\times 10^{-1}$)	-0.35 (0.39)	-0.08 (0.30)	-0.18 (0.29)	-0.16 (0.31)	0.30 (0.33)	0.08 (0.28)
Relative growth of money ($\times 10^{-1}$)	0.24 (0.94)	0.83 (0.74)	4.68 (1.13)**	1.45 (1.20)	1.79 (0.78)*	1.24 (0.65)
Variability of exchange rate vs. DM	0.63 (0.16)**	0.22 (0.13)	0.48 (0.08)**	0.32 (0.09)**	0.17 (0.09)	0.32 (0.08)**
Number of observations	120	120	120	120	120	120
R^2	0.34	0.33	0.51	0.28	0.50	0.49
F-test OCA variables $F_{4,110}$	4.6**	3.2*	2.8*	3.2*	4.2*	4.6**
F-test other variables $F_{4,110}$	3.5**	1.5	5.8**	1.2	5.7**	2.4

Notes: Standard errors are reported in parentheses. One and two asterisks indicate that the coefficient is significant at the 5 and 1 percent probability level, respectively. See the text for an explanation of the variables.

four OCA variables have their expected signs (except for the diversity of exports in the 1960s) and, as before, generally differ from zero at standard confidence levels. We cannot reject the null of zero coefficients on country size in the 1960s, and the same is now true for the nominal exchange rate in the 1970s and 1980s. (Note, however, that this coefficient regains its significance in the 1970s when we augment the specification to include additional country characteristics in Table 7.8.) The coefficients on our measure of export diversity are also generally insignificant. Overall, however, these results further support the predictions of OCA theory.

The coefficients on the OCA variables are again little affected when we include additional country characteristics. Those other characteristics remain significant as a group each of our three decades, at least for nominal rates. That is, the predictions of the theory of optimum currency areas do not by themselves provide a complete explanation for differences across countries in exchange rate variability. However, the sign and magnitude of the coefficients on those other variables are not stable across decades. Only the absolute difference in relative rates of money-supply growth has a consistent – and relatively significant – impact on exchange rate variability. Pairs of countries for which the average rate of growth of the money supply differs by more tend to have more variable exchange rates. (Note that this is different from the statement that countries for whom relative rates of growth of the money supply are more variable tend to have more variable exchange rates.) This effect plausibly reflects the constraints of the Snake and the ERM, which encouraged governments to harmonize their average rates of inflation and reduce the variability of nominal variables in pursuit of exchange rate stability.

Capital controls are associated with lower (nominal) exchange rate variability in the 1960s but higher variability in the 1980s. An interpretation is that the stringency of controls was a function of exogenous historical factors in the 1960s, giving European countries with more restrictive capital-account regimes additional levers with which to buttress the stability of their currencies. By the 1980s, in contrast, the incidence of capital controls had become more selective. They were maintained primarily by countries for which currency stability was a problem – Italy and Greece spring to mind – leading to the positive association between controls and exchange rate variability. Note that these patterns are different from those for all countries, among whom the association between controls and currency volatility is uniformly negative.

Finally, the "regime" or "system" variable (measured as the bilateral rate vis-à-vis Germany and taking on a value of zero for observations where Germany is one of the partner countries) enters with a positive coefficient in all three periods and consistently differs from zero at the 10 percent confidence level. This is in contrast to the results for the entire sample, where the analogous coefficients change sign over time. The coefficients for Europe suggest that the deutsche mark functioned as an anchor currency throughout the period, even in the 1960s. These results should not be interpreted as suggesting that there existed a nascent DM zone under Bretton Woods. There was a strong correlation between bilateral dollar and DM rates for other European countries in a decade when the dollar and the DM were stable vis-à-vis one another. When we use the variability of the bilateral rate against the dollar as the "system" variable in the 1960s, we continue to obtain a positive and significant coefficient for the European subsample. The notable difference from the estimates for all industrial countries is in the 1970s and 1980s, when there is no evidence of a tradeoff between stability vis-à-vis the anchor currency and stability vis-à-vis other bilateral rates. Another way of putting the point is that membership in the Snake and the ERM had a stabilizing influence on the entire grid of exchange rates among member countries, not just bilateral deutsche mark rates. The bottom line again is that not only individual country characteristics but also the broader international regime are important for exchange rate performance, although the relationship between the international regime and the stability of bilateral rates is different depending on the regime in question.

A final way of summarizing our results is to compare actual exchange rate variability with the variability predicted by the model. Tables 7.9 and 7.10 report residuals from the OCA model and the extended model in the 1980s. To aid comparison, positive residuals that are greater than $2\frac{1}{2}$ percent are shaded darkly, while their negative equivalents are shaded lightly. A predominance of negative residuals for European countries is evident. When we limit the specification to the four OCA variables, the variability of nominal rates against the DM is overpredicted for France, Italy, the United Kingdom, Austria, Denmark, Finland, Ireland, Norway, Spain, Sweden, and Switzerland; it is underpredicted only for Belgium, Greece, the Netherlands, and Portugal.[21] In many cases, as the shading indicates, the underprediction of exchange rate variability is large.[22]

An interpretation is that Europe moved toward currency stability in the 1980s before achieving the degree of economic convergence (in terms of variables like the symmetry of shocks and trade interdependence) typically associated with such behavior across the OECD as a whole. This interpretation is consistent with the difficulties these countries faced in holding their currencies stable starting in 1992–3. Note,

Table 7.9. Residuals – "OCA" regression

	US	JA	GR	FR	IT	UK	CA	AS	AU	BE	DE	FI	GC	IR	NT	NZ	NO	PO	SP	SW
US																				
JA	-0.01																			
GR	0.00	-0.01																		
FR	0.01	0.00	-0.04																	
IT	0.01	0.00	-0.04	-0.03																
UK	-0.01	-0.03	-0.04	-0.03	-0.04															
CA	0.04	0.00	0.01	0.02	0.02	0.01														
AS	-0.02	0.01	0.01	0.02	0.01	0.00	-0.02													
AU	0.02	0.02	-0.01	-0.03	-0.03	-0.02	0.04	0.04												
BE	0.04	0.02	0.02	0.02	-0.03	0.00	0.04	0.04	-0.02											
DE	0.04	0.00	-0.05	-0.06	-0.05	-0.02	0.05	0.06	-0.05	-0.06										
FI	0.01	0.00	-0.03	-0.03	-0.04	-0.01	0.03	0.02	-0.01	-0.01	-0.02									
GC	0.00	0.04	0.01	-0.01	0.00	-0.05	0.01	0.01	0.03	-0.01	0.01	0.02	-0.01							
IR	0.03	0.02	-0.01	-0.03	-0.04	0.05	0.03	0.03	-0.01	-0.01	-0.04	-0.04	-0.02	0.01						
NT	0.03	0.00	0.00	-0.02	-0.04	0.00	0.04	0.05	-0.04	0.04	-0.03	-0.03	-0.02	0.03	0.00					
NZ	0.02	0.00	-0.02	-0.01	-0.01	-0.04	0.00	0.03	0.01	0.01	0.04	-0.01	-0.01	0.00	0.02	0.01				
NO	-0.01	-0.02	-0.03	-0.05	-0.06	-0.03	0.01	0.02	-0.03	-0.04	0.02	0.02	-0.04	-0.03	-0.05	-0.01	0.02	-0.02		
PO	0.04	0.05	0.02	0.01	0.00	0.01	0.05	0.04	0.04	0.03	0.00	0.00	0.04	0.00	0.01	0.02	-0.01	-0.05	0.02	
SP	0.01	0.02	-0.01	-0.01	-0.02	-0.03	0.02	0.01	0.01	0.01	-0.02	-0.02	-0.03	-0.02	0.00	-0.01	0.01	-0.05	0.01	-0.04
SW	0.03	0.01	-0.01	-0.03	-0.02	-0.01	0.04	0.03	0.00	0.00	0.02	0.02	-0.02	-0.02	0.00	0.01	0.01	0.01	-0.01	0.02
SZ	0.04	0.02	-0.02	-0.01	-0.01	-0.01	0.05	0.05	-0.01	-0.01	-0.03	-0.03	0.03	-0.01	-0.04	0.02	-0.01	0.05	0.05	0.03

Key: US = United States; JA = Japan; GR = Germany; FR = France; IT = Italy; UK = United Kingdom; CA = Canada; AS = Australia; AU = Austria; BE = Belgium; DE = Denmark; FI = Finland; GC = Greece; IR = Ireland; NT = The Netherlands; NZ = New Zealand; NO = Norway; PO = Portugal; SP = Spain; SW = Sweden; SZ = Switzerland.

Table 7.10. Residuals – "general" regression

	US	JA	GR	FR	IT	UK	CA	AS	AU	BE	DE	FI	GC	IR	NT	NZ	NO	PO	SP	SW
US																				
JA	-0.02																			
GR	-0.01	0.00																		
FR	0.00	0.02	-0.02																	
IT	0.00	0.01	-0.02	-0.02																
UK	-0.03	-0.02	-0.03	-0.02	-0.03															
CA	0.03	0.01	0.02	0.04	0.03	0.03														
AS	-0.03	0.02	0.02	0.04	0.03	0.03														
AU	0.00	0.02	0.00	-0.02	-0.02	-0.02	-0.02													
BE	0.01	0.02	0.02	0.02	-0.02	0.00	0.03	0.03	-0.03											
DE	0.02	0.01	-0.04	-0.05	-0.04	-0.01	0.05	0.06	-0.05	-0.05										
FI	-0.01	0.00	-0.02	-0.02	-0.03	-0.01	0.02	0.02	-0.01	-0.01	-0.01									
GC	-0.01	0.04	0.02	0.01	0.01	0.04	0.02	0.02	0.03	0.03	0.03	0.00								
IR	0.00	0.02	-0.01	-0.03	-0.04	0.05	0.02	0.03	-0.02	-0.01	-0.04	-0.02	0.01							
NT	0.00	-0.01	0.01	-0.02	-0.04	-0.01	0.03	0.04	-0.05	0.04	-0.04	-0.02	0.00	-0.01						
NZ	-0.01	-0.01	-0.01	0.00	-0.01	-0.04	-0.01	0.03	0.00	0.01	0.03	-0.01	0.00	0.02	0.02					
NO	-0.03	-0.02	-0.02	-0.04	-0.05	-0.03	0.00	0.02	-0.03	-0.03	0.01	-0.04	-0.03	-0.05	-0.01	0.00				
PO	0.02	0.05	0.03	0.02	0.01	0.01	0.05	0.04	0.03	0.03	0.00	0.04	0.00	0.00	0.02	0.02	-0.02			
SP	-0.01	0.03	0.00	0.00	-0.01	-0.03	0.03	0.02	0.02	0.02	-0.01	-0.02	-0.01	0.00	0.01	0.00	-0.04	0.03		
SW	0.00	0.01	-0.01	-0.03	-0.01	-0.02	0.03	0.02	0.00	0.00	0.01	0.02	-0.02	-0.03	-0.01	0.00	-0.02	0.01	-0.04	
SZ	0.01	0.02	-0.02	-0.01	-0.01	0.00	0.04	0.04	-0.02	-0.02	-0.04	0.00	0.02	-0.01	-0.04	0.01	-0.02	0.05	0.02	0.02

Key: US = United States; JA = Japan; GR = Germany; FR = France; IT = Italy; UK = United Kingdom; CA = Canada; AS = Australia; AU = Austria; BE = Belgium; DE = Denmark; FI = Finland; GC = Greece; IR = Ireland; NT = The Netherlands; NZ = New Zealand; NO = Norway; PO = Portugal; SP = Spain; SW = Sweden; SZ = Switzerland.

however, that the countries for which the OCA model overpredicts exchange-rate variability are not limited to members of the ERM; they include also countries that shadowed the ERM (Austria, Switzerland, Finland, Norway, and Sweden). Two ERM members depart from the pattern; the OCA model does not overpredict exchange-rate variability for the Netherlands and Belgium (two small economies tied to Germany both by extensive bilateral trade and by other factors making for symmetrical business-cycle disturbances, characteristics that lead the model to predict low levels of exchange-rate variability). It is noteworthy that these two were among the countries least affected by exchange-market turbulence in 1992–3. Two other countries, Greece and Portugal, also display greater exchange rate variability than predicted by the OCA specification, suggesting that other factors, presumably originating in the political domain, also affected international monetary behavior.

Thus, the results for Europe further substantiate the empirical applicability of the theory of optimum currency areas. At the same time they suggest that OCA theory does not provide a complete explanation for differences in exchange rate behavior across countries. Not only is there a role for other country characteristics not directly associated with OCA theory, but the evidence for Europe provides particularly strong support for the notion that international and regional monetary arrangements independently influence exchange rate outcomes.

VII Conclusion

The point of departure for our analysis of exchange rate behavior and choice of exchange rate arrangements has been the literature on optimum currency areas. Contrary to the view that its empirical implications have little explanatory power, our investigation reveals robust correlations between observed exchange-rate behavior and OCA variables like asymmetric shocks, the importance of trade, and country size. OCA variables do not provide a complete explanation for the variability of bilateral exchange rates; we also find a role for other country characteristics not obviously associated with the theory of optimum currency areas. These other characteristics were relatively important in the 1960s, the OCA variables in the 1970s and 1980s.

We also find that the traditional approach of linking the characteristics of countries to their choice of exchange rate regime provides an incomplete explanation for the phenomenon at hand. Repeatedly, decisions to limit exchange rate variability have involved cooperative agreements among countries; the Snake and EMS are obvious examples, but one might also cite the General Arrangements to Borrow and the

Louvre and Plaza Accords, all of which involved bilateral or multilateral support. Small countries may be inclined to peg, but they are not equally inclined to do so vis-à-vis all potential partners; pegging to large countries offers access to the widest zone of monetary stability and will be particularly attractive when the partner offers exchange rate support. By definition, the exchange rate is the relative price of two national currencies; it should be analyzed in terms of economic conditions in both of the countries involved.

In addition, we find that the stability of bilateral exchange rates is significantly affected not just by the characteristics of the two countries whose currencies are directly involved but also by the structure of global and regional monetary arrangements. In the 1960s, when the anchor currencies were stabilized against one another, there existed no optimum-currency-area dilemma: stabilizing against one currency facilitated stabilizing against the rest. In the 1970s and 1980s, in contrast, the competing anchors, the dollar and the deutsche mark, were floating against one another: stabilizing against one meant varying against the other and greater variability against the currencies of third countries. Only within Europe, where the franc, the DM, and other currencies were stabilized vis-à-vis one another through the operation of a system that re-created Bretton-Woods-style stability on a regional scale, was this tradeoff attenuated.

Our results suggest, then, that there is more than has typically been suggested to the empirical implications of the theory of optimum currency areas. This has been obscured by the fact that OCA models have focused on the situation facing individual countries or limited groups. Our results also suggest that the choice of exchange rate regime and observed exchange rate behavior should be understood in a context of a broader model, one that transcends the single-country perspective and acknowledges that countries' choices of exchange rate regime are interdependent. A satisfactory analysis requires modeling this problem of collective action and introducing a role for the structure of the international system.

The hallmark of the current system of floating exchange rates is the flexibility it provides for countries to tailor their exchange rate arrangements to fit their needs. Our results can be read as suggesting that the industrial countries have used this flexibility to increasingly good effect over time. But flexibility has come at a cost insofar as countries have been forced to choose between alternative nominal anchors. Stabilizing against, say, the dollar implies floating against the yen and the deutsche mark, an unpleasant dilemma that did not arise under the more rigid Bretton Woods pegged exchange rate system. The swings in the international monetary pendulum over the last 150 years, from the stability of the gold standard to the variability of dirty floating in the 1930s, back to the stability of Bretton Woods and now to the flexibility of the current regime of floating rates, can be seen as reflecting changing assessments of the relative importance of stability and flexibility. The continuing controversy over the merits of alternative international monetary arrangements suggests that this debate is far from over.

DATA APPENDIX

The data on nominal exchange rates, broad and narrow money supplies, real GDP, nominal GDP, the GDP deflator, and total trade all came from the IMF's *International Financial Statistics*. Bilateral trade data came from the IMF's *Direction of Trade Statistics*. The source of the capital controls index was Grilli and Milesi-Ferrati (1995).

NOTES

We thank Benjamin Cohen, Reuven Glick, Linda Goldberg, Clas Wihlborg, and participants at a seminar held at the European University Institute for comments on a previous draft.

1. Another relevant study is Marion (1996), who relates traditional OCA variables such as openness and country size to the width of exchange-rate fluctuation bands.
2. In particular, most studies of choice of exchange rate regime in developing countries, the part of the world economy on which most of this literature has focused, take variables such as these as their point of departure. For references to this literature, see Section II below.
3. OCA theory has, however, occupied an important place in the debate over the European Monetary Union.
4. Vaubel (1978) also used exchange rate variability as a measure of optimum currency area suitability, using data on the European Community. However, his approach was to use exchange rate variability as an optimum currency area criterion, while we use it as a measure of the exchange rate regime.
5. There exist a number of reviews of the literature described below; recent examples are Edison and Melvin (1988), Honkapohja and Pikkarainen (1992), and Savvides (1993).
6. Capital controls also provide breathing space for governments to organize orderly realignments, protection from speculative pressures, and limited autonomy for national policy. See Eichengreen and Wyplosz (in press). Holden, Holden, and Suss (1979) anticipate the controversy, suggesting that theoretical models yield ambiguous conclusions about the effects of the degree of capital mobility on the desirability of fixed versus floating rates, and quoting Tower and Willett (1976) to this effect. Another author who explicitly acknowledges the ambiguity is Weil (1983).

7. For convenience, we refer to these periods as the 1960s, 1970s, and 1980s.
8. Results for real exchange rates, constructed from nominal rates using GDP deflators, are very similar. This is a stylized fact for industrial countries, although it is less true for developing countries. Glick and Wihlborg (this volume) similarly find that their trade equations are little affected when they substitute various measures of nominal and real rate variability. Annual data were used, as much of the other data used in the estimation were available only at this frequency, and as they appeared to illustrate the essential features of the historical record reasonably well.
9. More surprisingly, Spain also falls into this category. In addition, Finland devalued a month earlier, partly in response to the international financial turbulence caused by uncertainty about sterling.
10. Mundell (1961), McKinnon (1963), and Kenen (1969).
11. Technically it would be preferable to decompose relative output movements into relative supply shocks, relative demand shocks, and the respective economies' response to each. Elsewhere (Bayoumi and Eichengreen 1993) we have applied a methodology for distinguishing supply and demand shocks, but this is infeasible to implement with the relatively short time series utilized here.
12. Manufactured goods are defined as the total of basic manufactures, chemicals, machines, and transport equipment, miscellaneous manufactured goods, and other goods. Food is the sum of food and live animals, beverages and tobacco, and animal, vegetable oils, and fats. Minerals amalgamate data on crude materials excluding fuel with mineral fuels, etc. Data sources are given in the appendix.
13. A potential technical concern with this specification is that not all of the entries for the dependent variable are independent of each other. However, although it is true that *changes* in bilateral rates are not independent (the change in the bilateral rate between the dollar and the yen is equal to the change between the dollar and the deutsche mark and between the deutsche mark and the yen), the *standard deviations* of these rates are independent as the covariances can differ across pairs of countries.
14. Estimates of underlying exchange rate pressures can be constructed by adjusting observed exchange rate changes for the volume of reserve changes. See Holden, Holden, and Suss (1979), Glick, Kretzmer, and Wihlborg (1995), and Glick and Wihlborg (this volume).
15. The relative accuracy of these coefficient estimates implies that it would be possible to construct an index measuring the relative benefits of stabilizing exchange rates between countries.
16. See, for example, Mussa et al. (1995) and Corbo and Rojas (1995).
17. It ranges from zero to six, with larger values indicating more comprehensive controls. See Grilli and Milesi-Ferrati (1995) for details.
18. This is distinct from the tendency for two countries that trade disproportionately with one another to peg their exchange rate as a way of preventing exchange rate volatility from disrupting their commerce, a factor for which we have already controlled by including a measure of bilateral trade.

19. Below where we consider a subsample of European countries, we use the variability of the deutche mark rate to capture the influence of the broader exchange rate regime.
20. It should be noted, however, that the coefficient on the systems variable is insignificant in the 1960s in the real exchange rate equation.
21. The only case where the results for the DM rate are noticeably affected by moving from the OCA to the extended model is Spain, which is no longer an outlier in either direction when the extended specification is used.
22. Corresponding to these negative residuals for Europe are a number of positive residuals for Canada and Australia. We remain unclear as to why the estimation results for these two countries tend to underestimate actual exchange rate variability.

REFERENCES

Bayoumi, Tamim, and Barry Eichengreen (1993). "Shocking Aspects of European Monetary Unification." In Francisco Torres and Francesco Giavazzi (eds.), *Adjustment and Growth in the European Monetary Union*, pp. 193–229. Cambridge University Press.

Bosco, Luigi (1987). "Determinants of the Exchange Rate Regimes in LDCs: Some Empirical Evidence," *Economic Notes* 1, 110–43.

Branson, William, and Louka Katseli (1981). "Exchange Rate Policy for Developing Countries." In Sven Grassman and Eric Lundberg (eds.), *The World Economic Order: Past and Prospects*, pp. 391–419. New York: St. Martin's Press.

Corbo, Vittorio, and Patricio Rojas (1995). "Exchange Rate Volatility, Investment, and Growth: Some New Evidence," unpublished manuscript, Catholic University of Chile.

Corden, W. Max (1972). *Monetary Integration*, Princeton Studies in International Finance 93. International Finance Section, Princeton University.

Crockett, Andrew (1994). "Monetary Implications of Increased Capital Flows." In Federal Reserve Bank of Kansas City, *Changing Capital Markets: Implications for Monetary Policy*, pp. 331–64. Kansas City: Federal Reserve Bank of Kansas City.

Dreyer, Jacob S. (1978). "Determinants of Exchange-Rate Regimes for Currencies of Developing Countries: Some Preliminary Results," *World Development* 6, 437–45.

Edison, Hail, and Michael Melvin (1988). "The Determinants and Implications of the Choice of an Exchange Rate System," unpublished manuscript, Arizona State University.

Eichengreen, Barry (1995). "The Endogeneity of Exchange Rate Regimes." In Peter B. Kenen (ed.), *Understanding Interdependence: The Macroeconomics of the Open Economy*, pp. 3–33. Princeton: Princeton University Press.

Eichengreen, Barry, and Beth Simmons (1995). "International Economics and Domestic Politics: Notes on the 1920s." In Charles Feinstein (ed.), *Banking,*

Currency and Finance in Europe Between the Wars, pp. 131–50. Oxford: Oxford University Press.

Eichengreen, Barry, and Charles Wyplosz (in press). "What Do Currency Crises Tell Us about the Future of the International Monetary System?" In Fundad, *The Implications of the Mexican Crisis for the Future of the International System*, Amsterdam: Fundad.

Friedman, Milton (1953). "The Case for Floating Exchange Rates." In *Essays in Positive Economics*, pp. 157–203. Chicago: University of Chicago Press.

Glick, Reuven, Peter Kretzmer and Clas Wihlborg (1995). "Real Exchange Rate Effects of Monetary Disturbances Under Different Degrees of Exchange Rate Flexibility: An Empirical Analysis," *Journal of International Economics* 38, 249–74.

Goodhart, Charles (1995). "The Political Economy of Monetary Union." In Peter B. Kenen (ed.), *Understanding Interdependence: The Macroeconomics of the Open Economy*, pp. 450–505. Princeton: Princeton University Press.

Grilli, Vittorio, and Gian Maria Milesi-Ferrati (1995). "Economic Effects and Structural Determinants of Capital Controls,' *Staff Papers* 42, 517–51.

Heller, H. Robert (1978). "Determinants of Exchange Rate Practices," *Journal of Money, Credit and Banking* 10, 308–21.

Holden, Paul, Mule Holden, and Ester Suss (1979). "The Determinants of Exchange Rate Flexibility: An Empirical Investigation," *Review of Economics and Statistics* 61, 327–33.

Honkapohja, Seppo, and Pentti Pikkarainen (1992). "Country Characteristics and the Choice of Exchange Rate Regime: Are Mini-Skirts Followed by Maxi?" Centre for Economic Policy Research, Discussion Paper no. 774 (December).

International Monetary Fund (various issues). *International Financial Statistics*. Washington, DC: International Monetary Fund.

Kenen, Peter (1969). "The Theory of Optimum Currency Areas: An Eclectic View." In Robert A. Mundell and Alexander K, Swoboda (eds.), *Monetary Problems of the International Economy*, pp. 41–60. Chicago: University of Chicago Press.

Kenen, Peter (1988). *Managing Exchange Rates*. London: Royal Institute of International Affairs.

Levine, Ross, and David Renelt (1992). "A Sensitivity Analysis of Cross-Country Growth Regressions," *American Economic Review* 82, 942–63.

McKinnon, Ronald (1963). "Optimum Currency Areas," *American Economic Review* 53, 717–25.

McKinnon, Ronald (1979). *Money in International Exchange: The Convertible Currency System*. New York: Oxford University Press.

Melvin, Michael (1985). "The Choice of an Exchange Rate System and Macroeconomic Stability," *Journal of Money, Credit and Banking* 17, 467–78.

Mundell, Robert A. (1961). "A Theory of Optimum Currency Areas," *American Economic Review* 51, 657–65.

Mussa, Michael, Morris Goldstein, Peter Clark, Donald Mathieson, and Tamim Bayoumi (1995). *The Future of the International Monetary System: Constraints and Possibilities*, IMF Occasional Paper 116, Washington, DC: International Monetary Fund.

Sachs, Jeffrey D. (1995). "Alternative Approaches to Financial Crises in Emerging Markets," unpublished manuscript, Harvard University.

Savvides, Andreas (1990). "Real Exchange Rate Variability and the Choice of Exchange Rate Regime by Developing Countries," *Journal of International Money and Finance* 9, 440–54.

Savvides, Andreas (1993). "Pegging the Exchange Rate and Choice of a Standard by LDCs: A Joint Formulation," *Journal of Economic Development* 18, 107–25.

Tower, Edward, and Thomas D. Willett (1976). "The Theory of Optimum Currency Areas and Exchange Rate Flexibility," Special Papers in International Economics, no. 11, International Finance Section, Department of Economics, Princeton University.

Vaubel, Roland (1978). "Real Exchange Rate Changes in the European Community: A New Approach to Optimum Currency Areas," *Journal of International Economics* 8, 319–39.

Weil, Gordon (1983). "Exchange Rate Regime Selection in Theory and Practice," Monograph Series in Finance and Economics No. 1983–2, New York: New York University Graduate School of Business Administration.

Wickham, Peter (1985). "The Choice of Exchange Rate Regime in Developing Countries," *Staff Papers* 32, 248–88.

CHAPTER 8

Optimum currency area theory: Bringing the market back in

Benjamin J. Cohen

Dating back to the pioneering work of Peter Kenen (1969) and others, following Robert Mundell's seminal 1961 article (Mundell 1961), the theory of optimum currency areas (OCAs) has lately enjoyed something of a revival as a result of developments in Europe and elsewhere (Masson and Taylor 1993; Tavlas 1993, 1994). The purpose of this essay, in honoring Kenen, is to contribute to the continuing evolution of this important area of inquiry.

In its first incarnation, OCA theory was strikingly apolitical. Following Mundell's lead, most early contributors, including Peter Kenen, concentrated on a search for the most appropriate domain of a currency irrespective of existing national frontiers. The globe, in effect, was treated as a tabula rasa. The central issue was to find the right criterion for the organization of monetary space. But as the practical limitations of the so-called criterion approach (Tavlas 1994: 213) became clear, an alternative – and, in political terms, seemingly less naive – approach eventually prevailed, focusing instead on costs and benefits of state participation in a common currency area or its equivalent, a regime of irrevocably fixed exchange rates. No longer an irrelevance, the existence of sovereign nations now became the starting point for analysis. Reminding us that countries are not all alike – and thus that no single currency choice is likely to be suitable for all – OCA theory was deliberately reincarnated in a presumably more policy-relevant form.

In the process, however, the role of market forces in determining currency outcomes was unfortunately suppressed. Reflecting conventional political geography, configurations of monetary space typically have been assumed to result exclusively from government design. Currency arrangements are thus defined, like states themselves, in strictly territorial terms: physically distinct and mutually exclusive spatial enclaves; in effect, the monetary counterpart of customs unions or free-

216

trade areas in commercial relations. The world is portrayed as comprised of insular national moneys, which either remain wholly independent or may be formally merged into a currency union or its equivalent. Moneys, in effect, are treated like discrete building blocks, homogeneous products of state sovereignty to be combined or remain independent at the behest of governments.

The limitation of this approach is that it effectively ignores the existence of cross-border currency competition, a well-documented and pervasive phenomenon driven largely by market forces. In fact, the use of moneys outside their country of origin is commonplace. The domains within which individual currencies serve the standard functions of money frequently diverge quite sharply from the legal jurisdictions of issuing governments. In practice, therefore, configurations of monetary space involve a far greater role for private markets than acknowledged by standard OCA theory (Cohen 1994).

In this essay I aim to highlight the missing market dimension in OCA theory – in effect, to "bring the market back in" to the analysis of monetary space. In contrast to the traditional currency *area*, an explicit product of state action, I propose the competing notion of a currency *region*, a configuration that is functional rather than geographic in nature, bounded not by territorial frontiers but rather by the range of each money's effective use and authority; and thus defined by market networks of domestic and transnational transactions rather than by legal agreements or formal institutions. Though not easy to visualize physically – they certainly cannot be drawn casually on a map – currency regions are both pervasive in practice and frequently extensive in scope. They are important because they can have a significant impact on the balance of costs and benefits of participation in a formal currency area.

For reasons of brevity, my approach in this essay is deliberately informal. Following a short synopsis of OCA theory and the role of market forces in organizing currency space, an analysis is conducted in two stages. First, as in standard OCA theory, discussion is structured as a dichotomous comparison of two alternative policy choices: national monetary autonomy versus participation in a broader currency region. Welfare implications of a currency region are contrasted with the assumed status quo of an insular national money. Going beyond standard OCA theory, however, each effect in turn is viewed from not one but two perspectives: that of the home country – the nation whose currency forms the basis for a region; and that of host countries – the nations whose monetary jurisdictions are correspondingly invaded. For home and host countries, calculations of state interest in fact turn out to be quite different.

Second, discussion then turns to issues posed for the formation of a formal currency area, as traditionally defined in OCA theory, by the prior existence of market-determined currency regions. What happens if local currencies already face a high degree of competition from a widely used outside currency within the group's nominal monetary space? Again two alternatives may be compared: a government-organized monetary union or equivalent whose borders are contiguous with those of a currency region based on a major local currency versus one whose borders effectively overlap with the functional domain of an established outside currency. The degree of symmetry between currency area and currency region, we shall see, significantly influences the net gains of a monetary union for participating countries.

The essay concludes with a brief summary of the main results of the analysis and some implications for future research.

Conventional OCA theory

As developed over the last twenty years or so, conventional OCA theory has taken on a distinctly state-centric cast. Debate is deliberately structured to contribute to the formulation of public policy, highlighting the advantages or disadvantages, as seen from a single country's point of view, of abandoning monetary autonomy to participate in a currency union or its equivalent. Under what conditions, analysts ask, would a state surrender its right to alter the external value of its currency? The now standard approach identifies a number of key economic characteristics that may be regarded as instrumental in a government's decision. Kenen (1969) highlighted the importance of the degree of commodity diversification. Other factors stressed in the literature include: wage and price flexibility, factor mobility, geographic trade patterns, size and openness of economies, inflation trends, and the nature, source, and timing of potential payments disturbances. These diverse variables are singled out because each is assumed to influence, to a greater or lesser extent, material gains or losses for the nation as a whole. Exchange-regime choices are presumed to be based on a systematic calculus of potential costs and benefits.[1]

On the positive side, a common currency or equivalent is expected to yield certain distinct gains, including in particular possible improvements in the usefulness of money in each of its principal functions: as a medium of exchange (owing to a reduction of transactions costs as the number of required currency conversions is decreased), store of value (owing to a reduced element of exchange risk as the number of currencies is decreased), and unit of account (owing to an information saving as the number of required price quotations is decreased). Additional benefits might also accrue from a saving of international reserves due to an internalization through credit of what would otherwise be external trade and payments – effectively enhancing the foreign purchasing power of each participating currency – and from a broadening of the foreign-exchange market vis-à-vis third countries, decreasing currency volatility.

Against these advantages, governments are assumed to compare the disadvantages of the corresponding surrender of monetary autonomy: the potential cost of having to adjust to domestic disturbances or balance-of-payments shocks without the option of changing either interest rates or the exchange rate. In Paul Krugman's words, the question "is a matter of trading off macroeconomic flexibility against microeconomic efficiency" (Krugman 1993: 4).[2] Each of the variables identified by OCA theory arguably affects the magnitude of losses at the macroeconomic level by influencing either the severity of potential external imbalances or the ease of the consequent processes of adjustment. The basic premise is that, ceteris paribus, the lower the potential net economic cost to the country, the more governments should be willing to peg their exchange rates absolutely.

The contributions of OCA theory are considerable. In particular, the work serves to remind us that all money is *not* insular, that alternative spatial configurations of currency relations do (or could) exist, extending across the frontiers of individual nations. However, the debate also seems distinctly limited by its built-in state-centrism, which directs attention exclusively to monetary spaces that are the product of government design. In this respect, the standard approach greatly simplifies reality.[3] A desire to remain policy-relevant is of course understandable. But an economic theory that leaves out much of the influence of market forces must be regarded as, at best, somewhat incomplete.

The role of market forces

Standard OCA theory tends to ignore the existence of cross-border currency use and competition. In fact, insular national money is a very special case – the exception rather than the rule. Governments are not the sole determinants of the organization of currency space.

Global currency competition

For any money to be truly insular, its functional realm would have to coincide precisely with the political jurisdiction of the state. The currency would have to exercise an exclusive claim to all the traditional roles of money within the domestic economy. There could be no other currency accepted for transactions purposes or used for the denomination of contracts or financial assets. And the government would have to be able to exercise exclusive control over all aspects of the monetary system. In matters of commerce, the equivalent would be described as "autarky" – national self-sufficiency. In the real world, autarky is no more common in currency relations than it is in trade.

As a practical matter, cross-border currency use is commonplace. Several national moneys are widely employed outside their country of origin for transactions either between states (currency internationalization) or within foreign states (currency substitution). However, although both currency internationalization (CI) and currency substitution (CS) are familiar phenomena and frequently discussed in the technical literature,[4] their implications for OCA theory or for practical issues of monetary integration are only rarely addressed directly.

Currency internationalization ("international" currency use), as we know, can occur at two levels of operation: at the private level it occurs as a medium of exchange (a "vehicle") for foreign trade, as a unit of account for commercial invoicing, and as store of value for international investments; at the official level, it occurs as a reserve and intervention medium and as a peg for exchange rates.[5] In relation to OCA theory, however, only the exchange-rate link tends to receive much serious attention, mainly as an empirical indicator of emergent or informal currency "blocs" or "zones" (approaching – though not equivalent to – the notion of currency regions as defined below).[6] Other ways in which CI might influence prospects for a successful merger of national currencies have until recently been generally ignored.[7]

The same is also true of the literature on currency substitution ("foreign-domestic" use). Two key variants of CS are generally distinguished. One is the more or less symmetrical interchangeability of money or monetary assets characteristic of financial relations among industrial countries.[8] CS in this sense, though integral to the process of global portfolio diversification, has been formally addressed in relation to OCA theory almost exclusively in the context of the European Union (EU), as part of ongoing debates over alternative approaches to an eventual Economic and Monetary Union (EMU). For some Europeans, inspired by the laissez-faire views of Friedrich Hayek, a common currency would best be attained not by government fiat (the Maastricht strategy) but rather through a direct competition of moneys in the marketplace (Fratianni and Peters 1978; Vaubel 1978; Salin 1984; British Treasury 1989). To date, however, only a few sketchy attempts have been made to analyze systematically the effects of this variant of CS on monetary unification, with inconclusive results (Woodford 1991; Weil 1991; Canzoneri et al. 1993; De Grauwe 1994, chap. 6). Otherwise its possible relevance to OCA theory is mentioned only in passing, if at all (e.g., Wihlborg and Willett 1991: 283–4).

The other variant of CS refers to the asymmetrical situation of many developing or transition economies where local demand for desirable foreign currency is not matched by a counterpart demand from abroad for the less attractive domestic money. CS in this sense, which may be for any or all of the usual monetary purposes, has never to my knowledge been formally addressed in the context of OCA theory.

Both types of cross-border currency use, international and foreign-domestic, emerge from an intense process of market competition – a kind of Darwinian process of natural selection in which some moneys come to be seen as functionally superior to others. Analytically, the motivations for each can be easily appreciated. Internationalization (including the symmetrical variant of CS) derives from the economies of scale, or reduced transactions costs, to be gained from concentrating cross-border activities in just one or at most a few currencies with wide circulation networks ("thick markets"); or from cross-border variations of interest rates and currency expectations. Asymmetrical CS typically occurs as a result of a high or accelerating inflation rate, which encourages a country's residents to turn to some more stable foreign money as a preferred store of value and frequently even as a unit of account and medium of exchange. Both CI and CS represent a kind of Gresham's Law in reverse, where more attractive ("good") money drives out less attractive ("bad") money.[9] Neither is at all an irrational form of behavior. On the contrary, each may be regarded as a quite natural response to prevailing market structures and incentives.

Which currencies are likely to prevail in the Darwinian struggle? The principal qualities required for competitive success are familiar and hardly controversial (Cohen 1971a; Tavlas 1991; Krugman 1992). Two essential attributes, at least in the early stages of a currency's cross-border use, are widespread confidence in the money's future value and political stability in the country of origin. In addition, markets for the money should be sufficiently deep and resilient to ensure a high degree of liquidity and predictability of asset value. And, perhaps most important of all, the money must be widely employed commercially, since nothing enhances a currency's acceptability more than the prospect of acceptability by others – what analysts refer to as money's "network externalities" (Dowd and Greenaway 1993) or "thickness externalities" (Alogoskoufis 1993). None of these attributes, however, is a constant. We may also assume, therefore, that the outcome of the competitive process is quite likely to change substantially over time. No currency can be presumed to enjoy a permanent monopoly for either international or foreign-domestic use.

Empirical evidence

How well are these cross-border uses documented? Although comprehensive statistics do not exist, partial indicators abound that provide some measure of rough orders of magnitude. Representative samples of data for recent years, including indicators of both CI and CS, are available elsewhere (Cohen 1994; Thygesen et al. 1995). Taken together, these diverse data – however imperfect or incomplete – offer a composite picture that is strikingly at variance with the conventional assumption of insular national moneys.

Currency internationalization, for example, is evidently quite substantial in magnitude. Reflecting the economies of scale involved, it also appears to be highly concentrated in terms of numbers. Just a small handful of moneys account for the great bulk of use at both the private and official levels. The leading role of the U.S. dollar, though diminished from what it once was, is confirmed by its still dominant position in central-bank reserves and interventions, commercial banking claims and bond issues, and wholesale foreign-exchange market activity. Vying distantly for second place are the Deutsche mark (DM) – especially important in official reserves and exchange markets – and the Japanese yen, which ranks strongly in banking assets and securities. The only other international currencies of any particular significance are the pound sterling and French and Swiss francs, and beyond them the Netherlands guilder, Belgian franc, Italian lira, and Canadian dollar.

The main exception lies in the area of trade invoicing, where a noticeably less asymmetrical pattern of currency use seems to prevail. Ever since the pioneering empirical work of Swedish economist Sven Grassman (1973), it has been well known that the most favored vehicle for trade among industrial countries, particularly when involving manufactures, tends to be the exporter's own currency.[10] Yet even for this purpose some currencies clearly remain more important than others. In bilateral trade between developed and developing nations, for example, the currencies of the industrial countries still generally predominate, whatever the national identity of the exporter. Morever, even within the industrial world, the importance of home money in export invoicing tends to vary quite sharply depending on the issuing country's relative weight in world trade: the smaller the country, the smaller the share of exports denominated in local currency. And, in the vast area of trade in primary products (including, especially, oil), the dollar plainly remains the vehicle of choice. Though the selection of moneys for retail trade purposes may be less asymmetrical than in the wholesale foreign-exchange market or global banking and securities markets, international use still remains quite highly concentrated in just a small handful of major currencies.

A complementary picture of asymmetry emerges from available data on CS. Although less well documented than CI, the phenomenon of foreign-domestic use is known to be substantial in magnitude and also seems quite concentrated in terms of numbers. Only the most familiar and trusted international currencies tend to be used at all widely outside their own country of issue. On the other hand, the range of states where CS occurs is apparently very broad, encompassing many of the economies of the developing world and former Soviet bloc. The sample of popular currencies whose effective range extends beyond their national frontiers may be small; the world of currencies whose legal jurisdiction is correspondingly penetrated certainly is not.

In short, evidence of the pervasiveness of global currency competition is overwhelming. Three observations stand out. First, the scale of cross-border currency use is obviously extensive. Autarky in currency relations truly is a special case. Second, the number of moneys actually employed for either international or foreign-domestic purposes tends to be rather small. And third, conversely, the number of moneys that routinely face effective competition at home from currencies orginating abroad appears to be quite large. The population of currencies is distinctly hierarchical. Although all moneys enjoy nominally equal status as a matter of international law, some currencies (to paraphrase George Orwell) clearly are, as a matter of practical reality, far more equal than others. From these facts emerge currency regions – each region grouped around one of a small handful of elite "key" currencies.[11] Cross-border competition ensures that market forces too play a critically important role.

Currency regions

If the available data are to be believed, it would seem reasonable to assume that currency regions in practice are quite ubiquitous (reflecting the sheer scale of currency competition). It would also appear that they are limited in number (reflecting the small handful of moneys actually employed outside their own country of issue) but frequently broad in scope (reflecting the large number of currencies routinely facing cross-border competition). The organization of currency space, in short, can be assumed to mirror closely the hierarchical structure of the monetary population. In an Orwellian world, a few key currencies hog the scene.

Currency regions in practice

In fact, the list of regions is remarkably short. Topping the charts, of course, is the dollar, which remains by far the world's most popular money for both international and foreign-domestic purposes. In effect, the dollar's region spans the globe, from the Western Hemisphere (where the accepted synonym for currency substitution is "dollarization") to the former Soviet bloc and parts of the Middle East (where dollars circulate widely as a de facto parallel currency). Next comes the DM, which clearly dominates currency relations within Europe, including not only the EU but much of East Central Europe and the Balkans as well (Tavlas 1991). In francophone Africa, a smaller region has long existed centered on the French franc (Boughton 1993); and in the Far East, a limited grouping may now be starting to coalesce around the Japanese yen.[12] Elsewhere, however, only a few "micro"-regions can be identified clustered around such locally influential currencies as the South African rand, Indian rupee, or Australian dollar; noticeably absent from the list is Britain's pound sterling, once the proud leader of an extensive region of its own, today no more than a pale shadow of its former self (Cohen 1992). In total, currency regions can be counted on less than the fingers of two hands.

The scope of some of these regions, on the other hand, appears to be remarkably broad. Though few moneys may be chosen to lead currency regions, many appear called to follow. It is the rare country indeed that remains fully insulated from the effects of cross-border currency competition. For most governments, therefore – not just the governments of the few key currencies actually used for cross-border purposes – state interests clearly are affected. The challenge for public policy is real. It is also more or less universal.

Defining currency regions

Can we define currency regions more formally? To do so, we need an appropriate analytical "metric" that we can use to distinguish and contrast the international competitiveness of individual moneys.

At issue is a fundamental distinction between physical and functional notions of economic space. Currency regions are market-driven, reflecting the choices of private actors at least as much as the preferences of public officials, and may never be formalized in legal or institutional terms. Based not on geography but on practice, they are delimited not by territorial frontiers but rather by the range of each money's effective use and authority – "spaces-of-flows," in the language of political scientist John Ruggie (1993: 173), rather than the more traditional "spaces-of-places." The key lies in the network externalities that are so critical to the competitive success of individual moneys. Currency regions are rooted in the networks of domestic and transnational transactions centered on a single key currency.

The distinction between physical and functional space is not a new one. Nearly half a century ago, economic historian François Perroux (1950) underscored the contrast between "banal" notions of physical space and more abstract ideas of *economic* space, defined in his terms as a "field of forces." "Modern mathematics," he wrote, "has become accustomed to consider the abstract relations which define mathematical beings, and so to give the name 'spaces' to these structures of abstract relations" (91). Economists, he continued, should learn to do the same. And among the most important of these abstract spaces for economists, he maintained, was *monetary* space: a field of forces "seen more easily in terms of a 'network' of payments" (98). Only recently, however, in a relatively new literature on the "economics of networks," developed largely in France, have theorists finally begun to explore seriously the implications of this alternative, functional approach to the organization of spatial relations. Just two sources, to my knowledge, have as yet tried to apply the new network theory to the analysis of issues of monetary integration.[13]

A formal definition of currency regions can be readily constructed on the foundation laid by Perroux and the new network theory. Conceptually, what is at issue is what may be called the *authoritative domain* of each individual money. The term "domain" in this context refers directly to the range or network of transactions for which a given currency effectively performs the standard functions of money – its *economic space*, strictly speaking. But this is not the whole story, since currencies are still created and nominally managed by governments. No matter how important the role of markets may be, there is also a dimension of political authority to take into account. That is the purpose of the modifying adjective "authoritative," which refers to the range or network of transactions over which each issuing government is able to exercise effective control through its monetary and exchange-rate policies – the currency's *political space*, as it were. Both dimensions, the political as well as the economic, are integral to a comparative analysis of currency competitiveness.

To illustrate, consider a country where, for one reason or another, residents begin to favor a popular foreign currency for various international or even domestic monetary purposes. In effect, the economic space of home money is correspondingly diminished: international competition has directly eroded its authoritative domain while enhancing the authoritative domain of the foreign currency. Much the same effect, however, will also be achieved even in the absence of overt currency substitution if external financial linkages are sufficiently strong. The more capital markets at home are functionally tied to a strong currency abroad, the more control over domestic monetary management is in effect ceded to a foreign central bank. Local money may continue to function for the usual purposes within the national economy, preserving its economic space. The money's authoritative domain is nonetheless eroded in this case too (and the authoritative domain of the foreign currency enhanced), owing this time to the shrinkage of its *political* space. Cross-border use and competition may influence either dimension of a money's international standing.

The concept of authoritative domain provides the basis for a more formal definition of currency regions. *Currency regionalism occurs whenever a money's authoritative domain extends significantly beyond the legal jurisdiction of its issuing government.* Admittedly, the concept of authoritative domain is not easy to operationalize for objective empirical purposes. The data simply do not exist to capture accurately all facets of each currency's economic and political space. But it does at least provide a common, if subjective, standard for identification of currency regions like those centered on the dollar, Deutsche mark, and other key currencies. And it offers as well a useful focal point for the policy calculations of governments. Whether they recognize it or not, public officials mandated to manage a nation's money are speaking the language of authoritative domain.

The determinants of currency regions

What, then, determines the authoritative domain of currencies? Standard OCA theory assumes that governments are the dominant if not exclusive shapers of currency relations. Market forces enter into OCA theory only as input into the public decision process – exogenous considerations presumed to influence the costs or benefits of alternative currency choices. Assigning a central role to governments is a natural corollary of the notion of insular national money. In a world of extensive cross-border use, however, private actors are at least as important as state decision makers in determining the authoritative domains of currencies, through the choices they make of what vehicles to employ for various monetary purposes. Configurations of currency space are by no means established at the behest of governments alone.

Governments may try, of course. States generally are no less concerned about the creation and management of money than they are about other dimensions of their putative national sovereignty; and within limits set by power capabilities and the strategic environment of interstate rivalry, most more or less do actively seek to preserve as much monopoly control over currency issue as possible, either separately or as part of a formal monetary union. A national money is valued not only for its political symbolism or the macroeconomic flexibility it may provide but also as a source of seigniorage (otherwise known as the "inflation tax"). Public spending financed by money creation has been described as the "revenue of last resort" for governments (Goodhart 1995: 452) – the single most reliable instrument of policy available, especially in times of emergency, to appropriate resources from the private sector. If governments had their way, monetary spaces would indeed be defined in strictly territorial terms, coterminous with national boundaries, and would be as numerous as states themselves decide.

Markets, on the other hand, prefer the efficiency benefits of a smaller number of currencies, as amply demonstrated by the pervasiveness of CI and CS around the globe. How small a number? For some theorists, such as Roland Vaubel (1977), the number might be as small as one, owing to the power of economies of scale. Unfettered currency competition, Vaubel argues, will lead eventually to a single universal money – the ultimate expression of Gresham's Law in reverse. "Ultimately, currency competition destroys itself because the use of money is subject to very sizable economies of scale. . . . The only lasting result will be . . . the survival of the fittest currency" (437, 440). Such a view, however, is highly deterministic, not to say simplistic, and appears to be contradicted by both empirical evidence and theoretical considerations. Markets may prefer to reduce costs by driving out "bad" money, but a multiplicity of currency regions seems the more natural selection than one single money.

Historically, the Darwinian process of currency competition has never shown any tendency to concentrate favor exclusively on a single money, even in the presence of competitive disparities as great as those, for example, between sterling and the dollar in the decades after World War I. In Paul Krugman's words: "The impressive fact here is surely the inertia; sterling remained the first-ranked currency for half a century after Britain had ceased to be the first-ranked economic power" (1992: 173). Similar inertias have been evident for centuries, in the prolonged use of such international currencies as the Byzantine gold solidus or

Spanish silver peso long after the decline of the imperial powers that first coined them (Andrew 1904; Lopez 1951); and they can still be seen today in the continued popularity of the dollar despite America's shrinking economic predominance. Such immobilism cannot be accounted for merely by residual political influences.

Network theory, on the other hand, provides a quite workable explanation for what has been called the "paradox of the non-universality of money" (Thygesen et al. 1995: 41). Two distinct structures are recognized in the organization of "spaces-of-flows": the "infrastructure," which is the functional basis of a network; and the "infostructure," which provides needed management and control services. Economies of scale, by reducing transactions costs, promote a consolidation of networks at the level of infrastructure. At the infostructure level, by contrast, the optimal configuration is more decentralized and competitive in order to maximize agent responsibility. A natural trade-off exists, therefore, that is more likely to result in intermediate solutions than in either absolute centralization or decentralization – in short, currency regions rather than either a single universal money or insular national currencies.

A priori, no one intermediate configuration can be identified as optimal for all circumstances. Much more likely is the possibility of multiple equilibria, a conclusion consistent with other recent approaches to the analysis of international money (Krugman 1992; Matsuyama et al. 1993; Hartmann 1994). Particularly influential is the self-reinforcing impact of "mimesis": the rational impulse of market actors, in conditions of uncertainty, to minimize risk by imitative behavior based on past experience. Once a currency gains a degree of acceptance, its use is apt to be perpetuated – even after the appearance of powerful new competitors – by regular repetition of previous practice. In effect, a conservative bias is inherent in the dynamics of the marketplace. As one source has argued, "imitation leads to the emergence of a convention [wherein] emphasis is placed on a certain 'conformism' or even hermeticism in financial circles" (Orléan 1989: 81–3). In markets for money, as in other organized asset markets where choices are a function of interdependent expectations, any number of equilibrium configurations are in fact possible.

Ultimately, then, currency outcomes will depend on market psychology as well as political authority. Whereas governments generally seek to preserve as much monetary sovereignty as possible, either singly or in unions, markets promote a far greater consolidation of currency spaces. Governments and markets thus both play a critical endogenous role, not only acting independently but also reacting strategically to the initiatives of the other – sometimes reinforcing one another's choices, at other times constraining the opposite side's behavior. Practical outcomes, in the form of currency regions, will reflect the balance of influence and ongoing dialectic between political authority and markets and must in the end be assumed to be both mutually determined and highly contingent.[14]

The economics of currency regions

What are the advantages or disadvantages of currency regions for a single sovereign state? As indicated, discussion may be structured as in standard OCA theory – a dichotomous comparison of two alternative policy choices, national monetary autonomy versus participation in a broader currency region – but with one distinct difference. Analysis must take account of not one but two separate perspectives: that of the state whose money, the key currency, forms the basis for a region (the home country); and that of the states whose moneys' authoritative domains are correspondingly reduced (host countries).

Microeconomic effects

At the microeconomic level, the broad impact of a currency region is likely to be much the same as predicated in OCA theory for a common currency or equivalent. The wider the authoritative domain of the key currency, the greater will be the savings on transactions costs. The usefulness of money will be improved for all participants, whether in home or host country.

Such a result is not surprising. Currency regions are largely driven by the forces of market competition, which can ordinarily be expected (ceteris paribus) to generate some measure of efficiency gains. Indeed, if left entirely to themselves, market forces might conceivably maximize microeconomic efficiency, thus achieving in practice what Mundell, Kenen, and other early contributors to OCA theory set out to identify in principle: the economically most appropriate domains for currencies irrespective of existing national frontiers. Refocusing analysis on currency regions rather than currency areas, ironically, suggests that the first incarnation of OCA theory may not have been so naive after all.

Macroeconomic effects

At the macroeconomic level, the main impact of a currency region will be felt in the mechanism for balance-of-payments financing. Economists have long contrasted the relative ease of adjustment to interregional imbalances within countries with the frequently greater difficulties associated with payments adjustments between countries. One major differ-ence, early sources pointed out (Scitovsky 1958; Ingram 1959), is the greater scope for equilibrating capital flows within countries in the event of transitory disturbances, owing to the existence of a stock of "general-ized" short-term financial claims that can be readily traded between surplus and deficit regions. The development of these generalized claims, in turn, has traditionally been attributed to the existence of a single national currency, which removes all exchange risk. Such reasoning, of course, is based on the conventional assumption of insularity in national moneys. But the same logic applies even if that assumption is relaxed to allow for the possibility of a broader currency region.[15] The wider the authoritative domain of a given money, the greater will be the range for equilibrating capital flows, taking the form of purchases and sales of generalized claims denominated in the key currency. Other things being equal, these flows should reduce the collective cost of adjustment to unanticipated payments shocks.

This result too is unsurprising, since it largely replicates another of the benefits of a common currency or equivalent mentioned in OCA theory: the savings that accrue from internalization through credit of what would otherwise be external transactions.[16] But there is a crucial difference here that tends to be obscured by OCA theory's narrow state-centric ap-proach. If currency space can be assumed to be shaped predominantly if not exclusively by national governments, it is not unfair to conclude that all participating countries are apt to share in this benefit commensu-rately. The same is not true, however, when currency relations are shaped in larger part by market forces, which promote a hierarchy rather than a merger of national moneys. In this case, the home country will almost certainly gain disproportionately, to the extent that the area within which its currency can be used to finance imbalances is enlarged. Its macroeconomic flexibility is in effect enhanced. Host countries, by contrast, will find themselves less able to rely on equilibrating capital flows denominated in their own national moneys. Their room to maneu-ver will be effectively constricted. Thus costs of payments adjustment may indeed be reduced, but most if not all of the benefit is likely to go to just one participant, the home country.

The gain of macroeconomic flexibility for the home country may not be costless, of course. In principle, increased use of a money abroad could, if the total supply is fixed, actually lead to welfare losses insofar as it causes a shortage of local currency at home (Matsuyama et al. 1993). Likewise, monetary policy could conceivably be pegged to a misleading target (since a large but indeterminate part of the currency supply is in circulation abroad) or be destabilized by unanticipated variations of foreign demand for domestic money. On balance, however, the advantage here would appear to outweigh disadvantages.

For host countries, on the other hand, implications are more ambiguous. What is the significance of the constriction of their policy flexibility? At least two contrasting viewpoints are possible, as illustrated by some past and current discussions of the Euro-dollar in international currency relations. On one side is an early contribution of my own (1963), focusing on the emerging European Community (now European Union), which emphasized the disadvantages of widespread domestic use of a foreign currency. Already by the 1960s, I argued, the Euro-dollar had acquired some of the characteristics of a de facto common currency for the Europeans – "the informal common currency of the Common Market" (1963: 613). In effect, the Community had become part of a currency region centered on the dollar. But because this would have meant reliance for financing on a supply of assets managed by the Federal Reserve rather than by their own central banks, it appeared that the effectiveness of national monetary policies was bound to be reduced. "The problem," I wrote, "is not one of geography but of sovereignty.... Because the borders of the area within which the Euro-dollar circulates do not coincide with the borders of the Common Market, efforts to control liquidity within the union must inevitably [be compromised]" (1963: 614–15).[17]

The other side is illustrated by a more recent contribution by James Meigs (1993), focusing on the emerging states of East Central Europe and the former Soviet Union, which takes a more sanguine view of the potential role of the Euro-dollar. For these countries, Meigs notes, the challenge has been not to preserve monetary stability but to create it. And what better way might there be, he asks, than to "hire" a foreign currency for the job? "Using Euro-dollars, without exchange controls, would greatly speed up the clearing of international trade and capital transactions.... Evolution of the new trading and payments system would be market-driven [and] would provide an automatic, nonpolitical system for grading the republics on their performance" (Meigs 1993: 716–17). Quite clearly, there are indeed circumstances in which a loss of monetary autonomy may well be regarded more a blessing than a curse.

Seigniorage, domestic and international

At first glance, in addition to the gain of macroeconomic flexibility, the home country might also be expected to benefit from increased opportunities for the extraction of seigniorage, international as well as domestic. Within any national economy the key to seigniorage, viewed as an alternative source of revenue to government, is a lack of substitutes for domestic currency. The larger the currency's authoritative domain, the easier it should be for public officials to appropriate real resources through money creation at the expense of the private sector. Likewise, between national economies the key to seigniorage, viewed as an implicit international transfer, is the increased willingness of nonresidents to hold domestic money or use it outside the country of origin. Expanded cross-border circulation of a currency generates the equivalent of a subsidized or interest-free loan from foreigners – a real-resource gain for the nation as a whole.[18]

International seigniorage, however, can be exploited only so long as the home money continues to be held voluntarily or circulate abroad. Unfortunately, the superior competitiveness of a currency can never be permanently guaranteed. In fact, the benefit for the home country is apt to be greatest in the earliest stages of cross-border use, when its money is most popular. Later on, material gains as well as policy autonomy may well be gradually eroded – as they were historically for both sterling and the dollar – by the accumulation of an overhang of liquid foreign liabilities. Equilibrating capital flows may continue to provide an extra degree of macroeconomic flexibility to deal with transitory payments problems. Over time, however, policy will almost certainly be increasingly constrained by the need to discourage sudden or substantial conversions into other currencies. Ultimately, net international seigniorage may well be reduced to zero or even turn negative.[19]

The interesting question is: Where does the benefit go? It certainly does not go to host governments, which also suffer an erosion of their monopoly control of the effective money supply. Competition from currencies originating abroad necessarily reduces the capacity of host governments to rely on seigniorage at home, when needed, to extract resources from the private sector. In effect, the base for levying an inflation tax is shrunk. This not only means a deceleration of fiscal revenue, which for countries with underdeveloped tax systems could be a particularly acute problem (Tavlas 1993: 673). Unless budgetary deficits are reduced it could also mean an acceleration of inflationary pressures, since to finance the same level of expenditures, policy-makers would now have to speed up the rate of domestic money creation. The result might be "a vicious cycle of ever increasing inflation" (Brand 1993: 46) that could, in the end, be reversed only by a severe curtailment of public spending.

So where does the benefit go? Quite clearly, it goes from the public sector in general – home and host governments alike – to the private sector; in other words, from state to society. The capabilities of policy-makers everywhere are reduced: in the home country, by the burden of a currency overhang; in host countries, by the loss of a base for the inflation tax. The capabilities of market actors, in the aggregate, are correspondingly enhanced. Through the choices they make in the Darwinian struggle among currencies, private agents can exercise a degree of discipline over public policy that goes well beyond what would normally be tolerated in direct state-to-state relations (as the 1994 Mexican peso crisis amply demonstrated). This is what observers mean when they describe the impact of currency competition as a "market-enforced monetary reform" (Melvin 1988); Meigs had the same idea in mind when referring to "an automatic, nonpolitical system for grading [policy] performance" (1993: 717). Market forces not only help to shape currency space; they also exercise enormous influence over how governments behave within existing monetary arrangements.

In effect, therefore, the impact of currency regions is to amplify the shift in relative capabilities from states to markets that is now commonly associated with the increase of global capital mobility in recent decades (Cohen 1996). Few scholars today dispute the proposition that, as political scientist David Andrews phrases it, "the degree of international capital mobility systematically constrains state behavior by rewarding some actions and punishing others" (1994: 193). As true as that proposition is, however, it underestimates how deeply the discipline of the market truly penetrates into domestic political economies. A focus on capital mobility tends to highlight just a part of the story, relating solely to financial-market integration and cross-border use of moneys for store-of-value purposes. In fact, as already emphasized, international currency competition is far more extensive, involving all the standard functions of money and penetrating to the very core of what is meant by national political sovereignty. A focus on currency regions makes clear that much more is involved here than financial markets alone or just a few narrowly defined economic policies. It is, indeed, a matter of the effectiveness of government itself.

Currency regions versus currency areas

We now turn to issues posed for the formation of a formal currency area, as traditionally defined in OCA theory, by the prior existence of market-determined currency regions. Two alternative possibilities will be contrasted: first, a government-organized monetary union or equivalent whose borders are contiguous with those of a currency region based on a major local currency; and second, one whose borders effectively overlap with the authoritative domain of an established outside currency. At issue are the potential reactions by market agents in participating countries. Analytical implications of the two cases seem strikingly different.

Contiguous borders

First, imagine a group of countries so closely aligned on a single key currency, to the exclusion of all other moneys, that their collective borders effectively define a currency region. Put differently, the functional borders of the key currency's authoritative domain coincide more or less precisely with the territorial frontiers of the participating states. A formal monetary union in this case – in effect, formalization of an informal region – would encounter few economic obstacles, since little change of behavior would be required of local market agents, and would mainly affect the balance of costs and benefits between member governments and between state and society.

Collectively, a formal monetary union would add little to the microeconomic benefits already being enjoyed within the group; and would probably contribute only marginally to expansion of the stock of generalized claims available to ease adjustment to transitory disturbances. Assuming, however, that authority over monetary policy is transferred from the key currency to a central banking institution based on some form of collective decision making, two significant differences may be noted. On the one hand, the gain of macroeconomic flexibility previously captured by the home country will now be shared more equally among all the governments involved (just as assumed in standard OCA theory). On the other, the loss of state capacity to extract seigniorage, in home and host countries alike, will be at least partially redressed by the reduction of currency competition among the participants. Joint management of a single money will both broaden the distribution of adjustment savings available to the public sector and restore a measure of the monopoly control needed to successfully levy an inflation tax on the private sector.

From the point of view of host governments, therefore, a formal monetary union appears distinctly superior as compared with an informal currency region. For the home country, by contrast, implications are more ambiguous and would certainly involve some loss of policy autonomy in relation to other governments. Ceteris paribus, this might help explain why in the context of the European Union – which for some EU members already displays many of the characteristics of an informal currency region based on the Deutsche mark – France and other smaller countries have been so eager to pursue EMU while in Germany opposition has been steadily rising. Whereas host governments clearly have an incentive to acquire a role in the management of a common currency, the home country has every reason to resist giving up the historic advantages of a key currency. Even in the absence of any significant overlap with an established outside currency region, this is a recipe for discord if not outright conflict.

Overlapping borders

Matters become more complicated when there is indeed an overlap between regions within the same physical space. Imagine a group of countries where two key currencies are now in active competition: one issued by a locally dominant member (e.g., the DM in Europe) and one by a nonmember (e.g., the dollar). A formal monetary union in this case would encounter more serious economic obstacles, since market agents will now be under pressure to alter traditional patterns of behavior, and would almost certainly generate some degree of friction between the group and the outside home country.

At the microeconomic level, savings on transactions costs may be lost, at least initially, if residents are asked to substitute the new common money for a popular outside currency. Insofar as the outside currency was previously used within the group in preference to local moneys (including the local key currency), it must have been because of superior network externalities that were available for at least some cross-border purposes. Put differently, the reach of the outside currency's authoritative domain must already have made it a more efficient medium for some range of local market uses. Polly Allen (1993) calls this a currency's "in-place network externality," which in an uncertain world makes that currency obviously more attractive than a newly created and untested alternative. In her words:

> In a world of great uncertainty, the relative externalities of an in-place network become greater.... The expected network externalities from a new competing currency are likely to be small and uncertain.... [Hence] its lack of *in-place* network externalities and uncertain *current* externalities will dominate its still uncertain expected *future* network externalities. (172–3; emphasis in the original)

The advantage of the outside currency for residents will presumably be least for purely domestic transactions or for mutual trade within the group, especially if the new common money is supported by restrictive legal-tender legislation. But as a vehicle for exports to the outside home country or others, as well for import trade, or as a store of value in global banking and securities markets, the outside currency will undoubtedly enjoy an initial competitive edge, particularly if the new common money seems less credible than the local key currency it is meant to supplant. Reputations take time to develop, after all. Can widespread confidence in the new money's future value be instantly generated? Can political stability or a high degree of liquidity and predictability of asset value be immediately assured? In practice, it would not be at all irrational for market agents, at least at the outset, to prefer the tried-and-true to the experimental. Inertias similar to those that prolonged the life of other key currencies in the past, therefore, are highly likely to manifest themselves again.[20]

The persistent competitiveness of the outside currency, in turn, will also reduce other potential benefits of a monetary union. Continuing use of the outside currency will both inhibit growth of a stock of generalized local-currency claims that might ease payments adjustments vis-à-vis third countries and restrict the base for levying an inflation tax at home. Neither macroeconomic flexibility nor the capacity for seigniorage will be enhanced as much as it would be in the absence of a rival, overlapping currency region.

The magnitude of the challenge, quite plainly, will be a direct function of the *degree* of overlap between currency regions prior to formal union. If the overlap is minimal, with the local key currency already greatly favored by residents for most if not all cross-border purposes, the outside currency's in-place network externalities will be of relatively little consequence. However, the more extensive its use in any of the participating countries, the greater will be the tendency toward inertia in market practice, and hence the smaller will be the gains of a currency merger. At the extreme, where the outside currency faces no effective local rival, formal union might yield no significant benefits at all. The authoritative domain of the new common money would not exceed that of the combination of previous host currencies.

In time, of course, things could change. With accumulating experience could come increased credibility and confidence in the usefulness of the new money. Eventually, its network value to residents could even come to exceed that of the established outside currency, particularly if growing use within the group is reinforced by parallel adoptions elsewhere. As indicated, no single configuration of monetary space can be identified as optimal for all circumstances, and multiple equilibria are possible.

Getting from one equilibrium to another, however, can be costly and, given the conservative bias introduced by mimesis, will certainly be resisted initially unless promoted vigorously by participating governments. The problem is one of collective action: a coordination dilemma. Individual market actors have little incentive to switch from one currency to another, except where compelled to do so by legal-tender requirements, unless they have reason to expect many others to do the same. Governments can increase the probability of widespread acceptance by facilitating expansion of networks for cross-border use – for example, by sponsoring development of debt markets denominated in the new money or by subsidizing its use as a vehicle currency for third-country trade. This is one circumstance where in the ongoing dialectic between political authority and markets, public policy can make a real difference.

In doing so, however, participating governments would also pose a direct threat to the authoritative domain of the outside key currency, and thus put themselves on course for open confrontation with the outside home country. Policy initiatives from within could provoke countermeasures from without, as each side strives to defend or promote the competitiveness of its own money. In effect, therefore, members of the new union would be forced to make a choice: either tolerate considerable inertia in market practice, which might severely limit the gains of a formal merger; or else risk increased tensions in extra-union relations. This too would be a recipe for discord if not outright conflict.

Conclusions

Bringing the market back in, then, does make a difference. Explicit consideration of the implications of cross-border currency competition tends to cast the conclusions of standard OCA theory in a significant new light. The *informal* currency regions produced by market-driven CI and CS not only generate their own gains and losses, as compared with the hypothetical alternative of national monetary sovereignty. Even more importantly, they quite dramatically alter the calculus of state interests in the creation of a *formal* monetary union or equivalent. Within groups of countries where one money already functions as a key currency, efforts to create a common currency inevitably trigger tensions between the erstwhile home country and others. Within groups where there is significant overlap with an outside currency region, gains may be preserved only at the risk of triggering tensions with outsiders. Either way, the existence of functional monetary spaces quite distinct from the traditional territorial enclaves promoted by governments adds a whole new dimension to the analysis of optimum currency areas.

For future research, the discussion suggests both empirical and theoretical challenges. At the empirical level, it is clear that more and better data are needed to document the scale of cross-border currency use for both international and foreign-domestic purposes. Is it possible, in effect, to "map" the true dimensions of the world's main currency regions? At the theoretical level, more work is needed to sort out the implications of different dimensions of currency competition – CI in contrast to CS or the transactions role of currency in contrast to its portfolio role. Do costs and benefits vary systematically by monetary function? Are inertias likely to be greater for some types of competition than for others? And, perhaps most important of all, further inquiry is needed to understand the mutually endogenous roles of governments and markets in determining the overall organization of currency space. There is simply no excuse to continue analyzing international monetary relations as if the world remains comprised of insular national currencies.

NOTES

I am indebted to Polly Allen, Barry Eichengreen, Marc Flandreau, George Tavlas, and Tom Willett for helpful comments and suggestions. The able assistance of Kathleen Collihan is also gratefully acknowledged.

1. For more on the role of OCA theory in exchange-regime choices, see Chapter 7 in this volume, by Tamim Bayoumi and Barry Eichengreen. For more on the related issue of devaluation decisions, see Chapter 12, by Nancy Marion.
2. The loss of macroeconomic flexibility matters, of course, only insofar as monetary-policy instruments (the money supply or exchange rate) can be assumed to have a sustained influence on real economic variables (output and employment). In effect, there must be some lasting trade-off between unemployment and inflation (a negative slope to the Phillips curve). Many economists, inspired by Milton Friedman's natural unemployment-rate hypothesis and later by rational-expectations theory, have disputed this essentially Keynesian view of the world, arguing to the contrary that there is no such trade-off (no slope to the Phillips curve); money instead is said to be neutral with respect to real output, influencing only prices. In the "monetarist" view, the only benefit of an independent currency is an ability to choose one's own inflation rate. Empirical evidence, however, suggests that the monetary neutrality argument is valid, if at all, only in the relatively long term. Over periods of time more relevant to public officials, monetary policy does retain importance: its surrender can be assumed to represent a cost. For more, see Krugman 1993: 21; Tavlas 1993: 669–73.
3. OCA theory, in this respect, also stands as the direct opposite of the competitive-currency views of Friedrich Hayek and his followers (Hayek 1976; Vaubel 1977), who advocate absolute free choice in currency and unrestrained private production of money. For a useful recent discussion, see Selgin and White 1994.
4. For more on currency internationalization, see Krugman 1992, chap. 10; Black 1991, 1993. For more on currency substitution, see Calvo and Vegh

1992, 1993; Brand 1993; Giovannini and Turtelboom 1994; and Mizen and Pentecost 1996.

5. Modestly, I may claim credit for first introducing this analytical typology into the literature (Cohen 1971a), as has been acknowledged by, among others, Kenen 1983; and Krugman 1992, chap. 10.

6. See, e.g., Bénassy-Quéré and Deusy-Fournier 1994; Frankel and Wei 1995. Both sources estimate the relative importance of the U.S. dollar, Deutsche mark, and yen in the determination of the values of currencies of a diverse group of smaller countries, with quite similar results. The Deutsche mark dominates in Europe, the dollar in the Western Hemisphere and most of Asia, and the yen practically nowhere.

7. For an early exception, see Cohen 1963. For a much more recent discussion, see Thygesen et al. 1995.

8. Strictly speaking, this formulation, encompassing money substitutes as well as currency, defines "broad" or "indirect" CS, which in formal models is usually distinguished from "narrow" or "direct" CS, referring to the interchangeability of money alone (e.g., Copeland 1994, chap. 9). For the purposes of this essay, the broad definition is more appropriate.

9. Streissler 1992; Guidotti and Rodriguez 1992. The reversal of Gresham's Law in conditions of high inflation has been labeled "Thiers' Law" by Bernholz (1989), after the nineteenth-century French historian Louis Thiers, who noted the occurrence of the pattern at the time of the French revolution.

10. This pattern of home-currency preference is variously labeled the symmetry theorem (Carse et al. 1980) or Grassman's rule (Bilson 1983).

11. The term "key currency" was originated by economist John Williams at the end of World War II. See, e.g., Williams 1947.

12. Kwan 1994, chap. 9; Taguchi 1994. But cf. Frankel 1993; Frankel and Wei 1994; Bénassy-Quéré and Deusy-Fournier 1994.

13. Aglietta and Deusy-Fournier 1994; Thygesen et al. 1995. In fact, these two sources might be considered one, since the relevant texts are virtually identical and evidently owe their composition to one single scholar, Pierre Deusy-Fournier, who was a coauthor of both publications.

14. For more on the determinants of the organization of monetary space, see Cohen 1994.

15. The broader applicability of the logic was recognized by James Ingram in an early proposal for financial integration – in effect, a currency region based on firmly fixed exchange rates – among the industrial nations of Europe and North America (Ingram 1962), and more recently was revived as the basis for a possible alternative route to monetary integration in Europe (Kregel 1990). But the logic holds, obviously, only so long as all exchange risk is indeed removed. Between currencies whose exchange rates are not irrevocably pegged, capital flows may be anything but equilibrating.

16. Mundell (1973) called this the "internalization principle" – one of six "uncommon arguments for common currencies."

17. A good part of the credit for this early argument is in fact due to Peter

Kenen, who first planted the seed of the idea in my head while I was completing my doctoral dissertation under his supervision in 1962.

18. The magnitude of international seigniorage is of course a direct function of the size of current-account deficits financed in the home currency. Indirectly, it is also related to the size of fiscal deficits monetized by the national government (domestic seigniorage), but only to the extent that such budgetary shortfalls, by reducing net national savings, may be considered a contributing factor to external disequilibrium.

19. For an example, see Cohen 1971b.

20. This prediction accords with recent discussions of EMU and its possible impact on the relative standing of the dollar (Gros and Thygesen 1992; Bénassy et al. 1994; Johnson 1994). In the words of Gros and Thygesen: "The most visible effect of EMU at the global level will be the emergence of a second global currency . . . a serious competitor to the US dollar. . . . However, this does not imply that the introduction of the ecu as the common currency will cause sudden large shifts in international financial relations. History has shown that the international role of currencies changes only slowly. . . . The erosion of the dominant international position of the US dollar will be gradual" (1992: 295–6). Such judgments, however, tend to be more ad hoc than based on systematic theory.

REFERENCES

Aglietta, Michel, and Pierre Deusy-Fournier (1994). "Internationalisation des monnaies et organisation du système monétaire," *Economie Internationale* 59:3, 71–106.

Allen, Polly Reynolds (1993). "Transactions Use of the Ecu in the Transition to EMU: A Model of Network Externalities," *Recherches Economiques de Louvain* 59:1–2, 155–76.

Alogoskoufis, George (1993). "The ECU, the International Monetary System and the Management of Exchange Rates." In Leonce Bekemans and Loukas Tsoukalis, eds., *Europe and Global Economic Interdependence*, pp. 231–51. Brussels: European Interuniversity Press.

Andrew, A. Piatt (1904). "The End of the Mexican Dollar," *Quarterly Journal of Economics* 18:2 (May), 321–56.

Andrews, David M. (1994). "Capital Mobility and State Autonomy: Toward a Structural Theory of International Monetary Relations," *International Studies Quarterly* 38:2 (June), 193–218.

Benassy, A., A. Italianer, and J. Pisani-Ferry (1994). "The External Implications of the Single Currency," *Economie et Statistique*, Special Issue, 9–22.

Bénassy-Quéré, Agnes, and Pierre Deusy-Fournier (1994). "La concurrence pour le statut de monnaie internationale depuis 1973," *Economie Internationale* 59:3, 107–44.

Bernholz, Peter (1989). "Currency Competition, Inflation, Gresham's Law and Exchange Rate," *Journal of Institutional and Theoretical Economics* 145:3 (September), 465–88.

Bilson, John F. O. (1983). "The Choice of an Invoice Currency in International Transactions." In Jagdeep S. Bhandari and Bluford H. Putnam, eds., *Economic Interdependence and Flexible Exchange Rates*, chap. 14, pp. 384–401. Cambridge: MIT Press.

Black, Stanley W. (1991). "Transactions Costs and Vehicle Currencies," *Journal of International Money and Finance* 10, 512–26.

Black, Stanley W. (1993). "The International Use of Currencies." In Dilip K. Das, ed., *International Finance*, pp. 553–65. London: Routledge.

Boughton, James M. (1993). "The Economics of the CFA Franc Zone." In Paul R. Masson and Mark P. Taylor, eds., *Policy Issues in the Operation of Currency Unions*, chap. 4, pp. 96–107. Cambridge University Press.

Brand, Diana (1993). *Currency Substitution in Developing Countries: Theory and Empirical Analysis for Latin America and Eastern Europe*, Ifo-Studien zur Entwicklungsforschung No. 24. Munich and London: Weltforum Verlag.

British Treasury (1989). "An Evolutionary Approach to Economic and Monetary Union," Discussion Paper. London: HM Stationary Office, 2 November.

Calvo, Guillermo A., and Carlos A. Vegh, eds. (1992). *Revista de Analisis Económico*, Special Issue, "Convertibility and Currency Substitution," 7:1 (June).

Calvo, Guillermo A., and Carlos A. Vegh (1993). "Currency Substitution in High Inflation Countries," *Finance and Development* 30:1 (March), 34–7.

Canzoneri, Matthew, Behzad Diba, and Alberto Giovannini (1993). "Currency Substitution: From the Policy Questions to the Theory and Back." In Francisco Torres and Francesco Giavazzi, eds., *Adjustment and Growth in the European Monetary Union*, chap. 10, pp. 318–32. Cambridge University Press.

Carse, Stephen, John Williamson, and Geoffrey E. Wood (1980). *The Financing Procedures of British Foreign Trade*. Cambridge University Press.

Cohen, Benjamin J. (1963). "The Euro-Dollar, the Common Market, and Currency Unification," *Journal of Finance* 18:4 (December), 605–21.

Cohen, Benjamin J. (1971a). *The Future of Sterling as an International Currency*. London: Macmillan.

Cohen, Benjamin J. (1971b). "The Seigniorage Gain of an International Currency: An Empirical Test," *Quarterly Journal of Economics* 85:3 (August), 494–507.

Cohen, Benjamin J. (1992). "Sterling Area." In Peter Newman, Murray Milgate, and John Eatwell, eds., *The New Palgrave Dictionary of Money and Finance*, Vol. 3, pp. 554–5. London: Macmillan Press.

Cohen, Benjamin J. (1994). "The Geography of Money: Currency Relations Among Sovereign States," OFCE Working Paper No. 94–07. Paris: Observatoire Français des Conjonctures Economiques, October.

Cohen, Benjamin J. (1996). "Phoenix Risen: The Resurrection of Global Finance," *World Politics* 48:2 (January), 268–96.

Copeland, Laurence S. (1994). *Exchange Rates and International Finance*, 2nd ed. Reading, MA: Addison-Wesley.

De Grauwe, Paul (1994). *The Economics of Monetary Integration*, 2nd ed. New York: Oxford University Press.

Dowd, Kevin, and David Greenaway (1993). "Currency Competition, Network Externalities and Switching Costs: Towards an Alternative View of Optimum Currency Areas," *Economic Journal* 103:3 (September), 1180–9.

Frankel, Jeffrey A. (1993). "Is Japan Creating a Yen Bloc in East Asia and the Pacific?" In Jeffrey A. Frankel and Miles Kahler, eds., *Regionalism and Rivalry: Japan and the United States in Pacific Asia*, chap. 2, pp. 53–87. Chicago: University of Chicago Press.

Frankel, Jeffrey A., and Shang-Jin Wei (1994). "Yen Bloc or Dollar Bloc? Exchange Rate Policies of the East Asian Economies." In Takatoshi Ito and Anne O. Krueger, eds., *Macroeconomic Linkage: Savings, Exchange Rates, and Capital Flows*, chap. 12. Chicago: University of Chicago Press.

Frankel, Jeffrey A., and Shang-Jin Wei (1995). "Emerging Currency Blocks." In Hans Genberg, ed., *The International Monetary System: Its Institutions and Future*, chap. 5. New York: Springer-Verlag.

Fratianni, Michele, and Theo Peters, eds. (1978). *One Money for Europe*. London: Macmillan.

Giovannini, Alberto, and Bart Turtelboom (1994). "Currency Substitution." In Frederick Van Der Ploeg, ed., *The Handbook of International Macroeconomics*, chap. 12, pp. 390–436. Cambridge, MA: Blackwell.

Goodhart, Charles (1995). "The Political Economy of Monetary Union." In Peter B. Kenen, ed., *Understanding Interdependence: The Macroeconomics of the Open Economy*, pp. 448–505. Princeton: Princeton University Press.

Grassman, Sven (1973). "A Fundamental Symmetry in International Payment Patterns," *Journal of International Economics* 3:2 (May), 105–16.

Gros, Daniel, and Niels Thygesen (1992). *European Monetary Integration*. New York: St. Martin's Press.

Guidotti, Pablo E., and Carlos A. Rodriguez (1992). "Dollarization in Latin America: Gresham's Law in Reverse?" *International Monetary Fund Staff Papers* 39:3 (September), 518–44.

Hartmann, P. (1994). "Vehicle Currencies in the Foreign Exchange Market." Document de travail du seminaire Delta No. 94–13. Paris: Ecole Normale Superieure.

Hayek, Friedrich A. (1976). *Denationalisation of Money – The Argument Refined*. London: Institute of Economic Affairs.

Ingram, James C. (1959). "State and Regional Payments Mechanisms," *Quarterly Journal of Economics* 73:4 (November), 619–32.

Ingram, James C. (1962). "A Proposal for Integration in the Atlantic Community." In *Factors Affecting the United States Balance of Payments*, Compilation of Studies Prepared for the Subcommittee on International Exchange and Payments of the Joint Economic Committee of the Congress, pp. 175–207. Washington, DC: U.S. Government Printing Office.

Johnson, Karen H. (1994). "International Dimensions of European Monetary Union: Implications for the Dollar." International Finance Discussion Papers No. 469. Washington: Federal Reserve Board of Governors, May.

Kenen, Peter B. (1969). "The Theory of Optimum Currency Areas: An Eclectic View." In Robert A. Mundell and Alexander K. Swoboda, eds., *Monetary*

Problems of the International Economy, pp. 41–60. Chicago: University of Chicago Press.

Kenen, Peter B. (1983). *The Role of the Dollar as an International Currency.* Occasional Papers No. 13. Washington, DC: Group of Thirty.

Kregel, J. A. (1990). "The EMS, the Dollar and the World Economy." In Piero Ferri, ed., *Prospects for the European Monetary System*, chap. 12, pp. 236–51. New York: St. Martin's Press.

Krugman, Paul R. (1992). *Currencies and Crises.* Cambridge and London: MIT Press.

Krugman, Paul R. (1993). *What Do We Need to Know about the International Monetary System?* Essays in International Finance 190. International Finance Section, Princeton University, July.

Kwan, C. H. (1994). *Economic Interdependence in the Asia-Pacific Region: Towards a Yen Bloc.* London and New York: Routledge.

Lopez, Robert S. (1951). "The Dollar of the Middle Ages," *Journal of Economic History* 11:3 (Summer), 209–34.

Masson, Paul R., and Mark P. Taylor (1993). "Currency Unions: A Survey of the Issues." In Paul R. Masson and Mark P. Taylor eds., *Policy Issues in the Operation of Currency Unions*, chap. 1, pp. 3–51. Cambridge University Press.

Matsuyama, Kiminori, Nobuhiro Kiyotaki, and Akihiko Matsui (1993). "Toward a Theory of International Currency," *Review of Economic Studies* 60:2 (April), 283–307.

Meigs, A. James (1993). "Eurodollars: A Transition Currency," *Cato Journal* 12:3 (Winter), 711–27.

Melvin, Michael (1988). "The Dollarization of Latin America as a Market-Enforced Monetary Reform: Evidence and Implications," *Economic Development and Cultural Change* 36:3 (April), 543–58.

Mizen, Paul, and Eric Pentecost, eds. (1996). *The Macroeconomics of International Currencies: Theory, Policy and Evidence.* Cheltenham: Edward Elgar.

Mundell, Robert A. (1961). "A Theory of Optimum Currency Areas," *American Economic Review* 51:4 (September), 657–65.

Mundell, Robert A. (1973). "Uncommon Arguments for Common Currencies." In Harry G. Johnson and Alexander K. Swoboda, eds., *The Economics of Common Currencies*, chap. 7, 114–32. London: George Allen and Unwin.

Orléan, André (1989). "Mimetic Contagion and Speculative Bubbles," *Theory and Decision* 27:1/2, 63–92.

Perroux, François (1950). "Economic Space: Theory and Applications," *Quarterly Journal of Economics* 64:1 (February), 89–104.

Ruggie, John Gerard (1993). "Territoriality and Beyond: Problematizing Modernity in International Relations," *International Organization* 47:1 (Winter), 139–74.

Salin, Pascal, ed. (1984). *Currency Competition and Monetary Union.* The Hague: Martinus Nijhoff.

Scitovsky, Tibor (1958). *Economic Theory and Western European Integration.* Stanford: Stanford University Press.

Selgin, George A., and Lawrence H. White (1994). "How Would the Invisible

Hand Handle Money?" *Journal of Economic Literature* 32:4 (December), 1718–49.

Streissler, Erich W. (1992). "Good Money Driving Out Bad: A Model of the Hayek Process in Action." In Ernst Baltensperger and Hans-Werner Sinn, eds., *Exchange-Rate Regimes and Currency Unions*, chap. 10, pp. 203–23. New York: St. Martin's Press.

Taguchi, Hiroo (1994). "On the Internationalization of the Japanese Yen." In Takatoshi Ito and Anne O. Krueger, eds., *Macroeconomic Linkage: Savings, Exchange Rates, and Capital Flows*, chap. 13, pp. 335–55. Chicago: University of Chicago Press.

Tavlas, George S. (1991). *On the International Use of Currencies: The Case of the Deutsche Mark*. Essays in International Finance 181, International Finance Section, Princeton University, March.

Tavlas, George S. (1993). "The 'New' Theory of Optimum Currency Areas," *The World Economy* 16:6 (November), 663–85.

Tavlas, George S. (1994). "The Theory of Monetary Integration," *Open Economies Review* 5, 211–30.

Thygesen, Niels, et al. (1995). *International Currency Competition and the Future Role of the Single European Currency*. Final Report of a Working Group on "European Monetary Union–International Monetary System." London: Kluwer Law International.

Vaubel, Roland (1977). "Free Currency Competition," *Weltwirtschafliches Archiv* 113:3, 435–61.

Vaubel, Roland (1978). *Strategies for Currency Unification: The Economics of Currency Competition and the Case for a European Parallel Currency*. Tubingen: J.C.B. Mohr.

Weil, Phillipe (1991). "Currency Competition and the Transition to Monetary Union: Currency Competition and the Evolution of Multi-Currency Regions." In Alberto Giovannini and Colin Mayer, eds., *European Financial Integration*, chap. 10, pp. 290–302. Cambridge University Press.

Wihlborg, Clas, and Thomas D. Willett (1991). "Optimum Currency Areas Revisited on the Transition Path to a Currency Union." In Clas Wihlborg, Michele Fratianni, and Thomas D. Willett, eds., *Financial Regulations and Monetary Arrangements after 1992*, chap. 12, pp. 279–97. Amsterdam: Elsevier Science Publishers.

Williams, John H. (1947). *Postwar Monetary Plans and Other Essays*. New York: Knopf.

Woodford, Michael (1991). "Currency Competition and the Transition to Monetary Union: Does Competition Between Currencies Lead to Price Level and Exchange Rate Stability?" In Alberto Giovannini and Colin Mayer, eds., *European Financial Integration*, chap. 9, pp. 257–89. Cambridge University Press.

PART III
APPLIED POLICY ANALYSIS

CHAPTER 9

Labor market adjustment and trade: Their interaction in the Triad

Marina v.N. Whitman

Introduction

In a recent essay on the future of the Bretton Woods system, Peter Kenen and his coauthor Barry Eichengreen note that "the ability of governments to manage change internationally depends importantly on their ability to manage it domestically," especially as regards income distribution and the structure of the economy. They assert, furthermore, that throughout the industrialized world this ability to manage has fallen increasingly short since 1973, as virtually all these countries have been confronted with slower real growth, an increase in both the pace of structural change and the amplitude of business cycles, and intensified global competition (Kenen and Eichengreen 1994: 53–4).

The focus of this essay is on one particularly salient aspect of the link noted by Kenen and Eichengreen, namely, the responses of domestic labor markets to the challenges that have confronted the industrialized nations since the 1973 watershed and their feedback to trade pressures and policies. These responses are particularly crucial to the functioning of the international economy for two reasons. First, because the politics of trade and trade policy tend almost everywhere to focus heavily on the labor-market or "jobs" impact of such policies, and this focus has, if anything, intensified in the face of the increasing "footlooseness" of the other major factors of production: capital and technology. And second, because the reverberations in labor markets from post-1973 developments have been disquieting. They have included a near-universal (among industrialized countries) slowdown or stagnation in the growth of real incomes. Along with it have come either a significant increase in unemployment or underemployment (in Europe and Japan, respectively) or a substantial increase in wage dispersion and income inequality (in the United States and other non-European English-speaking countries).

The challenge confronting the leading industrialized nations that comprise the "triad" (the United States, Japan, and Western Europe)[1] is to find ways to maintain or enhance their flexibility to adapt to structural change while minimizing the social costs that such change imposes on individuals and communities – costs that economists frequently ignore but which politicians and policymakers cannot afford to. None has so far found a fully satisfactory way to accomplish these twin goals. In the United States, long known for its ability to adapt, companies are downsizing and restructuring and new forms of business organization are rapidly emerging. The result has been an acceleration of productivity growth and a restoration of competitiveness but, at the same time, a spreading sense of personal insecurity and of disquiet regarding the social effects of slowed wage growth and widening disparities in income. In Japan, where lifetime employment and extensive on-the-job training have traditionally been matched by workers' loyalty, flexibility, and active involvement in continuous improvement, companies are scaling back commitments in the face of growing underemployment and prolonged economic reverses. Meanwhile, Europeans confront labor market rigidities associated with high unemployment and low job creation and are reevaluating the scope and costs of their social safety nets.

The starting premise of this essay is that despite significant differences in the institutions and processes of labor market adjustment among the three areas of the triad, suggested briefly above and explored in more detail in the next section, developments in all three are converging toward relatively greater reliance on external (between-firm) as opposed to internal (within-firm) adjustment processes.

I demonstrate that this shift is a rational response to the changing economic environment. However, it also tends to move the costs of adjustment away from firms and toward workers, thus making them more visible and politically sensitive. One result has been the increased prominence of the view, honed to caricature in the rhetoric of Ross Perot and Pat Buchanan, that trade has a major negative impact on employment, wages, and the distribution of income in the United States and other industrialized countries.

The consensus that emerges from the numerous theoretical and empirical analyses summarized briefly in this essay is that these views are largely erroneous. But their impact on the public debate, together with the apparent tendency of trade protection documented here to be directed toward cushioning or retarding labor-market adjustments, poses a potential threat to the maintenance of an open global economy that cannot be ignored. The essay concludes with a discussion of some of the policy issues raised by the developments just outlined, as well as suggestions for further research directed at shedding light on some of the uncertainties that currently impinge on many of the central questions at issue.

Labor market institutions and adjustment processes

The nations of the triad have many common characteristics. All are advanced industrial democracies with market-oriented economies, relatively high average incomes, and a high degree of economic interaction with each other. The patterns and outcomes of labor-market adjustment to cyclical fluctuations and structural changes differ widely among them, however, at least in part because of differences in labor market institutions. I will describe the major differences among the United States, Japan, and Europe as regards these processes and institutions in a highly stylized fashion, of necessity simplifying many subtleties and focusing on those characteristics the major European countries have in common rather than on the many aspects in which they differ from one another.

The United States lies clearly at one end of the spectrum as regards the speed and sensitivity with which its markets, including its labor markets, respond to changing economic signals. In terms of geographical mobility, job turnover, relative volume of job accessions and separations, and short average duration of unemployment, it leads the industrialized world (Freeman 1993: 5). Wage-setting is highly decentralized, essentially unrestricted by government regulation, and increasingly less so by collective bargaining as union membership declines. Layoffs, too, are relatively unrestricted and are the major means of reductions in force required by changes in external conditions.

Japan lies at the opposite end of the spectrum as regards labor market institutions and their responses to both cyclical and structural developments (Dore 1986). Its rate of labor turnover is one of the lowest in the industrialized world (even when adjustments are made for firm size, as documented in Blinder and Krueger 1991), limited not so much by formal legislation as by a body of case law built up gradually over the years since World War II and by strongly entrenched custom and the set of mutual expectations among employers and employees described earlier. Given these constraints, Japanese firms make heavy use of alternatives to layoffs, including reduced overtime, work-sharing, attrition, and early retirement, as well as focusing on reduction of nonlabor costs when business deteriorates (Odagiri 1992; Fukao 1995).

More formal quantitative evidence shows that employment changes much less in relation to business output in Japan than in the United States (Abraham and Houseman 1989). The rate of total separations (the sum of those who quit and those who are laid off or dismissed) is lower in Japan than in the United States, whereas the ratio of workers who quit to those who are laid off or dismissed is higher. Furthermore, in the United States quits rise during economic expansions and fall during recessions, whereas layoffs show the opposite cyclical relationship. No such cyclical pattern is evident in the data for Japan (Hashimoto 1990).

To the extent that one can generalize about a heterogeneous group of countries, Western Europe appears to lie between the United States and Japan as regards the use of labor turnover (and its reciprocal, average job tenure within a given enterprise) as a mechanism of labor reallocation in response to economic change (OECD 1993; Houseman 1994: 16). Job security, in the form of restrictions on and/or high costs associated with layoffs or dismissals, is provided either directly through legislation or through a centralized industrywide process of collective bargaining underpinned by legislation that extends contract provisions to regular workers who are not actually members of the union. Requirements affecting conditions of work and the social safety net, including such matters as minimum wages, health, vacation and retirement benefits, and unemployment compensation tend to be both relatively generous and set by national governments, whether they are provided directly through taxes and government expenditures or indirectly through mandates on private employers.[2]

Not surprisingly, inflexibility in firm-level employment in response to exogenous shocks tends to be at least partially offset by greater flexibility in other components of labor input. Greater variability in hours worked in Japan appears to compensate in part for the greater rigidity of employment as compared with the United States. The utilization of work-sharing, attrition, and early retirement is also greater in the former than in the latter. Similarly, in those European countries where employment protection provisions are strictest, subsidies to short-time work, early retirement, and other alternative adjustment mechanisms are most liberal. The offsets are partial rather than complete, however; total labor inputs are still most responsive in the United States and least responsive in Japan (Houseman 1994).

The picture is less clear as regards the responsiveness of wages to exogenous shocks. The wage-setting process is clearly most decentralized in the United States and most centralized in a number of the countries of Western Europe (Freeman 1994: 18–20). But centralization and rigidity are not necessarily the same thing. The general view is that compensation, including wages, bonuses, and certain other nonwage items, is more responsive in Japan than in the United States and more rigid in Europe than in either of the other two areas. Detailed scrutiny of a number of studies suggests, however, that the evidence is more ambiguous (Boyer 1988, 238; Hashimoto and Raisian 1992: 84–7) and that, in Boyer's words, Europe may be "neither homogeneous nor significantly more rigid than the other countries" in this respect.[3]

It is even more difficult to discern a simple direct relationship between labor-market rules and institutions and the way such markets actually function. The widely held assumption on which the influential *OECD Jobs Study* (OECD 1994a) was predicated, for example, is that labor-market rigidities in Western Europe, particularly in the form of minimum wages, generous unemployment benefits, and restrictive employment protection laws, have been a significant factor in that region's persistent problems of high unemployment and low employment growth.

A number of empirical investigations bear out the negative relationship between the strength of job security provisions and both the rate of labor force participation in triad countries (OECD 1994b: II, 76) and the rate of employment growth in these countries over the 1980s (Bertola 1990), as well as the positive relationship between the generosity of unemployment benefits and the share of long-term unemployment in total unemployment (Bean 1994; Bertola 1990). But, with one exception, these same studies find no evidence of a systematic relationship between these apparent rigidities in labor market institutions and the aggregate unemployment rate (Buechtemann 1993: 33–4). Even more surprising is the finding that "The loosening of the employment security laws [in Europe] in the mid-1980's had no noticeable effect on the average monthly lag" of employment adjustment to output change in manufacturing (Blank 1993: 166).[4]

One explanation offered for these puzzling observations is that restrictive laws and regulations are frequently not binding for most firms, either because

> such government regulation frequently reflects codification of what is generally regarded by the private sector as best practice ... [or because] ... countries with stringent employment protection laws often have programs that lower the costs to companies of adjusting labor using alternatives to layoffs, such as short-time compensation and early retirement. (Houseman 1994: 20–4)

But resort to such alternatives, the same author notes, may often inhibit the hiring of regular workers and increase reliance on a secondary workforce of part-time or temporary workers not covered by protective legislation.

Another puzzle arises with respect to Japan. Overall, the external (that is, interfirm) processes of labor-market reallocation appear to be less responsive to market signals there than in the other nations of the triad. There is no evidence that Japan has been less exposed to external shocks or undergone less structural change in recent decades.[5] Yet despite its need to adapt and apparent lack of flexible response mechanisms, the Japanese economy has displayed greater macroeconomic stability over the past four decades than has the United States with its highly flexible labor markets. Variation in the real growth rate of GDP, adjusted for Japan's faster average growth rate (i.e., the coefficient of variation) has been smaller in Japan than in the United States. And, of the three triad areas, only Japan has combined reasonably strong growth in both employment and real wages while avoiding an increase in earnings inequality (Freeman 1993: 232–3).

Internal versus external adjustment processes

One frequent explanation for the apparent smoothness of the adjustment process in Japan is that Japanese firms adjust to structural change by relying heavily on *internal* rather than *external* processes to reallocate labor – that is, by diversifying output and redeploying workers within the firm to a far greater extent than do other countries in the triad. Anecdotal evidence for this behavior abounds, with steel firms diversifying into computers and semiconductors and textile producers into plastics and a variety of other products, for example.[6]

In particular, Japanese firms place heavy emphasis on anticipating declines in existing markets and planning for diversification, particularly when traditional markets are under stress. And, although mergers and acquisitions (M&A's) are rare in Japan, two types are increasing in frequency and importance: acquisitions to start operations overseas and acquisitions to diversify when industrial structure changes rapidly. Furthermore, M&A's are associated with diversification to provide internal growth to absorb labor (Odagiri 1992; Gerlach 1992).

This hypothesis of internal adjustment through diversification may appear to be contradicted by the fact that Japanese firms are on average less diversified than those in the United States. But the data on which this comparison is based do not take account of subsidiaries, a major mechanism by which the highly porous *keiretsu* structure is elaborated (Odagiri 1992). Furthermore, R&D activity is much more diversified than sales in Japanese firms (Odagiri 1992, table 5.4), suggesting the kind of "forward diversification" referred to above. And the proportion of R&D devoted to fields other than a firm's main business has also increased over time in Japan, as has the proportion of leading companies' output devoted to something other than the firm's main product (Goto 1981; Dore 1989: 63).

Some American firms, AT&T notable among them, have also responded to the challenges and opportunities of deregulation by diversifying, not always successfully, into new areas. But certain characteristics of Japanese firms make diversification easier. Enterprise-based as opposed to industry-based unions make labor-management relations less contentious and efforts to diversify smoother. Less narrow occupational specialization and greater job rotation among different functions within a firm for both blue-collar and white-collar workers also contribute. And, as noted earlier, Japanese firms have greater flexibility in compensation.

We can say much less about the use of internal mechanisms – that is, diversification and reallocation of labor within firms – to respond to structural change in Europe, in part because the very heterogeneity of European experience makes assembling and interpreting data much more difficult. In terms of formal mechanisms, the United Kingdom appears to lie at the external-adjustment end of the European spectrum, resembling the United States in that its external labor markets are relatively unconstrained by employment protection limitations (even before the advent of a conservative government in 1979); at the same time, its ability to reallocate internally is limited by quite rigid work rules and narrow job classifications (Sengenberger 1992: 156). Yet the United Kingdom has by far the lowest rates of both gross worker turnover and gross job turnover – two standard measures of external labor mobility – among all the European countries studied, an anomaly that the authors who report it are at a loss to explain (Centre for Economic Policy Research 1995: 8–22).

Germany lies at the opposite end of the European spectrum as regards labor-market adjustment processes. That is, it resembles Japan in that its use of external adjustment mechanisms is significantly limited, in this case by strong legislation regarding job protection, worker welfare, and the collective bargaining process. At the same time, it appears to have relatively flexible internal labor markets, characterized by broad job categories, heavy emphasis on on-the-job training and retraining, and hence relatively easy redeployment of workers within the firm. There is some evidence, furthermore, that German firms have also made substantial use of internal expansion and diversification of product mix in response to cyclical downturns or structural shocks (Sengenberger 1992: 158–9, 171–2).

In France and Italy, on the other hand, both external and internal labor adjustment appear to be significantly constrained. "Collective dismissal in Italy is considered almost impossible, and in France it has to be approved by the labor inspectors. In both countries, internal work organization and allocation are subject to collective work rules" (Sengenberger 1992: 156). Not surprisingly, in light of these double constraints, these two countries' unemployment rates are among the highest in Europe.

Internal versus external adjustment: Pros and cons

Of all the nations in the triad, Japan makes by far the greatest use of internal as opposed to external mechanisms to reallocate labor in response to market signals. It is also the nation with by far the best macroeconomic performance, by all of the commonly used measures, although this performance has faltered noticeably in the first half of the 1990s.

These observations do not tell us, however, whether the apparently less-disruptive adjustment process in Japan is a result of the greater use of internal reallocation mechanisms per se. It could also be due to the higher growth rate Japan has experienced until the early 1990s, a growth rate that had eased dislocation and rendered potential rigidities inherent in her labor market institutions nonbinding. Nor do we know what the relationship is between greater reliance on internal reallocation and the overall growth rate. Finally, we do not know if reliance on internal reallocation will survive the prolonged recession and major structural changes currently under way in Japan.

The picture is equally incomplete for the nation at the opposite end of the internal–external reallocation spectrum, the United States. The United States has done better than the other triad nations, except Japan, as regards job growth and the level and duration of unemployment. But it brings up the rear as regards the growth of labor productivity and real wages and increased dispersion in the distribution of income. In between, as already noted, there is no obvious systematic relationship between reallocation mechanisms and macroeconomic performance in Western Europe. Given the complexity of observed patterns, what can economic reasoning tell us about the implications of internal versus external reallocation for national economic welfare?[7]

The relative advantages and disadvantages of markets versus firms as allocative mechanisms have been explored extensively by Coase (1937), Williamson (1971, 1975), and others. Within the general framework they established, one can identify a variety of conditions under which labor hoarding, as exemplified in long-term employment commitments, may increase overall economic welfare. This would be the case if workers had firm-specific skills that would be lost when they left a firm or if the transactions costs of hiring and/or discharging were high (Oi 1962; Okun 1981). It would also be true if the costs of finding buyers and sellers were lower for firms than for individuals (Malmgren 1961), or if workers were risk-averse or less able than firms to bear or pool risks – in other words, if firms had better access to both capital and information regarding human capital investment than do workers (Rosen 1985; Williamson 1971, 1975; Blinder and Krueger 1991). Finally, labor hoarding may contribute to productivity increases through its effect on labor–management relations, employee morale, and an enhanced ability to recruit superior workers (Boyer 1993: 94–5).

Maintaining the size of a firm's workforce during economic downturns may also contribute to macroeconomic stability by reducing variation in overall employment. This result is not so obvious as it may sound; even though individual firms may try to retain their workers when demand for output falls, developments such as bankruptcies, layoffs of temporary or contract workers, or reduced hiring will affect the overall economy. But macroeconomic stabilization can occur when efforts are made to retain workers because income shares are thereby shifted away from profits and toward labor during periods of adversity. Then, because a large share of wages than of profits is devoted to consumption, the multiplier effect of expenditures will rise during downturns and fall during upturns. This effect could increase the efficiency of resource-utilization at the macro-level without necessarily showing up in firm-level profitability (Odagiri 1992).

Finally, overall economic welfare could be increased if a positive relationship between job tenure and the skill level of the labor force is created through on-the-job training. Indeed, an OECD study (*Employment Outlook* 1993), of leading industrialized nations finds just such a positive and mutually reinforcing relationship between job tenure and employer-provided training, both among countries and among industries within a given country. The existence of such a "virtuous circle," resulting in greater investment by both employers and workers in human capital in Germany and Japan, for example, than in the United States, has led some observers to posit a more comprehensive virtuous circle as well, whereby such investment in human capital both encourages higher growth and technical progress and is encouraged by them.

The preceding discussion describes conditions under which internalization of adjustment mechanisms can benefit economic welfare, but there are powerful arguments in the opposite direction as well. One of the often-cited advantages of the U.S. style of capitalism is the high external mobility of both labor and capital, that is, the speed with which firms can expand or contract and are born or disappear in response to market signals. Such responsiveness can increase static efficiency by substituting the "hard" disciplines of market competition for the "softer" budget constraints that are likely to prevail within a single organization. It can also encourage dynamic efficiency in the sense of advancing technological frontiers by increasing both the pressures for innovation and the flexibility to respond to structural changes.[8]

From firm flexibility to market flexibility: Patterns and reasons

Despite the absence of any clear-cut general conclusions regarding the relative merits of internal versus external adjustment in labor markets, the triad countries have recently been voting with their feet in favor of greater reliance on external or market mechanisms for labor reallocation. And there are sound analytical reasons for regarding this shift as a rational response to the economic forces that are impinging, to a greater or lesser extent, on all of them.

A number of cross-country studies of labor-market behavior have noted convergence among Western industrialized nations toward a weakening of employment stability and toward performance-related pay, which tends to be inversely related to job tenure (Koshiro 1992; Abraham and McKersie 1990; Buechtemann 1993; Hartog and Theeuwes 1993; Houseman 1994).

Probably the most universal manifestation of this tendency toward heavier reliance on market-mediated as opposed to within-firm reallocation mechanisms is the increased use of a "peripheral" or "contingent" workforce, consisting of temporary or part-time workers or contract services. In the United States, although the proportion of the workforce accounted for by part-time or self-employed workers has remained relatively stable, the share accounted for by temporary employees and business services has tripled over the period 1982–92, albeit from a very small base.[9] In Japan, the proportion of temporary employees has remained relatively stable, but part-time employment has grown substantially. And the importance of both part-time and temporary workers has increased in a number of European countries, particularly where restrictions on the use of such "atypical" arrangements have been relaxed (Houseman 1994; Bridgeford and Stirling 1994).

Regarding other aspects of the movement in the direction of external reallocation mechanisms, the manifestations are less systematic and vary widely among countries, although the overall direction is clear. For the

United States, the evidence regarding job tenure or duration is somewhat mixed for the post-1973 period as a whole. The virtually universal belief, bolstered by voluminous anecdotal evidence, that job tenure has been declining since 1973 is supported by some studies (Marcotte 1995; Rose 1995; Swinnerton and Wial 1995); others find no such decline in the aggregate (Diebold et al. 1994; Farber 1995), although all agree that it is true for less-educated workers.[10] But the job loss rate was higher during the "modest recovery" period of 1991–3 than during the severe recession of 1981–3, providing "very preliminary evidence consistent with the view that there has been a secular decline in job security" (Farber 1996: 13). In particular, Farber notes, job loss rates have risen sharply since 1989 for more educated workers and for reasons classified as "position/shift abolished," the category that has an intuitive link to corporate restructuring and downsizing.

Another manifestation of the internal-to-external shift in the United States is the tendency for U.S. manufacturing firms to become smaller and more specialized over the 1980s. A December 1993 article in *Fortune* (Stewart 1993) notes that

> businesses are more tightly focused: Conference Board figures show that between 1979 and 1991 the number of three-digit standard industrial classification (SIC) codes in which an average U.S. manufacturer does business dropped from 4.35 to 2.12. Companies are also smaller: Census data show that the number of employees in the average U.S. workplace is 8% lower than it was in 1980.

A recent study (Brynjolfsson et al. 1994), cited at some length in the *Fortune* article, suggests a link between decreases in firm size and organizational changes associated with advances in information technology (IT). Although there is no way to predict in the abstract whether IT will reduce external coordination costs more than internal ones, the fact that the authors find shrinkage in firm size to be positively associated with IT spending suggests that such spending is a factor in reducing external coordination costs relative to both internal coordination and production costs, thus encouraging outsourcing and reductions in vertical integration. The authors find a decline in firm size (over the 1980s) for manufacturing only; no such trend is evident as yet in the services sector, but the impact of IT indicated by their results suggests that we may anticipate such a development in the future.[11]

For Japan, at the other end of the internal–external allocation spectrum, the evidence is more anecdotal, partly because these developments appear to be relatively recent, having been greatly accelerated by the prolonged recession and significant weakening of the banking structure

M. v.N. Whitman

that have plagued Japan since 1991. Toyota's decision to hire automobile designers at high salaries under one-year contract, the tendency of some major Japanese firms to substitute performance-based pay for earnings based strictly on seniority, the unprecedented resort to layoffs by several large firms, and the fear that Japanese industry may be curtailing funds for "forward" diversification in the form of R&D in new areas have all been chronicled in the pages of the *Wall Street Journal.*

Shintaro Hori summarizes the situation in the *Harvard Business Review* (Nov.–Dec. 1993): since the bubble burst, the erosion of lifetime employment is under way, the seniority pay system is being replaced by performance evaluation and the emergence of pay gaps between good and poor performance. There is more job-changing, especially among the young, and a decline in loyalty revealed in interview surveys.

Some of the forces that underlie this shift in the labor-adjustment process have been felt throughout the nations of the triad during the period since 1973. One of the most important is the slowdown in aggregate growth rates, which demands greater flexibility for downward adjustments, thus increasing the need to exercise the "hard" disciplines of the marketplace. This is the reverse side of Boyer's observation that "there always exists an average long-term growth rate for which labor rigidity is not binding" (1993: 115). Another is the increased incidence of large and unanticipated economic shocks. Even the most enthusiastic supporters of internal labor markets note that, because custom exerts a strong inertial pull on allocative mechanisms in these markets, the efficiencies of internal markets are greater when change is gradual and predictable, less so when it is radical and unanticipated (Doeringer and Piore 1971: 63). Finally, the impact of technological change, particularly of rapid advances in information technology, has already been described.

Other forces have impinged to differing degrees on the nations or regions of the triad. In Japan, the gradual reduction since 1980 of capital market regulations that had effectively limited access to capital to existing firms with close ties to financial institutions, along with some loosening of cross-shareholding relationships, has worked against the dominance of existing firms and thus against the relative importance of internal expansion and diversification.

In addition, Japan is no longer coming from behind in terms of technology. This is not only a major factor in slowing the rapid growth that has been such an integral part of Japan's "virtuous circle" (Saxonhouse 1994), it is also making decisions about where to reallocate resources more uncertain and therefore making firms more eager to spread the risk around.

Finally, an increase in the intensity of global competition has intensified pressures to increase competitiveness by reducing labor costs. These pressures operate to eliminate the shared rents on which internal labor markets depend and thus, once again, to stimulate the substitution of hard external disciplines for softer internal ones. These pressures have been felt most strongly in Western Europe and, to a lesser but still significant extent, in the United States. More recently, they have begun to impinge on Japan as well.

A reallocation model

A simple model of imperfect competition[12] can help to elucidate why a shift away from internal toward external labor-market adjustment is a rational response to the three developments just mentioned: deregulation of capital markets, technological catch-up, and intensified global competition.

The model assumes two industries and a single factor of production. Industry 1 is a Cournot oligopoly with n identical firms, in all of which labor receives a fixed, above-market wage.[13] Industry 2 is perfectly competitive.

Initially, the oligopolistic industry specializes in good x, which it produces with constant returns to labor inputs (where the unit labor requirements equals 1) but with certain fixed costs that constitute a barrier to entry. The competitive industry produces good y under conditions of diminishing returns to labor.

The inverse demand function faced by the representative oligopolistic firm is:

$$p_x = p_x \big[X + x_m + x_f \big], \tag{9.1}$$

where X = output of good 1 by the remaining $(n - 1)$ domestic oligopolistic firms;
x_m = imports of good 1 (treated here as a shift parameter);
x_f = output of good 1 by the representative firm; and
functions are denoted by square brackets.

Note that the price depends only on the output of good x and not on the output of good y or of income.[14]

Now, assume that there is a reduction in demand for good x or, alternatively, an exogenous increase in X_m, as a result of which labor must be reallocated. This leads the firms in industry 1 to diversify into the production of good y. Thus labor can be reallocated either internally, within the firms in industry 1, or externally, from firms in industry 1 to those in industry 2.

Assume further that, although the oligopolistic firms have no market power as regards good y, they must pay the same wage, w_0, to their workers regardless of which good they are producing.[15] Each oligopolistic firm will then maximize the following profit function:

$$p_x\left[X + x_m + \left(l_{x0} - tl_y - tl_e\right)\right]\left(1 + s\right)\left(l_{x0} - tl_y - tl_e\right)$$
$$+ F_y\left[K_w, tl_y\right]\left(1 + s\right) - w_0\left(l_{x0} - tl_e\right), \tag{9.2}$$

where $p_y = 1$ and

l_{x0} = initial amount of labor in X production

tl_y = amount of labor transferred internally to y production

tl_e = amount of labor released by industry 1

s = per-unit subsidy paid to industry 1 (oligopolistic) firms

F_y = production function for good y, where $\dfrac{\partial F_y}{\partial tl_y} > 0$ and

$$\frac{\partial^2 F_y}{\partial\left(tl_y\right)^2} < 0$$

K_w = measure of stock of knowledge of rest of world related to production of good y

We assume that both F_y and $\partial F_y/\partial(tl_y)$ are increasing in K_w. The reasoning is that, if a country is behind the technology frontier, K_w is already large and the productivity of the country's firms in producing good y benefits from the world knowledge that is freely available to them. If, on the other hand, the country is already *on* the relevant technology frontier, this benefit to productivity is not available.

Since the n firms in industry 1 are identical, the first-order conditions, that marginal revenue should equal marginal cost in each activity, are as follows:

$$p_x\left[x_m + n\left(l_{x0} - tl_y - tl_e\right)\right]\left(1 + s\right)\left(1 - \frac{1}{n\varepsilon}\right) = w_0, \tag{9.3}$$

where ε = the price elasticity of demand for good x, assumed to be constant, and

$$F_y'\left[K_w, tl_y\right]\left(1 + s\right) = w_0, \quad \text{where } F_y' = \frac{\partial F_y}{\partial tl_y}. \tag{9.4}$$

Equation (9.3) defines a negative relationship between tl_y and tl_e: as more people are reallocated internally, marginal revenue for good x rises

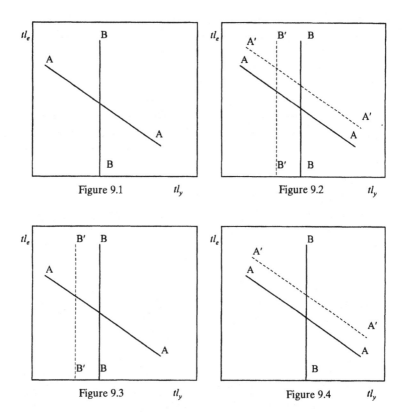

Figure 9.1

Figure 9.2

Figure 9.3

Figure 9.4

due to a reduction in x output, so that fewer people need to be released in order to keep marginal revenue equal to marginal cost. Equation (9.4) gives the value of tl_y, the only endogenous variable in that equation. It states that labor is reallocated internally until the marginal product of labor in y production equals the fixed wage, w_0.

Graphically, in Figure 9.1 the line AA plots all values of tl_y and tl_e that satisfy equation (9.3), and BB does the same for equation (9.4). We can now analyze the allocation effects of the three developments described at the beginning of this section using some simple graphics.

The effect of capital–market deregulation (which has the effect of a reduction in the subsidy to oligopolistic firms) is shown in Figure 9.2.[16] More workers now must be released to keep marginal revenue equal to marginal cost in production of good x, and fewer workers can be internally reallocated to the production of good y for the same reason, thus shifting AA to the right (A'A') and BB to the left (B'B'). The effect is to decrease tl_y and increase tl_e, that is, to reduce internal reallocation and increase external reallocation.

The effect of technology catch-up is shown in Figure 9.3. As the economy moves toward the technology frontier, K_w decreases, meaning that less "off the shelf" technology is available, thus reducing the productivity of industry 1 firms in good y. As the marginal productivity of labor in good y falls, less labor is reallocated internally and BB shifts to the left (B'B'). Once again, the effect is a shift from internal to external reallocation into industry 2, where the wage can fall in tandem with the marginal productivity of labor.[17]

Finally, Figure 9.4 depicts the effect of an exogenous increase in import competition in good x. When x_m increases, BB is unaffected, but AA shifts up (A'A'). That is, at the same level of tl_y, more workers must be released, increasing tl_e, so that the proportion of external reallocation increases.[18]

Trade, jobs, and wages: Beliefs and evidence

As the preceding discussion has demonstrated, the shift throughout the triad in the direction of more external (as opposed to internal) reallocation of labor can be interpreted as a rational response to various developments in the national or global economies since 1973. One effect of this shift, however, has been to make the dislocation impacts and distributional effects associated with such adjustments more explicitly visible and politically sensitive. At the same time, economic openness, as measured by the ratio of exports plus imports to GDP, has been increasing steadily in the United States and Western Europe and labor markets have been beset with difficulties throughout the triad nations.

Together, these developments have pushed to the forefront concerns about the impact of trade on labor markets, concerns variously subsumed under the rubrics of "deindustrialization" in the United States, "delocalization" in Western Europe, and "hollowing out" in Japan. And these concerns, skillfully exploited by Ross Perot and Pat Buchanan in the United States and their political counterparts in other triad countries, have disturbing implications for the future conduct of trade and trade-related policies, particularly because, as I describe below, the primary focus of trade protection has historically been to cushion or delay adjustments in labor markets.

Although the distinctions are seldom made clear, the concerns just cited actually relate to at least three different aspects of the "trade and jobs" issue: the total *quantity* of jobs (or the aggregate unemployment rate), the overall *quality* of jobs (generally measured by the average wage level), and the *income distribution* that results from a particular pattern of labor-market allocation. Because these different aspects are frequently intermingled in public discussion, it is worth considering each one separately in turn.

Several OECD studies, among others, have explored the employment effects of exogenous changes in trade volumes or trade balances by using input–output analysis for nine OECD countries over the period 1971–86 (OECD 1994b: 98–102).[19] In general, the relationship between trade and employment in tradable sectors was found to be positive but small, except for those countries – the United States and the United Kingdom – that experienced substantial deteriorations in their current accounts over the period. But the negative impact of trade deficits, which results directly from the input–output approach utilized, is somewhat beside the point, given that the employment effects of changes in domestic demand dominate the effects of changes in the trade balance in all the countries studied (Baldwin 1995: 15) and that, even given the factors that constrain fiscal policy in many of these countries, all of them have access to macroeconomic tools with which to impact the level of domestic demand.[20]

One might ask why a relationship that appears to economists to be a nonissue looms so large in the minds of politicians and the general public. The answer almost certainly lies in a confusion between the job displacement that accompanies any shift in the pattern of economic activity and a net reduction in aggregate employment and/or increase in unemployment for the country as a whole. Increases in trade, even if balanced, or changes in trade patterns certainly are associated with job displacement, and the net job impact on particular industries, communities, and even regions of a country can be substantial. Indeed, several cross-industry studies for the United States and Canada have found significant effects of import competition on employment at the industry level (Freeman and Katz 1991; Revenga 1992; Gaston and Trefler 1994). Manufactured imports from developing countries – a particularly fast-growing (albeit from a very small base) and politically sensitive component of triad-country trade – are particularly likely to cause displacement, because they tend to include a higher proportion of interindustry (as opposed to intraindustry) trade than do flows between industrialized countries.[21]

Such displacement, whatever its causes, creates a burden of adjustment, and this burden falls more heavily on individuals the greater is the reliance on external adjustment processes. Some studies have suggested, furthermore, that workers displaced by trade tend to bear a heavier burden of adjustment, in the form of longer periods of unemployment and larger permanent earnings losses than the average for all displaced workers (Richardson 1995: 46–7, and studies cited there).

The issue of trade and job *quality* has come to the fore particularly in the United States, where the increased role of trade and foreign direct investment are often blamed for the stagnation of real earnings since 1973 and for the elimination of "good" jobs, by which is generally meant well-paid production-worker jobs in manufacturing.

As regards the first point, careful empirical investigation (Lawrence and Slaughter 1993; Bosworth and Perry 1994) yields two major conclusions. First, that much of the slowdown in real compensation as generally measured is attributable to a slowdown in the growth of labor productivity over the same period. Second, that virtually all of the divergence between real wage growth and labor productivity growth in the United States is attributable to the fact that the price index of the market-basket American workers consume (the CPI) has risen much faster than the price index for the market-basket they produce (the GDP deflator for nonfarm output); when the same deflator is used for both series, they track almost perfectly (*Economic Report of the President* 1996: 61). The authors note, furthermore, that this divergence in the price indexes is *not* due to a net change in the external terms of trade for the United States, which have remained roughly constant, but rather primarily to the large drop in the price of computers and the large rise in the price of owner-occupied housing.

There is also evidence that expanded trade, rather than destroying "good" jobs, in fact creates them. Bernard and Jensen (1995) find that, holding other characteristics constant, U.S. exporting plants paid better, particularly to production workers, and experienced faster growth of both wages and employment than nonexporters over the period 1976–87.[22] Supporting evidence is found in Baily and Gersbach's (1995) study of productivity differences in manufacturing industries across Germany, Japan, and the United States, which concludes that global competition is essential "to stimulate operations to achieve the highest productivity; domestic competition alone is not enough" (346).

In an earlier study, Katz and Summers (1989) offer a complementary explanation for why exporting firms pay better than the overall or even the manufacturing average in the United States. They find that, even in the absence of unionization, labor rather than capital receives the major share of monopoly rents in the American economy, and that such labor-market rents are the primary factor in explaining interindustry wage differentials. Furthermore, they find, within manufacturing, export industries carry more rents than import-competing industries, thus reinforcing the benefits from trade, while import competition has affected primarily the low-wage parts of American manufacturing, with the exception of two previously high-rent industries, automobiles and steel – the two industries almost invariably cited in anecdotal evidence regarding the trade-induced disappearance of good jobs. Finally, they note that a similar pattern of exporting goods made by industries with high wage premiums and importing those from industries with low wage premiums is common to most industrialized countries, and that these industry wage patterns are very stable over time.

The issue that has generated the most controversy within the economics profession is whether globalization is making the rich richer and the poor poorer – that is, whether it has been a major factor in the growth of earnings inequality that has characterized a number of the triad countries since about 1980. The question of whether the effect of trade on factor prices implied by the Heckscher–Ohlin–Samuelson model is in fact causing the wages of skilled and unskilled workers to diverge in the triad countries has spawned an enormous theoretical and empirical literature, much of it focused on the United States, where the growth of income inequality has been by far the greatest.

In his recent comprehensive examination of this issue, Lawrence (1996) surveys the empirical results produced by three competing approaches to this question. The first utilizes data on the factor content of import and export industries to estimate the implicit change in relative factor endowments, and the associated change in relative factor prices in advanced countries, attributable to actual trade flows.

Other scholars argue, however, that by implicitly regarding exports and imports as exogenous rather than being simultaneously determined along with prices and wages, these studies ignore the fact that import competition can depress wages even without any actual change in import volumes and also fail to take account of the likely response of consumer demand to higher-priced domestic equivalents in the absence of imports. This second group turns instead to data on relative goods prices, arguing that an increase in wage inequality due to trade should be reflected in relative price declines for the goods produced by import-competing sectors that intensively utilize less-skilled labor. But, as Lawrence notes, the findings of different authors regarding movements in these relative prices are not consistent, and the overall implications are ambiguous. The latter point is reinforced by the observation that if trade were exerting downward pressure on unskilled wages in traded goods sectors, one would expect some displacement of these workers into the nontraded sectors. But the ratio of unskilled to skilled workers has been falling in these sectors as well, suggesting that other factors – most observers focus on skill-biased technical change – are dominant.

A third approach tries to get at the relationship through the impact of trade on concentration and oligopoly rents and the relationship of these rents to wages in different industries. Certainly, trade appears to have had a concentration-reducing effect on manufacturing industries in the United States during the period under consideration. Looking at the nation's most concentrated three-digit industries, for example (those in which the four largest firms accounted for more than 40 percent of the domestic output in that industry) the degree of concentration as conventionally measured shows no significant change between 1972 and 1987. If, however, import competition is taken into account by measuring these concentration ratios as shares of domestic consumption rather than domestic production, concentration decreased dramatically over the period in each of these high-concentration industries.[23]

If a substantial share of industry rents goes to labor (Katz and Summers 1989), an import-induced reduction in market power in concentrated industries might indeed affect the domestic earnings distribution. Borjas and Ramey (1994, 1995) offer as evidence that such an effect has in fact incurred the strong association between the growth in wage inequality among workers with different levels of education in the United States over the period 1963–88 and the durable-goods trade deficit as a percentage of GNP. They argue that increased import competition both causes wage premiums to decline in these highly concentrated sectors and reduces jobs in these sectors, pushing low-skilled workers out into more competitive sectors.[24] But Lawrence finds that these effects have been very small (he notes that wage premia have not in fact declined in any highly concentrated industries other than primary metals) and cannot account for "more than a trivial proportion" of education-related wage inequality (1996: 84).

After carefully evaluating the evidence generated by all these approaches, Lawrence argues persuasively that trade can account for only a small proportion – on the order of 10 percent or less – of the increase in earnings inequality that has characterized the United States in recent years, whereas skill-biased technical change appears to be a much more important – indeed, the dominant – factor.[25]

In sum, the evidence indicates that the beliefs regarding the negative effects of trade on labor markets that have achieved such prominence on the political landscape are wide of the mark. More specifically, three conclusions emerge from the wealth of theoretical modeling and empirical investigation. First, that there is no systematic relationship between trade volumes, trade balances, or trade patterns and aggregate levels of employment or unemployment in triad countries, but that trade can cause significant job displacement affecting particular industries or regions and that such displacement may carry greater adjustment costs for individuals when it arises from trade than when it arises from other causes. Second, that expanded trade tends to be positively rather than negatively associated with average wages and that the stagnation of real earnings in the United States is not due to trade effects. And third, that trade has played a much smaller role than is generally believed in the recent growth of earnings inequality in a number of triad countries, most noticeably the United States.

Labor markets and trade policies: Some current issues and areas for future research

Surprisingly, in light of the amount of concern and discussion the relationship between trade and jobs has generated among both economists and politicians, very little is known about the actual effects of trade policies on labor market adjustment. In the words of a recent survey of the literature on this exact issue, "to our knowledge, there are no cross-country studies which link changes in the trade regime with employment or wage effects at the aggregate economy-wide level" (Harrison and Revenga 1995: 14). One of the reasons, presumably, is the absence of satisfactory measures of trade policy, in the sense of level of restrictiveness or trade-distortion. Measures of economic openness in terms of the size of trade flows, comparisons of domestic and international prices, average tariff levels, and quantification of nontariff barriers are all fraught with severe methodological problems (Harrison and Ravenga 1995: 4–7).

Despite these difficulties, the authors note that a few partial-equilibrium analyses have attempted to measure the differential impact of trade reforms across subsectors within a country for the United States and Canada (such studies do not appear to exist for Europe or Japan). As one might expect for economies with relatively flexible labor markets, these studies all indicate that, in these two countries at least, trade policy changes lead to employment reallocation across industries, with very little effect on wages.

These findings lead naturally to the question of what kinds of industries and what sorts of workers are most likely to receive protection. Rodrick notes that "The [large number of] studies to date have focused on advanced industrial countries (mainly the U.S.), and have used many different indicators, including nominal and effective tariffs, non-tariff coverage ratios, and exemptions from multilateral trade liberalization" (1994: 31). Among the industry characteristics associated with higher levels of protection in these studies are that it is a labor-intensive, low-skill, low-wage industry, beset by high import penetration or an increase in import penetration, is in decline, is regionally concentrated, and engages in little intraindustry trade. The evidence as regards degree of concentration is more ambiguous: most studies find a positive relationship between industry concentration and protection, as would be expected given the presumption that free-rider effects should be important in lobbying, but some find the opposite (Rodrick 1994: 31–3).

One recent study (Deardorff and Haveman 1995) looks directly at the relationship between trade protection and income distribution in the United States over the period 1972–90. The authors seek to determine whether those industries that sought "administered protection" under U.S. trade laws had poverty rates above or below the national average.[26] They find that the industries that sought, as well as those that actually received, such protection were associated with lower than average poverty rates, suggesting that such protection tends to exacerbate rather than reduce income inequality. The industries seeking protection, furthermore, were characterized by above-average wage levels *and* above-average unemployment rates, suggesting the presence of wage premiums that tend to increase the costs of labor-market adjustments.

Despite inconclusiveness on some points, the pattern of protection indicated by the empirical work surveyed above suggests strongly that a major function of trade protection is to ameliorate – or perhaps delay – the transitional costs of labor-market adjustment. That is, protection appears to be focused on situations where labor reallocations are likely to be large, as in the case where interindustry rather than intraindustry trade is involved, or relatively expensive, as is the case with industries whose production is regionally concentrated. Protection also appears to be biased in the direction of those seen as most vulnerable and least able to bear the costs of adjustment, that is, low-skill low-wage workers in threatened or declining industries – although some of the work cited suggests that it is low-skill relatively *high*-wage workers (that is, those earning significant wage premiums) who suffer most from trade-related dislocation and are most likely to receive protection.[27]

The bottom line indicated by the studies just summarized is that, in those advanced industrialized countries for which these relationships have been investigated, old-fashioned protection aimed at cushioning adjustment in industries where a nation suffers a comparative disadvantage has dominated the more "strategic" variety, which would presumably be focused more on the support of high-productivity, high-technology industries in which the country has an actual or potential comparative advantage. It may be, of course, that these conclusions are distorted by the existence of forms of support for "strategic" industries, including a variety of subsidies, explicit or implicit, that are not easily measured or that do not generally fall under the rubric of trade policy. Certainly, anecdotal evidence of such measures abounds. But we must go with what we have.

This pattern of protection is particularly salient in light of current developments. The dominant trends in trade and trade patterns for the nations of the triad over the past two decades are clear: their increasing openness, as measured by the share of exports and imports in GDP, and the rapid growth of manufactured imports from newly industrializing countries. These developments have "more or less coincided with some disturbing trends in OECD labor markets: a sharp rise in wage inequality (especially in the United States) and a sharp rise in unemployment (mainly in Europe)" (Krugman 1995: 343). A similar sharp rise in unemployment, although not fully reflected in official statistics, appears to have been occurring in Japan.[28] And, despite the evidence from academic research that neither trade in general nor third-world exports in particular is a major cause of the problems in first-world labor markets (Krugman 1995: 344), there is a strong tendency in the minds of both politicians and the public to link these domestic trends to the international ones.

The movement in all three triad regions toward a relatively heavier reliance on external rather than internal labor reallocation that has been documented and analyzed in this essay forms the third leg of the triangle linking labor-market adjustment processes and attitudes toward trade and trade policies in the triad countries. The fact that this trend inevitably shifts some of the costs of adjustment away from firms and toward workers, thus making them more visible and politically sensitive, together with the labor-market difficulties the triad nations are currently experiencing and the fact that trade restrictions in these countries are apparently biased toward cushioning transitional costs of labor-market adjustment, all point to an enhanced vulnerability to protectionist pressures in these countries, pressures that have been submerged but not eliminated by the signing of the GATT and NAFTA agreements. It was not surprising, therefore, to hear Secretary of the Treasury Rubin comment in 1995 that, at the latest meeting of the G-7 finance ministers, every one of them had noted an increase in economic nationalism in his country.

At the very least, the interaction of these various developments is likely to make more difficult the expansion of those regional economic groups that currently consist primarily of high-wage industrialized countries, such as the European Union and the North American Free Trade Agreement, to include more relatively low-wage developing or Eastern

European countries. Trade expansion and liberalization can create significant opportunities for raising returns to labor in low-wage countries and thus for encouraging income convergence both interationally and within these poorer countries.[29] But the triad nations are likely to resist such developments if at the same time they continue to experience conditions, such as stagnating wages and/or high unemployment, that suggest that such convergence could involve downward pressures in some nations rather than differential rates of upward movement in all of them, or if the income *convergence* between nations is accompanied by persistent income *divergence* within the triad countries.

The increase in personal insecurity and social disquiet associated with labor-market developments in the triad nations is also likely to intensify pressures for harmonization or convergence of labor-market policies across countries as the price of allowing the benefits of increased trade and investment to be fully realized.[30] Pressures for harmonization tend to increase along with economic integration for a number of reasons. As barriers at the border (tariffs and NTB's) become less important, the distortions – or, to put it more neutrally, the modifications – in patterns of trade and investment created by differences in "domestic" policies become more prominent. As the pressures of global competition increase, firms become increasingly concerned about "fairness" and the competitive implications of an "unlevel playing field." Multinational corporations pursuing integrated global strategies often feel that facing consistent rules and conditions in the different markets in which thcy operate reduces complexity and therefore costs.

Governments, meanwhile, also worry that domestically popular labor-market policies might put their own firms at a competitive disadvantage and therefore seek to restrain a regulatory "race for the bottom." And all of these pressures are enhanced when economic insecurity and income inequality are important domestic political issues – witness the need to incorporate a "side agreement" on labor-market policies into the NAFTA as one of the political requirements for its passage.

There is no clear standard for determining the optimal degree of policy-harmonization among nations. The U.S. experience indicates that persistent differences among the states in labor-market conditions (Ehrenberg 1994) as well as real wages (Crandall 1993) are consistent with what is generally regarded as complete economic integration. But, in practical terms, there is a danger that harmonization pressures intensified by domestic labor-market problems could impede the potential benefits of international trade and investment. How do we decide when measures to ensure minimally acceptable global standards, such as a prohibition on imports of goods made by slave labor, cross the line into the disguised protectionism that developing countries so often complain about? How do we reconcile the dictum that the benefits of trade derive from differences among nations with the concern that some kinds of differences may have unacceptable distributional implications? How do we balance the desire to minimize distortions of trade and investment patterns with the very legitimate differences in tastes, needs, and priorities expressed by different bodies politic? And, finally, how do we avoid broadening the domain of trade issues, and therefore of trade disputes, to the point of overwhelming our capacities for negotiation and dispute-settlement?

There are no simple answers to these questions under the best of circumstances. But they are more likely to be resolved, at least implicitly, in ways that minimize both trade-related disputes and impediments to economic integration if the triad nations can find effective ways to mitigate the problems of labor-market adjustment that currently loom large in all of them. And this challenge, in turn, suggests avenues for future research urgently needed to help dispel some of the uncertainties that currently confront both analysts and policymakers who labor in this particular vineyard.

I have suggested in this essay some preliminary and partial conclusions about the relative merits of internal versus external adjustment processes in response to particular developments in the global economic environment since 1973. But the establishment of more systematic links between the nature of the external shock or structural change and the relative efficacy of different labor-adjustment processes would be a useful step in acquiring a better understanding of the relationship between a nation's macroeconomic performance and the microeconomic characteristics of its labor markets.

Another line of investigation has to do with determining how the increasing prominence of intraindustry and intrafirm trade affects the balance between internal and external adjustment. Is internal reallocation of labor more feasible, as some observers suggest, when trade-induced shifts occur within a single industry or firm rather than between them? Or has intrafirm trade in the form of outsourcing part or all of the production process to affiliates outside the home country's borders increased the pressures for external adjustment?

Most of the studies that have exonerated trade as a major factor in the labor-market problems of the triad nations have pointed to skill-biased technological change as the major source of increased earnings inequality. But in most of these studies, this result falls out as the unexplained residual, a situation that is always suspect. Investigations aimed at establishing directly the relative importance of technology as a factor affecting either the employability or the earnings position of less-educated work-ers would provide a sounder analytical foundation for policies to allevi-ate the problem, as would better insight on the interactions between trade patterns and the apparent skill-bias of technological change.

Finally, the major culprit in the slowing of wage growth continues to be the unexplained decline in the growth of labor productivity in many of the triad nations since 1973. Thus, some answers to the still-resistant "productivity puzzle" lie at the heart of the conundrum that confronts efforts to improve the performance of labor markets in all these countries.

These suggestions can be seen as opportunities for future Ph.D. can-didates and journal editors. But they also reflect an urgent need for a better understanding of the factors underlying the labor-market difficul-ties that are the focus of so much discussion and concern in the triad nations. In the absence of such understanding, a necessary first step toward devising effective policy responses, the widespread sense of inse-curity and social unease created by the increased pressure on labor-market adjustment processes since 1973 and the resulting breakdown of the "defining institutions" or implicit social contracts in these markets will continue to pose a potential threat to the maintenance and expan-sion of an open global trading system. And the reverberations of that threat are sure to be felt most sharply of all among those countries that have not yet made it into the "magic circle" of high-income industrialized nations.

NOTES

1. Where relevant studies incorporate Canada, I include it as well in the third leg of the triad.
2. The picture is complicated by substantial differences between de jure and de facto job stability – one study found a *negative* relationship between the stringency of employment protection rules and actual job tenure (OECD 1993: 146–7) – and by variations among European countries; the United Kingdom, for example, appears in many respects to be closer to the United States than to the countries of continental Western Europe. For detailed discussions of these issues see, Boyer (1988); Buechtemann (1993); Baglione and Crouch (1990); Hartog and Theeuwes (1993).
3. The multiplicity of earnings measures, including hourly versus annual earn-ings and nominal versus real earnings, contributes to the ambiguity sur-rounding empirical findings.
4. For evidence to the contrary, see Bean (1994: 610–11).
5. For evidence on this point, see Whitman (1994: 29).

6. For details, see Whitman (1994: 29).
7. The remainder of this section draws heavily on Whitman (1994).
8. For an opposing view, based on the premise that Leibensteinian increments in x-efficiency may be a more important source of technical change than Schumpeterian creative destruction, see Boyer (1993: 110–12).
9. This number is calculated by the Bureau of Labor Statistics on the basis of the number of employees on the day of the survey, averaged over the year, even though the number of employees who obtained temporary employment through staffing companies during 1992 was five to six times that number, or about 6.5 to 7.8 million employees. The even larger numbers cited in the popular press arise when the cumulative annual payroll of staffing companies, including individuals who appear on the rolls of more than one firm, are added together.
10. Marcotte (1995) surveys these studies and attempts to reconcile the different findings. For other evidence suggesting a reduction in job security see Osterman and Kochan (1990: 156–8).
11. Two observations may be germane in this connection: first, that this "delayed" response in the service sector may somehow be linked to the failure of measured productivity to increase in this sector despite intensive IT investment and, second, that many of the so-called mega-mergers of the 1990s are in service industries.
12. I acknowledge with thanks the role of my research assistant, Joy Mazumdar, now Assistant Professor of Economics at Emory University, in the formalization of this model.
13. Wages might be rigid, even in the absence of union activity, for a number of reasons, including the payment of "efficiency wages" to help maintain workers' performance or the provision of insurance to risk-averse workers (Blanchard and Fisher 1989, chap. 9; Solow 1979; Katz 1986). For evidence that high-profit oligopolistic industries, unionized or not, tend to share their rents by paying above-market wages, see Katz and Summers (1989). Note that the wage is fixed in terms of the y good.
14. This special assumption, adopted for the sake of simplicity, can be derived from several alternative simple utility functions. See, for example, Brander and Spencer (1984).
15. One might ask why, if oligopolistic firms have to pay above-market wages for the production of good y but have no market power to raise its price, there would be any internal reallocation at all. That is, if capital were introduced explicitly into the model, the rate of return to capital in y production would be lower for oligopolistic firms than for competitive firms that pay market wages, implying that capital would be reallocated to the competitive firms along with labor. However, even in a model incorporating capital explicitly, some internal reallocation would occur as long as capital was perfectly mobile within firms but imperfectly mobile between firms.
16. We assume that the capital subsidy to output is financed through lump-sum taxes. This subsidy can be interpreted as capital-rationing in favor of the

oligopolistic firms, even though capital does not appear explicitly in the model.

17. A lower K_w will also lower y-productivity for competitive firms. However, decreased productivity in this sector will lower the market wage without reducing the fixed wage that oligopolistic firms must pay, thus producing the result described in Figure 9.4.

18. Crandall (1993) notes that shifts in the locational patterns of production in the steel and auto industries within the United States over the 1970s and 1980s suggest that new firms are more likely than existing ones to be able to overcome the inherited disadvantages of location and industrial relations.

19. The word *exogenous* is crucial here. Because of the endogeneity of the trade balance over the business cycle – imports are more sensitive to changes in domestic income than are exports – observed patterns are counterintuitive: increases in trade deficits tend to be associated with a fall rather than a rise in the unemployment rate.

20. In the words of the OECD study just cited, "This empirical analysis does not, and cannot, measure the impact of changing trade patterns on *unemployment*" (105).

21. Such imports have increased from 0.22 percent to 1.30 percent of GDP in the European Union and from 0.28 percent to 1.91 percent in the United States over the period 1970–90 (Krugman 1995: 337). Although no such trend was visible for Japan over the period cited, the pressure exerted by the chronically overvalued yen toward the export of manufacturing activities from Japan to lower-wage Asian countries suggests that a similar trend may soon appear there as well.

22. A multicountry regression analysis performed for the OECD *Jobs Study* yielded somewhat contrary results: it found the relationship between export-intensity and relative wages to be insignificant overall, but negative for high-skill industries [OECD 1994b: I, 105].

23. Concentration ratios were obtained from the *Census of Manufactures 1987*; data on exports and imports in each industry were obtained from *Trade and Employment* and *U.S. Commodity Exports and Imports as Related to Output*, all published by the U.S. Department of Commerce.

24. The OECD *Jobs Study: Evidence and Explanations* (1994b: II, 31) found a similar link between concentration and wage premia; Gaston and Trefler (1994) note that their results also offer some support for the view that trade liberalization has led to more competition in labor markets and erosion of economic rents.

25. Lawrence's estimates are at the low end of the range, but his painstaking reconciliation of his findings with those of others lends credence to his views. For an alternative overview of the relevant literature, see the following contributions to a recent symposium in *The Journal of Economic Perspectives*: Freeman (1995), Richardson (1995), and Wood (1995).

26. The trade actions covered include escape clause (section 201 of U.S. trade law), unfair trade (sections 301 and 337), and countervailing and antidump-

ing duties (sections 701 and 731). The authors emphasize cases filed, rather than looking only at those that were ultimately successful in winning favorable decisions, on the grounds that "there is growing evidence that many trade actions that do not proceed all the way to an affirmative determination nonetheless result in collusive agreements that also restrain trade. Therefore, we judge that all trade actions have a certain amount of protective effect" (813).

27. Gaston and Trefler (1994) argue, in fact, that if proper adjustment is made for the endogeneity of protection, no such bias toward protection of low-wage industries is found. Their results suggest, in fact, that protection actually *causes* wages to be lower, but only in unionized industries. In another article, Trefler (1993) finds weak evidence that NTB's appear to protect the highest-income occupations (scientists and engineers) the most, whereas semiskilled labor receives very little.

28. As early as 1989, when the unemployment rates as conventionally measured were 2.2 percent as compared with 4.9 percent for the United States, a broader measure that takes account of discouraged and involuntary part-time workers yielded rates of 7.2 percent for Japan and 7.9 percent for the United States. In 1993, the comparable rates were 6.9 percent and 10.2 percent, respectively, for the United States and 2.6 percent and 5.7 percent for Japan (OECD, *Employment Outlook*, July 1995: 76).

29. For two recent investigations of the relationship between trade openness and growth rates that come to somewhat different conclusions, see Harison and Ravenga (1995) and Sachs and Warner (1995).

30. For a fuller discussion of these issues, see Ehrenberg (1994, esp. chap. 7).

REFERENCES

Abraham, K., and S. Houseman (1989). "Job Security and Work Force Adjustment: How Different Are U.S. and Japanese Practices?" NBER Working Paper No. 3155. Cambridge, MA.

Abraham, K. G., and R. B. McKersie, eds. (1990). *New Developments in the Labor Market: Toward a New Institutional Paradigm*, Cambridge, MA, and London: MIT Press.

Baglione, G., and C. Crouch, eds. (1990). *European Industrial Relations: The Challenge of Flexibility.* London: Sage.

Baily, M. L., and H. Gersbach (1995). "Efficiency in Manufacturing and the Need for Global Competition." *Brookings Papers on Economic Activity: Microeconomics*, 307–58.

Baldwin, R. E. (1995). "The Effect of Trade and Foreign Direct Investment on Employment and Relative Wages," NBER Working Paper No. 5037.

Bean, C. R. (1994). "European Unemployment: A Survey," *Journal of Economic Literature* 32(2), 573–619.

Bernard, A. B., and J. B. Jensen (1995). "Exporters, Jobs and Wages in U.S.

Manufacturing: 1976–87," *Brookings Papers on Economic Activity: Microeconomics*, 67–112.

Bertola, G. (1990). "Job Security, Employment and Wages," *European Economic Review* 34, 851–86.

Blanchard, O., and S. Fischer (1989). *Lectures on Macroeconomics*. Cambridge: MIT Press.

Blank, R. (1994). "Does a Larger Social Safety Net Mean Less Economic Flexibility?" In R. B. Freeman, ed., *Working Under Different Rules*, pp. 157–87. New York: Russell Sage Foundation.

Blinder, A. (1992). "More Like Them?" *The American Prospect* 8 (Winter), 51–6.

Blinder, A., and A. Krueger (1991). "International Differences in Labor Turnover: A Comparative Study with Emphasis on the U.S. and Japan." Paper prepared for the Council on Competitiveness and Harvard Business School Project on U.S. Corporate Investment and the Time Horizons of American Industry.

Borjas, G. J., and V. A. Ramey (1995). "Foreign Competition, Market Power, and Wage Inequality," *The Quarterly Journal of Economics* 110 (November), 1075–1110.

Borjas, G. J., and V. A. Ramey (1994). "Time Series Evidence on the Sources of Trends in Wage Inequality," *American Economic Review* 84(2), 10–16.

Bosworth, B., and G. Perry (1994). "Productivity and Real Wages: Is There a Puzzle?" *Brookings Papers on Economic Activity* 1, 317–35.

Boyer, R. (1988). "Defensive or Offensive Flexibility." In R. Boyer, ed., *The Search for Labour Market Flexibility: The European Economies in Transition*, pp. 222–51. Oxford: Clarendon Press.

Boyer, R. (1993). "The Economics of Job Protection and Emerging New Capital-Labor Relations." In C. F. Buechtemann, ed., *Employment Security and Labor Market Behavior*, pp. 69–125. Ithaca, NY: ILR Press.

Brander, J., and B. Spencer (1984). "Tariff Protection and Imperfect Competition." In H. Kierzkowski, ed., *Monopolistic Competition and International Trade*, pp. 194–206. Oxford: Clarendon Press.

Bridgeford, J., and J. Stirling (1994). *Employee Relations in Europe*. Oxford and Cambridge, MA: Blackwell.

Brynjolfsson, E., et al. (1994). "Does Information Technology Lead to Smaller Firms?" *Management Science* 40(12), 1628–45.

Buechtemann, C. F., ed. (1993). *Employment Security and Labor Market Behavior*. Ithaca, NY: ILR Press.

Centre for Economic Policy Research (1995). *Unemployment: Choices for Europe (Monitoring European Integration 5)*. London: CEPR.

Coase, R. (1937). "The Nature of the Firm," *Economica N.S.* 4, 386–405.

Crandall, R. W. (1993). *Manufacturing on the Move*. Washington, DC: The Brookings Institution.

Deardorff, A., and J. Haveman (1995). "The Effects of U.S. Trade Laws on Poverty in America," *Journal of Human Resources* 30(4), 807–25.

Diebold, F. X., et al. (1994). "Job Stability in the United States," NBER Working Paper No. 4859.

Doeringer, P. B., and M. J. Piore (1971). *International Labor Markets and Manpower Analysis*. Lexington, MA: Heath Lexington Books.

Dore, R. (1986). *Flexible Rigidities: Industrial Policy and Structural Adjustment in the Japanese Economy, 1970–1980*. London: Athalone Press.

Dore, R. (1989). *Japan at Work: Markets, Management and Flexibility*. Paris: OECD.

Economic Report of the President 1996. Washington, DC: U.S. Government Printing Office.

Ehrenberg, R. G. (1994). *Labor Markets and Integrating National Economies*, Washington, DC: The Brookings Institution.

Farber, H. S. (1995). "Are Lifetime Jobs Disappearing?: Job Duration in the United States: 1973–1993." Industrial Relations Section Working Paper No. 341, Princeton University.

Farber, H. S. (1996). "The Changing Face of Job Loss in the United States, 1981–1993." Princeton University, Industrial Relations Section Working Paper No. 360.

Freeman, R. B. (1993). "How Labor Fares in Advanced Economies" and "Lessons for the United States." In R. B. Freeman, ed., *Working Under Different Rules*, pp. 1–28 and 223–39. New York: Russell Sage Foundation.

Freeman, R. B. (1995). "Are Your Wages Set in Beijing?" *Journal of Economic Perspectives* 9(3), 15–32.

Freeman, R. B., and Katz, L. F. (1991). "Industrial Wage and Employment Determination in an Open Economy." In J. M. Abowd and R. B. Freeman, eds., *Immigration, Trade, and Labor Markets*, pp. 235–59. Chicago: NBER.

Fukao, M. (1995). *Financial Integration, Corporate Governance and the Performance of Multinational Firms*. Washington, DC: The Brookings Institution.

Gaston, N., and D. Trefler (1994). "Protection, Trade and Wages: Evidence from U.S. Manufacturing," *Industrial and Labor Relations Review* 47(4), 574–93.

Goto, Akira (1981). "Statistical Evidence on the Diversification of Japanese Large Firms," *Journal of Industrial Economics* 29(3), 271–8.

Harrison, A., and A. Revenga (1995). "The Effects of Trade Policy Reform: What Do We Really Know?" NBER Working Paper No. 5225.

Hartog, J., and J. Theeuwes, eds. (1993). *Labor Market Contracts and Institutions: A Cross National Comparison*. Amsterdam: North-Holland.

Hashimoto, M. (1990). *The Japanese Labor Market in Comparative Perspective with the United States*. Kalamazoo: Upjohn Institute.

Hashimoto, M., and J. Raisian (1992). "Aspects of Labor Market Flexibility in Japan and the United States." In K. Koshiro, ed., *Employment Security and Labor Market Flexibility: An International Perspective*, pp. 78–101. Detroit: Wayne State University Press.

Hori, Shintaro (1993). "Fixing Japan's White-Collar Economy: A Personal View," *Harvard Business Review* 71 (November–Demember 1993), 157–72.

Houseman, S. N. (1994). "Labor Market Adjustment in Europe, Japan, and the

United States." Paper prepared for the OECD Workshop on Labor Market Adjustment, Paris, October 4–5.

Katz, L. (1986). "Efficiency Wage Theories: A Partial Evaluation," *NBER Macroeconomics Annual*, 235–76.

Katz, L., and L. Summers, 1989, "Industry Rents: Evidence and Implications," *Brookings Papers on Economic Activity: Microeconomics*, 209–90.

Kenen, P. B., and Eichengreen, B. (1994). "Managing the World Economy under the Bretton Woods System: An Overview." In P. B. Kenen, ed., *Managing the World Economy: Fifty Years after Bretton Woods*," pp. 3–57. Washington, DC: Institute for International Economics.

Koshiro, K., ed. (1992). *Employment Security and Labor Market Flexibility: An International Perspective.* Detroit: Wayne State University Press.

Krugman, P. (1995). "Growing World Trade: Causes and Consequences," *Brookings Papers on Economic Activity* 1, 327–62.

Lawrence, R. Z. (1996). *Single World, Divided Nations? International Trade and OECD Labor Markets.* Washington, DC: The Brookings Institution for the OECD Development Centre.

Lawrence, R. Z., and Slaughter, M. J. (1993). "Trade and U.S. Wages in the 1980's: Giant Sucking Sound or Small Hiccup?" *Brookings Papers on Economic Activity: Microeconomics*, 161–226.

Levinsohn, J. (1993). "Testing the Imports-as-Market-Discipline Hypothesis," *Journal of International Economics* 35, 1–22.

Malmgren, H. (1961). "Information, Expectations and the Theory of the Firm," *Quarterly Journal of Economics* 125, 399–421.

Marcotte, D. E. (1995). "Declining Job Stability: What We Know and What It Means," *Journal of Policy Analysis and Management* (Fall), 590–8.

Odagiri, H. (1992). *Growth Through Competition, Competition Through Growth: Strategic Management and the Economy in Japan.* New York: Clarendon Press.

OECD (1993). "Enterprise Tenure, Labor Turnover and Skill Training," *OECD Employment Outlook* (July), 119–55.

OECD (1994a). *The OECD Jobs Study: Facts, Analysis, Strategies.* Paris: OECD.

OECD (1994b). *The OECD Jobs Study: Evidence and Explanations*, Parts I and II. Paris: OECD.

OECD (1995). *The OECD Jobs Study: Implementing the Strategy.* Paris: OECD.

Oi, W. (1962). "Labor as a Quasi-Fixed Factor," *Journal of Political Economy* 70, 538–55.

Okun, A. (1981). *Prices and Quantities: A Macroeconomic Analysis*, Washington, DC: The Brookings Institution.

Osterman, P., and T. A. Kochan (1990). "Employment Security and Employment Policy: An Assessment of the Issues." In Abraham and McKersie, *New Developments in the Labor Market: Toward a New Institutional Paradigm*, pp. 155–82. Cambridge, MA, and London: MIT Press.

Revenga, A. (1992). "Exporting Jobs: The Impact of Import Competition on Employment and Wages in U.S. Manufacturing," *Quarterly Journal of Economics* 7(1), 255–84.

Richardson, J. D. (1995). "Income Inequality and Trade: How to Think, What to Conclude," *Journal of Economic Perspectives* 9(3), 33–57.

Rodrik, D. (1994). "What Does the Political Economy Literature on Trade Policy (Not) Tell Us That We Ought to Know?" Council for Economic Policy Research Discussion Paper No. 1039. London: CEPR.

Rose, S. (1995). *The Decline of Employment Stability in the 1980's.* Washington, DC: National Commission on Employment Policy.

Rosen, S. (1985). "Implicit Contracts: A Survey," *Journal of Economic Literature* 23, 1144–75.

Sachs, J. D., and A. Warner (1995). "Economic Reform and the Process of Global Integration." *Brookings Papers on Economic Activity* 1, 1–95.

Saxonhouse, G. (1994). "Japan: Growing Old Gracefully?" *International Economic Insights* (January/February), 11–14.

Sengenberger, W. (1992). "Revisiting the Legal and Institutional Framework for Employment Security: An International Comparative Perspective." In Koshiro, ed., *Employment Security and Labor Market Flexibility*, 150–82.

Solow, R. (1979). "Another Possible Source of Wage Stickiness," *Journal of Macroeconomics* 1, 79–82.

Stewart, Thomas A. (1993). "Welcome to the Revolution," *Fortune* December 13, 66–77.

Swinnerton, K., and H. Wial (1995). "Is Job Stability Declining in the U.S. Economy?" *Industrial and Labor Relations Review* 48, 293–304.

Trefler, Daniel (1993). "Trade Liberalization and the Theory of Endogenous Protection: An Economic Study of U.S. Import Policy," *Journal of Political Economy* 101–11, 138–60.

Whitman, M. v.N. (1994). "Flexible Markets, Flexible Firms," *The American Enterprise* 5(3), 26–37.

Williamson, O. (1971). "The Vertical Integration of Production: Market Failure Considerations," *American Economic Review* 61, 112–23.

Williamson, O. (1975). *Markets and Hierarchies: Analysis and Antitrust Implications.* London: Collier Macmillan.

Wood, A. (1995). "How Trade Hurts Unskilled Workers," *Journal of Economic Perspectives* 9(3), 57–80.

CHAPTER 10

Do the G–3 countries coordinate monetary policy?

Kathryn M. E. Dominguez

I Introduction

Government officials from the United States, Germany, and Japan meet periodically to discuss shared economic problems and, on occasion, to coordinate economic policy. These policy agreements are often made public as communiqués. This essay examines public agreements to coordinate monetary policy in the period since the mid-1970s.

Economic theory suggests that countries often benefit from international policy coordination. For example, macroeconomic spillovers can create situations in which governments have incentives to coordinate monetary policies.[1] However, the empirical studies of the gains from policy coordination have generally found small, though nonzero, benefits.[2]

The subject of macroeconomic policy coordination has been a longstanding interest of Peter B. Kenen's. Indeed Kenen's Ph.D. dissertation (Kenen, 1960) examines British monetary policy from 1951–7, a period during which Britain coordinated its policies with the United States within the framework of the Bretton Woods System. In his book *Exchange Rates and Policy Coordination* (1989), Kenen suggests that the conventional models used by economists to study policy coordination may miss the point. Coordination is typically defined narrowly as involving clearly defined, noncontingent policy changes that countries would not have put in place in the absence of an agreement. Under this definition there have been few, if any, genuine policy coordination agreements between countries. Most policymakers define coordination much more broadly to include agreements to consult with other countries before making major policy changes, and agreements to work for common goals or to combat common dangers. It is Kenen's broader, more realistic definition of coordination agreements that will be used in this essay.

My previous joint work with Peter B. Kenen examines European monetary policy coordination in the context of the Basle–Nyborg Agreement.[3] The agreement signed at the Basle–Nyborg meeting provides participating central banks limited use of credit facilities for financing intramarginal intervention as long as they make fuller use of the EMS exchange rate band. Our paper shows that actual EMS exchange rate behavior was significantly different after the Basle–Nyborg Agreement than it was prior to the agreement. And, the paper concludes that the EMS governments honored the terms of their agreement. In the spirit of that earlier study, I now consider whether the G-3 governments mean what they say regarding monetary policy coordination agreements.[4]

There have been a number of case studies of particular policy coordination episodes. For example, Putnam and Henning (1989) study the coordination agreements made at the Bonn Summit of 1978. The political process by which countries arrive at economic policy agreements is examined by Putnam and Bayne (1987), Funabashi (1988), Dobson (1991), and James (1996). In an essay edited by Peter B. Kenen in the *Princeton Studies in International Finance*, Von Furstenberg and Daniels (1992) examine G-7 compliance with the economic policy declarations made at the yearly summit meetings from 1975 to 1989. They measure compliance with a complicated weighing scheme that takes into account (i) the degree of policy ambition, and (ii) random economic shocks that may confound policy influences.

The Brookings Institution, together with other organizations, sponsored a series of international collaborative projects in which researchers simulate G-7 policy coordination (and noncoordination) using each of the major multicountry econometric models.[5] Multicountry econometric models have also been used to estimate the benefits of moving to a target-zone system, where countries agree to coordinate macroeconomic policies in order to maintain target exchange rate levels.[6] These exercises indicate the possibility that G-7 policy coordination may enhance global welfare.

This essay differs from earlier studies in focus, sample, and methodology. It concentrates solely on monetary policy agreements between the G-3 countries. Communiqués from summits and all other official meetings are included in the sample. The time period extends from 1977 through 1993. Policy coordination is defined broadly and measured as a binomial process, and compliance is tested using standard time series techniques.

The first part of the essay describes the history of the coordination process during economic summits, G-7, G-5, and G-3 meetings. Monetary policy agreements reached at these meetings are identified and categorized over the period 1975 though 1993. The second part of the essay measures the degree to which countries follow through with these coordination commitments.

The essay also offers new measures of monetary policy changes. It is difficult to separate the effects of central bank policy changes from demand and supply shocks using data on individual countries' interest rates or monetary aggregates. As a consequence, cross-country correlations in these time series might suggest that countries coordinate policies when, in fact, they are simply subject to correlated economic shocks. In order to identify discretionary policy changes, the essay constructs monetary policy indexes using information on policy intentions available directly from the G–3 central banks. The U.S. monetary index appears in Boschen and Mills (1995) and is based on the minutes of FOMC meetings. The German and Japanese indexes are new, and are described in detail below, in Section IV.

The results indicate that the G–3 countries often mean what they say in the context of monetary policy coordination agreements. Perhaps surprisingly, the United States honors its international agreements more often than does either Japan or Germany. And Germany is the most likely of the three countries to defect from monetary agreements. On the other hand, Japan and Germany respond to U.S. policy changes, whereas the United States is generally unaffected by policy changes in Japan and Germany.

II The theory of international monetary policy coordination

When countries permit the values of their currencies to be market-determined, changes in foreign monetary policies may influence their domestic economies. In the Mundell–Fleming model, a monetary expansion in a foreign country reduces that country's real interest rate, depreciates its currency relative to others, raises import prices, and raises inflation and output. Other countries are affected because their currencies appreciate relative to the foreign country's (assuming that they do not match the foreign country's monetary policy), thereby reducing import prices and inflation, and possibly decreasing output. It is this terms-of-trade externality that encourages monetary policy coordination.

The question of whether to coordinate monetary policy with other countries can be modeled in a game-theoretic framework.[7] Theory suggests at least four potential equilibria that countries may choose in the face of macroeconomic externalities: noncooperation (Nash), international coordination (the process by which policymakers jointly choose the optimal noncooperative solution), cooperation, and some kind of

Stackelberg solution. Cooperative and Stackelberg solutions generally lead to higher global welfare compared to the Nash solutions, but they are difficult to achieve because both require a loss of sovereignty on the part of at least one country.[8] Theory therefore suggests that international coordination (and not cooperation) yields the greatest welfare in the class of feasible equilibria.

Game-theoretic models of international policy coordination assume that governments "policy optimize" in the sense that they choose to coordinate in order to exploit or mitigate the spillover effects of other country's policies on their own economies. Countries coordinate in order to maximize their own national welfares.[9] An alternative view of the coordination process, termed the regime-preserving or public-goods approach in Kenen (1990), postulates that countries coordinate in order to achieve global objectives. The scope for policy coordination is limited in this approach, since countries will not agree to coordinate if global objectives conflict markedly with national objectives.[10] This view of coordination is termed the public-goods approach because global objectives can be considered public goods. It is difficult to prevent countries from enjoying the fruits of coordination, even when they are not directly involved in the coordination effort.

These two approaches to understanding a country's motivation to engage in coordination can be illustrated in the context of a particular coordination episode, the G–5 Plaza Agreement. In the policy optimizing approach, the exchange rate agreement made at the G–5 Plaza meeting occurred because all the participating countries believed that a fall in the value of the dollar would serve their own national interests. In the regime-preservation approach, the Plaza Agreement reflects a consensus that the dollar was misaligned and, although some countries did not benefit from dollar depreciation, they participated in the Plaza Agreement in the interests of global welfare.

International policy coordination is difficult to define and even more difficult to measure. International monetary policy coordination can be narrowly defined to encompass joint changes in interest rates or money growth rates.[11] A broader definition of monetary policy coordination might include regimes in which there are consultations and information exchanges among countries.[12] Policy coordination may occur in the context of a rules-based system (for example, a target-zone system), or on an ad hoc basis.

This essay examines policy coordination episodes marked by joint statements of intent that appear in official communiqués. These statements can involve explicit commitments to changes in monetary policy (corresponding to a narrow definition of coordination), but more often are written in terms of global objectives rather than specific policies. For example, communiqués often state that countries have jointly committed to "vigilance against inflation" or "lower global interest rates."

Regardless of the reason that countries agree to coordinate policies, it is difficult to rationalize their willingness publicly to agree to coordinate if they did not intend to honor the agreement. However, ex post, countries may decide to renege on agreements if unanticipated events change the costs or benefits of implementing agreed-upon policies. Therefore, it would be surprising to find that countries always honor their public commitments to coordinate policies. On the other hand, if economic shocks are randomly distributed over time and across countries, it should be the case that, on average, countries honor their coordination agreements. The goal of this essay is to test the hypothesis that countries generally honor their coordination agreements.

III The measurement of G–3 monetary policy agreements

Throughout modern history countries have attempted to coordinate their economic policies.[13] In the interwar period there were numerous attempts to put an end to competitive devaluation policies and restore the gold standard. The Bretton Woods conference in 1944 created institutions to facilitate international coordination. There is controversy over just how much policy coordination actually occurred in the Bretton Woods system,[14] but member countries agreed in principle to follow economic policies that would maintain fixed exchange rate parities. In practice, this obliged foreign monetary authorities to follow U.S. monetary policy. In the early 1970s the fixed exchange rate system broke down when two countries in particular – Germany and Japan – refused to continue to follow the relatively expansionary course of U.S. monetary policy.

In 1973 finance ministers from the United States, Germany, France, and the United Kingdom met in the library of the White House to discuss post–Bretton Woods international monetary issues. This "Library Group" eventually added Japan and became known as the Group of 5 (G–5).[15] Although the original G–5 meetings did not result in any publicized commitments – indeed, they were marked by an absence of record keeping – the purpose of the meetings was to facilitate coordination of macroeconomic policies within the group.[16]

In 1975 French President Valery Giscard d'Estaing proposed the organization of another discussion group, based on the "Library Group" concept, for the heads of state of the largest industrial countries.[17] In its original conception, the purpose of the group meetings, termed summits, was to foster discussion of international policy coordination among the key heads of state in informal settings. But early on it was clear that such high-level discussions would be subject to intense media attention and public scrutiny. As a result, prior to the first summit in Rambouillet, personal representatives of the heads of state met three times in order to prepare for the meeting. By the third summit meeting in London any hope for informal and frank discussion gave way to involved political deal making and a formal pre-summit negotiation process.

The Group of 7 (G–7) was created at the 1986 Tokyo Summit in order to further institutionalize the process of international macroeconomic coordination.[18] The G–7 ministers and governors meet three times a year, typically early in the year and in conjunction with the semiannual meetings of the Interim Committee of the IMF and the Development Committee of the World Bank. The G–7 finance deputies meet more frequently during the year as common economic issues or crises arise, and it is at the deputy meetings that agendas are set for the three ministerial level meetings.

The heads of the central banks meet monthly at the Basle meetings of the Bank for International Settlements (BIS), and they are often involved in G–5 and G–7 meetings. But the central bankers are only occasionally involved in pre-summit preparations. This is problematic in that summit agenda often includes discussion of monetary policy. And, for most countries in the G–7, monetary policy decisions are made exclusively by the central banks. This leads to situations where the heads of state make commitments to certain policies that are not under their direct control.

The economic policy commitments made by the participating countries at summit and other official meetings are generally made public in the form of communiqués. Hajnal describes summit communiqués as, "scriptures, the central achievement whose creation consumes much of the summit preparatory activity during the preceding year" (1989: xxxi). Table 10.1 provides a brief summary of communiqué statements regarding monetary policy agreements at various summit, G–7, G–5, and G–3 meetings.[19] The communiqués from these meetings can generally be categorized as focusing on (i) inflation or (ii) lower real interest rates (economic growth). Although the language used in the communiqués is often extremely vague, and the policies discussed are not always within the legal jurisdiction of the particular meeting's participants, the communiqués provide a time series of public commitments to international coordination. The communiqués allow us to test whether these publicly declared commitments to coordination actually influence individual countries' policy decisions over time.

Table 10.1. *Selections from G–3, G–5, and G–7 communiqués*

Meeting	Communiqué statements
November 15–17, 1975 Rambouillet (Summit)	In consolidating the recovery, it is essential to avoid unleashing additional inflationary forces which would threaten its success . . .
June 27–28, 1976	Sustained economic expansion cannot be achieved in the context of high rates of inflation. [T]he relationship between the dollar and most of the main currencies has been remarkably stable.
San Juan (Summit)	However, some currencies have suffered substantial fluctuations. Our commitment to deliberate, orderly and sustained expansion, and to the indispensable companion goal of defeating inflation, provides the basis for increased stability.
May 7–8, 1977 London (Summit)	Our most urgent task is to create more jobs while continuing to reduce inflation. Inflation does not reduce unemployment. On the contrary, it is one of its major causes.
July 17, 1978 Bonn (Summit)	We must create more jobs, fight inflation, and achieve greater stability in exchange markets . . .
June 28–29, 1979 Tokyo (Summit)	no monetary policy commitments
June 22–23, 1980 Venice (Summit)	. . . monetary restraint is required to break inflationary expectations.
July 20–21, 1981 Ottawa (Summit)	We see low and stable monetary growth as essential to reducing inflation. Interest rates have to play their part in achieving this and are likely to remain high where fears of inflation remain strong.
June 4–6, 1982 Versailles (Summit)	. . . continuing fight against inflation will help bring down interest rates, which are now unacceptably high, and to bring about more stable exchange rates.
May 28–30, 1983 Williamsburg (Summit)	Our governments will pursue appropriate monetary policies that will be conducive to low inflation.

Table 10.1. *(cont.)*

Meeting	Communiqué statements
June 7–9, 1984 London (Summit)	We have agreed: To continue with and where necessary strengthen policies to reduce inflation and interest rates, to control monetary growth . . .
January 17, 1985 G–5 Ministers' Meeting	no monetary policy commitments
May 2–4, 1985 Bonn (Summit)	We will consolidate and enhance the progress made in bringing down inflation.
September 22, 1985 Plaza G–5 Ministers' Meeting	no monetary policy commitments
January 19, 1986 G–5 Meeting	No communiqué: Participants agreed that lower inflation worldwide and lower oil prices had created conditions for lower interest rates . . . (Funabashi 1988: 44).
February 10, 1986 Volcker-Pohl Meeting	No communiqué: United States and Germany agree to coordinated discount rate reductions (Funabashi 1988: 250).
March 6, 1986 G–5 Meeting	No communiqué: U.S., Germany and Japan agree to coordinated discount rate reductions (Funabashi 1988: 47).
April 18, 1986 United States– Japan Meeting	No communiqué: United States and Japan agree to coordinated discount rate reductions (Funabashi 1988: 50).
May 6, 1986 Tokyo (Summit)	no monetary policy commitments

Table 10.1. *(cont.)*

Meeting	Communiqué statements
September 27, 1986 G–7 Ministers' Meeting	Inflation is likely to remain low. [We have agreed] to continue to follow sound monetary policies supporting non-inflationary growth . . .
October 31, 1986 Baker–Miyazawa Accord	No communiqué: Japan agrees to lower interest rates in return for U.S. promises to reduce the budget deficit, enact tax reform and resist protectionist pressures (Funabashi 1988: 160).
February 22, 1987 Louvre Accord G–6 Ministers' Meeting	Monetary policy [in Germany] will be directed at improving the conditions for sustained economic growth while maintaining price stability. The Bank of Japan announced that it will reduce its discount rate by one half percent on February 23. Monetary policy [in the United States] will be consistent with economic expansion at a sustainable non-inflationary pace.
April 8, 1987 G–7 Ministers' Meeting	no monetary policy commitments
June 8–10, 1987 Venice, (Summit)	In view of the outlook for low inflation in many countries, a further market-led decline of interest rates would be helpful.
September 26, 1987 G–7 Ministers' Meeting	The Ministers and Governors commit themselves to take further appropriate actions as necessary to achieve the agreed goals set forth in the Louvre agreement. They will particularly intensify their efforts to . . . foster a high rate of sustained non-inflationary growth.
December 23, 1987 Telephone Accord G–7	no monetary policy commitments
April 13, 1988 G–7 Ministers' Meeting	no monetary policy commitments
June 19–21, 1988 Toronto (Summit)	We need to maintain vigilance against any resurgence of inflation.

Table 10.1. *(cont.)*

Meeting	Communiqué statements
September 24, 1988 G–7 Ministers' Meeting	no monetary policy commitments
April 2, 1989 G–7 Ministers' Meeting	The success of these efforts [coordinated noninflationary growth] depends on continued progress in controlling inflation.
July 16, 1989 Paris (Summit)	Until now, the threat of inflation in many countries has been contained, thanks to the concerted efforts of governments and monetary authorities. But continued vigilance is required . . .
September 23, 1989 G–7 Ministers' Meeting	no monetary policy commitments
April 7, 1990 G–7 Ministers' Meeting	no monetary policy commitments
May 6, 1990 G–7 Ministers' Meeting	They agreed that price pressures warrant continued vigilance.
July 11, 1990 Houston (Summit)	Inflation, although considerably lower than in the early 1980s, is a matter of serious concern in some countries and requires continued vigilance.
September 22, 1990 G–7 Ministers' Meeting	no monetary policy commitments
January 21, 1991 G–7 Ministers' Meeting	Implementation of sound fiscal policies, combined with stability-oriented monetary policies, should create conditions favorable to lower global interest rates.
April 28, 1991 G–7 Ministers' Meeting	The Ministers and Governors emphasized the importance of monetary and fiscal policies which provide the basis for lower real interest rates and a sustained global economic recovery with price stability.
June 23, 1991 G–7 Ministers' Meeting	The Ministers and Governors welcomed the reductions in interest rates that have taken place in a number of their countries and elsewhere.

Table 10.1. *(cont.)*

Meeting	Communiqué statements
July 17, 1991 London (Summit)	We therefore commit ourselves to implement fiscal and monetary policies . . . provide the basis for lower real interest rates.
October 12, 1991 G–7 Ministers' Meeting	The Ministers and Governors emphasized the importance of fiscal and monetary policies, which . . . provide the basis for lower real interest rates and sustained growth with price stability in a medium-term perspective.
January 25, 1992 G–7 Ministers' Meeting	Monetary policies should be directed to preserving the gains that have been achieved in reducing inflation while providing adequate scope to finance sustainable growth. Those countries which in the future experience better than expected inflation performance may have a basis for an easing of monetary conditions and interest rates without jeopardizing the commitment to price stability and exchange rate objectives.
April 26, 1992 G–7 Ministers' Meeting	On monetary policies, the Ministers and Governors welcomed the reductions in cost and price pressures in most of their countries, which have permitted significantly lower interest rates in several cases.
July 8, 1992 Munich (Summit)	. . . we [Heads of State and Governors of G–7] all would gain greatly from stronger, sustainable non-inflationary growth.
September 19, 1992 G–7 Ministers' Meeting	The Ministers and Governors will continue to cooperate and to monitor closely economic and financial conditions in their countries and will take appropriate additional actions as needed to achieve sustained growth and greater currency stability.
April 29, 1993 G–7 Ministers' Meeting	no monetary policy commitments
July 9, 1993 Tokyo (Summit)	Japan will implement fiscal and monetary measures as necessary, to ensure sustained non-inflationary growth led by strong domestic demand . . .
November 25, 1993 G–7 Ministers' Meeting	no monetary policy commitments

The information in Table 10.1 suggests that commitments tend to be episodic and are repeated using similar language in the communiqués over time. Unsurprisingly, concern over inflation, and commitments to fight inflation, coincide with periods in which the industrial countries experience relatively high rates of inflation. Participants committed to lowering inflation rates at the first summit in 1975 continued doing so through the London Summit in 1984 and again from mid-1988 to April 1989. (Inflation was not mentioned in the 1979 Summit communiqué, which focused on reducing oil imports, probably because of the uncertainty over possible additional oil price increases and their ramifications for inflation levels.) The focus shifted to economic growth and commitments to lower interest rates in 1986, 1987, 1991, and 1992.

In order to test whether monetary policy coordination occurs during periods when countries make public commitments, the information in Table 10.1 is summarized using two dummy variables. The inflation dummy variable takes on the value of 1 during the periods in which commitments to fight inflation are included in the communiqués. Likewise, the growth dummy variable takes the values of 1 during periods in which commitments to lowering interest rates are included in the communiqués. Table 10.2 lists the meetings in which policy commitments were made by the G–3 and categorizes types of commitment.

International policy coordination may serve a number of different political and economic purposes. Officials may choose policies that are politically convenient rather than economically sound. Further, officials may agree to certain economic policy changes in exchange for reciprocal agreements in other policy areas.[20] This essay measures the degree to which the G–3 countries coordinate monetary policy; it does not evaluate the rationality or the non-economic benefits of these commitments.

IV The measurement of monetary policy

Monetary policy is usually defined as a central bank's decision to expand or contract the domestic money supply. In principle it should be possible to quantify changes in monetary policy by examining data on monetary aggregates or interest rates. In practice, however, these data reflect changes in money demand in addition to policy decisions made by the central bank.

I measure monetary policy primarily on the basis of statements made by the G–3 central banks regarding their own policy decisions. Friedman and Schwartz (1963) is one of the first studies to identify major Fed policy changes using descriptive, rather than statistical, data. Tobin (1965) makes the point that if firms that plan to expand output increase

Table 10.2. *G–3, G–5, and G–7 monetary policy commitments*

Meeting	Inflation	Lower interest rates (growth)
November 15–17, 1975 Rambouillet (Summit)	X	
June 27–28, 1976 San Juan (Summit)	X	
May 7–8, 1997 London (Summit)	X	
July 17, 1978 Bonn (Summit)	X	
June 28–29, 1979 Tokyo (Summit)		
June 22–23, 1980 Venice (Summit)	X	
July 20–21, 1981 Ottawa (Summit)	X	
June 4–6, 1982 Versailles (Summit)	X	
May 28–30, 1983 Williamsburg (Summit)	X	
June 7–9, 1984 London (Summit)	X	
January 17, 1985 G–5 Ministers' Meeting		
May 2–4, 1985 Bonn (Summit)	X	
September 22, 1985 Plaza G–5 Ministers' Meeting		
January 19, 1986 G–5 Meeting		X
February 10, 1986 Volcker–Pohl Meeting		X United States and Germany
March 6, 1986 G–3 Meeting		X
April 18, 1986 United States–Japan Meeting		X United States and Japan
May, 6, 1986 Tokyo (Summit)		

Table 10.2. *(cont.)*

Meeting	Inflation	Lower interest rates (growth)
September 27, 1986 G–7 Ministers' Meeting		X
October 31, 1986 Baker–Miyazawa Accord		X Japan
February 22, 1987 Louvre Accord G–6 Ministers' Meeting		X
April 8, 1987 G–7 Ministers' Meeting		
June 8–10, 1987 Venice (Summit)		X
September 26, 1987 G–7 Ministers' Meeting		X
December 23, 1987 Telephone Accord G–7		
April 13, 1988 G–7 Ministers' Meeting		
June 19–21, 1988 Toronto (Summit)	X	
September 24, 1988 G–7 Ministers' Meeting		
April 2, 1989 G–7 Ministers' Meeting	X	
July 16, 1989 Paris (Summit)	X	
September 23, 1989 G–7 Ministers' Meeting		
April 7, 1990 G–7 Ministers' Meeting		
May 6, 1990 G–7 Ministers' Meeting	X	
July 11, 1990 Houston (Summit)	X	
September 22, 1990 G–7 Ministers' Meeting		
January 21, 1991 G–7 Ministers' Meeting		X

Table 10.2. *(cont.)*

Meeting	Inflation	Lower interest rates (growth)
April 28, 1991 G–7 Ministers' Meeting		X
June 23, 1991 G–7 Ministers' Meeting		X
July 17, 1991 London (Summit)		X
October 12, 1991 G–7 Ministers' Meeting		X
January 25, 1992 G–7 Ministers' Meeting		X
April 26, 1992 G–7 Ministers' Meeting		X
July 8, 1992 Munich (Summit)		X
September 19, 1992 G–7 Ministers' Meeting		X
April 29, 1993 G–7 Ministers' Meeting		
July 9, 1993 Tokyo (Summit)		X Japan
November 25, 1993 G–7 Ministers' Meeting		

their demand for money, the rate of money growth may rise before output rises even though monetary policy remains unchanged. Data on monetary aggregates alone, in this case, would lead the econometrician to conclude erroneously that expansionary monetary policy preceded the increase in output. Kareken and Solow (1963) also make the point that activist monetary policy may not result in changes in output if confounding shocks offset the effects of the money expansion. In this case, on the basis of the statistical data, the econometrician would erroneously conclude that monetary policy had no effect.

More recently Romer and Romer (1989) update the narrative approach by creating a U.S. monetary policy index variable that takes on the value 1 during periods in which the minutes from FOMC meetings and related records indicate that the Fed intends to contract the money supply in order to combat inflation. The Romer and Romer (1989) index ignores monetary expansions because the index is designed to test whether U.S. monetary policy affects U.S. output. The authors assume that the Fed does not contract the money supply in order to reduce output (it does so only to fight inflation), though it is reasonable to assume that the Fed expands the money supply to stimulate output.

This essay examines the influence of U.S., German, and Japanese monetary policies on each other, so is less sensitive to the simultaneity issues that arise in Romer and Romer (1989). Consequently, it is possible to examine the influence of both monetary contractions and monetary expansions. Boschen and Mills (1995) create a U.S. monetary policy index, largely following the Romer and Romer (1989) methodology, that includes monetary expansions and allows for different degrees of policy intensity. The Boschen and Mills index takes the value 2 (or –2) during periods when the Fed was strongly expansionary (contractionary) and the value 1 (or –1) during periods of mild expansion (contraction).[21] This essay uses the Boschen and Mills index to measure U.S. monetary policy changes.

The measurement of U.S. monetary policy intentions is relatively easy because the Fed makes publicly available (with a six-week lag) the minutes of the FOMC meetings where policy decisions are made. The Bank of Japan and the Bundesbank do not provide public records of their respective monetary policy directives. However, both banks provide ex post explanations for monetary policy changes; these explanations together with information gleaned from policy and money market data, are used to create German and Japanese monetary policy indexes that are analogous to the Boschen and Mills index for the United States. The next two sections of the essay describe the monetary policy changes that occurred in Germany and Japan, and how these policy changes are reflected in the respective country indexes.

A German monetary policy

The Bundesbank has sole responsibility for German monetary policy and is considered highly independent of the German federal government. The Bundesbank has a legal mandate to "safeguard the currency." Although the Bundesbank takes both economic growth and balance of payments issues into account in its monetary policy decisions, its sole and paramount responsibility is to maintain the purchasing power of the deutschemark.

The Bundesbank established a regime of monetary targeting in 1975. The main instrument that the Bundesbank uses to implement monetary policy is bank lending. Banks may borrow from the Bundesbank at three different interest rates: the discount rate,[22] the lombard rate,[23] and the repurchase (repo) rate.[24] Major changes in the monetary stance of the Bundesbank are typically initiated with changes in one or more of these interest rates, changes in the minimum reserve ratios, or a change in the monetary target ranges. The Bundesbank index is based on changes in these policy instruments, as well as official statements describing monetary policy objectives. An overview of major changes in Bundesbank monetary policy over the period from 1977 through 1993, and the ways in which the index reflects these decisions, follows.

German monetary policy was neither contractionary nor expansionary in 1977 and 1978. Bundesbank-controlled interest rate changes were small and generally represented reactions to movements in market interest rates. The 1977 and 1978 *Bundesbank Monthly Report*s indicate that although money growth rates exceeded their targets, inflation rates were below target, and official discussions of policy pay equal attention to growth and inflation. The Bundesbank monthly index is 0, signifying a neutral monetary policy stance, over this two-year period.

In January 1979 the Bundesbank raised the minimum reserve ratios for commercial banks and also raised the lombard rate. Over the next six months the lombard rate was raised two more times. The April 1979 *Bundesbank Monthly Report* describes the need to "restrain demand for credit" (5–6). In the second half of the year, the emphasis on controlling "domestic and external inflationary dangers" (*Bundesbank Monthly Report*, November 1979: 6) seems to have intensified. On September 1 limits on lombard borrowing were put in place, and the discount and lombard rates were raised three times in the next few months. In March 1980 the lombard limits were removed, and the intensity of the Bundesbank contraction seems to have eased. Consequently, the Bundesbank monthly index is –1 in the first half of 1979, it is decreased to –2 from July 1979 through February 1980, and it returns to –1 from March through August 1980.

Over the fall of 1980 and early 1981, "the Bundesbank gradually released the monetary brakes on account of the slower monetary growth and the increasing signs of a downturn in economic activity" (*Bundesbank Monthly Report*, December 1980: 11). The monthly index returns to 0, a neutral policy stance, in this period.

On March 4, 1981, the Bundesbank abruptly closed the lombard facility and replaced it with a special lombard rate three percentage points higher than the old lombard rate. The repo interest rate rose 2.9 percent in a volume-tender auction in April. Press reports described these dramatic interest rate moves as Germany's "effort to stabilize the mark against the dollar, [the increases] committed European leaders to a punishing interest-rate war with the United States" (*Business Week,* March 23, 1981). The monthly index falls to –2 from March through September 1981 to reflect the strong contractionary stance of policy.

In October 1981 the special lombard rate fell, but the usual lombard facility remained closed. The December 1981 *Monthly Report* characterized this period as a "gradual relaxation of monetary policy" (10). The Bundesbank monetary policy index returns to –1 in this period. In December 1981 the special lombard rate was lowered again and the Bundesbank signaled its intent to stop counteracting the fall of money market rates (*Bundesbank Monthly Report,* January 1982). The monetary policy index therefore rises to 0, or a neutral monetary policy stance, during December 1981.

In 1982 the special lombard rate was lowered twice and the usual lombard facility was reestablished in May at a lower rate. The lombard and discount rates were subsequently lowered three more times before the end of the year. The February *Monthly Report* states, "the range of this target [monetary growth] implied that the Bundesbank intended to encourage a somewhat more rapid monetary expansion than immediately before" (10). In March 1983 the Bundesbank intensified its expansionary stance by lowering the lombard and discount rates by one percentage point and stating that the rate cuts were designed to "bolster the expansionary forces." The monetary index is 1 for 1982 and the first two months of 1983; the index increases to 2 from March through August 1983.

The lombard and discount rates rose 50 basis points in September 1983 and June 1984, respectively, while rediscount quotas rose in June. Over the fall of 1983 through 1984 official interviews and *Monthly Reports* reflect a fairly neutral tone. The September 1984 *Monthly Report* suggests that the purpose of the (June) discount rate increase was to counteract the appearance that the increase of the rediscount quotas signaled a relaxation of monetary policy. The monetary index is 0 over this period.

In January 1985 the Bundesbank again raised the lombard rate, but this move was to "encourage the banks to reduce their lombard debt by switching transactions under repurchase agreements in securities at favorable interest rates, which were offered on an increased scale" (*Monthly Report,* February 1985: 9). Starting in early 1985 and continuing through May 1988, the pattern of repo rates and discount rate reductions suggests a change to a mild expansionary stance. Although the Bundesbank cut the rediscount quota and increased the minimum reserve requirement in February 1987, liquidity continued to increase over this period, as reflected in market interest rates and money growth rates. The monetary index is 1 over this three-year period.[25]

In June 1988 the Bundesbank raised both the discount and lombard rates. The September 1988 *Monthly Report* indicates that these moves reflected a change toward a neutral monetary stance. "In line with the changed overall economic conditions, in recent months the Bundesbank has sought to pursue a markedly less expansionary monetary policy" (10). The monetary index is 0 from June through November 1988.

Starting in December 1988 and extending through August 1992, the Bundesbank raised the lombard and discount rates nine times. Official statements and descriptions in the *Monthly Report*s all indicate that Bundesbank monetary policy was mildly contractionary over this period. After German reunification, policy statements were focused on inflationary pressures and money growth targets. The monetary index is –1 over this period.

On September 14, 1992, the Bundesbank lowered the lombard and discount rates for the first time in over five years. Likewise, the repo rate was lowered in October by volume-tender. In the first six months of 1993 the lombard and discount rates were lowered three times. The February 1993 *Monthly Report* states, "the Bundesbank has been cautiously exploring the scope for interest rate reductions. This has not involved any modification of its basic, stability-oriented course, nor would any such change be warranted, given the price and money stock trends" (12). The decidedly cautious tone of official statements suggests a neutral, rather than expansionary, monetary stance over this period. Consequently, the monetary index is 0 over this period.

Starting in July 1993 official statements and descriptions in the *Monthly Report* suggest that the Bundesbank changed to a mildly expansionary stance, largely due to slow M3 growth and reduced fears of inflationary pressures. The lombard and discount rates fell three times between July and October. The monetary index is 1 from July through December 1993.

B *Japanese monetary policy*

Bank of Japan Law authorizes the Policy Board, which includes representatives of the Ministry of Finance, to formulate, direct, and supervise monetary policy. Over the last twenty years, the Ministry of Finance's (MOF) influence on Bank of Japan (BOJ) policy decisions varies with changes in top personnel and economic conditions. Typically, when the BOJ wants to change the discount rate (its main monetary policy tool), it consults with the MOF, the finance minister, and the prime minister before coming to a decision.[26] The objectives of Japanese monetary policy have undergone substantial changes over the last two decades, focusing alternatingly on economic growth, the value of the yen, the balance of payments, and inflation. The BOJ has no legal mandate to maintain price stability.

Major changes in the monetary policy stance of the BOJ are typically initiated with changes in the discount rate, the interest rate at which commercial banks can borrow funds from the BOJ. The BOJ also uses window guidance, the reserve progress ratio,[27] changes in the reserve requirement, and the call money rate[28] to signal to the market and other governments changes in monetary policy intentions. The BOJ monetary policy index is based on changes in these four policy instruments, as well as official statements describing monetary policy objectives. An overview of major changes in BOJ monetary policy over the period 1977 through 1993, and the ways in which the index reflects these decisions, follow.

In early 1977 Japanese economic growth had stalled, industrial production growth was shrinking, and inflation was low. On March 12, 1977, the BOJ announced a 50-basis-point reduction in the discount rate, indicating that the aim of the rate reduction was to encourage economic growth. In October 1977 the reserve requirement for commercial banks was reduced. The BOJ lowered the discount rate three more times over the next two years, and after each rate reduction gave "economic growth" as the rationale. The BOJ monetary index takes on the value 1, signifying a mild expansionary stance, over this period.

It was not until April 1979 that the BOJ ended its relatively loose monetary policy stance. On April 17, 1979, the BOJ raised the discount rate 75 basis points with an accompanying statement indicating that it had done so in reaction to rising inflation and a depreciating yen. In addition, the BOJ "tightened its window guidance of financial institutions term by term in line with the intention of the official rate hike" (BOJ *Annual Report*, 1979: 3) The BOJ intensified its contractionary stance in July 1979 with a 1 percent increase in the discount rate. Between July 1979 and August 1980 the discount rate was increased three times, raising it from 6.5 percent to 9 percent. In April 1980 the BOJ raised the reserve requirement rate for commercial banks. In late August 1980 the BOJ reduced the discount rate 75 basis points, but Bank of Japan Governor Hauro Mayekawa took pains in a press conference speech to emphasize that the rate slash "does not mean the start of monetary relaxation or stimulation of the economy."[29] The BOJ monetary index, therefore, takes on the value −1 starting in April 1979, signifying a mild contraction. The index changes to −2, indicating a strong contraction, over the period from July 1979 through July 1980. The index then returns to −1 through October 1980.

In November 1980 the BOJ returned the reserve requirement on commercial banks to its level prior to the April 1980 increase. The BOJ index is 0, indicating neither expansion nor contraction, between November 1980 and February 1981.

In March 1981 the BOJ indicated that it had officially changed to a mildly expansionary policy stance in an effort to spur economic growth. On April 1, 1981, the BOJ reduced the reserve requirement. And over the next three years the BOJ lowered the discount rate three times and repeatedly emphasized the need for "economic stimulation." The 1982 BOJ *Annual Report* describes the policy stance as "maintaining monetary relaxation" (3). And the 1983 BOJ *Annual Report* states, "the Bank kept its easy monetary stance ... maintaining a flexible window guidance posture" (3). Consequently, the BOJ index is 1 over this three year period.

In early 1984, despite lackluster economic growth, a surge in the yen's value against the dollar, and financial market expectations of another discount rate cut, the BOJ declined to change interest rates. The central bank governor told a news conference, "Japan has no immediate plan to change monetary policy," and, in particular, to stem the rise in the yen.[30] In November 1985, Governor Satoshi Sumita stated that, "Japan will avoid widening the interest-rate spread between Japan and the United States at any cost."[31] The BOJ monetary policy stance in 1984 and 1985 was largely neutral; consequently the index is 0 over the period.[32]

The BOJ cut the discount rate for the first time in almost two years in January 1986, citing the need to encourage economic growth. Indeed, statements by the Governor, Mr. Satoshi Sumita, indicate that the BOJ monetary policy was mildly expansionary starting in 1986 and continuing through the first few months of 1988. Over this period the discount rate was reduced four times, from 4.5 percent down to 2.5 percent. The BOJ index is 1 over this time period.

In May 1989 the BOJ raised the discount rate 75 basis points, but in subsequent interviews the BOJ Governor emphasized that the increase should not be interpreted as a change toward tighter money. The discount rate was increased two more times in 1989, but after both changes officials indicated that these increases were to keep discount rates in line with market interest rates, and should not be taken as signals of a change in policy stance. The BOJ index is 0 for most of 1989 and early 1990.

On March 20, 1990, in reaction to a 3 percent depreciation of the yen against the dollar in one month and a dramatic stock market drop on the previous day, the BOJ abruptly changed course and raised the discount rate a full percentage point. Monetary policy remained relatively contractionary through June 1991. The BOJ index is −1 over this period.

Starting in mid-summer 1991, official statements suggest that the BOJ had relaxed its contractionary stance. The discount rate was lowered by 50 basis points three times through the fall of 1991, but after each rate reduction official statements indicate that these changes should not be considered expansionary. The BOJ index, therefore, returned to 0 over this period.

In the spring of 1992 the BOJ announced a 75-basis-point reduction in the discount rate one day after the government announced a package of emergency "pump-priming" measures to bolster the economy. The discount rate was cut two more times over the next year. Then, in September 1993, the BOJ intensified its expansionary stance by lowering the discount rate to a historic low of 1.75 percent. The BOJ index is 1 starting in April 1992, then jumps to 2 in September 1993, and remains at 2 for the rest of 1993.

The Boschen and Mills (1995) index of Fed monetary policy changes is fundamentally an ex ante measure. The index is based on the policy intentions of the FOMC as documented by the minutes of each FOMC meeting. The German and Japanese indexes are not directly comparable to the U.S. index because they measure policy intentions with hindsight. These indexes are, by necessity, based on after-the-fact accounts of policy in central bank publications and on historical movements in monetary aggregates and interest rates. But the common feature of the three indexes is that they are, at least partially, based on descriptive information provided by each central bank.

V Time series evidence of G–3 monetary policy coordination

In order to examine the degree to which the G–3 coordinated monetary policies over the period from 1977 through 1993, three approaches are used. The first approach measures simple correlations between the monetary policy indexes. The second tests whether monetary policies are influenced by policies in the other two countries. The first two approaches identify any systematic relationships between monetary policies in the United States, Germany, and Japan without offering information on the underlying reasons for policy interdependence. The third approach examines the relationship between monetary policies and coordination agreements, considering whether, and how, the coordination agreements are related to changes in monetary policy in each of the G–3 countries.

Table 10.3. *Cross-correlation matrices*

	U.S. monetary policy index	German monetary policy index	Japanese monetary policy index
I. Sample: 1977–1993			
U.S. monetary policy index	1.00	0.32	0.31
German monetary policy index	0.32	1.00	0.56
Japanese monetary policy index	0.31	0.56	1.00
II. Sample: 1977–1984			
U.S. monetary policy index	1.00	0.66	0.60
German monetary policy index	0.66	1.00	0.45
Japanese monetary policy index	0.60	0.45	1.00
III. Sample: 1985–1993			
U.S. monetary policy index	1.00	0.26	0.25
German monetary policy index	0.26	1.00	0.59
Japanese monetary policy index	0.25	0.59	1.00

Note: Matrix entries are the cross-correlation coefficients for each pair of series. The data are monthly and the sample period is denoted above each matrix.

Table 10.3 presents correlations between U.S., German, and Japanese monetary policy indexes over the full period and two subperiods. The first subperiod is 1977–1984 and the second subperiod is 1985–1993. The sample is split in 1985 to test whether interdependence among the G–3 increased after the United States became a more active participant in international coordination efforts. The elements in the first correlation matrix indicate that monetary policies in Germany and Japan are relatively highly correlated, and U.S. monetary policy is slightly more correlated with German policy than Japanese policy over the full sample period. Further investigation indicates that the correlation between German monetary policy at time t with Japanese monetary policy at time $t -$ 12 through $t + 12$ (where time is measured in months, so that $t + 12$ is one

Table 10.4. *Bivariate Granger-causality tests*

Dependent variables	Independent variables		
	U.S. monetary policy index	German monetary policy index	Japanese monetary policy index
I. Sample: 1977–1993			
U.S. monetary policy index		0.584	0.751
German monetary policy index	0.086[†]		0.127
Japanese monetary policy index	0.091[†]	0.053[†]	
II. Sample: 1977–1984			
U.S. monetary policy index		0.739	0.601
German monetary policy index	0.009**		0.418
Japanese monetary policy index	0.101	0.469	
III. Sample: 1985–1993			
U.S. monetary policy index		0.127	0.223
German monetary policy index	0.057[†]		0.650
Japanese monetary policy index	0.034*	0.124	

Note: Matrix entries are the significance levels of *F*-statistics from tests of the null hypothesis that the independent variable (the monetary policy index) is zero in a bivariate regression of the dependent variable on own lags and lags of the independent variable. The number of lags in each bivariate regression is selected using the Akaike criterion. ** denotes significance at the 0.01 level; * denotes significance at the 0.05 level; and [†] denotes significance at the 0.10 level. The data are monthly and the sample period is denoted above each matrix.

year ahead) is always positive. On the other hand, U.S. monetary policy at time *t* appears to be negatively correlated with German and Japanese monetary policy at time *t* + 8, suggesting that when the United States expands, Germany and Japan initially also expand, but reverse their policies after approximately eight months.[33] If we exclude these reversal periods, the correlation between U.S. and German monetary policy rises

Table 10.5. *Cross-correlation matrices*

Policy commitments	G–3 policy indexes		
	U.S. monetary policy index	German monetary policy index	Japanese monetary policy index
I. Sample: 1977–1993			
Inflation	−0.37	0.05	−0.13
Growth	0.62	0.09	0.18
Oil prices	−0.07	−0.07	−0.25
II. Sample: 1997–1984			
Inflation	−0.54	0.02	−0.31
Growth	na	na	na
Oil prices	−0.16	−0.11	−0.51
III. Sample: 1985–1993			
Inflation	−0.42	−0.15	−0.30
Growth	0.60	0.07	0.25
Oil prices	−0.11	−0.13	−0.14

Note: Matrix entries are the cross-correlation coefficients for each pair of series. The data are monthly and the sample period is denoted above each matrix. There were no G–3 growth commitments during the sample period 1977–1984.

to 0.38 and the correlation between the United States and Japan rises to 0.46. Interestingly, the subperiod results suggest that the correlation between U.S. monetary policy and the policies of Germany and Japan is larger in the earlier subperiod, whereas the correlation between German and Japanese policies is slightly stronger in the second subperiod.

Granger's (1969) regressions allow us to test the direction of causality among the G–3 monetary policies. One variable Granger causes another if forecasts of the second variable can be improved using past observations of the first variable in addition to past observations of the second variable. The Granger-causality test results presented in Table 10.4 support the hypotheses that U.S. monetary policy influences Germany and Japan, and German policy influences Japan – but these tests do not support the hypothesis that Japanese policy influences U.S. or German policy over the full sample period.

The simple correlations presented in Table 10.3 suggest a stronger relationship between the monetary policies of Germany and Japan than the relationship between U.S. monetary policy and those of either Germany or Japan. But the causality tests suggest that it is U.S. policy that influences both Germany and Japan. Combined, the results in Tables 10.3 and 10.4 suggest that monetary policies in the United States, Germany, and Japan are related, and that causality runs from the United States to Germany and Japan. We now turn to the question of whether the interdependence of G–3 monetary policies is, in turn, related to the coordination commitments made by these countries.

Table 10.5 presents correlations between monetary policy indexes and the coordination commitment dummy variables over the full period and two subperiods. In cases where commitments involved unilateral monetary policy changes (e.g., Japan's commitment to lower interest rates as part of the Baker–Miyazawa Accord in October 1986), the coordination dummy variable is adjusted accordingly. We should expect that a commitment to lower inflation would lead to a monetary contraction, and, indeed we find this to be the case for the United States and Japan. Perhaps surprisingly, given Germany's inflation-fighting reputation, the German monetary policy index is (weakly) positively related to inflation commitments over the full period. Commitments to reduce interest rates (and stimulate growth) should be associated with monetary expansions – and monetary policies in all three countries are positively correlated with these commitments.

The final row in each matrix in Table 10.5 presents correlations between monetary policies and changes in oil prices. This is intended as a robustness test. Large oil price movements in the sample period should be negatively correlated with monetary policies, and indeed this is the case for all three countries.

The results presented in Table 10.5 suggest that monetary policies in the United States, Japan, and Germany are sometimes strongly correlated with the coordination commitments made public by these countries since the mid-1970s. But simple cross-correlations do not demonstrate causality. Table 10.6 presents results from bivariate Granger-causality tests of the influence of commitments on monetary policies in the three countries over the full period and the two subperiods. These tests suggest that U.S. and Japanese monetary policies are influenced by public commitments to reduce inflation and interest rates over the full sample period. German monetary policy appears to be unaffected by public commitments over all sample periods. Changes in oil prices influence only Japanese monetary policy.

The classification of the communiqué statements into "inflation" or "growth" oriented monetary policy commitments is necessarily subjective. Two sets of sensitivity analyses provide tests of the robustness of the results presented in Tables 10.5 and 10.6. One sensitivity analysis considers whether any individual coordination commitment had undue influ-

Table 10.6. *Bivariate Granger-causality tests*

Dependent variables	Independent variables		
	Inflation	Growth	Change in oil prices
I. Sample: 1997–1993			
U.S. monetary policy index	0.031*	0.017*	0.264
German monetary policy index	0.740	0.263	0.431
Japanese monetary policy index	0.053†	0.072†	0.034*
II. Sample: 1977–1984			
U.S. monetary policy index	0.042*	na	0.282
German monetary policy index	0.465	na	0.247
Japanese monetary policy index	0.100†	na	0.000**
III. Sample: 1985–1993			
U.S. monetary policy index	0.076†	0.049*	0.318
German monetary policy index	0.512	0.301	0.668
Japanese monetary policy index	0.251	0.048*	0.227

Note: Matrix entries are the significance levels of F-statistics from tests of the null hypothesis that the independent variable (the coordination commitments or changes in oil prices) is zero in a bivariate regression of the dependent variable on own legs and lags of the independent variable. The number of lags in each bivariate regression is selected using the Akaike criterion. ** denotes significance at the 0.01 level; * denotes significance at the 0.05 level; and † denotes significance at the 0.10 level.

ence on the time series results. Each of the correlations in Table 10.5, and each Granger-causality test in Table 10.6, was recalculated a number of times, each time dropping a different coordination dummy variable from the sample in order to check whether the results depend heavily on a single coordination episode. The results from these tests did not reveal any significant outliers. A second sensitivity analysis separates those coordination agreements made at regularly scheduled meetings (the yearly summit and the two G–7 ministerial level meetings in the fall and spring) from those made at meetings called unexpectedly in order to confront specific crises (e.g., the Plaza and Louvre Agreements). Again, the correlations and Granger-causality tests were repeated excluding the nonregularly scheduled meetings. (The bulk of these meetings occurred during 1985–7.) These tests also indicate that the results presented in the tables are not unduly influenced by agreements made at nonregularly scheduled meetings.

VI Conclusions

This essay examines the relationship between monetary policy decisions in the United States, Germany, and Japan. Theory suggests that it may sometimes be in a country's best interest to coordinate its monetary policy. And, in practice, the G–3 occasionally announce their intention to coordinate policies. The first part of this essay documents the occasions in which the G–3 made public commitments to coordinate monetary policies. The second part of the essay tests whether the G–3, on average, honored these commitments. Using monetary policy indexes based on central bank descriptions of monetary policy stances, empirical tests suggest that the G–3 monetary policies are interdependent. But interdependence appears to run from the United States to Germany and Japan, with little evidence to suggest that German and Japanese policy decisions influence the United States. The United States and Japan generally honor their commitments to reduce inflation and interest rates. However, German policy is unaffected by any of the coordination commitments.

The conclusion that Germany is the least likely of the G–3 countries to be influenced by coordination agreements should not be surprising. Indeed, Henning (1994) concludes that, of the three countries, Germany has the most "consistent" monetary policy objectives. Germany consistently stresses price stability as its main monetary policy objective, whereas the monetary policy objectives of the United States and Japan vary with changes in administrations and currency movements. The monetary policy coordination agreements over this period may have been incompatible with Germany's domestic policy objectives. Consequently, the puzzle is why Germany agreed to many of the coordination commitments in the first place, not why German policy was unaffected by the commitments.

Countries publicly commit to coordination agreements for numerous economic and political reasons. And public commitments may not accurately reflect implicit agreements among the participating countries. Therefore, one explanation for Germany's unilateral approach may be that it was an unwilling participant in many of the coordination agreements, but signed on as a gesture of political unity. This would also explain why the United States and Japan continued to include Germany in coordination agreements after it had ignored previous commitments.

Unanticipated shocks or changes in domestic politics are often understood among participating countries to be grounds for "involuntary" defections. Another possible explanation for Germany's unilateral approach is that it was subject to a greater number of unanticipated shocks than the United States or Japan. Of the three countries, Germany was the only one with a formal commitment to exchange rate (and therefore monetary policy) coordination with another group of countries, members of the European Monetary System (EMS). An implicit understanding among the G–3 may exist over the precedence of EMS coordination for Germany. Likewise, unification presented Germany with numerous unanticipated shocks that may have led to legitimate defections from G–3 coordination agreements.

Another puzzle that arises from the results in the essay is the surprisingly strong performance of U.S. monetary policy in the context of the coordination agreements. The likely explanation is that the United States was the dominant force in the coordination process over this period. Indeed, Henning (1994) suggests that German and Japanese authorities often declined to pursue coordination agreements when the United States was an unwilling participant. If the coordination agreements mainly reflect monetary policies that are in the best interests of the United States, then it is unsurprising that the United States consistently honors the commitments.

Although the goal of this study was to evaluate the economic performance of the G–3 coordination process, the economic record cannot be fully understood without taking into account the politics of international monetary agreements.[34] The data suggest that Germany is the most frequent defector from G–3 monetary coordination agreements, but the more likely culprit is the political process in which the agreements are made.

NOTES

I thank an anonymous referee, Barry Eichengreen, Marina Whitman, and especially Benjamin Cohen for useful comments and suggestions. Donald Redl and Belinda Weir provided outstanding research assistance. I am grateful to the National Science Foundation for providing financial support for this project under grant number SBR–9311507.

1. See, for example, Hamada (1976, 1985), Cooper (1985), and Canzoneri and Henderson (1991).
2. The Oudiz and Sachs (1984, 1985) estimates of the gains from cooperation are quite small. Currie, Levine and Vidalis (1987) find that benefits increase markedly in cases where governments have strong reputations for policy consistency and external shocks are large and persistent. Hughes Hallett, Holtham, and Hutson (1989) find that gains from exchange rate targeting may be as high as 1.7 percent of GNP. See Currie, Holtham, and Hughes Hallett (1989) for a survey of this literature.
3. Dominguez and Kenen (1992).
4. The G–3 consists of Germany, Japan, and the United States; the G–5 adds France and the United Kingdom; and the G–7 adds Canada and Italy.
5. The results of these simulations are presented in Bryant, Currie, Frenkel, Masson, and Portes (1989), Bryant, Henderson, Holtham, Hooper, and Symansky (1988), and Bryant, Hooper, and Mann (1993).
6. The target-zone model proposal is described in Williamson and Miller (1987). Currie and Wren-Lewis (1990) provide an empirical assessment of the proposal for the G–3. Hughes Hallett (1992) examines how much international policy coordination would be introduced by a target zone system in practice.
7. Canzoneri and Henderson (1991) provide a comprehensive game-theoretic examination of international policy coordination.
8. The Nash (noncooperative) solution to the dilemma (in which policy makers maximize national welfare, taking other countries' policies as given) is generally inefficient because countries playing Nash do not internalize foreign monetary policy spillovers. The cooperative solution (in which policymakers maximize weighted averages of national welfares so that no single country can be made better off without making another worse off) and the Stackelberg solution (in which the leader commits to a given policy and then maximizes national welfare taking into account the follower reaction, and the follower maximizes national welfare given the leaders' policy commitment) are both usually welfare-improving relative to Nash. But both the cooperative and Stackelberg equilibria may also be inefficient in the presence of third-party effects (Rogoff, 1985), time consistency problems, or uncertainty over the underlying economic model. Further, in the Stackelberg equilibria the improvement over Nash will not necessarily be symmetric for the leader and follower countries, leading to sustainability problems.
9. However, coordination may not always be welfare-improving. Currie and Wren-Lewis (1990) suggest that the "lack of coordination" between the

United States, Germany, and Japan in the early 1980s may have been a deliberate welfare-improving cooperation strategy. The intuition is that G–3 inflation rates were highly divergent prior to the U.S. contraction; by equalizing inflation rates, the (noncoordinated) Volcker monetary contraction increased global welfare.

10. Another explanation for the small number of coordination agreements is uncertainty over the correct economic model (Frankel and Rockett 1988; Holtham and Hughes Hallett 1987, 1992), or over the terms of the agreements (e.g., initial positions, weights on target variables, policy multipliers), Frankel (1988).

11. These changes need not be "harmonized" in the sense that all countries move in the same direction; indeed, optimal policies will typically require countries to do different things.

12. Currie, Holtham, and Hughes Hallett (1989) and Bryant (1995) emphasize that consultations and information exchanges are important aspects of international policy coordination. Canzoneri and Edison (1990) find that gains from information sharing tend to be larger than the incremental gains in moving from a Nash to full-scale cooperative equilibria.

13. See Eichengreen (1990) and James (1996) for some historical examples.

14. See Bordo (1993) for a discussion of the controversy.

15. Initially this group included the finance ministers, one additional support official from each country, and occasionally the central bank governors.

16. Putnam and Bayne (1987) provide an excellent history of the "Library Group."

17. The first summit meeting, held in Rambouillet, included France, Germany, Italy, Japan, the United Kingdom, and the United States. Canada was invited to attend the 1976 summit and the President of the European Commission began attending in 1977. The politics of summit invitations is discussed in James (1996) and Putnam and Bayne (1987).

18. G–7 meetings may include finance ministers, finance deputies, and central bank governors from each of the seven industrial countries that attend the summit meetings, as well as the Managing Director of the IMF. In most cases the G–7 deputy is the senior Finance Ministry (or Treasury) official in each member country who is responsible for international affairs. See Dobson (1991) for the names of these deputies over the period 1985–9.

19. Monetary policy coordination between the United States, Germany, and Japan also takes place in the context of meetings at the IMF, the OECD, and the Bank for International Settlements (BIS). However, the commitments made at these meetings are generally not made public. Table 10.1 includes five coordination commitment agreements made in 1986 that were not accompanied by communiqués, but were widely reported by the financial press.

20. Currie and Levine (1991) describe these as one-off agreements. The 1978 Bonn Summit is an example of one such agreement where Germany agreed to a fiscal expansion in exchange for changes in U.S. oil policy and Japanese trade policy.

21. The Romer and Romer (1989) index differs conceptually from the Boschen and Mills (1995) index in that it is intended to measure U.S. monetary policy innovations directly, while the Boschen and Mills index attempts to describe the current state of monetary policy.

22. The discount rate is typically below the market interest rate. Banks are rationed at the discount window according to a preset quota, but they are allowed to borrow discount credit upon request up to their quota.

23. The Lombard rate is always above the market interest rate so that there is no need to ration this credit under normal circumstances. Lombard credit can be thought of as a last resort source of funds for banks when there is excess demand for central bank money.

24. Repos are loans to banks that are collateralized by securities. The Bundesbank auctions repos once a week. The auctions can be either volume or interest tenders. In volume tenders the Bundesbank fixes the interest rate and banks bid for quantities. Generally under 50 percent of bids are successful. The Bundesbank reportedly uses volume tenders as a means of signaling information to the market about changes in interest rates. In interest rate tenders banks bid both quantities and prices (interest rates).

25. This is one of the few periods in which data and official statements provide some mixed messages. There is some evidence to suggest that the Bundesbank monetary stance was neutral, rather than mildly expansionary, starting in March 1996. The time series tests presented in the next section were performed using both the index described in the text and one that characterizes this period as neutral. The qualitative implications of the results did not change with this alternative specification.

26. See Henning (1994: 70–1 and especially footnote 22) for a discussion of the "fiction of BOJ independence."

27. The reserve progress ratio is the cumulative sum of daily reserves held by commercial banks from the beginning of the current reserve accounting period relative to the required reserves of the period. This ratio is expected to start at 0 and to increase by about 3.3 percent every day to reach 1 at the end of the month. If the BOJ wants to loosen or tighten its monetary policy stance, it can alter the rate of change in the reserve progress ratio by increasing or decreasing its lending to banks.

28. The call market rate is similar to the Federal Funds market rate in the United States: it is the interest rate that banks offer each other to borrow short term funds. Although the BOJ does not have direct control over the call rate, it is widely believed that, especially prior to 1988, the BOJ exerts strong influence over the call market.

29. Nihon Keizai Shimbun, *Japan Economic Journal*, August 26, 1980, p. 21.

30. Kyodo News Service, *Japan Economic Newswire*, March 8, 1984.

31. Jiji Press Ticker Service, November 13, 1985.

32. The BOJ increased short-term interest rates (but not the discount rate) in October 1985, shortly after the Plaza Agreement. "This move, which was not subject to MOF approval, touched off a sharp domestic and international

dispute . . . critical reactions compelled BOJ to reverse its policy course only a few weeks later" (Henning 1994: 146). Because this policy change and subsequent reversal occurred within the month, it does not appear in the monthly data.

33. Ljung-Box Q-statistics indicate that the monetary policy correlations between the pairs of countries are highly statistically significant over various combinations of leads and lags.

34. For a recent evaluation of the politics of G–7 cooperation see Bergsten and Henning (1996). Fischer (1988) and Currie (1993) describe the prospects for future international monetary cooperation.

REFERENCES

Bank of Tokyo (Nition Ginko), *BOJ Annual Report*. Economic Research Department, Tokyo, Japan (various issues).

Bergsten, Fred C., and C. Randall Henning (1996). *Global Economic Leadership and the Group of Seven*. Washington, DC: Institute for International Economics.

Boschen, John F., and Leonard O. Mills (1995). "The Relation between Narrative and Money Market Indicators of Monetary Policy," *Economic Inquiry* (January), 24–44.

Bordo, Michael (1993). "The Bretton Woods International Monetary System: A Historical Overview." In *A Retrospective on the Bretton Woods System: Lessons for International Monetary Reform*, Michael Bordo and Barry Eichengreen, eds., pp. 3–108. Chicago: University of Chicago Press.

Bryant, Ralph C. (1995). "International Cooperation in the Making of National Macroeconomic Policies: Where Do We Stand?" In *Understanding Interdependence: The Macroeconomics of the Open Economy*, Peter B. Kenen, ed., pp. 391–447. Princeton: Princeton University Press.

Bryant, Ralph C., David A. Currie, Jacob A. Frenkel, Paul R. Masson, and Richard Portes, eds. (1989). *Macroeconomic Policies in an Interdependent World*. Washington, DC: Brookings Institution, Centre for Economic Policy Research, and International Monetary Fund.

Bryant, Ralph C., Dale W. Henderson, Gerald Holtham, Peter Hooper, and Steven A. Symansky, eds. (1988). *Empirical Macroeconomics for Interdependent Economies*. Washington, DC: Brookings Institution.

Bryant, Ralph C., Peter Hooper, and Catherine L. Mann, eds. (1993). *Evaluating Policy Regimes: New Research in Empirical Macroeconomics*. Washington, DC: Brookings Institution.

Business Week (March 23, 1981). Cited in Japan Economic Newswire (NEXIS), 1984.

Canzoneri, Matthew, and Hali Edison (1990). "A New Interpretation of the Coordination Problem and Its Empirical Significance." In Peter Hooper, Karen H. Johnson, Donald L. Kohn, David E. Lindsey, Richard D. Porter, and Ralph W. Tryon, eds., *Financial Sectors in Open Economies: Empirical Analy-*

sis and Policy Issues, pp. 399–433. Washington, DC: Board of Governors of the Federal Reserve System.

Canzoneri, Matthew, and Dale Henderson (1991). *Monetary Policy in Interdependent Economies: A Game Theoretic Approach*. Cambridge: MIT Press.

Cooper, Richard (1985). "Economic Interdependence and Coordination of Economic Policies." In *Handbook of International Economics*, Vol. 2, Ronald Jones and Peter B. Kenen, eds., pp. 1195–1234. Amsterdam: North Holland.

Currie, David (1993). "International Cooperation in Monetary Policy: Has It a Future? *The Economic Journal* 103 (January), 178–87.

Currie, David, Gerald Holtham, and Andrew J. Hughes Hallett (1989). "The Theory and Practice of International Policy Coordination: Does Coordination Pay?" In Ralph C. Bryant et al. 1989, pp. 14–46.

Currie, David, and Paul Levine (1991). "The International Co-ordination of Macroeconomic Policy." In *Companion to Contemporary Economic Thought*, D. Greenway, M. Bleaney, and I. M. T. Stewart, eds., pp. 100–23. London: Routledge.

Currie, David, Paul Levine, and Nic Vidalis (1987). "International Cooperation and Reputation in an Empirical Two-Bloc Model." In Ralph C. Bryant and Richard Portes, eds., *Global Macroeconomics: Policy Conflict and Cooperation*, pp. 73–121. London: Macmillan.

Currie, David, and Simon Wren-Lewis (1990). "An Appraisal of Alternative Blueprints for International Policy Coordination," *European Economic Review* 33, 1769–85.

Deutsche Bundesbank, *Bundesbank Monthly Report*. Frankfurt, Germany (various issues).

Dobson, Wendy (1991). *Economic Policy Coordination: Requiem of Prologue?* Washington, DC: Institute for International Economics.

Dominguez, Kathryn, and Jeffrey Frankel (1993). *Does Foreign Exchange Intervention Work?* Washington, DC: Institute for International Economics.

Dominguez, Kathryn, and Peter B. Kenen (1992). "Intramarginal Intervention in the EMS and the Target-Zone Model of Exchange-Rate Behavior," *European Economic Review* 36 (December), 1523–32.

Eichengreen, Barry (1990). *Elusive Stability: Essays in the History of International Finance, 1919–1939*. Cambridge University Press.

Fischer, Stanley (1988). "Macroeconomic Policy." In *International Economic Cooperation*. Martin Feldstein, ed., pp. 11–43. Chicago: University of Chicago Press for NBER.

Frankel, Jeffrey A. (1988). *Obstacles to International Macroeconomic Policy Coordination*, Princeton Studies in International Finance 64, International Finance Section, Princeton University, December, 1–41.

Frankel, Jeffrey A., and Katherine Rockett (1988). "International Macroeconomic Policy Coordination When Policy-makers Do Not Agree on the True Model," *American Economic Review* 78, 318–40.

Friedman, Milton, and Anna J. Schwartz (1963). *A Monetary History of the United States, 1867–1960*. Princeton: Princeton University Press.

Funabashi, Yoichi (1988). *Managing the Dollar: From the Plaza to the Louvre.* Washington, DC: Institute for International Economics.

Granger, Clive (1969). "Investigating Causal Relations by Econometric Models and Cross-Spectral Models," *Econometrica* 37, 424–38.

Hajnal, Peter (1989). *The Seven-Power Summits: Documents from the Summits of the Industrialized Countries, 1975–1989.* Millwood, NY: Kraus International.

Hamada, Koichi (1976). "A Strategic Analysis of Monetary Interdependence," *Journal of Political Economy* 84, 677–700.

Hamada, Koichi (1985). *The Political Economy of International Monetary Interdependence.* Cambridge: MIT Press.

Henning C. Randall (1994). *Currencies and Politics in the United States, Germany and Japan.* Washington, DC: Institute for International Economics.

Holtham, Gerald, and Andrew J. Hughes Hallett (1987). "International Policy Cooperation and Model Uncertainty. In *Global Macroeconomics: Policy Conflict and Cooperation*, Ralph C. Bryant and Richard Portes, eds., pp. 128–77. London: Macmillan.

Holtham, Gerald, and Andrew J. Hughes Hallett (1992). "International Macroeconomic Policy Coordination When PolicyMakers Do Not Agree on the True Model: Comment," *American Economic Review* 82(4) (September), 1043–51.

Hughes Hallett, Andrew J. (1992). "Target Zones and International Policy Coordination: The Contrast Between the Necessary and Sufficient Conditions for Success," *European Economic Review* 36(4) (May), 893–914.

Hughes Hallett, Andrew J., Gerald Holtham, and Gary Hutson (1989). "Exchange Rate Targeting as a Surrogate for International Policy Coordination." In *Blueprints for Exchange Rate Management*, Marcus Miller, Barry Eichengreen, and Richard Portes, eds., pp. 239–78. London and New York: Academic Press.

James, Harold (1996). *Monetary Cooperation since Bretton Woods.* Washington, DC, and New York: IMF and Oxford University Press.

Japan Economic Journal (NEXIS) (Nition Keizai Shimbun), August 26, 1980, p. 21.

Japan Economic Newswire (NEXIS) (Kyodo News Service), March 8, 1984.

Jiji Press Ticker Service (NEXIS), November 13, 1985.

Kareken, John, and Robert M. Solow (1963). "Lags in Monetary Policy." In Commission on Money and Credit, *Stabilization Policies*, pp. 14–96. Englewood Cliffs, NJ: Prentice Hall.

Kenen, Peter B. (1960). *British Monetary Policy and the Balance of Payments 1951–1957*, Harvard Economic Studies 116. Cambridge: Harvard University Press.

Kenen, Peter B. (1989). *Exchange Rates and Policy Coordination.* Manchester, U.K.: Manchester University Press.

Kenen, Peter B. (1990). "The Coordination of Macroeconomic Policies." In *International Policy Coordination and Exchange Rate Fluctuations*, William

Branson, Jacob Frenkel, and Morris Goldstein, eds., pp. 63–102. Chicago: University of Chicago Press for NBER.

Oudiz, Gilles, and Jeffrey Sachs (1984). "Macroeconomic Policy Coordination among the Industrial Economies," *Brookings Papers on Economic Activity* 1, 1–64.

Oudiz, Gilles, and Jeffrey Sachs (1985). "International Policy Coordination in Dynamic Macroeconomic Models." In *International Economic Policy Coordination*, Willem Buiter and Richard Marston, eds., 274–319. Cambridge University Press.

Putnam, Robert D., and Nicholas Bayne (1987). *Hanging Together, Cooperation and Conflict in the Seven-Power Summits*. London: Sage Publications.

Putnam, Robert D., and C. Randall Henning (1989). "The Bonn Summit of 1978: A Case Study in Coordination." In *Can Nations Agree?* Richard Cooper, Barry Eichengreen, Gerald Holtham, Robert D. Putnam, and C. Randall Henning, eds., pp. 12–140. Washington, DC: The Brookings Institution.

Rogoff, Kenneth (1985). "Can International Monetary Policy Coordination Be Counterproductive?" *Journal of International Economics*, 18 (May), 199–217.

Romer, Christina, and David Romer (1989). "Does Monetary Policy Matter? A New Test in the Spirit of Friedman and Schwartz." In Olivier J. Blanchard and Stanley Fischer, eds., pp. 121–70. *NBER Macroeconomics Annual 1989*. Cambridge: MIT Press.

Tobin, James (1965). "The Monetary Interpretation of History: A Review Article," *American Economic Review* 55, 464–85.

Von Furstenberg, George, and Joseph Daniels (1992). *Economic Summit Declarations, 1975–1989: Examining the Written Record of International Cooperation*, Princeton Studies in International Finance 72, International Finance Section, Princeton University, February, 1–55.

Williamson, John, and Marcus Miller (1987). *Targets and Indicators: A Blueprint for the International Coordination of Economic Policy*, Policy Analyses in International Economics No. 22. Washington, DC: Institute for International Economics.

CHAPTER 11

Fundamental determinants of Mexico's exchange-rate crisis of 1994

Polly Reynolds Allen

A theme throughout Peter Kenen's long and highly influential career has been the relationship between exchange rates and the real side of the economy. In theoretical models, empirical studies, or direct policy analysis, Kenen has always sought insight toward building sound economic and exchange-rate policies. In our joint work fifteen years ago on the asset-market approach to exchange rates (Allen and Kenen 1980), we examined links between the short-run determination of exchange rates in the financial markets and the ultimate importance of real factors in the current account for the long-run equilibrium exchange rate, focusing on the implications for economic integration.

The goal of this essay – to better understand some of the fundamentals leading up to the Mexican exchange-rate crisis in late 1994 – is sympathetic to Kenen's approach, at least in spirit, if not always in letter. The NATREX model that follows focuses on the real fundamentals of investment, saving, and long-run capital flows. Understanding the relationships of these flows to the real exchange rate and to the stability of an economy is a prerequisite for sound economic policy, particularly in countries facing rapid institutional changes, relatively inflexible prices, and volatile behavior of foreign investors.

In December 1994 Mexico's exchange-rate crisis and subsequent economic contraction sharply reversed a period of slow growth and optimism about the economy's imminent takeoff. The crisis followed a seven-year period of widely praised reforms by the Mexican government. Aspe (1993) describes Mexico's program for bringing down inflation, which had peaked at almost 600 percent per year in one month of 1987. Mexico rejected the standard neoclassical prescription of contractionary monetary and fiscal policies in favor of a program of structural reforms, including liberalization and reform of the financial markets, trade liberalization culminating with NAFTA, privatization

316

of state-owned industries, and tax and fiscal reforms. At the core of the program was a series of pacts among business, labor, agriculture, and the government to control wages and prices and to stabilize the nominal exchange rate. Inflation fell from 160 percent per year in 1987 to 45 percent in 1988 and to less than 20 percent in subsequent years.

A key factor in the pacts was the promise of limited and controlled nominal depreciation of the peso against the dollar, cumulatively totaling 56 percent from 1988 to November 1994, far short of Mexico's cumulative price increases of some 250 percent. Dornbusch and Werner (1994), measuring Mexico's real exchange rate in several ways, show a real appreciation of the peso from 1987–93 in the range of 60 to 80 percent. This appreciation occurred in spite of a 14 percent fall in Mexico's terms of trade, a large component of the real exchange rate. Mexico also ran overall balance-of-payments surpluses from 1990–93, accumulating over U.S.$7 billion of reserves in 1993 alone. Left to the markets, the real appreciation would have been even greater. Then, in 1994, increased concern about Mexico's political situation reduced capital inflows, leading to large reserve losses. In December, the government devalued, stimulating further speculation that sent the peso into a free-fall.

Eight months before the crisis, Dornbusch and Werner summarized the opposing views of economists. On one side, the "equilibrium view" maintained that Mexico's investment opportunities, increased productivity, fiscal restraint, and newly liberalized trade and capital flows justified the continuing real appreciation. On the opposite side, Dornbusch and Werner argued that the rising current-account deficit, slow growth of output, and real appreciation relative to purchasing power parity showed an increasingly overvalued peso. The exchange-rate crisis in December and the subsequent 40 percent depreciation of the peso seemingly support Dornbusch and Werner's assessment. Their model of an incomes policy provides insight into Mexico's growing disequilibrium.

But even in retrospect there is no consensus about the underlying causes of the economic crisis. Many economists adhere to the acceptance of an overvalued real exchange rate and accompanying large current-account deficit as the basic problem, in line with Dornbusch and Werner. Many exchange-rate-based stabilization (ERBS) policies have faced similar problems of real overvaluation. Edwards (1996) describes the similarities between the inflation inertia and real appreciation of Chile in the 1970s and Mexico in the 1980s. A literature on speculative attacks on currencies pegged to a currency of a country with lower inflation came out in the late 1970s (Salant and Henderson 1978; Krugman 1979).

Flood, Garber, and Kramer (1995) extend these monetary-type speculative-attack models with no sterilization to a portfolio model with sterilization of reserve changes to explain the 1994 collapse of the peso.

Other economists have emphasized problems of expectations about Mexico's ERBS policy as more important than inflation inertia. Obstfeld and Rogoff (1995) provide empirical evidence of a lack of credibility of Mexico's policies, without discussing the underlying causes of this lack of credibility. Mendoza and Uribe (1996) use a model in which uncertain duration of the currency peg leads to boom-recession cycles, a worsening external deficit, and strong real appreciation, in the presence of flexible prices and perfect capital mobility. Applying this model to the Mexican situation, their quantitative numerical exercise produces fluctuations similar in magnitude to those seen in Mexico. They conclude that uncertainty about the duration of the currency peg is more important than lack of credibility in explaining Mexico's crisis.

One source of doubt about the overvaluation of the peso was Mexico's overall balance-of-payments surplus during most of the period. A speculative attack in 1993 was financed and weathered with little problem, and the Mexican authorities apparently believed the same would be true when capital began to flow out in early 1994 after the Colosio assassination and the uprising in Chiapas raised political uncertainties. Gil-Díaz and Carstens (1996) argue that the fundamentals in Mexico were basically sound throughout 1994 and stress political events as the major explanation of the crisis. Lustig (1996) discusses ongoing political weaknesses in Mexico that may continue to hinder recovery and growth. Sachs, Tornell, and Velasco (1996) conclude that the fundamental conditions of the Mexican economy cannot account for the extent of the crisis, attributing the crisis to unexpected shocks, inadequate policy response, vulnerability to panic, and panic itself.

However, the composition of the evolving financial portfolios during the period of borrowing was also a major contributor to the crisis. Calvo and Mendoza (1996, in press) point to imbalances in the financial markets, between the money supply and the stock of reserves, and between the privately held short-term public debt and reserves, as well as to herd behavior on the part of financial investors as the major causes of the crisis in December 1994. Lustig (1995) agrees that the major problem was the outstanding short-term public debt, which was converted into dollar denominations in early 1994, making the Mexican financial situation even more vulnerable. Newly liberalized capital markets allowed for a strong inflow of short-term lending by foreigners to a newly liberalized and weak banking system. McKinnon and Pill (1995) point to the weaknesses in the financial system as the major problem, emphasizing the moral hazard of deposit insurance, which allowed the banks to take too much risk.

Many economists (e.g., Feldstein 1995; Summers 1995) have noted Mexico's low saving rate and the implications for Mexico's growth of such low saving. In this essay I argue that Mexico's saving behavior was a crucial problem, leading the economy away from an equilibrium trajectory. More important for the crisis than the level of Mexico's saving were the dynamics of its national saving rate, which fell from 18 percent of GDP in 1988 to only 15 percent in 1992 and 1993. In spite of the positive fundamentals of Mexico's reforms, such as growing investment and increased government saving, Mexicans were borrowing to finance consumption more than investment.

The argument presented here – that Mexico's falling saving and appreciating real exchange rate suggest a fundamentally unstable trajectory – does not contradict other explanations of the timing and severity of the peso collapse. Before the crisis, Mexico's future looked promising to most observers, with the frequently heard assertions that Mexico's fundamentals were right. And many of the analyses done after the fact assume explicitly or implicitly that the basic fundamentals were not at issue; instead, they focus on some aspect of the exchange-rate policy, the dynamics of expectations, or the financial markets.

The purpose of this essay is to point out the problems with the underlying fundamentals. The inflation inertia and rapid appreciation, the imbalances in the financial markets, the political uncertainty, and the fickleness of foreign investors all contributed to the crisis and possibly played a role in the rapid decline of Mexico's saving. But ultimately the unstable trajectories of the basic fundamentals, unless reversed, were bound to lead to trouble for the Mexican economy.

It is widely acknowledged that a country cannot borrow indefinitely to finance consumption. But Mexico's growing borrowing for consumption has been little emphasized in the post mortems on Mexico's crisis. The NATREX model that is laid out below provides a theoretical foundation for describing an economy's *equilibrium* responses to changes in saving and in investment. NATREX models have provided encouraging empirical support for the hypothesis that medium-run to long-run movements of equilibrium real exchange rates in countries with fairly flexible prices can be explained by the fundamentals of productivity, thrift, and exogenous terms of trade (Crouhy-Veyrac and Saint Marc 1995; Lim and Stein 1995; Stein 1995a, 1995b; Stein and Sauernheimer 1995).

The changes in Mexico's investment, saving, current account, and real exchange rate are inconsistent with the equilibrium trajectories of the NATREX model and more closely resemble the trajectories of the unstable case, where saving continues to rise in the face of rising debt to foreigners. For Mexico, then, the NATREX model is useful in identifying a fundamental problem: increased borrowing from foreigners in the face of declining national saving, exacerbated by an overvalued and appreciating real exchange rate.

A simple NATREX model

The NATREX model is a basic macro growth model of a stable equilibrium economy through time, borrowing for either investment or consumption. The model assumes stabilizing behavior and does not consider short-run deviations from equilibrium due to price rigidities, speculation, and other lags in market adjustment. The short-run deviations from equilibrium, many of which contributed to the Mexican crisis, are ignored in this model in order to focus on the longer-run fundamentals. However, the stability constraints of the model are important in identifying a fundamental problem in the trajectory of the Mexican economy.

An equilibrium model can be useful as a benchmark for analyzing an economy in disequilibrium. The equilibrium trajectories of the NATREX model reflect underlying fundamentals that ultimately constrain any economy. The NATREX trajectories are benchmarks against which to compare the trajectories of a disequilibrium economy and to evaluate the causes of the disequilibrium.

The model is a real, medium- to long-run model with high capital mobility, in which the goods market is cleared by the real exchange rate. Investment and capital flows lead to changes in the stocks of capital and net foreign debt, which in turn influence the demand and supply for goods. The equilibrium real exchange rate (the NATREX) continually clears the market for goods in the medium run. As investment and capital flows alter the stocks of capital and foreign debt, the economy gradually evolves until it reaches a steady state, where the stocks of capital and debt (per unit of effective labor) are constant. For simplicity, we shall consider here the case of a stationary economy with zero long-run growth, implying zero saving and investment and a balanced current account in the steady state. In a growing economy, the steady-state values of these flows need not be zero, but are limited by the long-run growth rate of the economy.

The real exchange rate, R, is defined as the foreign-currency price of domestic currency, E, multiplied by the ratio of domestic to foreign price levels, P/P^* (GDP deflators),

$$R = \frac{EP}{P*}. \tag{11.1}$$

A rise in R indicates real appreciation of the currency.

This general purchasing power definition of the real exchange rate, equal to unity with purchasing power parity, can be written in terms of the domestic and foreign relative prices of nontradeables to exportables and the terms of trade. Define the price levels as

$$P = P_n^a P_2^b P_1^{(1-a-b)} \quad \text{and} \tag{11.2}$$

$$P* = P_n^{*a*} P_1^{*b*} P_2^{*(1-a*-b*)}, \tag{11.2'}$$

where good n is nontradeable, good 1 is exported, and good 2 is imported by the home country. The asterisk denotes foreign variables. Assuming the law of one price for tradeable goods,

$$P_1 E = P_1^*, \text{ and} \tag{11.3}$$

$$P_2 E = P_2^*, \tag{11.3'}$$

the real exchange rate for the home country can be written as a geometric average of the relative price of nontradeables to exportables in each country, R_n and R_n^*, and the home country's terms of trade, T:

$$R = R_n^a R_n^{*a*} T^{(1-b-b*)} = z R_n^a \tag{11.1a}$$

where

$$R_n = \frac{P_n}{P_1}, \quad R_n^* = \frac{P_n^*}{P_2^*}, \quad T = \frac{P_1}{P_2}, \quad \text{and } z = R_n^{*a*} T^{(1-b-b*)}.$$

This general formulation for the real exchange rate (Allen 1995), allowing for the effects of changes in the relative prices of nontradeables to tradeables and in the terms of trade, can be applied to a variety of models, and is empirically measurable.

The model describes a hypothetical medium-run equilibrium, where output is at its natural level and the basic balance of payments is in equilibrium. Cyclical, speculative, and short-run expectational factors are assumed to be played out in the medium run and are ignored. Stocks of capital and net foreign debt are held constant in the adjustment to this medium-run equilibrium, but then begin to change as a result of investment and capital flows. Since changing stocks of capital and foreign debt continue to alter market equilibrium, the NATREX is a moving equilibrium real exchange – an equilibrium trajectory rather than level.

The basic NATREX model can be summarized in three equations: a medium-run market-clearing equation (11.4), and dynamic equations for the stocks of capital and foreign debt, equations (11.5) and (11.6).[1] All stocks and flows are written in terms of the export good 1.

First, market equilibrium requires that national investment, I, minus national saving, S, plus the current account, CA, sum to zero.

$$I - S + CA = 0. \tag{11.4}$$

The current account is assumed to respond to changes in the real exchange rate, declining in the face of real appreciation. Market equilibrium is achieved through adjustments in the real exchange rate, which bring the current account (CA) to equal the difference between national saving and national investment $(S - I)$.[2]

Assuming that the securities markets clear and that central banks do not intervene in the foreign-exchange market in the medium run, equation (11.4) can be read either as zero excess demand for goods or as basic balance-of-payments equilibrium, where the current account is offset by nonspeculative long-term net capital flows. National investment and national saving include both public and private flows, no distinction being made between public and private.

Perfect long-term capital mobility assures that the country can borrow freely at r^*, the world real long-term interest rate. Behaviors of both investors and consumers are derived from optimizing behavior based on all current information, but without perfect foresight. Given the uncertainty of future real disturbances, the trajectory of the real exchange rate cannot be predicted, even when the underlying structure of the model is known. Market participants know that the real exchange rate will change but cannot – and do not – predict its trajectory. As a consequence, long-term capital mobility equates the domestic with the foreign long-term real interest rate.

The remaining two – dynamic – equations describe the trajectories of the capital stock and net debt to foreigners. National investment, I, leads to changes in the capital stock, k, whereas net capital inflows, $I - S$, lead to changes in the net debt to foreigners, F.

$$\dot{k} = I, = 0 \text{ in the steady state, and} \tag{11.5}$$

$$\dot{F} = I - S, = 0 \text{ in the steady state.} \tag{11.6}$$

In the medium run, the desired rates of saving, investment, and the current account depend on the existing levels of k, F, and R, given exogenous factors X, so that

$$I\left(k; X\right) - S\left(k, F; X\right) + CA\left(R, k, F; X\right) = 0, \tag{11.4a}$$

$$\dot{k} = I(k; X), \tag{11.5a}$$

$$\dot{F} = I(k; X) - S(k, F; X). \tag{11.6a}$$

Saving equals GNP (output less interest payments to foreigners, $y - rF$) minus consumption,

$$S = S(k, F; X) = y(k) - rF - C(w; X); \tag{11.7}$$

the domestic real interest rate equals the foreign rate,

$$r = r^*, \tag{11.8}$$

and wealth equals the capital stock minus net debt to foreigners,

$$w = k - F. \tag{11.9}$$

The important behavioral responses are negative responses of investment to the capital stock, $I_k < 0$, and of the current account to the real exchange rate, $CA_R < 0$; positive responses of consumption to wealth, $C_w > 0$, and of output to the capital stock, $y_k > 0$; and, most problematic for many net debtor countries, a positive relation of saving to foreign debt, $S_F > 0$. A rise in net debt to foreigners, F, raises net interest payments to foreigners, lowering GNP. The negative effect of the rising debt (falling wealth) on consumption must be greater than the increase in net interest payments, in order for saving to rise. This positive effect of foreign debt on saving is essential for stability.

The exogenous fundamentals, X, include the marginal productivity of capital, u, which raises investment; the world interest rate, r^*, which determines the domestic interest rate, with negative effects on both investment and GNP; the rate of time preference, σ, which raises consumption and lowers saving; and the terms of trade, T, which, as a component of the real exchange rate, contributes directly to real appreciation.

Fundamental disturbances in productivity and time preference

The NATREX model is designed to show the trajectories of the fundamental national variables – saving, investment, the current account, output, and the real exchange rate – of a stable, equilibrium economy, in response to changes in the exogenous real fundamentals, X. The model emphasizes, first, that the equilibrium real exchange rate, the NATREX, is itself a trajectory, responding not only to changes in exogenous fundamentals, but also to endogenous, ongoing changes in the stocks of capital and debt. Purchasing power parity, where $R = 1$, does not measure the equilibrium real exchange rate, which is a moving equilibrium reflecting both exogenous and endogenous real fundamentals. The second emphasis is on the differences in the various trajectories for a country borrowing for consumption and for one that is borrowing for investment. Any exogenous increase of borrowing (not fully offset by increased demand for imports) will induce medium-run real appreciation. The subsequent responses of the exchange rate, output, consumption, and saving depend crucially on the purpose of the borrowing.

Basic trajectories for three fundamental disturbances are described: (1) a rise in borrowing for consumption (increased rate of time preference); (ii) a rise in borrowing for investment (increased marginal productivity); and (iii) an exogenous fall in the terms of trade. The trajectories of the major variables are graphed for each disturbance.

Borrowing for consumption

The initial fall in saving at time t_0 leads to a net capital inflow and a real appreciation, producing the decline in the current account needed to clear the goods market. In response to the rising debt to foreigners, saving must gradually increase until negative saving is eliminated. The accompanying decline in borrowing and the increasing interest payments to foreigners lead to gradual real depreciation. In the new steady state, the trade balance must move into surplus to offset the interest payments to foreigners, implying a long-run real depreciation. Moreover, the increased rate of time preference will have increased consumption only temporarily; in the new steady state, with higher debt and increased interest payments to foreigners, both GNP and consumption will have fallen.

Figure 11.1 shows the trajectories of investment, saving, and the equilibrium real exchange rate, in response to an exogenous increase of consumption and decrease of saving at time t_0.

Borrowing to finance investment

We see a different set of trajectories and long-run outcomes when the country borrows to finance new investment (due to a rise in the marginal product of capital). Investment financed from abroad increases both the capital stock and debt to foreigners – equations (11.5) and (11.6) – producing more complex and possibly nonmonotonic trajectories. Before predicting the trajectories, we need to know what goods are produced and traded, which goods are capital goods, and in which industry productivity increases.

For Mexico, let us take the case of a small country, producing two

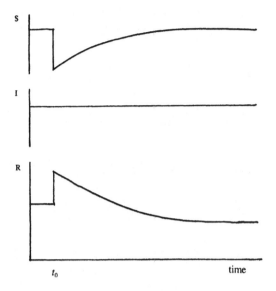

Figure 11.1. Trajectories of saving (S), investment (I), and the real exchange rate (R) in response to a rise in time preference (decrease of saving).

kinds of goods: tradeable goods, $t = 1, 2$, sold at world prices, and nontradeable goods, n. The terms of trade, determined by world prices $(T = P_1^*/P_2^*)$, are exogenous. Only the relative price of nontradeables, $R_n = P_n/P_1$, is endogenous, adjusting to medium-run equilibrium and providing the endogenous adjustment in the NATREX. In equation (11.1a), endogenous changes in R are proportional to changes in R_n.

With the tradeables markets always clearing at world prices, the trade balance, TB, equals the country's excess supply of tradeable goods,

$$TB = y_t - E_t, \tag{11.10}$$

where E_t is expenditure for tradeables for either investment or consumption and y_t is output of tradeables. As the country's demand for tradeables is always fulfilled at world prices, any excess demand for goods must come from nontradeables. From the national-income-accounting definitions and equation (11.10), equation (11.4) can be rewritten as

$$
\begin{aligned}
I - S + CA = E - y + TB &= E_t + E_n - y_t - y_n + \left(y_t - E_t \right) \\
&= E_n - y_n \\
&= E_n\left(k, F, R_n; X\right) - y_n\left(k, R_n; X\right) = 0, \tag{11.4b}
\end{aligned}
$$

where E denotes investment plus consumption expenditure for all goods; E_n, expenditure for good n; and y_n, output of good n. For a small country facing fixed world prices of tradeables, equations (11.4a) and (11.4b) are two ways of looking at the same market-clearing condition. A rise in the relative price of nontradeables to tradeables, R_n, will lower both the excess demand for nontradeables, reducing the aggregate demand for goods, and the country's net supply of tradeables, reducing the trade balance. Since R_n is proportional to the equilibrium real exchange rate, R, a real appreciation clears the goods market and reduces the current account.

Borrowing for new investment induces real appreciation at time t_0, to the extent that the new capital goods are produced domestically rather than being imported. Assuming that investment is profitable, wealth increases, and, gradually, consumption rises. Output gradually increases with the rising capital stock. Through time, investment and purchases of capital goods decline to zero (in a stationary economy).

If the productivity increase occurs in the tradeable goods industry, as assumed here, then the trade balance gradually increases through rising output of tradeables, and excess consumption demand for nontradeables gradually rises due to rising incomes. Both are consistent with pressures for long-run appreciation. The initial medium-run appreciation came from the borrowing to finance investment; by contrast, the long-run appreciation comes from the increased output of tradeables, higher wage rates in the economy, reallocation of labor from nontradeables to tradeables, and the resulting rise in the relative price of nontradeables. Since the medium-run and long-run responses of the exchange rate depend on different variables, their relative sizes are specific to each case. Moreover, the trajectory between the medium and long run is probably nonmonotonic.[3]

Through time, borrowing to invest in tradeable goods implies higher output and income, greater wealth, increased consumption, and real appreciation. Compared to the first disturbance (borrowing for consumption), the outcomes are quite different. When the borrowing was for consumption, output remained constant, wealth and consumption gradually declined, and the NATREX ultimately depreciated.

Figure 11.2 shows the trajectories of investment, saving, and the real exchange rate, in response to an exogenous increase of investment at time t_0. The possible paths are numerous and the trajectories are probably more complex than drawn in Figure 11.2, especially for the real exchange rate. What can be said from the model is that investment will first rise and gradually return to zero; the cumulation of net savings over the full trajectory will be positive; and the real exchange rate will have appreciated both at time t_0 and in the long run.

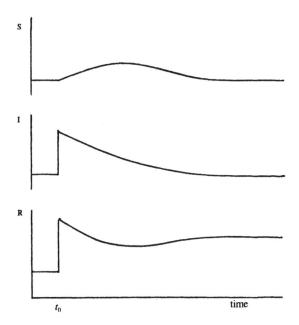

Figure 11.2. Trajectories of saving (S), investment (I), and the real exchange rate (R) in response to a rise in productivity (increase of investment).

A fall in the terms of trade

Finally, an exogenous decline in the terms of trade will almost surely depreciate the real exchange rate, R. It may either raise or lower the relative price of nontradeables to exportables, R_n, depending on the various cross elasticities of demand and supply between nontradeables, exportables, and importables. But the primary influence of the terms of trade on the real exchange rate R is its contribution as a direct component of the real exchange rate.

$$R = R_n^a R_n^{*a^*} T^{(1-b-b^*)}. \tag{11.1a}$$

It is unlikely that any rise in R_n would be sufficient to offset the direct effect of a fall in the terms of trade.

An unstable economy

The NATREX model can also be used to examine an unstable case, where saving does not rise in response to rising debt to foreigners, but continues to fall, $S_F < 0$. This occurs when consumption is not cut back enough, in response to falling wealth, to offset the rising interest pay-

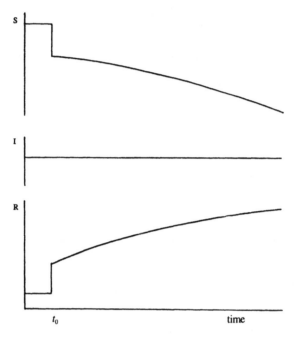

Figure 11.3. Unstable case: Trajectories of saving (S), investment (I), and the real exchange rate (R) in response to a rise in time preference (decrease of saving).

ments to foreigners. The likelihood of instability would be even higher, if the country were required to pay a risk premium on borrowing from foreigners, one which rose in the face of increased debt to finance consumption. Stability would then require an even greater response of consumption and saving to the declines in wealth.

Figure 11.3 shows the paths of investment, saving, and the exchange rate in response to an exogenous rise in time preference in an unstable economy. Such trajectories are unsustainable and, if continued, lead to crisis.

Evidence of fundamental disequilibrium in Mexico

Table 11.1 shows Mexico's balance of payments from 1988 through the third quarter of 1994. The current-account deficit had grown to 8 percent of GDP by 1992. Foreign direct investment remained fairly steady, at only 1 to 2 percent of GDP, slightly less than the increase of reserves for 1990–3. Almost 90 percent of the net foreign investment from 1988–93

Table 11.1. *Mexican balance of payments (m. of U.S.$)*

Year	Curr. Acct. +	Dir. Inv. +	Port. Inv. +	Errors =	Chg. in Res.
1988	−2,374	2,011	−6,506	−3,193	−10,062
1989	−5,825	2,785	−1,675	4,504	−211
1990	−7,451	2,549	5,892	1,228	2,218
1991	−14,888	4,742	20,397	−2,278	7,973
1992	−24,442	4,393	23,010	−852	1,745
1993	−23,400	4,389	28,850	−3,128	7,232
1994	−28,784	7,978	4,796	−1,636	−17,666

Source: International Monetary Fund, *International Financial Statistics*, various years.

Table 11.2 *Mexican real investment, saving, and current-account deficit (m. of M$) (deflated by GDP deflator and population index, 1990 = 100)*

Year	I	S	CA[a]	ΔI	ΔS	ΔCA[a]
1987	127,433	137,585	10,152	—	—	—
1988	135,873	121,254	−14,629	8,440	−16,331	−24,771
1989	143,947	119,570	−24,377	8,074	−1,684	−9,758
1990	150,272	121,885	−28,387	6,325	2,315	−4,010
1991	155,810	118,837	−36,973	5,538	−3,048	−8,586
1992	164,186	106,767	−57,419	8,376	−12,070	−20,446
1993	152,999	104,513	−48,486	−11,187	−2,254	8,933
Sum of changes:				25,566	−33,072	−58,638

[a] CA = Exports − Imports − Net factor payments from the National Accounts.
Source: International Monetary Fund, *International Financial Statistics*, various years.

was in the form of portfolio investment, much of it short-term and indexed to the dollar. Reserve inflows turned negative in 1994, with capital inflows falling sharply in the second quarter.

To see whether net foreign investment (NFI) in Mexico financed new investment or new consumption, we can look at the changes in national investment and national saving that accompanied the current-account deficit, keeping in mind that NFI = $-CA = I - S$. Table 11.2 shows Mexico's national investment, national saving, and current-account defi-

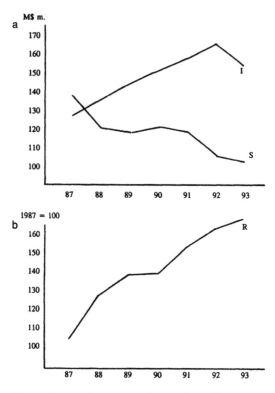

Figure 11.4. (a) Mexican national saving (S) and investment (I), 1987–1993. *Source: International Financial Statistics* (deflated by GDP deflator and population index, 1990 = 100). (b) Mexico's real exchange rate, 1987–1993. *Source:* Dornbusch and Werner (1994).

cit, measured in real terms and deflated by an index of population growth, as well as the year-to-year changes in these three flows, for the period 1987–93. The sum of the decreases in saving for 1988–93 totaled M$ 33,072 m., while the sum of the increases in investment totaled only M$ 25,566 m. The declines of saving over the period were one-third greater than the increases of investment. When saving and investment are taken as ratios to GDP, the differences are even more striking. The sum of declines in S/GDP (0.58) are over twice the sum of the increases in I/GDP (0.027) and are almost exactly equal to the increases of private consumption (C_p/GDP).

Figure 11.4 shows the trajectories of Mexico's investment and saving (11.4a) and of the real exchange rate (11.4b). While the investment ratio was rising during the five years, saving fell even more, with a resulting steady increase of the current account deficit.

On the positive side, Mexico saw rising investment for five of the six years before the crisis. In a stable economy, higher investment in tradeable goods leads to real appreciation in both the medium and long run. But the strength of equilibrium appreciation over time is correlated with the productivity of new investment. In spite of Mexico's increasing investment, growth of output was slow, averaging only 2.65 percent per year for 1988–93.

Even more important in Mexico's trajectories were the large and continued declines of saving. The NATREX model suggests that increases of investment should give rise to a period of higher saving, so the fall in Mexico's saving cannot be seen as an endogenous response to the higher investment. The declines in Mexico's saving presumably come either from exogenous increases of time preference or from a perverse response of saving to rising foreign debt. It makes little difference which. Either shows an economy that is failing to exhibit the necessary stable response to rising debt – an increase of saving. Mexico's trajectories for saving and the real exchange rate (Figure 11.4) can be compared with the stable (Figure 11.1) and unstable (Figure 11.3) trajectories of a response to a fall in saving in the model. The Mexican trajectories are quite different from the stable case, which shows rising saving and a depreciating real exchange rate. But they are remarkably similar to the unstable case, with continually falling saving and an appreciating real exchange rate.[4] As foreign debt increased, Mexico's declining saving rate necessitated more borrowing from abroad. As long as the markets were willing to lend to Mexico, this increasing borrowing produced pressures for an appreciating real exchange rate. But such a trajectory is unstable and cannot be considered an equilibrium trajectory.

Conclusion

This essay does not attempt a full explanation of the Mexican exchange-rate crisis of 1994. Rather, it points out the contributing role of Mexico's rapidly rising consumption, financed by borrowing from abroad. Whether Mexico imported consumption or capital goods is not the issue. The question is the degree to which the increases in the current-account deficit reflected increases in investment or decreases in saving. In Mexico's case, well over half the net foreign investment financed increased consumption. At the same time, in spite of a 14 percent decline in the terms of trade, the real exchange rate appreciated from 60 to 80 percent.

During the period from 1987 to 1993, Mexico's widely praised reforms raised expectations about the future performance of the economy. To many observers, the fundamentals appeared to have been in line. But the combination of saving falling more than investment rose, slow growth, and strong real appreciation suggests an unstable trajectory. Minus the other factors contributing to the 1994 Mexican crisis, had these trends in saving, investment, output, and the real exchange rate not been reversed, a crisis would have been inevitable at some point. How long the markets are willing to finance rising consumption depends on many factors. For emerging economies with poor track records, weak institutions, and political instability, the time frame is much shorter than for an industrialized country such as the United States.

Most of the exchange-rate literature of the last twenty-five years has focused on explaining short-run movements in exchange rates, with a notable lack of success (Meese and Rogoff 1983; DeGrauwe 1989). Much of the problem lies in the difficulty of estimating and explaining exchange-rate expectations, which play such an important role in short-term exchange-rate movements. The suggestion here is that the longer-run movements in response to basic fundamentals, such as productivity and thrift, can explain much of the longer-run movements of real exchange rates.

Expectations become less important when looking at real factors in the longer run for several reasons: the long-run average annual changes in the real exchange rates are much smaller than the short-run volatility; prices of goods and services have had time to adjust, so that the real exchange rate reflects the fundamentals rather than changes in the nominal exchange rate; the cyclical and speculative pressures on the real exchange rates tend to cancel out over time, leaving the long-run fundamentals to influence the real exchange rate; and the future changes in the fundamentals that determine the real exchange rate are impossible to predict. As a result, market participants put much less weight on expectations of the real exchange rate in their long-run decisions.

More work is needed to estimate the fundamental determinants of real exchange rates and to have a better understanding of this complex process. Empirical evidence will come largely from countries where prices are relatively flexible, allowing for adjustment to the equilibrium real exchange rate. In such countries, the real exchange rate adjusts to equilibrium regardless of the nominal-exchange-rate policy. But in countries where prices respond only slowly to market signals, the government's choice of nominal-exchange-rate policy becomes crucial in determining the equilibrium real exchange rate. For these countries an understanding of the fundamental trajectories of saving, investment, and the real exchange rate is essential for good policy.

APPENDIX

Specification and solution of the NATREX model

The three goods are nontradeables, n, and tradeables, 1 and 2. All flows are denominated in good 1, the export good. Since the terms of trade, T, is exogenous and exogenous changes in T are not considered here, goods 1 and 2 are treated together as tradeables, t, and the influence of T on the functions is not explicitly shown. As productivity increases are considered only for the tradeables industry, $u = u_t$. Throughout, $R = zRn$, where $z = R_n^{*a^*} T^{(1-b-b^*)}$.

I *Production*

$$
\overset{+\ \ +\ \ -}{(1)\quad y_n = y_n(k,\ R_n;\ u_t),} \text{ output of nontradeables (in units of good 1)}
$$

$$
\overset{+\ -\ +}{(2)\quad y_t = y_t(k,\ R_n;\ u_t),} \text{ output of tradeables}
$$

A rise in k, given R_n and u_t, is allocated to both industries; a rise in R_n increases profitability of y_n, inducing a reallocation of capital and labor from industry t to industry n. A rise in productivity in tradeables induces reallocation of factors in the opposite direction, from nontradeables to tradeables.

$$
\overset{+}{(3)\quad y = y(k)} \text{ total production or GDP, in units of good 1.[1]}
$$

II *Investment demand*

$$
(4)\quad I = I\left[\overset{+}{\frac{f(k)}{r^*}};\ \overset{+}{u_t}\right] = I(\overset{-}{k};\ \overset{-}{r^*},\ \overset{+}{u_t}),
$$

where $f(k) = y' > 0$ is the marginal product of capital and $f' < 0$.

$$
(5)\quad I_n = x_n\overset{?}{(R_n)}\,I, \text{ proportion of investment spent on nontradeables,}
$$

$$
(6)\quad I_t = x_t\overset{+}{(R_n)}\,I, \text{ proportion of investment spent on tradeables, where}
$$
$$
x_n + x_t = 1.
$$

[1] Clearly, y is positively affected by R_n, when it is measured in units of good 1, since a rise in R_n increases the value of nontradeables. However, for our purposes, y appears in the model only in the definition of saving and the effect of R_n on $S = y - r^*F - C$ is far more ambiguous. For simplicity, S is assumed to be independent of R_n and omitting R_n from the function for y further simplifies the notation.

III *Consumption demand*

(7) $C = C(\overset{+}{k} - F;\ \overset{+}{\sigma})$, national consumption expenditure,

(8) $C_n = m_n(\overset{?}{R_n})\ C$, proportion of consumption spending on good n,

(9) $C_t = m_t(\overset{+}{R_n})\ C$, proportion of consumption spending on good t,

where $m_n + m_t = 1$. For both equations (5) and (8), a rise in R_n raises the value of given expenditure for good n, but also may induce substitution away from good n into good t.

IV *Expenditure for nontradeables and tradeables*

(10) $E_n = I_n + C_n = E_n(\overset{?}{k},\ \overset{-}{F},\ \overset{?}{R_n};\ \overset{+}{u_t},\ \overset{+}{\sigma},\ \overset{-}{r^*})$, total expenditure for good n

(11) $E_t = I_t + C_t = E_n(\overset{?}{k},\ \overset{-}{F},\ \overset{+}{R_n};\ \overset{+}{u_t},\ \overset{+}{\sigma},\ \overset{-}{r^*})$, total expenditure for good t

(12) $E = E_n + E_t$, total expenditure for all goods

V *Saving, trade balance, and current account*

(13) $S = y - r^*F - C$, national saving
(14) $B = y_t - E_t$, trade balance, for small country facing perfectly elastic world demands and supplies for tradeables at world prices,
(15) $CA = B - r^*F$, current account

VI *Market equilibrium*

(16) $I - S + CA = E - y + B = E_n - y_n = 0$,

(16a) $E_n(\overset{?}{k},\ \overset{-}{f},\ \overset{?}{R_n};\ \overset{+}{u_t},\ \overset{+}{\sigma},\ \overset{-}{r^*}) - y_n(\overset{+}{k},\ \overset{+}{R_n};\ \overset{-}{u_t}) = 0$,

where $\dfrac{\delta E_n}{\delta R_n} - \dfrac{\delta y_n}{\delta R_n} = E_{nR} - y_{nR} < 0$, as long as goods are gross substitutes.

VII *Dynamics*

(17) $\dot{k} = I$, $= 0$ in the steady state, and
(18) $\dot{F} = I - S$, $= 0$ in the steady state.

VIII *Medium-run responses to a rise in time preference, σ, and a rise in productivity in the tradeables industry, u_t (holding k and F constant)*

$$(19) \quad \frac{dR_n}{du_t} = -\frac{E_n u}{\left(E_{nR} - y_{nR}\right)} > 0$$

$$(20) \quad \frac{dR_n}{d\sigma} = \frac{E_{n\sigma}}{\left(E_{nR} - y_{nR}\right)} > 0.$$

Either disturbance appreciates R in the medium run, proportional to the increase of demand for nontradeables.

IX *Long-run responses of k^s, F^s, w^s, and R_n^s to a rise in time preference, σ, and a rise in productivity in the tradeables industry, u_t*

A *Rise in u_t*

$$(21) \quad \frac{dk^s}{du_t} = \frac{(-I_u)}{I_k} > 0,$$

$$(22) \quad \frac{dF^s}{du_t} = -\frac{I_u(C_w - y')}{I_k(C_w - r^*)} > 0,$$

unless the marginal product of capital, y', is greater than C_w, in which case income and saving rise sufficiently to repay the debt and move to a net lending position.

$$(23) \quad \frac{dw^s p}{du_t} = \frac{dk}{du_t} - \frac{dF}{du_t}$$

$$= -\frac{I_u(y' - r^*)}{I_k(C_w - r^*)} > 0.$$

Stability conditions guarantee that the denominator is positive and $y' - r^* > 0$ during the period of positive investment.

$$(24) \quad \frac{dR_n^s}{du_t} = \left[\frac{m_n C_w}{(y_{nR} - m_{nR}C)}\right]\frac{dw}{du_t} - \left(\frac{y_{nk}dk}{du_t}\right) + y_{nut} > 0.$$

$$(25) \quad \frac{dR^s}{du_t} = \frac{z dR_n^s}{du_t} > 0.$$

B *Rise in σ*

$$(26) \quad \frac{dk^s}{d\sigma} = 0,$$

$$(27) \quad \frac{dF^s}{d\sigma} = -\frac{dw}{\sigma} = \frac{C_\sigma}{(C_w - r^*)} > 0,$$

$$(28) \quad \frac{dR_n^s}{d\sigma} = -\frac{r^*}{(C_w - r^*)} < 0,$$

$$(29) \quad \frac{dR^s}{d\sigma} = z\frac{dR_n^s}{d\sigma} > 0.$$

NOTES

1. A more detailed exposition of the NATREX approach can be found in Stein, Allen et al. (1995, chaps. 1–3). The NATREX approach encompasses several variations of the basic model, adapted to meet the specific characteristics of the economy described. Variations include alternative assumptions about what goods are produced; whether they are consumer, capital, or intermediate goods; the degree of capital mobility; the rate of growth of the economy; and how large the country is in various markets, including the possibility of modeling interacting large economies. But the basic shape of the simple model presented here and the major conclusions typify all NATREX models.
2. The assumption that I and S are independent of the real exchange rate is a simplification, though probably not a serious one. All flows are denominated here in terms of the export good, so that a rise in the relative price of nontradeables, R_n (a component of R), will increase the value of aggregate flows, to the extent that they include nontradeables. In the case of aggregate output, a rise in R_n will increase production of nontradeables as well as their value in terms of the export good, so aggregate output is positively related to R_n. But substitutability between consumption goods would shift consumption away from nontradeables in the event of a rise in R_n, so the effect on overall consumption is ambiguous, depending on the elasticities of substitution. The effect of the real exchange rate on investment is thoroughly ambiguous, depending on which industry is the target of investment and which good is the capital good. On balance, the assumption that both I and $I - S$ are independent of the real exchange rate is not unreasonable, unless one is modeling a specific country where it is possible to sign the direction of the influence.
3. The argument that increased productivity in the tradeables sector appreciates a country's real exchange rate has traditionally been based on rising wages in both sectors (Balassa 1964; Samuelson 1964; Bhagwati 1984). Although this argument is consistent with the response in the NATREX model, it does not consider investment, net capital flows, or the change in debt, and leaves out the responses emphasized in the NATREX approach.
4. Gil-Díaz and Carstens (1996) argue that Mexico's saving rate should be measured as GDP minus consumption rather than GNP minus consumption – that is, before net factor payments to foreigners are subtracted. Measuring saving from GDP would obviously produce a higher saving rate for Mexico. Such a measure violates the essential concept of saving, that of forgoing consumption

out of *available* income. Measuring saving in terms of GDP also fails to capture a major stability question for countries with rising debt: Can the country reduce its consumption enough to finance the rising interest payments to foreigners?

REFERENCES

Allen, Polly Reynolds (1995). "The Economic and Policy Implications of the NATREX Approach." In Stein, Allen, et al., chap. 1, 1–37.

Allen, Polly Reynolds, and Peter B. Kenen (1980). *Asset Markets, Exchange Rates, and Economic Integration: A Synthesis*. Cambridge University Press.

Aspe, Pedro (1993). *Economic Transformation: The Mexican Way*. Cambridge: MIT Press.

Balassa, Bela (1964). "The Purchasing Power Parity Doctrine: a Reappraisal," *Journal of Political Economy* 84 (December), 1161–76.

Bhagwati, Jagdish N. (1984). "Why Are Services Cheaper in the Poor Countries?" *Economic Journal* 94 (June), 279–86.

Calvo, Guillermo A., and Enrique G. Mendoza (1996a). "Petty Crime and Cruel Punishment: Lessons from the Mexican Debacle," *American Economic Review: Papers and Proceedings* 86(2) (May), 170–5.

Calvo, Guillermo A., and Enrique G. Mendoza (in press). "Mexico's Balance-of-Payments Crisis: A Chronicle of a Death Foretold," *Journal of International Economics*.

Crouhy-Veyrac, Liliane, and Michèle Saint Marc (1995). "The French Franc and the Deutsche Mark, 1971–1990." In Stein, Allen, et al., chap. 4.

DeGrauwe, Paul (1989). *International Money: Post-War Trends and Theories*. Oxford: Oxford University Press.

Dornbusch, Rudiger, and Alejandro Werner (1994). "Mexico: Stabilization, Reform, and No Growth," *Brookings Papers on Economic Activity* 1994(1), 253–97.

Edwards, Sebastian (1996). "Exchange-Rate Anchors, Credibility, and Inertia: A Tale of Two Crises, Chile and Mexico," *American Economic Review: Papers and Proceedings* 86(2) (May), 176–80.

Feldstein, Martin (1995). "Global Capital Flows: Too Little, Not Too Much," *The Economist* 335 (June 24, 1995), 72–3.

Flood, Robert P., Peter M. Garber, and Charles Kramer (1995). "Collapsing Exchange Rate Regimes: Another Linear Example." International Monetary Fund Research Department, August.

Gil-Díaz, Francisco, and Agustín Carstens (1996). "One Year of Solitude: Some Pilgrim Tales about Mexico's 1994–1995 Crisis," *American Economic Review: Papers and Proceedings* 86(2) (May), 164–9.

Krugman, Paul (1979). "A Model of Balance-of-Payments Crises," *Journal of Money, Credit, and Banking* 2 (August), 311–25.

Lim, Guay C., and Jerome L. Stein (1995). "The Dynamics of the Real Exchange Rate and Current Account in a Small Open Economy: Australia." In Stein, Allen, et al., chap. 3.

Lustig, Nora (1995). "The Outbreak of Pesophobia," *The Brookings Review* 13(2) (Spring), 46.

Lustig, Nora (1996). "Mexico: The Slippery Road to Stability," *The Brookings Review* 14(2) (Spring), 4–9.

McKinnon, Ronald I., and Huw Pill (1995). "Credible Liberalizations and International Capital Flows: The Overborrowing Syndrome." Unpublished manuscript. Stanford University, June.

Meese, Richard, and Kenneth Rogoff (1983). "Empirical Exchange Rate Models of the Seventies: Do They Fit Out of Sample?" *Journal of International Economics*, 14, 3–24.

Mendoza, Enrique G., and Martín Uribe (1996). *The Syndrome of Exchange-Rate-Based Stabilizations and the Uncertain Duration of Currency Pegs*. International Finance Discussion Papers no. 548 (April). Washington, DC: Board of Governors of the Federal Reserve System.

Obstfeld, Maurice, and Kenneth Rogoff (1995). "The Mirage of Fixed Exchange Rates," *Journal of Economic Perspectives* 9(4), 73–96.

Sachs, Jeffrey, Aaron Tornell, and Andrés Velasco (1996). "The Collapse of the Mexican Peso: What Have We Learned?" *Economic Policy* 22 (August), 13–63.

Salant, Stephen, and Dale Henderson (1978). "Market Anticipations of Government Policies and the Price of Gold," *Journal of Political Economy* 86 (August), 627–48.

Samuelson, Paul (1964). "Theoretical Notes on Trade Problems," *The Review of Economics and Statistics* 46, 145–54.

Stein, Jerome L. (1995a). "The Fundamental Determinants of the Real Exchange Rate of the U.S. Dollar Relative to the G7," IMF Working Paper 95–81. Washington, DC: International Monetary Fund.

Stein, Jerome L. (1995b). "The Natural Real Exchange Rate of the United States Dollar, and Determinants of Capital Flows." In Stein, Allen et al., chap. 2, 38–84.

Stein, Jerome L., Polly Reynolds Allen, and associates (1995). *Fundamental Determinants of Exchange Rates*. Oxford: Oxford University Press.

Stein, Jerome L., and Karlhans Sauernheimer (1995). "The Equilibrium Real Exchange Rate of Germany," *Journal of International and Comparative Economics* 4.

Summers, Lawrence (1995). "Summers on Mexico: Ten Lessons to Learn," *The Economist* 337 (December 23, 1995), 46–8.

CHAPTER 12

Devaluation cycles and adjustment costs

Nancy P. Marion

I Introduction

Peter Kenen has been an important contributor to the debate on the appropriate exchange-rate policy for a single country. Some of his earliest work focused on the role of structural characteristics in influencing this choice. In recent years, he has helped shape the debate on the costs and benefits of moving to a common currency in Europe. This essay focuses on the decision to make an adjustment in the fixed exchange rate, given that a country has already made the decision to have a fixed exchange-rate regime. It draws on insights and themes in Kenen's own work to detect whether some of the economic factors that influence the choice of exchange-rate regime might influence the size and timing of devaluations as well.

Exchange-rate pegs do not last forever. A developing country often pegs its exchange rate to a single currency, such as the U.S. dollar, even though it faces a higher inflation rate than the country to which it is pegged. Eventually a growing real exchange-rate misalignment drives the cost of sticking with the peg above the cost of reneging. A devaluation occurs and the process begins anew. The purpose of this essay is to learn more about devaluation cycles by studying the costs associated with abandoning a peg.

Models of collapsing fixed exchange rates often assume that the policymaker bears a *fixed cost* of taking action and devaluing the currency. This study examines a model where devaluation costs can include both a lump-sum component and a component that is proportional to the size of the realignment. The model shows how these devaluation costs influence the optimal size and timing of devaluations. The study then uses data from Latin American peg episodes to test whether the model is supported empirically. The analysis also examines whether the cost of

339

taking action increases with the openness of the economy or with changes in other structural characteristics.

In order to isolate the role of devaluation costs, I use the framework developed in Flood and Marion (1995). The policymaker adopts a fixed exchange rate and capital controls and chooses the size and expected timing of future devaluations in order to minimize the expected value of a loss function. The loss function includes the cost of taking no action, namely tolerating real exchange-rate misalignment, and the costs of periodically adjusting the exchange rate.

In the special case where the real exchange rate is the monitored variable and follows regulated Brownian motion with negative trend, the policymaker's loss minimization problem can be solved for the band of inaction within which the real exchange rate fluctuates without triggering a devaluation and for the expected time when the real exchange rate hits the bottom of the band, causing a devaluation. The devaluation of the nominal exchange rate moves the real exchange rate back to the top of the band, so the band size is equivalent to the optimal devaluation size.

Flood and Marion (in press) found empirical support for a model with lump-sum devaluation costs but made no effort to impose any structure on the costs of devaluation or have them vary across peg episodes or across different-sized devaluations. The current study examines more closely the nature of these adjustment costs.

Since the optimal devaluation policy depends, in part, on the cost of taking action, it is important to consider the appropriate specification of the adjustment cost. Take the most extreme case. If there were no cost of changing the nominal exchange rate, the policymaker would continuously adjust it to keep the real exchange rate at its desired level. When action is costly, this strategy is not optimal.

If the cost of exchange-rate adjustment is some fixed amount, say c_1, then it is not worth correcting small misalignments of the real exchange rate. When the discounted value of misalignment costs reaches a critically large level, then a discrete devaluation takes place that moves the real exchange rate back to an optimally chosen point. Consequently, lump-sum adjustment costs imply periodic discrete devaluations.

If, in addition to the lump-sum component, the cost of exchange-rate adjustment includes a component that is proportional to the size of devaluation, say c_2 times the size of devaluation, then once again it is not worth adjusting the peg to correct small misalignments. As the misalignment grows, however, the gain from moving the exchange rate to reduce the misalignment eventually exceeds the cost. However, the currency will be devalued only up to the point where the marginal gain from moving the exchange rate another small unit distance is equal to the marginal cost, c_2. Consequently, the combination of both proportional and lump-sum cost components implies a range of inaction and sudden discrete devaluations when the extreme of the range is reached. But the exchange rate is adjusted only to the point where the marginal benefits of a further devaluation equal the marginal cost (see Dixit 1993).

The plan of the essay is as follows. Section II specifies a model where the policymaker considers the lump-sum and proportional costs of devaluation when choosing the optimal size and expected timing of devaluation. Section III introduces the hypothesis that these devaluation costs are themselves linear functions of structural characteristics of the economy. The set of structural characteristics investigated is guided by the optimal currency literature (e.g., McKinnon 1963; Kenen 1969; Heller 1978; and Melvin and Edison 1990). Since there is evidence that certain structural characteristics, such as openness, trade concentration, and size, influence the decision of whether or not to peg the exchange rate (Flood and Marion 1992), the hypothesis here is that these structural characteristics influence the costs of abandoning the peg as well. Section IV presents the empirical evidence, relying on nonlinear techniques for cross-section data to demonstrate the role of structural characteristics in determining the costs of peg adjustment. Section V concludes.

II The model

Suppose a policymaker pegs the home currency to that of another country and imposes capital controls to prevent speculative attacks on the fixed exchange rate. The real, or price-adjusted, exchange rate is defined as $q_t = e_t p_t^*/p_t$, where e is the nominal exchange rate (home currency/ foreign currency), p^* is the foreign price level, and p is the domestic price level. Ideally, the policymaker should be able to choose the rate of domestic inflation, and thus affect the trend of the real exchange rate, along with choosing the size and expected timing of nominal exchange-rate adjustments. More realistically, there is a policy hierarchy, with the government deficit determining the rate of monetization and inflation and the policymaker taking that rate of inflation as given in setting exchange-rate policy. Consequently it is assumed here that the policymaker cannot affect the trend of the real exchange rate; the policymaker can influence real exchange-rate behavior only by adjusting the nominal exchange rate.

Figure 12.1 illustrates the basic story. The desired level of the real exchange rate, q^*, is taken as exogenous with respect to the policymaker's behavior. The policymaker sets the initial value of the real exchange rate at q_0 by pegging the nominal exchange rate at e_0. The

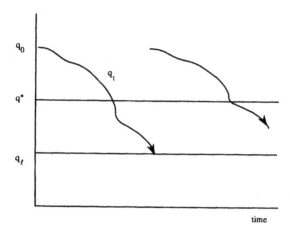

Figure 12.1. The real exchange-rate path.

policymaker then monitors the real exchange rate over time. The real exchange rate follows a stochastic process and, assuming the rate of inflation at home exceeds that in the country to which it is pegged, the real exchange-rate process has a negative trend. The policymaker is assumed to know the trend and variance of the real exchange-rate process.

The policymaker allows the real exchange rate to deviate from its desired level until it reaches some critical lower bound, q_ℓ. At that point a nominal devaluation occurs that moves the real exchange rate back to q_0. The policymaker devalues the currency because having q deviate too much from q^* is costly. However, the policymaker does not devalue too frequently because the cost of adjusting the real exchange rate through a nominal devaluation is also costly.

The policymaker's problem can be specified by means of a loss function. The policymaker minimizes the expected discounted stream of a set of costs arising from real exchange-rate misalignment and periodically adjusting the nominal exchange rate. The policymaker minimizes the expected discounted costs by appropriate choice of the initial real exchange rate and its lower bound. Thus q_0 and q_ℓ in Figure 12.1 are set optimally. The chosen exchange-rate band (q_0-q_ℓ) represents the real exchange-rate appreciation allowed over a peg episode. The band also measures the size of devaluation. With the band chosen, the probability distribution of possible times when the real exchange rate hits the lower barrier can be determined. Then the expected hitting time, or expected time of devaluation, can be calculated.

Computing the loss function in order to do the minimization problem is a hard problem analytically because the times when the real exchange rate hits the lower barrier and requires the policymaker to incur the adjustment costs are stochastic. It is possible to calculate the loss function and obtain a closed-form solution to the policymaker's problem if two assumptions are made: (i) the real exchange rate follows regulated Brownian motion, and (ii) the policymaker monitors only the real exchange rate (the one state variable) in determining exchange-rate policy. Although neither assumption is completely realistic, each is required to derive an analytical framework that is potentially useful for thinking about devaluation decisions.

To keep the policymaker's problem comparable to the stochastic flow problems analyzed by Harrison, Selke, and Taylor (1983) and Harrison (1985), we normalize by setting the lower barrier at zero. We set:

$$0 = q_\ell - q_\ell \qquad x^* = q^* - q_\ell$$
$$x_0 = q_0 - q_\ell \qquad x_t = q_t - q_\ell \qquad (12.1)$$

Now zero is the normalized lower barrier, x_0 is the normalized starting value for the real exchange rate as well as the size of the band, x^* is the normalized equilibrium real exchange rate, and x_t is the normalized real exchange rate at time t.

In the absence of intervention by the policymaker, the real exchange rate follows (μ, σ) Brownian motion with negative trend:

$$x_t = x_0 + \mu t + \sigma w_t \qquad (12.2)$$

where w is a Wiener process with independent incremental shocks that are normally distributed with mean zero and unit variance. It follows that μ and σ^2 are the nonstochastic trend and variance of x, respectively, with $\mu < 0$.

Letting $x_0 \geq 0$, consider the processes (ℓ, z) that are obtained from x by imposing a lower control barrier at zero. The variables ℓ and z have the following properties:

$$\ell \text{ is increasing, with } \ell_0 = 0, \qquad (12.3)$$

$$\ell \text{ increases only when } z = 0, \text{ and} \qquad (12.4)$$

$$z_t \equiv x_t + \ell_t \geq 0 \text{ for all } t \geq 0. \qquad (12.5)$$

In the terminology of Harrison (1985), z_t is a *regulated* Brownian motion, whereas x_t is *unregulated* Brownian motion. We can interpret ℓ_t as the cumulative increase in the real exchange rate effected by the policymaker up to time t.

The policymaker's objective is to minimize the expected present value of costs incurred over an infinite planning horizon by fixing the nominal exchange rate and periodically readjusting it. The policymaker can increase the real exchange rate by any amount desired but is obliged to keep $z_t \geq 0$.

When discounting is continuous at interest rate λ, the policymaker's problem amounts to the minimization of:

$$k(x_0) \equiv E_{x_0}\left\{\int_0^\infty e^{-\lambda t}\left[\beta(z_t - x^*)^2 dt + c_1 I(d\ell) + c_2 d\ell\right]\right\}; \quad x_0 \geq 0 \quad (12.6)$$

where $I(d\ell) = 0$ if $d\ell = 0$ and $I(d\ell) = 1$ if $d\ell > 0$.

In terms of notation, $k(\cdot)$ is the expected present value of costs and E_{x_0} is the expectations operator conditional on setting the real exchange rate at x_0 at the start of the peg episode. Misalignment of the real exchange rate is measured by the square of the deviation of the actual real exchange rate from its desired level, $(z_t - x^*)^2$. The parameter β in (12.6) is the weight attached by the policymaker to the cost of misalignment. Misalignment due to real exchange-rate appreciation is costly since domestic goods and services become less competitive, worsening the current-account balance and reducing employment in the tradeable sector. Misalignment due to real exchange-rate depreciation is also costly as imports become more expensive for consumers and higher-priced imported inputs push up production costs.

Devaluation costs are incurred by the policymaker whenever the nominal exchange rate is adjusted. In the loss function specified by (12.6), devaluation costs are assumed to have a lump-sum component c_1 and a component c_2 that is proportional to the size of devaluation. These costs may be interpreted as the economic and political costs incurred when the economy reacts to a large, sudden change in the terms of trade or when domestic agents bear the social costs associated with the redistribution of gains and losses. In addition, these costs may be thought of as the policymaker's lost reputation or credibility, possibly even loss of office.

Because z_t is a regulated Brownian motion, the method for obtaining a closed-form solution to equation (12.6) has been provided by Harrison, Selke, and Taylor (1983). The solution and its derivation are provided in the appendix.

The policymaker has rational expectations and minimizes the loss function in (12.6) with respect to x^* and x_0. Recalling the normalization in (12.1), this means that the policymaker chooses an initial value for the real exchange rate (q_0) and a lower barrier (q_ℓ) so as to minimize expected discounted costs, given the desired real exchange rate q^*.

The chosen exchange-rate band $(x_0 = q_0 - q_t)$ represents the optimal real appreciation over a peg spell. If the real exchange rate continues to be characterized by the same stochastic process, then the exchange-rate band represents the optimal size of devaluation.[1] From the first-order conditions we find that the optimal band width is x_0, and it obeys:

$$\frac{-\alpha(\lambda)\delta}{x_0} - \alpha(\lambda)\gamma + \frac{\gamma}{x_0}\left(1-e^{-\alpha(\lambda)x_0}\right) + \frac{\alpha(\lambda)x_0\left(1+e^{-\alpha(\lambda)x_0}\right)}{\lambda\left(1-e^{-\alpha(\lambda)x_0}\right)} = \frac{2}{\lambda} \qquad (12.7)$$

where

$$\alpha(\lambda) \equiv \left(\frac{1}{\sigma^2}\right)\left[\left(\mu^2 + 2\sigma^2\lambda\right)^{\frac{1}{2}} + \mu\right] > 0 \qquad (12.8)$$

δ is the lump-sum cost of peg adjustment *relative* to the weight attached to misalignment costs $(\delta = c_1/\beta)$ and γ is the proportional cost of peg adjustment *relative to* the weight assigned the misalignment costs $(\gamma = c_2/\beta)$. Examining (12.7) and (12.8), we find that the optimal band width depends on these relative costs of peg adjustment, δ and γ, as well as on the trend and variance of the real exchange-rate path and the interest rate used for discounting.

Now consider the special case where the policymaker pays only a lump-sum cost to adjust the peg. In order to determine the band width, or equivalently, the devaluation size, the policymaker minimizes (12.6) when $c_1 > 0$ and $c_2 = 0$. The desired devaluation size is x_0 and obeys:

$$\frac{-\alpha(\lambda)\delta}{x_0} + \frac{\alpha(\lambda)x_0\left(1+e^{-\alpha(\lambda)x_0}\right)}{\lambda\left(1-e^{-\alpha(\lambda)x_0}\right)} = \frac{2}{\lambda} \qquad (12.9)$$

Comparing (12.7) and (12.9), we see that the size of devaluation is influenced by the type of adjustment costs assumed.

The expected time of devaluation and the exchange-rate band are jointly determined outcomes of optimizing behavior, since the expected time of devaluation is based on a probability distribution of possible times when the real exchange rate will hit the optimally chosen lower barrier. Let $T(0)$ denote the first time $t > 0$ at which $x_t = 0$, that is, the first time that the real exchange rate hits the lower barrier, triggering a devaluation. Calculating the Laplace transform $E_{x_0}[e^{-\lambda T(0)}]$ yields:[2]

$$E_{x_0}\left[e^{-\lambda T(0)}\right] = e^{-\alpha(\lambda)x_0}, \qquad x_0 > 0 \qquad (12.10)$$

where $\alpha(\lambda)$ is defined in (12.8) and x_0 is given by (12.7) or (12.9), depending on the nature of the adjustment costs. We see that the expected time of devaluation is also influenced by the relative costs of peg adjustment, as well as by the trend and variance of the real exchange rate and the interest rate.

We now examine how an increase in these relative adjustment costs affects the devaluation cycle. When the cost of devaluation is purely lump-sum in nature, the band width is characterized by (12.9) and the effects of a higher adjustment cost on the size and timing of devaluations are straightforward. Differentiating (12.9) and the actual hitting time with respect to δ yields:[3]

$$\frac{\partial x_0}{\partial \delta} > 0, \qquad \frac{\partial T}{\partial \delta} = \frac{\alpha}{\lambda} \frac{\partial x_0}{\partial \delta} > 0 \qquad (12.11)$$

The results in (12.11) indicate that the policymaker facing a greater lump-sum devaluation cost will prefer to undertake bigger devaluations less frequently. As the lump-sum cost increases, the policymaker wants to reduce the number of times the cost is incurred. At the margin, the policymaker is willing to widen the band and tolerate greater misalignment costs in order to incur the devaluation cost less frequently. The wider band in turn implies a delay in the time when the real exchange rate hits the lower barrier.

When devaluation costs involve both lump-sum and proportional components, the band width is characterized by (12.7) and an increase in either of these components has the following effects:

$$\frac{\partial x_0}{\partial \delta} > 0, \qquad \frac{\partial x_0}{\partial \gamma} > 0,$$

$$\frac{\partial T}{\partial \delta} = \frac{\alpha}{\lambda} \frac{\partial x_0}{\partial \delta} > 0, \qquad \frac{\partial T}{\partial \gamma} = \frac{\alpha}{\lambda} \frac{\partial x_0}{\partial \gamma} > 0 \qquad (12.12)$$

For a given lump-sum cost, a larger γ means that the greater the size of devaluation, the more the policymaker pays, but also the less frequently the policymaker has to face the adjustment cost. There is an obvious tradeoff and, for plausible parameter values, an increase in γ increases the band size. The effects of an increase in the lump-sum component are straightforward. For a given proportional cost, a larger δ raises the cost of any size devaluation. At the margin, the policymaker prefers to accept more misalignment in order to incur the larger adjustment cost less frequently. Consequently a larger δ increases both the band size and the time interval between devaluations.

III Adjustment costs and economic structure

We now set out the hypothesis that devaluation costs, again relative to the weight attached to misalignment costs, are linear functions of structural characteristics of the economy. Let

$$\delta = \delta_0 + \sum_{j=1}^{n} \delta_j \theta_j$$

$$\gamma = \gamma_0 + \sum_{j=1}^{n} \gamma_j \theta_j \qquad (12.13)$$

where θ_j is a particular structural characteristic of the economy. For example, suppose that a larger value for θ_j increases the lump-sum cost of peg adjustment relative to the cost of a given misalignment. Then in an estimation, the coefficient δ_j should have a positive sign, and by (12.11) or (12.12) an increase in the value of structural characteristic θ_j will increase the size and timing of devaluations. Of course, it is possible that a larger value for structural variable θ_j will increase proportionately the cost of exchange-rate adjustment and the weight attached to a given misalignment, will have no noticeable effect on relative adjustment costs. In that case, coefficient δ_j should not be significantly different from zero, and a change in the structural variable will not affect the devaluation cycle.

The set of structural characteristics used in (12.13) is guided by the optimal currency literature. That literature considers the role of structural characteristics in influencing the decision of whether or not to peg the exchange rate in the first place. The idea here is that these structural characteristics influence the relative cost of abandoning the peg as well.

For example, McKinnon (1963) claimed that the economy's degree of openness was the principal criterion determining the domain of the optimum currency area. He argued that if a small open economy issued its own currency and allowed the currency to float against that of its larger trading partner, the likely volatility in the exchange rate would tend to undermine the domestic currency in performing its monetary functions and would encourage agents in the economy to substitute foreign currency for the domestic currency. The country would be better off adopting a fixed exchange rate.

The degree of openness may influence the devaluation cycle as well. Openness influences the impact of exchange-rate changes on the general price level. A more open economy will experience a greater impact on its price level for any sized devaluation and the policymaker may therefore face higher economic and political costs of peg adjustment. All else equal, greater openness should then increase the size and time of devaluations. On the other hand, greater openness may increase the cost of a given misalignment, which in turn reduces the size and time of devaluations.

Kenen (1969) argued that diversification in trade should be considered a major determinant of whether a country should opt to form an independent currency area or not. A country with a low level of export diversification, for example, may find that shocks experienced in one export sector are not easily offset by opposite shocks in different sectors. Consequently a country with less diversified trade might prefer a flexible exchange rate. On the other hand, a country highly concentrated in a few exports may find it advantageous to peg its exchange rate and finance changes in export receipts, thereby cushioning the impact of export fluctuations on the economy. Similarly, a country with a higher geographic concentration in its international trade may find that shocks to trade flows with one partner country are not offset by opposite shocks in flows to other countries and may prefer a flexible exchange rate. Alternatively, it may find that it can best achieve output stability by pegging its exchange rate to the currency of its major training partner. As with openness, greater commodity or geographic trade concentration may influence devaluation cycles by increasing adjustment costs, increasing the cost of a given misalignment, or some combination of the two.

Other contributors to the literature have suggested additional criteria, such as the degree of factor mobility (Mundell 1961), the similarity of inflation rates, country size, and the degree of financial integration. The survey by Melvin and Edison (1990) reports on the empirical work in this area, including that of Heller (1978), Dreyer (1978), and Holden, Holden, and Suss (1979). The early empirical work suggested that a country is more likely to fix its exchange rate the smaller its GNP, the higher its degree of openness, and the higher the degree of trade concentration. Some later studies, however, found that size of the economy did not matter for the choice of exchange-rate regime and that lower, not higher, degrees of trade concentration were associated with pegging. In the analysis that follows, I focus on the role of four structural characteristics in affecting the relative costs of peg adjustment. Empirically, these four structural characteristics have been important determinants of the choice of exchange-rate regimes. I consider the role of openness, size, geographic trade concentration, and commodity trade concentration.

IV Empirical evidence

In this section I use monthly data from many fixed exchange-rate episodes in seventeen Latin American countries over the 1957–90 period in order to test whether the selected structural characteristics affect devaluation costs. I proceed in two stages. First, I consider simple linear regressions to check whether the structural characteristics, along with the trend and variance of the real exchange rate, help explain devaluation cycles. Since the results from the linear regressions suggest that structural characteristics matter, I then use the exact model specification for the size of devaluation to determine whether devaluation costs in the Latin American peg episodes are influenced by structural characteristics. I also assess whether devaluation costs are best described as lump-sum in nature or have components that are both lump-sum and proportional to the size of devaluation.

The data are taken from actual dollar peg episodes in Latin America that begin on or after January 1957 and end on or before January 1991. The nominal exchange rate must be fixed for at least three months to be included in the sample. In addition, all peg episodes must be characterized by a negative trend in the real exchange rate. Based on these requirements, I end up with a sample of 80 peg episodes from 17 Latin American countries.[4]

To construct the measure of band width, I subtract the bilateral real exchange-rate index at the end of the last full month on the peg from the index observed at the end of the month in which the exchange rate is initially fixed. The index itself is based on end-of-the-month nominal exchange rates and monthly average consumer price indices for the home country and the United States. It is normalized to 100 at the start of the episode. To measure the devaluation time, I use the number of complete months during which the nominal exchange rate is fixed. I calculate the trend in the real exchange-rate index over each peg episode by regressing the first difference of the monthly real exchange-rate index on a constant and use the variance of the residuals from that regression to measure the variance of the real exchange rate.

Data on structural characteristics are generally available only on an annual basis. In order to obtain the average value of the structural characteristic over the peg episode, I weight the annual data by the fraction of total months on the peg accounted for by that year. For example, if a peg episode runs over the last six months of 1985 and the first three months of 1986, the 1985 annual data are weighted by $\frac{2}{3}$ and the 1986 data are weighted by $\frac{1}{3}$.

I consider the influence of four structural characteristics. The first is openness (OPEN). It is measured as the ratio of trade (exports plus imports) to GDP. The second structural characteristic considered is relative size (SIZE), measured as GDP in the home country relative to that in the United States. The third is geographic trade concentration (GEO).

Table 12.1. *Structural characteristics (percentage)*

Variable	Mean	Standard deviation	Median	Minimum	Maximum
OPEN	39.60	22.49	32.42	11.56	115.70
SIZE	1.75	2.53	0.61	0.12	14.43
GEO	29.43	14.40	30.12	1.93	66.32
EXP2	60.88	15.60	59.09	18.51	95.5

Variables: OPEN = exports plus imports relative to GDP (percentage); SIZE = GDP in the home country relative to GDP in the United States; GEO = exports to the United States plus imports from the United States relative to total exports and imports; EXP2 = the value of the largest two-commodity export categories relative to total commodity exports, measured at the two-digit SITC level.
Sources: Summers and Heston, *Penn World Tables* (Mark 5.6a); International Monetary Fund, *Directions of Trade*; United Nations, *Yearbook of International Trade Statistics*.

It is measured as the share of total trade with the United States. The fourth structural characteristic is commodity trade concentration (EXP2). It is measured at the two-digit SITC level and is represented by the value of the largest two export categories as a percentage of total commodity exports.[5]

Table 12.1 provides some information about the structural characteristics in the sample. The average openness over a peg episode is 39.6 percent, although the standard deviation around the mean is considerable. The smallest measure of openness associated with a peg episode is 11.6 percent, and the largest is over 100 percent. In the sample, relative size averages 1.7 percent. The average geographical concentration is 29.4 percent but ranges from a low of around 2 percent to a high of 66 percent. The average commodity concentration is 60.9 percent, with a low of 18.5 percent and a high of 95.5 percent.

We now turn to linear cross-section estimations of the size and timing of devaluations in order to see if structural characteristics play a role. We start with equations for band width and time until devaluation when the only regressors are the trend real exchange rate and its variance. The results are reported in Table 12.2, equations (1) and (2). The signs on the trend and variance coefficients are sensible since the theory says a more negative trend or bigger variance in the real exchange rate should increase band width and may increase or decrease time spent on the peg.[6] Together the trend and variance of the real exchange rate explain about 22 percent of the variation in band width and 10 percent of the variation

Table 12.2. *Effects of structure on size and timing of devaluation (linear regressions)*

Dependent variable	(1) Band	(2) Time	(3) Band	(4) Time
Observations	80	80	80	80
Constant	21.6141**	41.4049**	29.3612**	33.1847
	(2.95)	(7.58)	(11.05)	(40.68)
μ	−1.8290*	6.6318**	−1.5167	6.6568**
	(1.07)	(1.98)	(1.00)	(2.36)
σ^2	0.1293	0.4492**	0.0879	0.4179*
	(0.16)	(0.22)	(0.13)	(0.21)
OPEN			−0.1569**	−0.1807
			(0.08)	(0.22)
GEO			−0.3700**	−0.0287
			(0.18)	(0.27)
SIZE			−1.4043*	−3.0728
			(0.78)	(2.49)
EXP2			0.2159*	0.3617
			(0.13)	(0.38)
R^2	0.242	0.128	0.363	0.180
adjR^2	0.222	0.105	0.311	0.113

Notes: Standard errors in parentheses. The values are heteroskedastic-consistent.
**(*) Signifies significance at the 95 (90) percent confidence level.
Regressions are based on a cross-section of peg spells.
Sources: Summers and Heston, *Penn World Tables* (Mark 5.6a); IMF, *Directions of Trade*; IMF, *International Financial Statistics*; United Nations, *Yearbook of International Trade Statistics*.

in time until devaluation. The fact that trend and variance explain more of the variation in band width than in time should not be too surprising in light of the fact that the time variable in equation (2) is *actual* time until devaluation rather than expected time. Consequently the error term in the time regression also includes a rational expectations error, the difference between actual and expected time until devaluation.

In order to introduce devaluation costs explicitly into the linear regressions, we would like an equation of the form:

$$y(i) = \beta_0 + \beta_1 \, \text{trend}(i) + \beta_2 \, \text{variance}(i) + \beta_3 \, \text{cost}(i) + \varepsilon(i) \qquad (12.14)$$

where $y(i)$ is the band width or time of devaluation in peg episode i, trend(i) is the trend of the real exchange rate in peg episode i, variance(i)

is the variance of the real exchange rate in episode i, cost(i) is the devaluation cost at the end of episode i, and $\varepsilon(i)$ is an error term that is uncorrelated with the right-hand side variables. Because the devaluation cost is not observed, we proxy it with a linear function of the four structural variables:

$$\cos t(i) = \sum_{j=1}^{4} \kappa_{ji}\theta_{ji} + u_i \tag{12.15}$$

where θ_{ji} is structural variable j in episode i and $u(i)$ is uncorrelated with the structural variables. Consequently we actually estimate:

$$y(i) = \beta_0 + \beta_1 \text{trend}(i) + \beta_2 \text{variance}(i) + \beta_3 \sum_{j=1}^{4} \kappa_{ji}\theta_{ji} + \omega_i \tag{12.16}$$

where $\omega_i = (\varepsilon_i + \beta_3 u_i)$ and is uncorrelated with the regressors. Equations (3) and (4) in Table 12.2 introduce the four structural characteristics as additional regressors.

Examining the adjusted R^2 and calculating the F-statistic for the regressions with and without structural characteristics – equations (1) and (2) versus equations (3) and (4) in Table 12.2 – two observations can be made. First, the signs on the coefficients attached to structural variables are reasonable in the sense that a structural characteristic that reduces the cost of devaluation simultaneously reduces band width and time between devaluations. Second, the structural variables together add to the explanatory power of the band regression but not to the time regression. In the band regression, equation (3), greater openness, geographical concentration in trade and relative size reduce devaluation costs and hence band size, whereas greater concentration in commodity exports increases them.

Multicollinearity may be a problem. There is a fairly strong correlation between trend and variance ($r = -0.82$), between openness and size ($r = -0.51$), between size and export commodity concentration ($r = -0.35$), and between geographical concentration and the real exchange-rate process ($r_{\mu,\text{geo}} = 0.31$; $r_{\text{var,geo}} = -0.30$).

So far we have just examined the role of structural characteristics in linear regressions for band width and time of devaluation. We now turn to nonlinear estimation of the exact band specification (7) in order to identify the role of structural characteristics in determining devaluation costs and to assess whether devaluation costs include both a lump-sum component and a component proportional to the size of devaluation.

Table 12.3 contains the results of the nonlinear estimations. Specification (1) reports the results of estimating the cost components δ and γ

Table 12.3. *Estimations for devaluation size (band width) Nonlinear regressions*

Band width (x_0)
Lump-sum plus proportional devaluation costs

$$\frac{-\alpha(\lambda)\delta}{x_0} - \alpha(\lambda)\gamma + \frac{\gamma}{x_0}\left(1 - e^{-\alpha(\lambda)x_0}\right) + \frac{\alpha(\lambda)x_0\left(1 + e^{-\alpha(\lambda)x_0}\right)}{\lambda\left(1 - e^{-\alpha(\lambda)x_0}\right)} = \frac{2}{\lambda} + \varepsilon_i$$

1. Log likelihood = 552.647 $n = 80$
$\delta = -260.040$ s.e. = 219.530
$\gamma = 0.423316E + 08**$ s.e. = 0.474664E + 07
$\lambda = 0.259199E - 06**$ s.e. = 0.209321E - 07

2. Log likelihood = 615.947 $n = 80$
$\delta_0 = 375.126$ s.e. = 572.379
$\delta_1 = -16.0792*$ s.e. = 9.55761
$\delta_2 = 21.3524$ s.e. = 12.8984
$\delta_3 = -6.70072$ s.e. = 49.4507
$\delta_4 = -12.8708$ s.e. = 9.27355
$\gamma_0 = 0.540692E + 08**$ s.e. = 0.590437E + 07
$\gamma_1 = -45988.1$ s.e. = 80516.1
$\gamma_2 = -0.145384E + 07**$ s.e. = 176993
$\gamma_3 = -0.306346E + 07**$ s.e. = 0.106161E + 07
$\gamma_4 = 344692**$ s.e. = 105833
$\lambda = 0.375713E - 06**$ s.e. = 0.302102E - 07

3. Log likelihood = 657.81 $n = 80$
$\delta_0 = 2882.81**$ s.e. = 885.20
$\delta_1 = 10.445$ s.e. = 11.6052
$\delta_2 = -49.8582**$ s.e. = 20.8616
$\delta_3 = -110.221$ s.e. = 110.356
$\delta_4 = -32.4373**$ s.e. = 13.4545
$\delta_5 = -247.487**$ s.e. = 31.4436
$\delta_6 = 89.5985**$ s.e. = 41.8245
$\delta_7 = -1657.35**$ s.e. = 601.816
$\delta_8 = 84.0019**$ s.e. = 33.8778
$\gamma_0 = 0.444258E + 08**$ s.e. = 0.399694E + 07
$\gamma_1 = -0.115753E + 07$ s.e. = 0.250042E + 07
$\gamma_2 = 0.168142E + 07$ s.e. = 0.328063E + 07
$\gamma_3 = 0.207127E + 07$ s.e. = 0.201184E + 08
$\gamma_4 = -651313$ s.e. = 0.182071E + 07
$\gamma_5 = -0.196754E + 07$ s.e. = 0.251687E + 07
$\gamma_6 = -0.227046E + 07$ s.e. = 0.328734E + 07
$\gamma_7 = 0.195858E + 07$ s.e. = 0.202080E + 08
$\gamma_8 = 177709$ s.e. = 0.182605E + 07
$\lambda = 0.457330E - 06**$ s.e. = 0.378910E - 07

simultaneously with the interest rate λ. A priori, we expect δ, γ, and λ to be positive. The results are not completely satisfactory. Although γ and λ are positive and precisely estimated, δ is not significantly different from zero. The estimated value for the interest rate is also smaller than one would expect.

Specification (2) reports results when δ and γ are each assumed to be linear functions of the structural variables, as set out in (12.13). The coefficients δ_1 and γ_1 are attached to the openness variable, δ_2 and γ_2 are associated with geographic concentration in trade, δ_3 and γ_3 with relative size, and δ_4 and γ_4 with commodity export concentration. A likelihood ratio test indicates that the structural variables as a group do help explain adjustment costs associated with devaluation cycles. In addition, the results indicate that, at the 95 percent confidence level, greater geographic concentration in trade and greater relative size reduce the cost component γ while greater commodity concentration in exports increases it. In addition, the coefficient γ_0 is a large positive number and highly significant, suggesting a sizable fixed element to the cost component that is proportional to the size of devaluation. The coefficient δ_0 attached to the lump-sum cost component is positive but not precisely estimated. Greater openness appears to affect the lump-sum cost of adjustment, but only at the 90 percent confidence level. It is possible that greater openness increases both the cost of devaluation and the weight attached to misalignment costs. If that is the case, then greater openness could have little impact on the devaluation cycle.

It may be the case that the linkage between devaluation costs and the size and timing of devaluation is more pronounced for some subset of episodes. Since theory predicts that longer episodes have bigger adjustment costs, we next isolate the effects of those peg episodes by constructing a dummy variable (DUM) that takes on a value of one when the time until devaluation is greater than the sample median and zero otherwise. The dummy variable is used interactively with each of the structural variables. Coefficients δ_i and γ_i for $i = 5,6,7,8$ are attached to the variable θ_j*DUM, where θ_j is structural variable j (j = open, geo, size, exp2).

Specification (3) reports the results of the estimation with the interactive dummy. The results indicate that there are positive and highly significant fixed elements to the lump-sum and proportional costs of adjustment ($\delta_0 > 0$, $\gamma_0 > 0$). Moreover, for the longer spells, greater openness reduces the lump-sum cost of adjustment, as does greater relative size, whereas greater concentration in trade, whether geographic or commodity, increases the lump-sum cost. The effects of relative size and commodity concentration in trade therefore appear to be robust to alternative specifications. An increase in relative size reduces devaluation costs, and an increase in commodity concentration increases them.

We next turn to the nonlinear estimates in the special case where devaluation costs are only lump-sum in nature. When δ and λ are estimated simultaneously, both δ and λ are positive, but only λ is estimated precisely. These results are not very satisfactory.

We introduce the hypothesis that δ is a linear function of the structural parameters to check whether this modification yields more satisfactory results. Of the various structural characteristics, only commodity concentration appears to influence the lump-sum cost of adjustment and hence the devaluation cycle. The results suggest that greater commodity concentration increases lump-sum devaluation costs.

When we examine how structure might influence costs in the longer spells, we find again that commodity concentration is the only structural variable that matters. As before, greater commodity concentration in trade increases lump-sum devaluation costs.

Two major conclusions can be drawn from the nonlinear estimations. First, structural variables do influence the costs of adjusting exchange-rate pegs. Of the four structural variables considered, greater commodity concentration in trade always increases devaluation costs. Greater relative size reduces them in almost all estimations. Surprisingly, the openness of the economy rarely affects devaluation costs in the estimations. Without more identifying restrictions, however, we are unable to determine whether greater openness increases the cost of devaluation and the cost of misalignment proportionately, thereby having no significant effect on *relative* adjustment costs, or whether greater openness has no effect on either.

Second, although both the lump-sum-plus-proportional costs of adjustment specification and the lump-sum cost specification perform less than satisfactorily when the cost components are estimated as simple constants, both specifications do better when structural variables are introduced. Although the assumption of a lump-sum devaluation cost is not rejected by the Latin American data, the data also support the more general specification in which devaluation costs include a lump-sum component and a component proportional to the size of devaluation.

V Conclusion

This essay shows how devaluation costs influence devaluation cycles: the optimal size and timing of devaluations. Data from Latin American devaluation cycles support the notion that there is a lump-sum cost associated with devaluation. In addition, the data suggest that there is a cost component that is proportional to the size of devaluation.

Borrowing from the optimum currency literature, we also show that structural characteristics thought to influence the decision of whether or not to peg the exchange rate can influence the size (and timing) of devaluations as well. In the Latin American devaluation cycles, greater commodity concentration in trade increases the relative costs of peg adjustment and causes devaluations to be bigger and less frequent. Greater relative size as measured by country GDP relative to U.S. GDP reduces the relative costs of peg adjustment, making for smaller and more frequent devaluations. Surprisingly, the degree of openness has little effect on devaluation cycles, perhaps because it increases the cost of a given misalignment along with the cost of adjusting the exchange rate.

The framework used in this paper can be expanded in a number of directions. For example, the model yields explicit solutions for the optimal size and timing of devaluations by assuming that the policymaker monitors one state variable, the real exchange rate, in making decisions about the exchange-rate peg. Yet it is more realistic to believe that the policymaker tracks many state variables. Although one cannot obtain a closed-form solution in a model with many state variables, their effects on devaluation cycles can be uncovered using simulation methods. In addition, the current model could be extended to the case where capital is mobile internationally. In a world of high international capital mobility, the markets can influence the path of the monitored variables and, along with the policymaker, play a role in the determination of devaluation cycles. Finally, more work needs to be done to identify the costs associated with devaluations. The current study focuses on the role of structural characteristics in influencing devaluation costs. It is possible that devaluation costs also vary in systematic ways with the type of nominal and real shocks hitting the economy or with changes in the political environment.

APPENDIX

The policymaker minimizes the following loss function (equation (12.6) in text):

$$k(x_0) \equiv E_{x_0}\left\{\int_0^\infty e^{-\lambda t}\left[\beta(z_t - x^*)^2 \, dt + c_1 I(d\ell) + c_2 d\ell\right]\right\}; \qquad x_0 \geq 0 \qquad (12.\text{A}1)$$

where $I(d\ell) = 0$ if $d\ell = 0$ and $I(d\ell) = 1$ if $d\ell > 0$.

In (12.A1), $k(x_0)$ is the solution to a second-order differential equation with some particular boundary conditions. That differential equation is $\lambda k(x_0) - \mu k'(x_0) - (\frac{1}{2})\sigma^2 k''(x_0) = (x - x^*)^2$, subject to the "value-matching" condition that

$k(0) = k(x_0) + \delta + \gamma x_0$, where $\delta = \frac{c_1}{\beta}$ and $\gamma = \frac{c_2}{\beta}$. In the value-matching condition, δ is the lump-sum cost of peg adjustment relative to the weight attached to mis-alignment costs, while γ is the proportional cost of peg adjustment relative to the weight assigned to misalignment costs. The value-matching condition requires that the expected costs incurred when x is at the lower barrier of zero must be equal to the expected costs incurred when x is again at its optimal point above the barrier, plus the relative control costs of moving x there. The solution to (12.A1) is:

$$k(x_0) = g(x_0) + k(0)e^{-\alpha(\lambda)x_0} \tag{12.A2}$$

where

$$g(x_0) \equiv E_{x_0}\left\{\int_0^T e^{-\lambda T}(x_t - x^*)^2 dt\right\}, \tag{12.A3}$$

$$k(0) = k(x_0) + \delta + \gamma x_0, \tag{12.A4}$$

$$\alpha(\lambda) \equiv \left(\frac{1}{\sigma^2}\right)\left[(\mu^2 + 2\sigma^2\lambda)^{\frac{1}{2}} + \mu\right] > 0. \tag{12.A5}$$

T is the first time the real exchange rate hits the lower boundary, and $g(x_0)$ is the expected discounted value of misalignment costs up to the first hitting time. Since T is stochastic, the calculation of $g(x_0)$ in (A3) requires the Ito stochastic calculus.

Using Harrison (1985), pp. 44–48, the $g(x_0)$ function in (A3) is equal to:

$$g(x_0) = f(x_0) - f(0)e^{-\alpha(\lambda)x_0}; \qquad x_0 \geq 0 \tag{12.A6}$$

where, using Fubini's theorem,

$$f(x_0) \equiv E_{x_0}\left[\int_0^\infty e^{-\lambda t}(x_t - x^*)^2 dt\right] = \int_0^\infty e^{-\lambda t} E_{x_0}\left[(x_t - x^*)^2\right] dt \tag{12.A7}$$

To calculate (12.A7), use the expression in (12.2) of the text for x_t, and derive the expected squared deviation of the real exchange rate from its equilibrium value:

$$E_{x_0}(x_t - x^*)^2 = (x_0 - x^*)^2 + \mu^2 t^2 + 2(x_0 - x^*)\mu t + t\sigma^2 \tag{12.A8}$$

Substituting (12.A8) into (12.A7) gives:

$$f(x_0) = (x_0 - x^*)^2 \int_0^\infty e^{-\lambda t} dt + \mu^2 \int_0^\infty e^{-\lambda t} t^2 dt + [2(x_0 - x^*)\mu + \sigma^2]\int_0^\infty e^{-\lambda t} t dt \tag{12.A9}$$

Integrating (12.A9) yields the following expression for $f(x_0)$:

$$f(x_0) = \frac{(x_0 - x^*)^2}{\lambda} + \frac{2\mu^2}{\lambda^3} + \frac{2(x_0 - x^*)\mu + \sigma^2}{\lambda^2} \tag{12.A10}$$

Substituting (12.A10) into (12.A6) and also evaluating the function $f(x_0)$ at $x_0 = 0$ gives:

$$g(x_0) = \frac{(x_0 - x^*)^2}{\lambda} + \frac{2\mu^2}{\lambda^3} + \frac{\{2(x_0 - x^*)\mu + \sigma^2\}}{\lambda^2}$$
$$- \left[\frac{x^{*2}}{\lambda} + \frac{2\mu^2}{\lambda^3} + \frac{(\sigma^2 - 2x^*\mu)}{\lambda^2}\right]e^{-\alpha x_0} \tag{12.A11}$$

With the solution of $g(x_0)$ in hand, we can then rewrite the expected discounted costs in (12.A2) as:

$$k(x_0) = \left\{\frac{(x_0 - x^*)^2}{\lambda} + \frac{2\mu^2}{\lambda^3} + \frac{[2(x_0 - x^*)\mu + \sigma^2]}{\lambda^2}\right.$$
$$\left. - \left[\frac{x^{*2}}{\lambda} + \frac{2\mu^2}{\lambda^3} + \frac{(\sigma^2 - 2x^*\mu)}{\lambda^2} - \delta - \gamma x_0\right]e^{-\alpha x_0}\right\}\{1 - e^{-\alpha x_0}\}^{-1} \tag{12.A12}$$

The first term in curly brackets in (12.A12) is the sum of the two types of costs: (i) the expected discounted flow costs of letting the real exchange rate fall from x_0 to the lower barrier one time, and (ii) the discounted relative control costs of resetting the exchange rate back above the barrier one time. The second term in curly brackets capitalizes the value of an infinite sequence of these flow costs and control costs.

NOTES

I would like to thank Polly Allen, B. J. Cohen, Avinash Dixit, Hank Farber, Bob Flood, Tim Jenkinson, and Costas Michalopoulos for helpful comments. Any remaining errors are mine.

1. If the exchange-rate process is expected to change with peg resetting, perhaps because repegging is combined with other policies, then the policymaker would reoptimize at the time of resetting by minimizing the loss function with the new view about the exchange-rate process.
2. See Harrison (1985), pp. 38–44, for details.
3. In order to calculate the actual time when the real exchange rate hits the lower barrier, we invoke rational expectations so that the expected time is equal to the actual time adjusted for an error term, ε_t, that is uncorrelated with x_0:

$$E_{x_0}\left[e^{-\lambda T(0)}\right] = e^{-\alpha(\lambda)x_0}e^{\varepsilon_t}$$

Substituting this expression into (12.10), taking logs of both sides and rearranging terms yields:

$$T(0) = \frac{\alpha(\lambda)x_0}{\lambda} + \frac{\varepsilon_t}{\lambda}$$

The comparative statics are done on this expression for the actual hitting time.

4. The countries are Argentina, Bolivia, Brazil, Chile, Colombia, Costa Rica, Dominican Republic, Ecuador, El Salvador, Guatemala, Jamaica, Mexico, Nicaragua, Panama, Peru, Uruguay, and Venezuela. In all peg episodes, the home price of the U.S. dollar increases when the peg is adjusted. Most peg episodes end with a discrete devaluation, but some end with a move to a crawl or a float. These peg spells were first identified in Klein and Marion (in press) and analyzed further in Flood and Marion (in press).

5. Alternative measures of these four structural characteristics were also explored but were found to be inferior to the measures reported in the text. For example, openness was also measured as the ratio of exports to GDP, the ratio of imports to GDP, and the ratio of imports to consumption. (The various openness measures were highly correlated, with the correlation coefficients ranging between $r = 0.95$ and $r = 0.99$.) Geographical trade concentration was also specified as the share of total exports going to the United States or the share of total imports coming from the United States. Alternative commodity trade concentration measures considered were the value of the largest export category as a percentage of total commodity exports, the value of the largest import category relative to total commodity imports, and the value of the two largest import categories relative to total commodity imports.

6. The intuition is as follows. *For a given band size,* a more negative trend or a bigger variance of the real exchange rate means that the real exchange rate will hit the lower barrier more frequently and hence the policymaker will bear the adjustment cost more often. To reduce the number of times the adjustment cost is incurred, the policymaker is willing to widen the band and accept greater misalignment costs at the margin. The ambiguity regarding trend and variance on the time of devaluation is due to opposing forces. *For a given band size,* a larger negative trend or bigger variance reduces the time spent on a peg since the real exchange rate hits the lower barrier more quickly. However, a larger negative trend or bigger variance also increases the band size and could therefore delay the time when the real exchange rate hits the barrier, triggering a devaluation.

REFERENCES

Dixit, Avinash (1993). *The Art of Smooth Pasting*. Chur, Switzerland: Harwood Academic Publishers.

Dreyer, Jacob (1978). "Determinants of Exchange-Rate Regimes for Currencies of Developing Countries: Some Preliminary Results," *World Development* 6 (April), 437–45.

Flood, Robert, and Nancy Marion (1992). "Exchange Rate Regime Choice." In Peter Newman, ed., *The New Palgrave Dictionary of Money and Finance*. London: Macmillan.

Flood, Robert, and Nancy Marion (in press). "The Size and Timing of Devaluations in Capital-Controlled Economies." NBER Working Paper No. 4957, December 1994, revised for the Eighth Inter-American Seminar on Economics, November, 1995. Bogota, Colombia: NBER and Fedesarrollo. *Journal of Development Economics.*

Harrison, J. Michael (1985). *Brownian Motion and Stochastic Flow Systems.* New York: Wiley.

Harrison, J. Michael, Thomas Selke, and Allison Taylor (1983). "Impulse Control of Brownian Motion," *Mathematics of Operations Research* 8, 454–466.

Heller, Robert (1978). "Determinants of Exchange Rate Practices," *Journal of Money, Credit, and Banking* 10 (August), 308–21.

Holden, Paul, and Merle Holden, and Esther Suss (1979). "The Determinants of Exchange Rate Flexibility: An Empirical Investigation," *The Review of Economics and Statistics* 61 (August), 327–33.

International Monetary Fund, *Directions of Trade.*

International Monetary Fund, *International Financial Statistics.*

Kenen, Peter (1969). "The Currency Area Problem." In Robert Mundell and Alexander Swoboda, eds., *Monetary Problems of the International Economy,* pp. 41–60. Chicago: University of Chicago Press.

Klein, Michael, and Nancy Marion (in press). "Explaining the Duration of Exchange-Rate Pegs," *Journal of Development Economics.*

McKinnon, Ronald (1963). "Optimal Currency Areas," *American Economic Review* 53 (September), 717–25.

Melvin, Michael, and Hali Edison (1990). "The Determinants and Implications of the Choice of an Exchange Rate System." In William Haraf and Thomas Willett, eds., *Monetary Policy for a Volatile Global Economy,* pp. 1–44. Washington, DC: AEI Press

Mundell, Robert (1961). "A Theory of Optimum Currency Areas," *American Economic Review* 51 (September), 657–65.

Summers, Robert, and Alan Heston (1995). *The Penn World Tables* (Mark 5.6a).

United Nations, *Yearbook of International Trade Statistics.*

CHAPTER 13

Payments problems in the Commonwealth of Independent States

Constantine Michalopoulos

I Introduction

Integration of the previously centrally planned countries into the international economy has presented some of the most difficult challenges of transition to the market. State control of trade and foreign exchange, vastly distorted prices, and insufficiently developed financial institutions left countries in East-Central Europe and the former Soviet Union ill prepared to participate and benefit from international trade and finance. At the same time, their governments realized that without integration into the international economy, the transition to a market system would never be complete or successful.

In 1990, Peter Kenen prepared a report for the IMF that focused on the implications of price liberalization and moving to international prices and convertible currencies for trade and financial relationships among the countries of East-Central Europe that were members of the soon-to-be-defunct CMEA (Kenen 1991). He concluded that the needed economic reforms would worsen these countries' terms of trade and drive them into a current-account deficit with the USSR. He recommended the extension of medium-term financing from the USSR to individual countries and additional external financing from the international community to cope with the terms of trade shock.[1]

In 1992, the USSR itself collapsed and in its place fifteen new countries emerged, all proceeding with price liberalization and moving to international prices and convertibility at a different pace. The problems of economic relations between East-Central Europe and the USSR were quickly overshadowed by the problems of the countries of the former Soviet Union (hereafter FSU) itself: inadequate payments arrangements and a poorly functioning banking system constrained trade and payments with the rest of the world, but especially with each other. Price

361

liberalization resulted in a severe terms of trade shock for energy importers within the former USSR, such as the Baltics, Ukraine, and Belarus,
and contributed to the emergence of large intra-FSU balance of payments disequilibria. With the exception of the Baltics, monetary instability combined with institutional weaknesses have impeded countries'
efforts to cope with these financing difficulties.

Since then, East-Central Europe has dealt remarkably well with international trade problems arising in the context of transition: there were
few financing difficulties with the USSR, in part because of supply declines in Russian and other FSU exportables, and in part because of a
rapid reorientation of East-Central Europe's trade to the OECD. Additional international financing, as suggested by Kenen, also became available to most countries (Bosworth and Ofer 1995).

The integration of the FSU countries into the international economy
has been far less smooth: several years after independence trade among
these countries is at a fraction of previous levels and a substantial
share of it is conducted under barter arrangements. Payments problems
still appear to plague trade in many countries with the exception of the
Baltics; and no solution is in sight for the financing problems created in
countries like Belarus and Ukraine by large imbalances in intra-FSU
trade.

The purpose of this essay is threefold: (a) to analyze the adverse
impact of payments problems on trade among the FSU countries, using
a framework similar to the one Kenen used in the context of the Eastern
European countries; (b) to consider what could have been done to
address these problems and why it was not done; and (c) to recommend
appropriate institutional and policy reforms to address the remaining
problems, including ways to deal with the intractable intra-FSU
financing difficulties.

The essay concludes that the payments problems need to be addressed
– first, through more effective stabilization measures, to enhance prospects of convertibility, and second, by strengthening institutional arrangements to permit efficient settlements via correspondent bank
accounts. A multilateral clearing arrangement, though once a potentially
appealing option, would no longer be appropriate in these countries'
changed economic circumstances. Consistent with Kenen's conclusion
about East-Central Europe, the essay argues that a payments union
would not have been a good idea for addressing the problems of intra-
FSU trade either in the past or at present. There is also a need for
increased external financing for many of these countries, which however,
should be conditioned on continued progress in stabilization and structural reform.

II Trends in trade and payments

The trade decline

In the aftermath of independence, there was a decline in trade between the new independent states of the FSU and the rest of the world, but trade with each other apparently collapsed. Official estimates using market exchange rates show a decline in exports to the rest of the world of about 20 percent between 1991 and 1992. By 1995 these exports had recovered, whereas 1995 exports to other FSU countries were only 14 percent of their 1991 level (Table 13.1). Russia is by far the largest trading country in absolute terms, its trade with the rest of the world accounting for over 50 percent of the FSU total in 1995, with Ukraine a distant second at about 8 percent. There are many problems with these estimates: first, they clearly overstate the actual decline in 1992 because the exchange rate used to convert rubles to dollars in 1991 was substantially overvalued. (On the other hand, in subsequent years the ruble and some of the other new currencies were substantially undervalued using purchasing power parity and wages-in-dollars comparisons [Michalopoulos and Tarr 1994a]). Second, there is evidence that the implicit exchange rates used in the conduct of intra-FSU trade in 1992–3 involved a much smaller ruble devaluation vis-à-vis the dollar. Third, the absence of customs posts meant that a lot of trade was unrecorded; at the same time, there were many barter transactions, often at artificial exchange rates. Although the statistical agencies tried to adjust for unrecorded and barter trade, it is doubtful that the adjustments made captured all the amounts involved.

Data on intra-FSU trade (hereafter "interstate trade") published by individual countries are incomplete and contradictory. The constant price series presented in Table 13.2 is based in part on World Bank estimates. They show a somewhat smaller decline for interstate trade than the series in U.S. dollars, which, however, remains substantial. In most countries exports fell by 70 to 90 percent. Even Belarus and Kazakstan, which suffered the smallest declines over the period, still experienced drops of 36 and 55 percent, respectively. The fact that interstate trade declined substantially is also corroborated by firm level surveys (Bull 1994).

By 1995, trade with the rest of world had recovered in almost all FSU countries, with the notable exception of Ukraine. In part this was because most countries, and especially Russia, pursued a conscious policy to shift energy and raw material exports to the OECD in order to earn hard currency and avoid payments problems associated with FSU trade.

Table 13.1. *Foreign trade of the New Independent States of the former Soviet Union, 1991–1995 (millions of current U.S. dollars at market exchange rates)*

	1991 Exports	1991 Imports	1992 Exports	1992 Imports	1993 Exports	1993 Imports	1994 Exports	1994 Imports	1995 Exports	1995 Imports
*Trade with the rest of the world**										
Armenia	70	830	40	95	29	188	57	188	104	340
Azerbaijan	487	1,248	774	333	402	401	354	279	322	424
Belarus	1,661	1,957	1,061	755	737	777	1,053	690	1,415	1,696
Estonia	50	204	242	254	462	652	724	1,253	1,151	1,969
Georgia	30	480	161	269	222	460	86	189	68	167
Kazakstan	1,183	2,546	1,489	961	1,529	1,269	1,327	1,694	2,173	1,135
Kyrgyz Republic	23	785	77	71	112	112	112	88	137	165
Latvia	125	478	429	423	501	472	486	747	683	1,009
Lithuania	345	475	557	342	696	486	859	1,525	1,063	1,949
Moldova	180	656	157	170	181	179	152	176	260	258
Russia	53,100	45,100	41,600	37,200	43,900	33,100	49,530	27,567	60,812	31,866
Tajikistan	424	706	111	132	263	374	319	306	484	311
Turkmenistan	146	618	1,145	543	1,156	749	487	688	574	448
Ukraine	8,500	11,300	6,000	5,500	6,300	4,700	4,648	4,347	5,713	5,790
Uzbekistan	1,257	2,048	869	929	1,466	1,280	912	1,106	1,792	1,601
Former Soviet Union	67,581	69,431	54,711	47,977	57,957	45,199	61,105	40,844	76,751	49,128

Trade with countries of the former Soviet Union

Armenia	3,823	4,686	243	292	124	159	159	206	167	335
Azerbaijan	9,091	7,013	797	665	591	1,036	283	499	222	242
Belarus	23,151	20,375	1,939	2,128	3,092	3,348	2,085	2,990	3,292	3,868
Estonia	3,836	2,996	147	146	343	244	575	407	536	634
Georgia	5,594	4,806	144	224	295	433	156	280	75	110
Kazakstan	14,285	16,949	2,141	2,463	3,126	3,576	2,014	2,042	2,874	3,435
Kyrgyz Republic	5,163	4,293	236	344	282	378	325	402	272	357
Latvia	5,920	4,365	451	472	539	488	503	495	601	637
Lithuania	9,268	6,251	505	624	929	1,111	1,160	1,276	1,396	1,381
Moldova	6,190	5,525	313	470	303	452	413	483	485	583
Russia**	108,571	83,333	10,954	9,246	15,752	10,546	15,407	10,978	16,586	14,493
Tajikistan	3,456	4,361	93	172	118	198	170	252	265	488
Turkmenistan	6,314	3,684	616	410	1,731	876	1,689	1,002	1,434	1,024
Ukraine	49,598	61,217	5,262	6,425	5,669	9,185	5,543	7,593	7,289	9,032
Uzbekistan	13,761	14,100	628	827	2,085	2,225	1,408	1,086	1,317	1,292
Former Soviet Union	268,022	243,954	24,468	24,907	34,980	34,253	31,891	29,991	36,811	37,911

* The rest of the world refers to countries outside the former Soviet Union.

Sources: IMF *Direction of Trade Statistics*, 1995. Annual for the following countries and periods: Armenia 1994–95; Azerbaijan 1992–95; Estonia 1993–95; Kazakstan 1994–95 (FSU only); Latvia 1993–95; Lithuania 1994–95; Moldova 1993–95; Russia 1994–95, Ukraine 1995. For all other countries, national official statistics and World Bank staff estimates were used. For further information on sources and methods, see C. Michalopoulos and D. Tarr, *Trade in the New Independent States*, 1994. Studies of Economies in Transformation No. 13. World Bank, Chapter 1 and Appendix; Belkindas, M. and O.V. Ivanova, *Foreign Trade Statistics in the USSR and Successor States*, 1996. Studies of Economies in Transformation No. 18. World Bank, Chapter 8.

Table 13.2. Volume of interstate trade, 1991–1995 (1991 = 100)

	1992		1993		1994		1995	
	Exports	Imports	Exports	Imports	Exports	Imports	Exports	Imports
Armenia	70.5	35.3	30.2	25.8	19.9	18.2	14.4	16.2
Azerbaijan	50.7	46.6	24.6	23.4	10.8	18.4	6.1	7.1
Belarus	77.8	76.1	59.2	61.8	42.0	45.3	64.8	57.2
Estonia	37.9	38.7	21.5	17.6	13.2	18.8	15.4	25.8
Georgia	24.3	37.5	22.7	33.0	11.1	13.8	5.2	5.3
Kazakstan	95.8	110.1	63.8	72.3	32.4	30.8	45.3	32.1
Kyrgyz Republic	45.8	56.1	22.8	31.5	18.5	21.5	15.1	18.6
Latvia	79.6	80.4	23.5	25.1	17.0	23.1	20.2	24.4
Lithuania	48.2	71.1	28.9	28.3	14.5	18.5	17.0	19.6
Moldova	52.1	61.3	45.9	46.9	28.5	27.0	32.1	29.6
Russia	72.2	86.2	46.7	54.2	32.5	44.9	33.8	58.2
Tajikistan	26.1	32.2	15.1	16.2	16.5	13.4	25.1	25.4
Turkmenistan	95.5	114.7	54.5	100.0	48.2	23.0	40.0	23.0
Ukraine	64.8	79.3	39.8	56.5	24.9	26.3	27.2	24.8
Uzbekistan	45.0	49.4	43.3	43.6	28.9	18.2	26.4	21.1
Former Soviet Union	67.4	77.4	43.7	52.1	29.0	32.7	31.5	36.7

Sources: 1992–1993: Michalopoulos and Tarr, 1994a. 1994–95: World Bank staff estimates.

In the CIS this shift was virtually always undertaken within an overall trade regime that initially restrained exports which itself had significant adverse effects on output and welfare (Gros 1994a).

There is a question as to whether the decline in interstate trade should be of concern. This is an issue because there is strong evidence that under central planning the FSU countries – then simply regions of the Soviet Union – traded excessively with each other. Trade with the "rest of the world," that is, foreign trade of the Soviet Union, was totally controlled. Under central planning "imports were a necessary evil – the source of last resort for basic raw materials and other inputs that could not be produced at home in quantities sufficient to meet domestic needs. Exports were needed to pay for imports, but they were released reluctantly, because of domestic shortages" (Kenen 1991, p. 246). Moreover, production was highly concentrated, with some goods produced by a single producer or very few producers.

Consequently, trade among the then Republics absorbed an unusually high proportion of total trade.[2] At 67 percent of total exports, Russia had the lowest dependence on trade with the other republics in 1991; for the others, such exports amounted to between 85 percent (Ukraine) and almost 100 percent (Kyrgyz Republic) of the total (Table 13.3).

There is no consistent detailed information on the evolution of the commodity composition of this trade after independence. The information available (presented in Table 13.4) suggests the following general pattern: energy in the form of oil and gas exports is a large part of Russia's and Turkmenistan's exports; Ukraine exports primarily semifinished industrial products (steel) and processed agricultural commodities; Uzbekistan and Kazakstan exports are dominated by raw materials; Belarus and the smaller countries tend to export a variety of manufactured commodities.

The patterns of trade that developed reflected in part natural resource endowment. But some of the trade, especially in manufactures, was the result of decisions to locate production on the basis of political or other considerations unrelated to economic efficiency. Some other parts of trade simply involved inefficient production that could not be expected to meet international competition once a market system was adopted. Losing this trade could be welfare-enhancing rather than welfare-reducing.

Gravity models suggest that in the long run, following market reforms, the share of total trade accounted for by FSU interregional trade would decline to about 15 to 30 percent of the total, depending on the country (Kaminski et al. 1996). In practice, the share seems to have fallen more or less to about what would have been predicted. However, the shift has

Table 13.3. *Distribution of interstate trade, 1991–1995 (percent)*

	1991		1992		1993		1994		1995	
	Exports	Imports	Exports	Imports	Exports	Imports	Exports	Imports	Exports	Imports
Country share of total interstate trade										
Armenia	1.4	1.9	1.0	1.2	0.4	0.5	0.5	0.7	0.5	0.9
Azerbaijan	3.4	2.9	3.3	2.7	1.7	3.0	0.9	1.7	0.6	0.6
Belarus	8.6	8.4	7.9	8.5	8.8	9.8	6.5	10.0	8.9	10.2
Estonia	1.4	1.2	0.6	0.6	1.0	0.7	1.8	1.4	1.5	1.7
Georgia	2.1	2.0	0.6	0.9	0.8	1.3	0.5	0.9	0.2	0.3
Kazakstan	5.3	6.9	8.8	9.9	8.9	10.4	6.3	6.8	7.8	9.1
Kyrgyz Republic	1.9	1.8	1.0	1.4	0.8	1.1	1.0	1.3	0.7	0.9
Latvia	2.2	1.8	1.8	1.9	1.5	1.4	1.6	1.7	1.6	1.7
Lithuania	3.5	2.6	2.1	2.5	2.7	3.2	3.6	4.3	3.8	3.6
Moldova	2.3	2.3	1.3	1.9	0.9	1.3	1.3	1.6	1.3	1.5
Russia	40.5	34.2	44.8	37.1	45.0	30.8	48.3	36.6	45.1	38.2
Tajikistan	1.3	1.8	0.4	0.7	0.3	0.6	0.5	0.8	0.7	1.3
Turkmenistan	2.4	1.5	2.5	1.6	4.9	2.6	5.3	3.3	3.9	2.7
Ukraine	18.5	25.1	21.5	25.8	16.2	26.8	17.4	25.3	19.8	23.8
Uzbekistan	5.1	5.8	2.6	3.3	6.0	6.5	4.4	3.6	3.6	3.4
Former Soviet Union	100.0	100.0	100.0	100.0	100.0	100.0	100.0	100.0	100.0	100.0

Trade with the rest of the world as a share of total trade

Armenia	1.8	15.0	14.1	24.6	19.2	54.2	26.4	47.7	38.4	50.4
Azerbaijan	5.1	15.1	49.3	33.3	40.5	27.9	55.6	35.9	59.2	63.7
Belarus	6.7	8.8	35.4	26.2	19.2	18.8	33.6	18.8	30.1	30.5
Estonia	1.3	6.4	62.2	63.5	57.4	72.8	55.7	75.5	68.2	75.6
Georgia	0.5	9.1	52.8	54.5	43.0	51.5	35.4	40.3	47.6	60.3
Kazakstan	7.6	13.1	41.0	28.1	32.8	26.2	39.7	45.3	43.1	24.8
Kyrgyz Republic	0.4	15.5	24.5	17.0	28.4	22.9	25.6	18.0	33.5	31.6
Latvia	2.1	9.9	48.8	47.2	48.2	49.2	49.1	60.1	53.2	61.3
Lithuania	3.6	7.1	52.5	35.4	42.8	30.4	42.5	54.4	43.2	58.5
Moldova	2.8	10.6	33.3	26.6	37.4	28.4	26.9	26.7	34.9	30.7
Russia	32.8	35.1	79.2	80.1	73.6	75.8	76.3	71.5	78.6	68.7
Tajikistan	10.9	13.9	54.3	43.5	69.0	65.4	65.2	54.9	64.6	38.9
Turkmenistan	2.3	14.4	65.0	57.0	40.0	46.1	22.4	40.7	28.6	30.4
Ukraine	14.6	15.6	53.3	46.1	52.6	33.9	45.6	36.4	43.9	39.1
Uzbekistan	8.4	12.7	58.1	52.9	41.3	36.5	39.3	50.5	57.6	55.3
Former Soviet Union	20.1	22.2	69.1	65.8	62.4	56.9	65.7	57.7	67.6	56.4

Source: Shares based upon data in current dollars in Table 13.1.

Table 13.4. *Commodity composition of interstate trade of selected FSU countries, 1993 (percent of total exports/imports)*

	Russia	Ukraine	Belarus	Kazakstan	Uzbekistan	Turkmenistan
Total exports	100.0	100.0	100.0	100.0	100.0	100.0
Oil and gas	37.4	0.5	8.7	19.9	42.5	78.5
Coal and other fuels	0.5	1.5	—	21.1	7.7	—
Raw materials	15.2	35.6	25.6	42.4	41.0	—
Agriculture and food	4.4	22.6	5.3	11.2	—	—
Manufactured goods and other	42.4	39.8	60.5	5.4	8.9	21.5
Total imports	100.0	100.0	100.0	100.0	100.0	100.0
Oil and gas	2.5	58.1	59.6	31.4	32.4	—
Coal and other fuels	1.5	1.1	1.6	4.9	3.0	—
Raw materials	31.6	15.7	24.9	28.5	0.0	—
Agriculture and food	12.6	3.5	9.0	7.8	14.6	—
Manufactured goods and other	51.7	21.6	5.0	27.4	50.0	—

Source: World Bank staff estimates.

Table 13.5. *Terms of trade in interstate trade, 1994 (1990 = 100)*

	Hypothetical changes in moving to world prices (1)	Actual changes (2)
Armenia	68.3	75.6
Azerbaijan	73.9	88.8
Belarus	80.1	86.2
Estonia	68.2	83.2
Georgia	55.2	64.3
Kazakstan	98.5	94.8
Kyrgyz Republic	87.3	81.1
Latvia	75.7	80.0
Lithuania	65.2	77.8
Moldova	46.6	56.2
Russia	137.6	118.9
Tajikistan	75.3	77.1
Turkmenistan	134.7	139.5
Ukraine	86.2	93.0
Uzbekistan	91.0	90.9

Sources: Column 1: Tarr, 1994; Column 2: Dikhanov, 1995.

occurred very rapidly and within the context of substantial declines in total trade. Not all of this decline resulted in welfare reductions: some resulted simply in reduced waste and better allocation of resources.

Interstate trade, however, declined significantly both in countries that implemented extensive market reforms such as the Baltics and in slow reformers such as Ukraine, in countries that consciously reoriented exports, and in countries that did not. Thus, it can be argued that the rapid decline in interstate trade had an impact on output because of the highly interlinked production structure of the former Soviet Union. Failure to supply needed inputs in interstate trade led to the reduction of output in downstream industries. And this output decline led to further declines in trade due to the reduction in the production of exportables.

The decline in trade was compounded by a very adverse terms-of-trade shock for the energy and raw material importing states (Tarr 1994). During 1992 the major energy exporters, Russia and Turkmenistan, raised previously heavily subsidized prices for interstate shipments of oil and natural gas close to world levels. Table 13.5 presents estimates of the terms-of-trade change on interstate trade. The first column reproduces Tarr's estimates (Tarr 1994) of the hypothetical change in the terms of trade that would have occurred if prices moved to international levels based on the 1990 trade pattern derived from Tarr's analysis (Tarr 1994). The second column provides estimates, prepared by Dikhanov (Dikhanov 1995), of terms-of-trade changes actually experienced through 1994.

The worst losers were the Baltic states, Georgia, Armenia, and Moldova, which were estimated to experience a loss on their terms of trade of between 20 and 40 percent. The table shows that what actually happened was pretty close to what had been predicted; and that most of the terms-of-trade changes had been completed by the end of 1994. The table also shows that the terms-of-trade shock experienced by the FSU energy importers was larger than the terms-of-trade shock that Kenen estimated for Eastern Europe (because the former had obtained energy imports at a fraction of the price paid by the latter) and substantially larger than that experienced by oil-importing countries after the oil shock of 1973.

Payments problems

Payments problems, with economic agents either unwilling or unable to use the banking system to pay for goods and services from other countries, may well have been the most serious impediment to interstate trade. Two distinct subperiods can be identified: first, the two-year period from independence in late 1991 to late 1993–early 1994, by which time almost all FSU countries had established their own currencies; second, the period from early 1994 to the present.

The first two-year period was truly chaotic. There were three sets of interrelated problems:

(a) Correspondent accounts between commercial banks in each of these countries could not be used to handle interstate trade transactions because there were disincentives or restrictions in their use and because of technical shortcomings and delays in making cross border payments. At the same time enterprises did not wish to pay for imports from other FSU countries with scarce hard currencies, and thus were unwilling to use foreign correspondent banks for interstate trade.

(b) The attempt to operate a common ruble zone failed (see below), and foreign exchange markets in the new currencies issued by new independent states took some time to be established.

(c) In the interim, the Central Bank clearing and payments system, established by the Central Bank of Russia (CBR) to control unlimited financing of bilateral trade deficits, imposed further uncertainties and constraints on the trading system (Michalopoulos and Tarr 1992a, 1994a).

In market economies, the existence of an effective banking system and the operation of foreign exchange markets gives enterprises access to the currencies through which they can make and/or receive payments to and from enterprises in trading partner countries. At the time of the break-up of the Soviet Union and the establishment of fifteen new independent states, such a system for making decentralized payments across borders did not exist. The ruble was the common currency, but it was losing value rapidly on account of high inflation, leading to the introduction of many quasi-currencies (e.g., in Ukraine). Payments took a lot of time to complete, were not always final, and were made without regard as to whether the payer had sufficient funds.

In February 1992, in an effort to monitor and facilitate interstate payments, the CBR and the other central banks established a system of official correspondent accounts through which payments were to be channeled. During this period Russia alone could create cash rubles, but the central banks of the other independent FSU states could expand the aggregate money supply by creating credit in rubles. It was a classic case in which many sovereign countries had an incentive to "free-ride" by issuing unlimited supplies of rubles, since the cost of inflation was shared but the benefit of seignorage accrued to the country that printed the money (Casella and Feinstein 1989; Flandreau 1993).

In this respect, the experience during the breakup of the FSU was similar to that following the breakup of the Austro-Hungarian Empire (Garber and Spencer 1994). Much like that earlier situation, in the absence of a coordinated monetary policy, the conflicting demands for seigniorage led to a break-up of the ruble zone. First, different so-called non-cash rubles emerged in different countries with different exchange rates among them and the Russian ruble. Concurrently, in the absence of monetary coordination among the central banks, governments saw no value in exporting in the ruble zone. All they gained for the exports were ruble credits in their banking system, something their central banks could create independently and had too much of in any case. Governments, including the Baltics, quickly responded by imposing export licensing requirements on interstate trade that were typically more severe than in their trade outside the FSU (Michalopoulos and Tarr 1994a).

The payments situation deteriorated further after July 1992. Russia began to accumulate large surpluses on its bilateral trade balances with most of the new independent states. To avoid unlimited financing of these trade surpluses and stem the outflow of goods, Russia imposed credit limits on the central bank correspondent accounts of these countries. When correspondent balances with the CBR were exhausted, they were either replenished by borrowing in the form of so-called technical credits or the CBR suspended payments by the central bank that had run out of ruble balances. Also, because the accounts at the CBR were bilateral, it was not possible to offset deficits with surpluses generated with other FSU countries. The system was still plagued by huge uncertainties and long delays (about three months) in a highly inflationary environment. Since the CBR could refuse to clear the payments orders of enterprises in a country that exceeded its limit, this meant that Russian exporters would not be paid for the goods they shipped, even if the importer had funds in its commercial bank to cover the payments order.

In early 1993, the Russian authorities decided to curb further financing of the other FSU states through the CBR and informed them that after the bilateral credits already negotiated were exhausted, they would have to obtain loans through the budget. This was followed in June 1993 by a resolution of the Supreme Soviet formally discontinuing access to other FSU countries to financing from the CBR and the demonetization of the pre-1993 ruble soon thereafter. The latter formally put an end to the ruble zone and forced the remaining non-Russian members (Armenia, Azerbaijan, Belarus, Georgia, Kazakstan, Moldova, Turkmenistan, Tajikistan, and Uzbekistan) into a dilemma: introduce their own currencies or accept monetary union with Russia, with monetary policy largely determined by the CBR.

All these countries but Tajikistan had introduced their own currencies by early 1994; the latter did so in 1995. These countries had stayed in the ruble zone essentially for two reasons. First, and perhaps most important, there was the expectation that membership would provide them with easy sources of financing. Second, for political reasons they did not want to "offend" Russia, on which they depended in a variety of ways, not the least of which was access to energy and raw material imports on, hopefully, subsidized terms. When it appeared that financing on easy terms would no longer be available, that energy imports would become more expensive over time, that monetary instability in Russia continued, and that they would not face political sanctions, they opted out of the zone. In so doing, they joined the Baltics, the Kyrgyz Republic, and Ukraine, which had launched their own currencies in 1992 and 1993.[3]

During this two-year period of unsettled monetary and exchange policy, the decentralization of payments through correspondent banks was hindered in a variety of ways. Processing of payments by the central banks was being done at a more appreciated exchange rate between the Russian ruble and the "national non-cash rubles" than was usually available to commercial banks. In addition, between August 1992 and July 1993, the CBR did not permit the opening of new accounts for correspondent banks in countries that did not have national currencies. Russian banks, facing both credit and exchange risk, were not interested in holding balances in other countries using the ruble; on the other hand, banks from other FSU countries wanted to build precautionary balances in accounts they had in Russia – a practice that some states prohibited in order to stem the outflow of capital to Russia.

The disarray in payments during this period had a devastating impact on interstate trade. Some large enterprises, especially in Russia, were able to continue to do business in other FSU countries, using partly rubles and partly hard currency. In 1992 and 1993 financial firms in several CIS member countries were offering to intermediate payments in other CIS members for fees ranging up to 20–30 percent of the value of the transactions (Gros, 1994a). But most enterprises either stopped trading or resorted to barter.

At the beginning of 1994, the start of the second period, the introduction of new currencies and the progressive elimination of controls on correspondent bank accounts improved the opportunities for decentralized financing of trade. Countries no longer had to fear that direct trade between enterprises facilitated through the commercial banking system would result in trade surpluses that had no value. A growing network of correspondent accounts among commercial banks spread through some countries (Russia and Ukraine), providing potentially fast turnaround on payments.

While this network started to facilitate some trade, a host of new issues emerged: first, the new currencies, with few exceptions (the Baltics, Kyrgyz Republic), were not fully convertible. The markets for these currencies were not developed and could not be used in trade. Trade between Russia and the CIS countries was usually denominated in rubles, but this entailed considerable foreign exchange risk because of the ruble's instability. Use of correspondent accounts was further constrained by the general weaknesses of the commercial banking system. Many countries were also facing a serious foreign exchange shortage and were unwilling to use foreign exchange for the denomination or settlement of interstate trade transactions.

Over time, the payments situation improved, but the improvements have been uneven and much remains to be done in many countries. The banking system and payments were probably functioning best in the Baltics and Russia, although banking crises of varying intensity had erupted even in these countries. Correspondent banks were being used for the conduct of trade in practically all countries without significant restrictions, but there were considerable weaknesses: clearances could be time consuming, trade finance was limited, and importers frequently have had to make payments in advance in full, and letters of credit were not being used extensively to finance interstate trade transactions. Although foreign exchange markets were operating in practically all countries, there were restraints to convertibility, and barter continued to be an important instrument of trade among most of the new states. As of late 1995, about a quarter to a third of total interstate transactions occurred through barter; slightly less in trade with Russia and slightly more in trade among the other countries.

III Financing constraints

The information on the amount of financing made available in support of interstate trade is quite incomplete. It is not possible to develop information on what has happened in the provision of financing for interstate trade on an annual basis and for all the countries. The information that is available is the amount of outstanding ex post credits that were provided primarily by Russia to the other countries – except the Baltics. In some of the cases (and especially for the most important creditors and debtors) it is possible to confirm the information by obtaining data from both the creditors and the debtors. In other cases no information is available.

Table 13.6 presents the latest World Bank staff estimates available. The first column shows the cumulative deficit or surplus countries have had on interstate trade during the period 1992–4. The remaining data show the total amount of outstanding credits that existed, mostly as of mid-1995, among these countries.[4]

Despite the incompleteness of the data, the table brings out the salient characteristics of financing of interstate trade. First, it shows quite clearly that Russia and Turkmenistan are the main creditors, and Ukraine, Kazakstan, and Belarus are the main debtors in absolute terms. Relative to the size of their economy, however, Tajikistan and Georgia have also accumulated a large amount of debt in interstate trade.

As with other aspects of the trade and payments situation during this period, financing was quite chaotic. The bulk of financing, approximately 80 percent, was forced, in the sense that it did not result from a contrac-

Table 13.6. *Interstate trade balances and financing among the CIS members, 1992–1994 (in millions of $ U.S.)*

	Cumulative trade balance, 1992–1994	Cumulative known net financing, 1992–1994*	Cumulative credits from Russia				Cumulative credits		
			Total	Technical credits, 1992–1993	State credits, 1993–mid-1995	For natural gas deliveries	From Turkmenistan	From Kazakstan	From Uzbekistan
Armenia	−229	138	86	45	41	—	51	—	—
Azerbaijan	42	148	82	82	—	—	66	—	—
Belarus	−1,350	925	925	385	81	459	—	—	—
Georgia	−342	662	150	135	12	3	489	22	—
Kazakstan	−1,290	1,154	1,320	1,250	68	2	—	—	—
Kyrgyz Rep.	−280	434	390	113	21	256	—	28	16
Moldova	−283	122	122	89	33	—	—	—	—
Russia	14,007	−8,977	—	—	—	—	—	—	—
Tajikistan	−240	471	254	127	127	—	—	18	199
Turkmenistan	2,000	−1,390	134	134	—	—	—	—	23
Ukraine	−6,728	5,922	4,981	2,500	204	2,277	940	1	—
Uzbekistan	−16	390	533	418	115	—	—	96	—
Total		8,977	8,977	5,278	702	2,997	1,547	166	238

* Includes some financing for 1995.

Sources: Data on trade balances for 1992–1994 are from Table 13.1. Data on financing are World Bank staff estimates, based on information supplied by member countries.

tual arrangement by individual countries to seek or provide credit. Instead, it was either the result of arrears (usually for natural gas shipments by Turkmenistan and Russia) that were subsequently consolidated or it was the result of the provision of overdraft facilities or "technical" credits by the CBR that were subsequently formalized in the form of a credit usually denominated in dollars at a LIBOR-linked interest rate and with a variety of maturities. Several of the consolidated credits, especially between Turkmenistan and Ukraine and some of the other small natural gas importers, also involve repayments in kind or in the form of equity participations in the debtor's enterprises. Some of the credits outstanding (e.g., from Russia to Tajikistan) are not, strictly speaking, financing for trade but have been incurred for the provision of currency by Russia.

The interest rates and amortization periods on which the forced financing has been consolidated are close to commercial. They have generally been extended without an assessment of the countries' creditworthiness. A number of countries in the region (the Kyrgyz Republic, Tajikistan) have found it difficult to meet these obligations and have sought rescheduling.

Beyond this forced financing – which occurred largely in 1992–3 and, in the case of Turkmenistan, also in 1994 – few new credits are known to have been extended during this period, perhaps no more than $700 million. These were provided by Russia to, for example, Belarus, Kazakstan, and the Kyrgyz Republic. In addition to these credits, there has been some $250 million of net financing by Russian enterprises directly to enterprises in the rest of the FSU in the form of excess of receivables over payables. A few of the main credit and financing arrangements related to interstate trade and payments of the past few years are worth noting:

- By far the largest amounts involve Russia's providing financing to Ukraine. The total of close to $5 billion is more than 50 percent of the total financing obtained by the ten net debtor countries. There are two major components to this debt, that related to CBR overdrafts and technical credits and that related to debt linked to shipments of natural gas by the Russian monopoly Gazprom (which is now a private company). Separate agreements have been signed for servicing each component of this debt.
- Turkmenistan's forced financing of natural gas exports accounts for the bulk of the remaining known financing. Turkmenistan

has reached agreements for the servicing of this debt (involving essentially consolidation of arrears) with most of its debtors, the most important of which are Ukraine and Georgia.

- Ukraine and to a much lesser extent Kazakstan and Belarus obtained the bulk of the financing and are the largest debtors. Ukraine is likely to have provided some credits to a number of the smaller FSU countries on which, however, there is no information.
- In addition to Ukraine and Belarus, Tajikistan and Georgia are major debtors that are likely to require extensive rescheduling of their debt on concessional terms – this has not formally happened yet. The total amount of outstanding debt of Tajikistan, including amounts owed to non-CIS creditors, is in excess of $800 million.
- Kazakstan and Uzbekistan appear to be in a net debtor position with Russia but are net creditors with other Central Asian economies.

This information with regard to the financing made available on interstate trade in the period 1992 through mid-1995 can be compared to the total amount of financing provided to these countries in 1992–5 from the rest of the world, primarily the OECD countries (Table 13.7). The table shows that the official development finance (which includes official grants as well as loans on both concessional and commercial terms) made available to these countries from the rest of the world was substantially more in the aggregate than the amount of new financing extended inside the FSU, primarily by Russia and Turkmenistan. Upon closer examination, however, it is important to note that the bulk of the assistance recorded here involves grants given to Russia by Germany to deal with the costs of relocation of Russian troops. If one excludes his financing, the remaining amounts provided to the whole FSU actually fall far short of the amounts of internal financing provided by Russia and Turkmenistan. Moreover, most of the new external credits from the rest of the world went to Russia. In addition, of course, Russia received very substantial financing in the form of deferral of its own debt payments, while it extended an unknown amount of de facto deferrals on interest and principal to developing countries which have not been servicing fully their obligations to the FSU.[5] All of this financing is also substantially less than the capital flight that has occurred from most FSU countries in this period and has variously been estimated at $30–50 billion.

Table 13.7. *Aggregate net resource flows to the CIS members, 1992–1995 (in millons of $U.S.)*

	Total CIS	Russia	Ukraine Belarus Moldova	Armenia Azerbaijan Georgia	Central Asia*
Official development finance	21,385.0	14,878.3	3,146.4	1,044.9	2,315.4
Official development assistance	13,906.0	10,927.8	1,847.9	532.8	597.5
Official grants	12,652.8	10,400.0	1,540.1	469.9	242.8
Official concessionary loans (net)	1,253.2	527.8	307.8	62.9	354.7
Bilateral	1,009.4	467.0	269.1	5.1	268.2
Multilateral	243.8	60.8	38.7	57.8	86.5
Official non-concessionary loans (net)	7,479.0	3,950.5	1,298.5	512.1	1,717.9
Bilateral	3,920.3	2,142.9	376.9	222.8	1,177.7
Multilateral	3,558.7	1,807.6	921.6	289.3	540.2
Private flows	23,769.6	17,790.3	3,105.4	160.3	2,713.6
Private loans (net)	15,941.3	13,483.0	1,313.4	40.3	1,104.6
Foreign direct investment	7,421.0	3,900.0	1,792.0	120.0	1,609.0
Portfolio equity investment	407.3	407.3	0.0	0.0	0.0
Memorandum item					
Net use of IMF credit	12,164.3	9,462.7	2,062.7	244.9	394.0
Interstate known financing	10,367.0	—	6,970.0	948.0	2,449.0

* Kazakstan, Kyrgyz Republic, Tajikistan, Turkmenistan, Uzbekistan.
Sources: OECD and World Bank staff estimates.

IV Alternative solutions

Following independence many believed it worthwhile to try to preserve, as much as possible, the previously integrated monetary and trade system of the Soviet Union. Divergent political and economic interests, however, made this impossible. From the very beginning the Baltic countries made it very clear that they wished to introduce market-based reforms quickly and to reorient their economies away from the FSU. Ukraine, primarily for political reasons, also declared early on its intention to issue its own currency and pursue an independent monetary and economic policy. Attitudes in the other CIS countries ranged from the desire to collaborate closely with Russia (Belarus) to the more independent – yet cautious – policies of some of the countries in Central Asia and the Caucasus.

The lack of monetary cooperation throughout 1992 and the likely unraveling of the ruble zone, with the resulting adverse effects on trade, led many analysts to recommend the establishment of a clearing and/or payments union (Dornbusch 1992; van Brabant 1991). The same arguments that were used in the context of East-Central Europe a few years earlier and the parallel with the European Payments Union were again presented in support of the establishment of a clearing and/or payments union for the CIS members (i.e., excluding the Baltics, especially Estonia and Latvia, which moved quickly in the course of 1992 to establish convertible currencies).

Indeed throughout this period the CIS countries agreed to implement a number of cooperative arrangements in the field of trade and payments, ranging from complete monetary union to a multilateral clearing arrangement to a customs union (Gros 1994a). A customs union among Russia, Belarus, and Kazakstan is in the process of implementation, but no region-wide arrangements have been put in place so far. In the payments field the closest anything came to implementation was a multilateral clearing arrangement that was to be established under the Interstate Bank. Ten countries actually ratified the treaty for setting up this bank in 1993, but, in the end, the bank (and multilateral clearing) did not get established, for reasons discussed below, in the section on "Clearing arrangements and the Interstate Bank."

The question nonetheless remains as to whether a clearing and/or payments union would have been useful in addressing the payments and financing problems that impeded interstate trade at the time and, more generally, whether such arrangements would be useful in the circumstances of these countries.

Convertibility and trade

Enterprise-to-enterprise trade and payments are facilitated in a single currency area, and there is a large literature discussing the requirements and conditions for establishing optimum currency areas (Goldberg in press). This literature stresses the benefits resulting from reduced transactions costs of trade within an optimum currency area compared with the potential costs in terms of macroeconomic adjustment that could result from the lack of exchange rate policy within the area. Whatever this balance may be, an essential precondition for any currency area is control over aggregate money creation within the area.

In the context of the break-up of the Soviet Union, there were strong forces of devolution of political and economic power to the individual states. These forces contributed to the lack of coordination and free-rider problems that led to the break-up of the ruble zone in 1993. As a consequence, it was not practical then and is not practical now to aim for a reestablishment of an area-wide single currency arrangement. There are two basic reasons, one political and one economic. On the political side, the new independent states, and especially Ukraine and the Baltics, look at the reestablishment of a single currency area as a vehicle for possible continued political domination by Moscow – something that, with few exceptions, they wish to avoid. On the economic front, the pace and orientation of reforms varied substantially, as did the value attached to stabilization. The Baltics wanted to and did stabilize quickly; other countries lagged significantly in stabilizing and at present conduct very different fiscal and monetary policies. This does not mean, however, that there may not be isolated cases where countries might find it advantageous to seek to establish very close monetary coordination or even a monetary union. Indeed, there have been numerous discussions and some concrete progress aiming at the establishment of a monetary union between Belarus and Russia.

If there are different currencies, convertibility of these currencies, especially for current account transactions, is the policy that would best facilitate trade. The examples of Estonia and Latvia and more recently in the Kyrgyz Republic, Lithuania, and Russia suggest that currency convertibility is feasible for both small and large countries, for countries with significant foreign exchange reserves and for those without, and that it can be achieved through the use of a fixed exchange rate system, a freely floating one, or even a managed float, such as the one that has been used by Russia.

Even when currencies are not convertible, trade need not be impeded if commercial banks establish correspondent accounts in hard currency in banks in developed market economies and trade is denominated and settled in hard currency. Such arrangements indeed were made by commercial banks in all FSU countries early on, and in some cases even before independence. These arrangements, however, have not been fully utilized to support interstate trade. The most serious impediment to hard-currency-based transactions has been the limitations on access to hard currency. Auctions or markets for hard currencies have existed in many countries, but the supply of hard currency has been limited because of taxes, exchange surrender requirements, and the general incentive of enterprises that earn foreign exchange to hold on to it as a store of value and hedge against inflation or use it in transactions with the hard currency areas. Moreover, governments have imposed constraints on access to these markets that limit the convertibility of domestic currencies into dollars for the purpose of conducting trade.

The conduct of trade in hard currencies through a network of correspondent accounts, of course, is not costless: banks will need to accumulate hard currency balances to satisfy the transactions demand for hard currency trade. There is an interest cost for maintaining these deposits that is equal to the difference between the interest earned on the accounts and the opportunity cost of these funds. For countries or banks whose cost of borrowing dollars on international markets is quite high, these costs may be substantial. In addition, fees must be paid to commercial banks in developed market economies for processing the transactions.

Clearing arrangements and the Interstate Bank

Despite the examples of Estonia and Latvia, there was considerable doubt throughout 1992–3 whether convertibility was achievable for most of the countries in the former ruble zone. It was also felt that hard currency shortages and weaknesses in the commercial banking system made it desirable to consider the establishment of a central-bank-based multilateral clearing arrangement, especially since the alternative appeared to be either bilateral clearing or barter.

The main objective of multilateral clearing through central banks would be to facilitate trade by providing efficient and secure settlement of payments for enterprise-to-enterprise transactions on a multilateral basis; a secondary objective could be savings in the use of scarce hard currency resources and overcoming the problems that scarcity of foreign exchange and ineffective or constrained foreign exchange markets pose for international trade.

In the context of the turbulent situation prevailing in 1992–3 and perhaps through 1994, such an arrangement made a lot of sense: unlike the situation in East-Central Europe reviewed by Kenen (Kenen 1991), trade among the states involved was a very substantial portion of total trade.[6] Moreover, currencies were inconvertible, clearing was inefficient and bilateral and there was general hard currency scarcity. A multilateral clearing arrangement through the central banks would also have permitted the clearing of a much larger volume of transactions than was feasible through the correspondent bank accounts. It has been estimated that the reductions on trade that would have been needed solely to achieve bilateral trade balance – and by inference the gains from multilateral clearing – amounted to 5–6 percent of incomes for CIS countries other than Russia. This would have produced a benefit several times larger than the benefits from multilateral clearing that accrued to the countries of the European communities in 1958 (Gros 1994b).

Such a multilateral clearing arrangement came very close to becoming operative in late 1993. An agreement to establish an Interstate Bank of mutilateral clearing and settlements among ten CIS countries was reached in January 1993; and it was actually ratified by the parliaments of most countries (with the notable exception of Ukraine).

The agreement was intended to be implemented by the CBR using a multilateral payments mechanism on the basis of the Russian ruble for clearance of trade transactions among the member states' central banks. Each day the CBR would inform the Interstate Bank of the amount of imports from the other states that they wanted to pay for. The Interstate Bank would provide a multilateral clearing service and inform member states of their cumulative debtor or creditor position. A two-week settlement period was established, with full settlement of all outstanding balances to be made in rubles or hard currency.

The system was to run on an initial credit line from the Central Bank of Russia (fixed at 300 billion rubles), but there was to be no additional credit, except interim finance amounting to one-month's exports. Central banks running up against their debt limit were expected to hold the amounts of imports they wanted to pay through the system to the exports declared by the other partner countries (or face expulsion). Thus the Interstate Bank was explicitly designed *not to address the financing problems of major FSU debtor countries*. It was also foreseen that the Interstate Bank would operate in parallel to the commercial banking system and would never be made obligatory (see Gros 1994b for details).

Following the January 1993 agreement, little happened to implement it, as the bank's future became tangled up in the uncertainty over the evolution of the ruble zone. After that issue was resolved in the summer of 1993, an effort to put the bank in place was re-initiated in December 1993 with a meeting of the central bank presidents. At the time, it was anticipated that the bank would operate as a clearing mechanism for the emerging new – but not yet fully convertible – currencies. Following that meeting, however, no additional steps were taken and the Interstate Bank never became operational.

The demise of the bank occurred essentially for political economy reasons: Russia did not want the institution because it had a convertible currency and was in a trade surplus position with practically all other CIS countries. It felt that it had no trouble conducting trade in rubles and was afraid that the clearing arrangement would be used to perpetuate its financing of the deficits of the other member countries of the bank; that is, that the bank would become a payments' union with Russia as its main creditor. The other countries had a free-rider problem: no individual country had a large enough incentive to invest the political capital needed to push for the Interstate Bank, since the institution would work only if everybody participated and the benefits would accrue to all.

Although a clearing arrangement such as the one under the proposed Interstate Bank may have been desirable at that time, the question remains whether it would be useful to deal with the continuing problems faced by countries in interstate trade. The main change over the last several years is that countries have made progress toward establishing currency convertibility, and the commercial banking system – although not fully effective – has also been strengthened. Trying to establish a new multilateral arrangement carries risks: one risk is that doing so could distract from efforts to promote convertibility, as well as efforts to strengthen clearing and settlements through correspondent bank arrangements. Moreover, the political economy reasons that prevented the establishment of the Interstate Bank are just as present today as they were a few years back. Thus, the time for a clearing arrangement is long past. The best course is to push ahead with convertibility and strengthen the institutional capacity of the banking system to expand the use of correspondent commercial banks and thereby facilitate payments.

Commercial banks in smaller CIS countries have opened correspondent ruble accounts in Russia, and Russian commercial banks maintain correspondent ruble accounts in those countries. These types of arrangements have been used to conduct some of the trade between Russia and the other FSU countries for some time now; they are less used in trade among the other countries. In the context of such trade, Russian firms have been insisting on receiving payments in rubles or hard currencies. Denominating trade in rubles poses a number of difficulties for some of the other countries.

The most important problem is the continuing inflation in Russia, which discourages exporters from accepting payment in rubles.[7] An additional risk involves ruble-denominated payments for contracts in the future. The absence of effective futures markets in most of the CIS makes it difficult for traders to hedge against an adverse movement in the exchange rate on futures contracts even in dollar-denominated contracts. The establishment of a band for the ruble helped the situation, but the absence of a well-functioning futures market is still a problem that needs to be addressed.

Another problem that has plagued interstate trade is the relative absence of mechanisms to deal with risks of nonpayment by buyers and nonperformance by sellers. Such risks are typically handled through insurance services, trade contract enforcement, and appropriate methods of payments (notably letters of credit) – mechanisms that are not widely available in Russia and most of the other states of the former Soviet Union. Letters of credit guaranteed by Western banks for dollar-denominated transactions are available, however, and this mechanism is already used to guarantee payment for imports from Western countries. In contrast, traders that use the ruble as the basis of interstate payments through commercial bank correspondent accounts in the former Soviet Union take risks that can be avoided if the dollar and Western banks are employed. Development of similar mechanisms to deal with ruble-denominated trade through the commercial banks is another area that needs to be addressed. More broadly, institutions need to be developed to facilitate direct trade among individual agents without government foreign exchange rationing.

Payments unions and financing

All of the measures discussed above could help facilitate trade and payments. But they would not deal with the fundamental financing problems that have emerged in interstate trade. The establishment of a payments union had been proposed early on – especially as the demise of the ruble zone appeared inevitable – in order to address the emerging financing problems that were perceived to hamper interstate trade. Subsequently, the establishment of a payments union was agreed in principle by CIS members in late 1994, and all twelve CIS members agreed to establish an Interstate Currency Committee in May 1995 as a first step in implementing a payments union – although not much has happened since then.

The main difference between a strictly multilateral clearing arrangement such as the Interstate Bank and a payments union is the provision of more extensive financing for deficits arising in interstate trade, based on some prearranged rules. In a payments union, only part of the multilateral balance needs to be paid until a country exhausts its credit limit.

Proponents of the establishment of a payments union in the FSU – just as they did in the case of East-Central Europe a few years earlier – have based their arguments on the successful contribution of the European Payments Union (EPU) in revitalizing intra-European trade in the 1950s (van Brabant 1991). A payments union in the FSU was recommended in the hope that it would accomplish one or more of the following three objectives: promote clearing among countries with inconvertible currencies, stimulate regional trade, or provide financing and balance of payments support (Williamson 1992).

There is a broad consensus, which includes Kenen (1991), that the EPU was helpful in stimulating European trade in the 1950s. The question is whether it was or is appropriate for countries of the FSU.

The basic problem with a payments union in the FSU is that superior policy instruments are available to attain each of the three objectives of clearing, trade expansion, and financing; and it is well established in economic theory that it is preferable to use the instrument that most directly attacks the problem at hand.[8]

If the problem impeding trade is making payments in the context of inconvertible currencies, convertibility or a multilateral clearing arrangement would suffice; the additional financing provided by the payments union would not be necessary to deal with the problem.

Assuming that clearing arrangements are in place, trade incentives can be provided more effectively and at less cost to intraregional trade by preferential treatment through tariffs and related trade measures than through the provision of aggregate balance-of-payments financing to countries with an overall debtor position on intraregional trade. This is because the relative "softness" of payments to countries within the union (i.e., the availability of financing) is perceived by the central bank of government authorities but is not internalized in the decision making of importing enterprises unless the central bank imposes foreign exchange rationing or other trade diverting controls on payments outside the union. But in these circumstances, preferential trade arrangements are the most direct and transparent means of stimulating trade with partner countries. This is not the place to discuss in detail the advantages and disadvantages of trade preferences for FSU countries. Suffice it to say that such arrangements may be beneficial or harmful to some or all of the countries in the region, depending on their design; and a number of preferential arrangements are already in place – these however, do not meet the standard conditions for efficient customs unions or free trade areas. The only point that needs to be emphasized here is that a payments union is not the preferred approach to provide preferential trade treatment (Michalopoulos and Tarr 1994b).

Finally, case-by-case financing through the IMF or World Bank conditioned on appropriate policies is arguably a better alternative than a payments union in addressing the financing problems facing some countries on interstate trade. This conclusion is based on the following considerations. In assessing the effectiveness of a payments union for addressing FSU interstate financing problems it is necessary first to determine the expected creditor–debtor position of the various countries that might participate in a potential arrangement. Based on the trade patterns of the last several years (see Table 13.6) it would appear that Russia and Turkmenistan would emerge as major creditors, and Ukraine and Belarus as the major debtors in absolute terms, but with a number of the other smaller CIS countries, such as Georgia, Tajikistan, the Kyrgyz Republic, Moldova, and Armenia showing relatively smaller deficits in absolute terms but large relative to their total trade. Azerbaijan and Uzbekistan would show small surpluses or deficits for interstate trade in both absolute and relative terms.[9]

The question would then arise as to whether Russia and Turkmenistan, the likely persistent creditors in a payments union with the rest of the FSU, would be willing to provide the necessary credit. Notwithstanding the 1994 agreement to establish a CIS-wide payments union, there is little evidence that they would: Russia has had persistent balance-of-payments difficulties and has been unable to service its external debt without extensive debt rescheduling. Its attitude during the discussions of the Interstate Bank clearly showed that it had no interest in providing significant financing for interstate trade, especially of the automatic unconditional variety likely to be needed for a payments union. Turkmenistan is a poor country, with very large energy potential, that is keen on utilizing its foreign exchange earning capacity to modernize and develop its economy; it is also highly unlikely that it would voluntarily enter an understanding in which it would provide external financing for an indefinite period to other FSU countries. Both Russia and Turkmenistan are, in fact, trying to reduce the arrears owed to them by other FSU countries.

At the same time it is important to recognize that for a variety of technical reasons – for example, difficulties in diverting sales of natural gas to other markets in the short run due to very large costs of pipeline construction – both countries are likely to continue to supply natural gas and be net creditors with most FSU countries, almost indefinitely. In the past they have been provided financing without consideration of capacity to repay. Credits have been provided primarily through the conversion of arrears. By comparison to that haphazard and ad hoc approach, a payments union with clear a priori limits established and adhered to may have been an improvement. Russia was not interested however, for a variety of reasons: it used the extension of credits as a leverage in the variety of political and other issues it faced with Ukraine and other countries, something that could not be done if transparent credit limits were pre-agreed; Gazprom, for example, was prepared to provide natural gas in exchange for gaining a foothold in transit and distribution assets of the importing countries' gas industry. Russia also feared that pre-agreed limits would not be adhered to and there would be pressure for additional financing.

Should donor nations or multilateral institutions step in to provide the credit? And, if so, should they do so in the context of a payments union or on a case-by-case basis and in the context of agreed programs of reform supported by the IMF and the World Bank?

The problem of providing external financial support through a payments union is that the rules of payments unions typically allow access to credit unconditionally and on the basis of predetermined credit limits. Under these circumstances countries that are pursuing the worst macroeconomic policies may run the largest deficits and draw most heavily on the credit. Should a payments union have been concluded, let us say in 1992–3, among the CIS countries, the bulk of the benefits would have accrued to Ukraine and Belarus, arguably two of the countries that have been among the slowest to reform (DeMelo et al. 1995). Perversely, balance-of-payments support would have gone to the countries whose adjustment programs appeared least worthy of support. In this way, a payments union may prolong inappropriate macroeconomic policies; in particular, it may prolong the period during which the country operates without a convertible currency. Although it is conceivable that conditionality regarding macroeconomic adjustment could have been introduced through a hypothetical payments union, it is highly unlikely that such conditionality would have been more effective in stimulating the introduction of macroeconomic adjustment than the direct involvement of the IMF with each of the countries. Moreover, some of the potential participants, for example, Uzbekistan, had a greater need for balance-of-payments support to finance imports from outside the payments union, but the credit provided to the payments union is restricted to balance-of-payments support within the region.

Although a payments union was not and is not the answer to the financing problems of some of the countries of the region, the financing needs of these countries are quite real and need to be addressed. Outside Russia very little external financing has been directed to these countries in the aggregate. At the same time, the reform process in some of them (Ukraine, Uzbekistan) only started in earnest in 1994; others continued to be plagued by war and insurrection through most of the period (Tajikistan, Georgia, Azerbaijan, Armenia). Thus, it is hard to make judgments as to whether additional financing should have been made available during this period or, if it had been made available, whether it would have been utilized effectively.

V   Conclusions and recommendations

Payments problems constrained interstate trade among the CIS countries over the period 1992–5, and especially during the long, drawn-out demise of the ruble zone. The solution to these problems should be sought in two general directions: more effective stabilization measures that would enhance the prospects of convertibility for the countries in the region; and strengthening of the institutional arrangements that would permit payments and settlements through correspondent bank accounts. The latter involves strengthening the commercial banks themselves, liberalizing foreign exchange markets, and promoting the use of letters of credit and other mechanisms that increase the security of trade transactions.

Although a multilateral clearing arrangement operated among central banks would have been a useful alternative to the chaotic payments conditions prevailing in the earlier part of the period, such arrangements are no longer needed because there has been considerable progress toward convertibility. A payments union was not desirable earlier, nor is it at present, to deal with continuing financing problems prevailing in some of the countries, especially energy importers.

It is best to deal with these problems on a case-by-case basis and in the context of well-defined programs of reforms supported by external financing from the IMF, the World Bank, and bilateral donors. IMF-supported stabilization programs have been put in place in practically all the countries. The most effective means of mobilizing private financing is the establishment of macroeconomic stability and transparent and stable rules regarding inflow of private capital.

Similarly, the World Bank and many bilateral donors have been providing a variety of assistance programs in support of reforms in all countries. Some of the financing problems could be eased by the pursuit of more effective adjustment policies by the recipients. For example, domestic energy prices in some energy importers continue to be below world prices. This would imply that balance-of-payments requirements could be eased through measures that will reduce the demand for energy imports.

One of the problems with public assistance has been that its rate of disbursement has been quite slow. For example, although World Bank financing commitments under these programs have reached almost $10 billion – more than half of the total going to Russia – disbursements have been less than half that amount. A key challenge for public resource flows is to improve the capacity of countries to absorb quickly large amounts of already committed finance. This would require action both by donors to expedite procurement and other administrative procedures and by recipients to address the problems of governance and institutional weaknesses that delay the disbursement of committed funding.

Irrespective of the pace and scope of reform, countries like Ukraine, Belarus, the Kyrgyz Republic, Tajikistan, and Georgia are likely to continue to run significant deficits on interstate trade. Russia and Turkmenistan are likely to continue to be major creditors within the FSU while net debtors with the rest of the world. Both countries need to develop an appropriate financing strategy as well as transparent credit facilities for the financing that they are likely to continue to extend to FSU countries. This strategy needs to take into account the creditworthiness of the recipient so as to ensure that repayment will be made and there will not be a need to reschedule soon after the credits are extended.

Finally, there is an urgent need to provide debt relief for two of the poorer countries that have a large amount of intra-FSU debt: Georgia and Tajikistan. Given the limited creditworthiness and financing problems faced by these two countries, long-term and concessionary debt relief is needed. Yet some of the creditors themselves (for example, Uzbekistan) have financing problems. Their ability to provide concessional financing depends to some extent on the amount of financing they are able to obtain from sources outside the FSU.

VI Implications for future research

Perhaps the greatest impediment to future research on countries of the former Soviet Union is the absence of reliable statistics. There are serious data limitations regarding both intraregional trade and payments. Regarding the period covered by this analysis, it is probably too late to develop more reliable statistics, as the raw data simply do not exist. Thus, strengthening of the statistical systems for the countries of the region is the highest priority for the future. The development of reliable statistical series will permit far more intensive analysis than has been possible to date in a number of areas. For example, reliable breakdowns on the commodity composition of trade will permit a much closer examination of the structural changes that transition has brought about in the patterns of production and the direction and composition of trade. Such information is also needed in order to undertake more systematic analyses of the costs and benefits of different forms of trade integration and to assess the implications of various proposals that are being developed in this area. Finally, reliable information on financial flows is needed in order to develop analyses of debt burdens and the development of a debt management strategy for practically all the countries in the region.

NOTES

I would like to thank David G. Tarr of the World Bank, with whom I have collaborated extensively on analyzing trade and payments in the former Soviet Union, for his contributions to my thinking about many issues covered in this paper, as well as for his comments on an earlier draft. I am also grateful to Benjamin J. Cohen of the University of California at Santa Barbara, Marina von Neumann Whitman of the University of Michigan, Kathryn Dominguez of Harvard University, and Basil Kavalsky of the World Bank, for their comments; to Misha Belkindas and Timothy Heleniak of the World Bank, for developing the statistical material; and to my assistant, Maria Luisa de la Puente, for processing this report. The findings, interpretations, and conclusions expressed in this essay are entirely those of the author and should not be attributed in any manner to the World Bank.

1. I had reached similar conclusions in my paper with David Tarr (Michalopoulos and Tarr 1992a).
2. It was a high proportion of GDP, but the estimates are somewhat distorted by the artificial exchange rate used to value international trade.
3. The IMF early on had supported the notion of a ruble-based monetary union. It abandoned the idea as soon as it became apparent in early 1992 that monetary coordination among the Central Banks was impossible. Thereafter, both the IMF and the World Bank, the sources of most of the external financial support to these countries over this period, were keen to promote stabilization policies in these countries and felt that such policies had a better chance of succeeding if they were in a position to pursue an independent monetary policy.
4. In interpreting the table please note that trade and current-account imbalances in intra-FSU transactions can be quite different from intra-FSU financing, as imbalances in these transactions may be financed by extra-FSU credits.

5. Russia took over under the "zero" option all of the old obligations and assets of the FSU. Unlike the predictions made early on, Russia also now has a debt amounting to about $25 billion to former CMEA countries. This was the result of the fact that despite a substantial terms of trade of improvement with the rest of the CMEA countries – as Kenen had predicted – the volume of Russia's exports in 1991–2 declined substantially, whereas shipments of the former CMEA countries did not.

6. It was this lack of intraregional trade links that weighed significantly in Kenen's recommendation against a clearing and/or payments arrangement among the East-Central European countries.

7. The monthly rate of inflation of the Russian ruble was 18 percent as of January 1995 (almost 800 percent annually), but declined to about 4 percent by the end of the year.

8. This has been developed by a number of authors, most notably Jagdish Bhagwati, Harry Johnson, V. Ramaswami, and T. N. Srinivasan. See, for example, Jagdish Bhagwati (1971).

9. The Baltics are excluded from this analysis, as they have never had the political interest in maintaining strong ties with the other FSU countries.

REFERENCES

Bhagwati, Jagdish (1971). "The Generalized Theory of Distortions and Welfare." In J. Bhagwati et al., eds., *Trade Balance of Payments and Growth: Essays in Honor of Charles Kindlberger*. Amsterdam: North-Holland.

Bosworth, Barry P., and Gur Ofer (1995). "Reforming Planned Economies in an Integrating World Economy." Washington, DC: Brookings Institution.

Bull, Greta (1994). "A Firm's Eye View of Foreign Trade in Ukraine." In C. Michalopoulos and D. Tarr, eds., *Trade in the New Independent States*. Washington, DC: World Bank.

Casella, Alexandra, and Jonathan Feinstein (1989). "Management of a Common Currency." In M. De Cecco and A. Giovannini, eds., *A European Central Bank?* (IMPG/CEPR) Cambridge University Press.

DeMelo, Martha, Alan Gelb, and Cevdet Denizer (1995) "From Plan to Market: Patterns of Transition." *Policy Research Working Paper.* Washington, DC: World Bank.

Dikhanov, Yuri (1995) "Measuring the Terms of Trade in the Countries of the Former Soviet Union." In Misha V. Belkindas and Olga V. Ivanova, eds., *Foreign Trade Statistics in the USSR and Successor States*. Washington, DC: World Bank.

Dornbusch, Rudiger (1992). "A Payments Mechanism for the Soviet Union and Eastern Europe." In D. Gross, J. Pisani-Ferry, and A. Sapir, eds., *Interstate Economic Relations in the Former Soviet Union*. Centre for European Policy Studies Working Document 63. Brussels.

Flandreau, Marc (1993). "On the Inflationary Bias of Common Currencies: The Latin Union Puzzle." *European Economic Review* 37, 501–6.

Garber, Peter M., and Michael G. Spencer (1994). *The Dissolution of the Austro-Hungarian Empire: Lessons for Currency Reform.* Essays in International Finance No. 191. International Finance Section. Princeton University.

Goldberg, Linda S. (in press). "Is Optimum Currency Area Theory Irrelevant for Economies in Transition?" In Richard Sweeney, Clas Wihlborg, and Thomas Willett, eds., *Currency Policies for Emerging Market Economies.* Boulder, CO: Westview Press.

Goldberg, Linda S., Barry Ickes, and Randi Ryterman (1995). "The Political Economy of Introducing New Currencies in the Former Soviet Union." In B. Crawford, *Markets, States, and Democracy: The Political Economy of Post-Communist Transformation.* Boulder, CO: Westview Press.

Gros, Daniel (1994a). "Comment on Russian Trade Policy." In Constantine Michalopoulos and David G. Tarr, eds., *Trade in the New Independent States.* Washington, DC: World Bank.

Gros, Daniel (1994b). "The Genesis and Demise of the Interstate Bank." In C. Michalopoulos and D. Tarr, eds., *Trade in the New Independent States.* Washington, DC: World Bank.

Kaminski, Bartlomiej, et al. (1996). "Foreign Trade in the Transition: The International Environment and Domestic Policy." *Studies of Economies in Transformation,* No. 20. Washington, DC: World Bank.

Kenen, Peter (1991). "Transitional Arrangements for Trade and Payments Among the CMEA Countries." *IMF Staff Papers* 38 (June), 235–57.

Michalopoulos, Constantine, and David Tarr (1992a). "Trade and Payments Arrangements in the Post-CMEA Eastern and Central Europe." In A. Hillman and B. Milanovic, *The Transition from Socialism in Eastern Europe.* Washington DC: World Bank.

Michalopoulos, Constantine, and David Tarr (1992b). "Trade and Payments Arrangements for the States of the Former USSR." *Studies of Economies in Transformation,* No. 2. Washington DC: World Bank.

Michalopoulos, Constantine, and David Tarr (1994a). "Summary and Review of Development since Independence." In Constantine Michalopoulos and David Tarr, eds., *Trade in the New Independent States.* Washington, DC: World Bank.

Michalopoulos, Constantine, and David Tarr (1994b). "Policy Recommendations." In Constantine Michalopoulos and David Tarr, eds., *Trade in the New Independent States.* Washington, DC: World Bank.

Michalopoulos, Constantine, and David Tarr (1994c). *Technical Note on Alternate Payments Arrangements for Trade Among the New Independent States.* Washington, DC: World Bank.

Tarr, David G. (1994). "The Terms-of-Trade Effects of Moving to World Prices on Countries of the Former Soviet Union." *Journal of Comparative Economics* 18, 1–24.

Williamson, John (1992). *Trade and Payments after Soviet Disintegration,* Washington DC: Institute for International Economics.

van Brabant, Josef (1991). "Convertability in Eastern Europe through a Payments Union." In John Williamson, ed., *Currency Convertibility in Eastern Europe.* Washington, DC: Institute for International Economics.

Index

Abraham, Katherine, 250, 256
Akhtar, Ahkbar, 125, 127
Allen, Polly R., 5, 235, 316, 321
Alogoskoufis, George, 221
Andrews, A., 228
Andrews, David, 233
Arize, Augustine, 128
Aspe, Pedro, 316
Asseery, A., 128

Baily, Martin N., 127, 264
balance of payments: among countries of
    former Soviet Union, 362, 372–7;
    among former Soviet countries, 362,
    374–6; financing in currency region,
    229–30; levels of Mexican, 317–18, 328–
    31
Baldwin, Richard, 60, 67–8, 263
banking system: former Soviet countries,
    361, 372–6, 383–5; Mexico, 318–19;
    proposed CIS multilateral clearing
    under Interstate Bank, 381, 384–5; ruble
    accounts among CIS countries, 35–6
Bank of Japan (BOJ), 298–301
Barro, Robert J., 94, 102, 178–9
Basle–Nyborg Agreement, 281
Bayne, Nicholas, 281
Bean, C. R., 251
Becker, Gary S., 32
Bellagio Group, 7, 16–17
Bernard, A. B., 264
Bertola, G., 251
Bhagwati, Jagdish, 57, 77, 79
Blank, R., 251
Blinder, Alan, 249, 255
Bohm-Bawerk, E. von, 33
Borjas, George, 266
Boschen, John F., 282, 295, 301

Boschen–Mills index, 295, 301
Bosco, L., 187
Bosworth, Barry, 264, 362
Boughton, James M., 224
Bowen, Harry, 32, 43, 51
Boyer, R., 251, 255, 258
Brada, Josef, 127
Brady Plan, 18
Brand, Diana, 232
Branson, William, 190
Bretton Woods system: exchange-rate
    pegging under, 186; exchange rate
    volatility under, 202, 210–11; monetary
    policy coordination under, 284
Bridgeford, J., 256
Brynjolfsson, E., 257
Buechtemann, C. F., 251, 256
Bull, Greta, 363

Calvo, Guillermo A., 318
Cameron, David, 90, 91, 92
Campa, J., 157, 160, 179
Canzoneri, Matthew, 221
capital (*see also* human capital): flows into
    and out of Mexico, 317–18; flows within
    currency region, 229–33; as intermediate
    factor (Kenen), 31–2, 45–51; in Kenen's
    three-factor, three-good production
    model, 36–40, 51; mobility in
    international macroeconomics, 14–16; in
    model of exchange rates and
    investment, 160–4; relation to exchange
    rate of marginal profitability of, 160–4;
    role in international trade (Kenen), 33–
    4; role in production function (Kenen),
    33–4
Carstens, Agustín, 318
Casella, Alexandra, 373